THE FREE NEGRO IN NORTH CAROLINA

John Hope Franklin received his B.A. from Fisk University and his graduate degrees from Harvard and has taught at numerous universities here and abroad. Since 1964 he has been professor of American history at the University of Chicago. In 1967 he became chairman of the department and in 1969 he was named John Matthews Manly Distinguished Service Professor. His books include *From Slavery to Freedom: A History of American Negroes; The Militant South;* and *Reconstruction After the Civil War.*

The Free Negro

In North Carolina

1790-1860

BY JOHN HOPE FRANKLIN

The Norton Library
W · W · NORTON & COMPANY · INC ·
NEW YORK

TO MY FATHER

AND IN MEMORY OF MY MOTHER

Preface

IN STUDYING the free Negro in North Carolina before the Civil War, perhaps nothing is more striking than the similarity between the attitude of the ante-bellum community and the attitude of various communities today, including the United States, toward certain smaller groups within their midst. These attitudes, in both cases, interestingly enough, sprang not so much from the belief that the smaller group was inherently incapable of accommodating itself to its environment as from a profound conviction that it was socially and economically undesirable. In the wake of this conviction there followed a train of manifestations and rationalizations—unconscious, subconscious, and conscious—which reflected this undesirability. The larger community, thereupon, was determined to make adjustment for the smaller group impossible. These reactions, in the period before the Civil War, did much to make the free Negro a "problem" and to create the complexities that make his status so difficult to ascertain and to understand.

My interest in the problem of the free Negro was first aroused while I was working at Fisk University under Professor Theodore S. Currier. Though my early efforts to study the group were meager, I was impressed with the scarcity of thorough studies on the subject and was encouraged by Professor Currier to continue my investigation. As a student of Professor Arthur M. Schlesinger, whose wise counsel and historical scholarship were among the greatest inspirations of my educational experience, I began to make definite plans for the present study. Finally, the work was carried to completion largely as a result of the constant encouragement and able criticism of Professor Paul H. Buck, under whose direction it was done. To these individuals I wish to express my most sincere gratitude.

A list of all the institutions and individuals to whom I am indebted for assistance would be unreasonably long. I feel obliged, however, to acknowledge gratefully the kind assistance rendered by staff members of the following libraries: the Widener Library of Harvard University, the National Archives, the Library of Congress, the Library of the University of North Carolina, the Duke University Library, St. Augustine's College Library, the Library of the University of Pennsylvania, the North Carolina Supreme Court Library, and the North Carolina State Library. I am also indebted to the North Carolina Historical Commission and the Historical Records Survey of North Carolina.

Drs. Guion Johnson, Albert R. Newsome, and Howard K. Beale of the University of North Carolina made many helpful suggestions, and Dr. C. C. Crittenden and Mr. David L. Corbitt of the North Carolina Historical Commission were always willing to coöperate, suggest, and advise at every stage of the work. Dr. Joseph Houchins of the Bureau of the Census and Professor Roy W. Wilson of Delaware State College were of great assistance to me at the Bureau of the Census. My colleagues, Professors E. H. McClenney, Ivan E. Taylor, C. D. Halliburton, and Paul McStallworth made many suggestions with regard to analysis and style that were of much value, and my assistants, Messrs. Robert L. Clarke and John Blue, Jr., performed a most helpful service in attending to innumerable details.

The major portion of the research for this book was made possible through the generosity of the Julius Rosenwald Fund in awarding me two fellowships and two grants-in-aid between 1937 and 1940, and of Harvard University in granting an Edward Austin Fellowship in 1937 and 1938. The publication of this work has been made possible through the generosity of the American Council of Learned Societies, the Carnegie Corporation of New York, and the Alpha Phi Alpha Fraternity. To these institutions I am deeply grateful.

Finally, I am especially grateful to my wife, whose able assistance, good nature, and constant encouragement have been important incentives to the completion of this work.

JOHN HOPE FRANKLIN.

Raleigh, North Carolina,
November 12, 1942.

CONTENTS

CHAPTER   PAGE

Preface   vii

I Introduction   3

II Growth of the Free Negro Population   14
     NUMBERS AND DISTRIBUTION   14
     MANUMISSION   19
     MISCEGENATION   35
     RUNAWAY SLAVES AND IMMIGRANT FREE NEGROES   39
     MAINTAINING THE STATUS OF A FREE MAN   48

III Legal Status of the Free Negro   58
     THE PROBLEM OF DISCIPLINE   58
     THE FREE NEGRO IN COURT   81
     CITIZENSHIP IN THE LARGER SENSE   101

IV The Free Negro in the Economic Life of North Carolina   121
     THE FREE NEGRO WORKER   121
     THE FREE NEGRO PROPERTY OWNER   150

V Social Life of the Free Negro   163
     EDUCATION   164
     RELIGION   174
     SOCIAL RELATIONSHIPS   182

VI An Unwanted People   192
     NORTH CAROLINA "LIBERALISM"   192
     THE COLONIZATION MOVEMENT   199
     THE GROWING HOSTILITY TO FREE NEGROES   211

VII Conclusions   222

Appendices   227

Bibliography   247

Index   259

MAPS

I The Free Negro Population in 1800   15

II The Free Negro Population in 1830   16

III The Free Negro Population in 1860   17

IV The Vote to Disfranchise Free Negroes in the
Convention of 1835   113

V The Vote to Equalize Representation in the House of
Commons, in the Convention of 1835   114

VI North Carolina in 1860   226

TABLES

I White Population in North Carolina in 1790   6

II Population of North Carolina, 1790-1860   18

III Free Negroes in Leading North Carolina Towns in 1860   18

IV Free Negro Apprentices in Craven County, 1800-1860   125

V Occupations of Free Negroes in North Carolina in 1860   134-135

VI Contributions of Citizens of North Carolina to the
American Colonization Society   204

VII Emigrants to Liberia, 1851-1860   209

THE FREE NEGRO IN NORTH CAROLINA

CHAPTER I

Introduction

History is the life of nations and of humanity. To seize and put into words, to describe directly the life of humanity or even of a single nation, appears impossible.

Tolstoy, *War and Peace,* second Epilogue.

MORE THAN a quarter of a century has elapsed since the appearance of John H. Russell's *Free Negro in Virginia.* This was the first exhaustive study of the subject by a trained historian;[1] and the only other work of similar scope and quality, James M. Wright's *The Free Negro in Maryland,* appeared twenty years ago. In addition to these detailed accounts, there have appeared from time to time brief sketches on the free Negro in certain areas and on individual free Negroes; but none has approached the standards set by Professors Russell and Wright in their pioneer efforts.[2] The enthusiasm and zeal so characteristic of the trained student of American history in the pursuit of knowledge concerning so many problems have been almost entirely lacking in the study of the free Negro.

The reluctance of historians to study the free Negro more seriously is not altogether understandable. Perhaps it is simply one of the several phases of our history that has not appeared especially attractive to students who are engaged in research and writing. The very nature of the problem, however, may serve to explain the preference of many for other tasks. As a group whose status, politically, economically, and socially was as indeterminable as it was unenviable, the free Negro as a subject for historical treatment abounds in elusive and difficult problems. The materials from which the picture must be drawn are scattered in scores of unsuspected places; and no small portion of the story calls for a type of sobriety and skill which emphasize the presump-

1. In 1899 Herbert E. Bolton wrote a doctoral dissertation at the University of Pennsylvania entitled, "The Free Negro in the Antebellum South," which has never been published. Since this work dealt, for the most part, with the status of the free Negro as reflected in legislative enactments and since the copy which the writer examined contains sections which are incomplete, it cannot be described as exhaustive or definitive.

2. See Bibliography.

tuousness of undertaking such a task. The results, however, are well worth the effort; for as a distinct, indeed an anomalous, group in the social structure the free Negro presents a picture that is at once fascinating and informative.

For several reasons there seems to be a real need for a more careful study of the free Negro in the ante-bellum South. The story of the section and the period cannot be completely told until there is available an adequate account of these quarter of a million people who often influenced the attitudes and policies of the communities in which they lived to a degree all out of proportion to their numbers. A more adequate story of the free Negro will constitute, moreover, another important step in the direction of understanding the relationship which exists between a minority group—in this instance, caste-like in its attributes—and the larger community. The problems which existed during the pre-Civil War period frequently have important bearings on our social attitudes in contemporary race relations. Many of the problems of the chief minority group in America have their roots not in the period of Reconstruction and after but in the earlier period when there was a large slave population and when the treatment of the free Negro by the whites in the community was conditioned by that fact.

We often get our cues for the present from the past in much the same way that a judge is almost invariably influenced by the principle of *stare decisis*. Any information concerning the genesis of a particular problem is most valuable in understanding it in its present stage. If many of our problems of racial adjustments had their origins in the difficult atmosphere of slavery, they present certain psychological factors that would have been different had they begun in an atmosphere of freedom, difficult though that also might have been immediately after the Civil War. This study of the free Negro makes no pretense of pointing the way to any satisfactory adjustment of race relations as they exist today. Nor is its primary purpose to show how much of the problem had its origin in the period under observation. It seeks merely to clarify and to explain the status of the free Negro in ante-bellum North Carolina as it was related to the larger community. The fuller understanding and solution of existing problems may be left to those whose wisdom and insight are greater than any claimed by the humble student of history.

Few areas possess the variety of geographical features that have played so important a part in the growth of North Carolina and have contributed so much to the development of a distinctive history. The poor harbor facilities in the East prevented the province from becoming an important center of import and export.[3] However, its interior provided accommodations for almost every type of settler. The corn and tobacco planter found in the coastal plain wide stretches of relatively unobstructed land suitable for his crops. In this same area the rich growth of pine forests afforded added wealth in the development of naval store industries. For the less enterprising farmer, or one with fewer means, the piedmont yielded a satisfactory crop of tobacco, wheat, corn, and the like. In the mountainous Appalachian region, sheep and cattle walks were obtained with comparative ease. The western part of the State, moreover, offered an excellent opportunity to those of the East who naturally rebelled against its strait-laced system of law and order.

North Carolina was essentially a rural state during the entire period under observation. Her shifting sand bars and shallow sounds prevented the rise of a Charleston; and, at best, Wilmington and New Bern were hardly satisfactory as ports of entry for a great interior that often looked to cities outside the province to furnish certain necessaries of life. Her lack of navigable rivers and her consequent relative isolation prevented the rise of a Richmond or a Memphis; and Fayetteville became and remained at best a leading village and a serviceable county seat. Thus, North Carolina presents one of the best examples in our history of the extent to which geography may play an important role in the development of an area.

No small factor, however, in the development of North Carolina was the racial and cultural characteristics of the people who lived there. Of the aborigines, the Tuscaroras on the seaboard, the Catawbas in the lower piedmont, and the Cherokees in the west were the most important.[4] Though these Indians showed marked differences in customs and tribal practices, each group easily manifested a remarkable achievement in accommodation to life in the Carolina wilderness and did a great deal to assist the white population to adjust itself to life in the new world.[5]

The group that constituted the white population of early Carolina represented an even wider variety of racial, national, and cultural backgrounds than did the Indians. There were not only the English, who in 1790 comprised more than 80 per cent of the white population, but there were also the Germans, French, Scotch-Irish, and Dutch. The

3. Guion G. Johnson, *Ante-bellum North Carolina*, p. 4.

4. *Ibid.*, p. 8.

5. There is a lengthy and reliable discussion of the Indians of North Carolina in John Brickell, *Natural History of North Carolina* (Dublin, 1737), pp. 277 ff. For a more recent account, see James C. Milling, *Red Carolinians* (Chapel Hill, 1940), *passim*.

following table is illuminating on the subject of white population in North Carolina in 1790:

TABLE I. WHITE POPULATION IN NORTH CAROLINA IN 1790[6]

Nationality	Number	Per cent of total
English...........................	240,309	83.1
Scotch...........................	32,388	11.2
German...........................	8,097	2.8
Irish.............................	6,651	2.3
French...........................	869	.3
Dutch...........................	578	.2
All other........................	290	.1

A knowledge of racial and national stock alone is inadequate in an attempt to understand the development of North Carolina in the early period. The white population represented at once a diversity of national stock and a relative economic and social homogeneity. The early and subsequent history of the State seems to uphold the point of view that the majority belonged to the yeomanry and that there were very few who could rank with the Byrds and Lees of Virginia or the Pinckneys and Laurenses of South Carolina. Peopled by a hard-working group of English, Scotch-Irish, and Dutch yeomanry and influenced culturally by Quakerism, Lutheranism, and Moravianism, North Carolina was to present a picture somewhat different from that of her neighbors in her attitude on many public questions and in her treatment of the races and classes of men found in her midst.

Just as there were important variations in the racial, economic, and social pattern of North Carolina, there were also interesting conditions peculiar to the free Negro of North Carolina. The free Negro population in Virginia and in Maryland was numerically greater than that of North Carolina; but the economic and social conditions in those states provided ways of life for the free Negro that differed markedly from conditions in North Carolina. In no State south of North Carolina were there half as many free Negroes as in that State. One can be sure, therefore, that because of these circumstances the problem of the free Negro in North Carolina will be different from that in any of the neighboring states.

A further distinction between the free Negroes of North Carolina and those of other states can be made. The free Negroes in other sections were essentially an urban group. In South Carolina, the majority

6. United States Census Office, *A Century of Population Growth* (Washington, 1909), p. 117.

was in or near Charleston. In Maryland, they lived in Baltimore or other towns. In Virginia, they were in Richmond, Norfolk, Fredericksburg, and Petersburg. In North Carolina, however, there were no such urban centers. The free Negroes of North Carolina, moreover, did not congregate in what urban centers there were. They, like most of the other North Carolinians, were rural and, therefore, agricultural. This condition had a most profound effect on the development of the free Negro in North Carolina. The isolation and general backwardness that were the results of rurality played an important part in the development of the social and economic pattern in which the free Negro had to live. This disadvantage was offset, in part, at least, however, by the protection from the public attack which the rurality afforded.

The year 1790 has been chosen as a starting point for several reasons. In the first place, the information concerning the free Negro in the earlier period is wholly inadequate for any kind of detailed treatment of the subject. It is impossible, for example, to obtain even a satisfactory estimate of the number of free Negroes before the first decennial census. In the second place, the year seems to coincide, roughly at least, with the period in which North Carolina was developing a policy toward free Negroes that reflected the point of view of the *people,* rather than that of the Crown, Council, and Assembly. Finally, North Carolina was by that time beginning to develop the way of life and approach to its problems that were to distinguish it from its neighbors in later years.

Very early in the history of North Carolina, Negroes came to be looked upon as a permanent element in the population. Indeed, in the "Fundamental Constitutions of Carolina," drawn up by John Locke in 1669, the English philosopher and political theorist showed that he expected Negroes to constitute a part of the population of the Ashley colony by remarking that, "Every freeman of Carolina, shall have absolute authority over his negro slaves, of what opinion or religion soever."[7] Already the Lords Proprietors had made the generous offer of fifty acres of land for every slave over fourteen years old imported into the colony.[8] As immigrants came into North Carolina, a number of those from Virginia and South Carolina brought slaves with them,

7. William L. Saunders, *The Colonial Records of North Carolina,* I, 204. This leads one to believe that the status of the first Negroes in North Carolina was that of slaves, in contrast to the status of the first ones in Virginia, which is still open to some question. See John H. Russell, *Free Negro in Virginia, 1619-1865,* pp. 16 ff.

8. Saunders, *Colonial Records,* I, 86.

recognizing, as did the proprietors, the value of slaves in settling the lands.

Into the northeastern part of the colony, before the end of the seventeenth century, a large number of younger members of Virginia's leading families came to build fortunes for themselves where the land was cheaper. Having seen how invaluable the slave had been in the development of their native colony, they brought a large number of black men with them, in the hope that their wealth and prosperity would come more easily.[9] In this way, the northeastern part of the colony was gradually peopled with blacks and whites who slowly moved southward into the rich stretches of land in Brunswick, Anson, Bladen, and Cumberland counties. The Scotch-Irish, Germans, and Dutch who moved into the piedmont section and into western North Carolina brought almost no slaves with them and constituted the group that in many instances resisted, though not altogether successfully, the movement of slavery westward.

The number of slaves in North Carolina grew very slowly in the early period, as did the population in general. The desirability of slaves to clear the lands and later to till the soil on the tobacco and rice plantations of the coastal plains, however, caused a steady growth in numbers, which Professor Bassett estimates at between 800 and 1,000 by 1700.[10] The strong resistance of the Indians in the early years of the eighteenth century, the economic impracticability of the plantation system in some portions of North Carolina, and the strong resistance offered by some groups having religious scruples against it were factors which tended to check the development of slavery. The growth of the number of slaves in the colony, however, can be seen clearly by the fact that there were 22,600 black taxables in 1767, over against 29,000 white taxables.[11] In the preceding decade, in 1755, the eastern counties were found to be far ahead of the rest of the province in slave population. New Hanover had 1,374 slaves; Craven, 934; Edgecombe, 924; Northampton, 834; and Beaufort, 567.[12]

The greatest increase in the slave population was from 1790 to 1800, when the foreign slave trade was still allowed. (See Table II.) After the beginning of the nineteenth century, there was a decided decrease in the growth of the slave population. The movement of large numbers of slaveholders into the cotton kingdom and the demand for slaves

---

9. See John S. Bassett, *Slavery in the Colony of North Carolina*, p. 18.

10. *Ibid.*, p. 20 n.

11. Saunders, *Colonial Records*, VII, 539.

12. *Ibid.*, V, 575.

in that area constituted a drain on the slave population of the older regions.[13]

Slavery in North Carolina never achieved the degree of importance that it did in Virginia,[14] or in South Carolina.[15] Seventy-three per cent of the families in North Carolina had no slaves in 1850, and more than half the slaveholders had less than ten slaves.[16] Although the slaves constituted about one third of the total population in North Carolina in 1860 (see Table II), it cannot be said that slavery was a growing institution. The rate of increase had steadily fallen off during the ante-bellum period, and the lack of profits, apparent even to the most rabid proslavery spokesman, heralded its demise as a constructive factor in the economic life of the State.[17]

It is impossible to indicate the date on which free Negroes first appeared in the colony of North Carolina. Some free Negroes, few though they may have been, were present by the beginning of the eighteenth century. In the March term of the General Court in 1703, it was ordered "that Tho. Symons pay unto ye petition^r ye sum of five pounds, as he being Executor of Charles Jones Deced itt being for ye bringing up a negro boy."[18] It may be that the Negro boy was free, for it would have been quite unusual for such a disposition to have been made of a slave, who would, in all probability, have passed by law to the "nearest heirs or assigns." A complaint lodged by North Carolinians with the Lords Proprietors of Carolina in 1705 leaves no doubt as to the presence of free Negroes in the colony as early as 1701:

We ... humbly represent to your lordships ... That it is one of the fundamental Rights and unquestionable Privileges belonging to Englishmen That all Elections of their Representatives to serve in Parliament ought to be free and indifferent and that no Alien born out of allegiance to the Crown of England, unless he be otherwise especially qualif'd ought to Elect for, or be elected to serve as a member of Assembly. But in 1701 the votes of many unqualify'd Aliens were taken ... and also several free Negroes were Receiv'd, and taken for as good Electors as the best freeholders in the Province.[19]

13. Bassett, *Slavery in North Carolina*, p. 78. See also Rosser H. Taylor, *Slaveholding in North Carolina: An Economic View*, Ch. 4.

14. James C. Ballagh, *A History of Slavery in Virginia*, pp. 25-26.

15. Census Office, *Century of Population Growth*, p. 135.

16. Johnson, *Ante-bellum North Carolina*, p. 469.

17. After an extensive study of the economic aspects of slavery in North Carolina, one historian concludes that it was not generally profitable. Taylor, *Slaveholding*, p. 98.

18. Saunders, *Colonial Records*, I, 585.

19. *Ibid.*, II, 903.

From the beginning of the eighteenth century to the end of the colonial period, the presence of free Negroes in North Carolina was acknowledged; and the growing concern of the Colonial Assembly as well as that of the public officials seems to suggest that the number of free Negroes was increasing as the other groups in the colony increased. In the laws enacted in 1715, free Negroes were prevented from voting[20] and from intermarrying with whites.[21] The latter law carried with it a fine of fifty pounds on any white man or woman who violated it and a similar fine on any cleric celebrating such a marriage. The laws of 1723 regulating manumission,[22] and the subsequent laws of the colonial period seeking to regulate every aspect of life for the free Negro simply bear witness to the growing concern of the whites for this group that was increasing in numbers. Added to this was the growing realization that free Negroes in a slave society must be carefully regulated lest their very presence serve to overturn the system.

Perhaps there is no definite connection between the end of the French and Indian War (there could hardly be) and the beginning of a more liberal attitude toward Negroes in North Carolina; but it is interesting to observe that the two coincided. In 1763, thirty-one men of Granville County signed a petition asking that the law of 1723[23] which heavily taxed free Negroes upon marriage be repealed. The petitioners "humbly shewed"

> That many Inhabitants of the s^d Counties [of Northampton, Edgecombe, and Granville] who are Free Negroes and Mulattoes and persons of Probity and good Demeanor and cheerfully contribute towards the discharge of every public Duty injoined them by Law. But by reason of being obliged by the said Act of Assembly to pay Levies for their wives and Daughters . . . are greatly Impoverished and many of them rendered unable to support themselves and families with the Common Necessaries of Life.[24]

This petition by the citizens of Granville is the first of a series of manifestations of a more liberal attitude toward free Negroes that culminated in the period of the American Revolution and immediately after. In the proceedings of the Safety Committee in Wilmington in July, 1775, it was brought out that John Collet, Commander at Fort Johnston, had given encouragement to Negroes to run away from

20. *Ibid.*, II, 214 ff.
21. Walter Clark, ed., *The State Records of North Carolina*, XXIII, 65.
22. *Ibid.*, XXIII, 107. These laws will be treated in greater detail in later sections.
23. *Ibid.*, XXIII, 106.
24. Saunders, *Colonial Records*, XI, 592, from Ms. records in the office of the Secretary of State.

their masters and promised to protect them.[25] While this greatly in-
flamed the people of Wilmington, they were careful to contain themselves, since they also were fighting for freedom.

It was in the following year that the liberal attitude was revealed
by an increase in the number of Negroes manumitted. In 1776, the
Yearly Meeting of the Society of Friends appointed a committee to aid
Friends in emancipating their slaves. The forty slaves thus set free
were declared by the courts still to be slaves and were resold under a
statute of 1777, passed *after* the slaves had been set free.[26] The action
of the courts in this instance could not thwart a movement that was
well under way and that gave many Carolinians an opportunity to
square their revolutionary philosophy with their own consciences. In
1778, the Moravians began to manumit Negroes;[27] and about the
same time numbers of individuals began to emancipate their slaves.[28]
So extensively had the Jeffersonian philosophy been practiced by those
who desired consistency that the Assembly passed the following act
in 1787:

> Whereas divers persons from religious motives, in violation of
> the law that slaves are to be set free for meritorious services only
> continue to liberate their slaves, who are now going at large to the
> terror of the people of this State. . . .
> Be it enacted by the General Assembly of . . . North Carolina
> . . . That if any slave hath been liberated contrary to the before
> recited Act (and is known to be lurking about) the Justice of the
> Peace is impowered and required immediately to issue his warrant
> . . . to the Sheriff, commanding him to make diligent search and
> apprehend all such slave or slaves and to commit him, her, or them
> to the gaol of the county. . . .[29]

It is interesting to observe, however, that the same Assembly that
was exhibiting so much concern over the increasing number of free
Negroes was contributing in a real way to the growth of this group.
Just before the passage of the act mentioned above, the Assembly had
passed five acts of emancipation in which seven slaves were set free.
Various circumstances prompted the passage of these acts: Four slaves
were emancipated in compliance with the wills of deceased slave-

25. *Proceedings of the Safety Committee for the Town of Wilmington, North Carolina* (Raleigh, 1844), p. 43.
26. P. M. Sherrill, *The Quakers and the North Carolina Manumission Society*, p. 32.
27. Adelaide Fries, *The Records of the Moravians in North Carolina*, III, 1236.
28. The records of the Courts of Pleas and Quarter Sessions show the extent to
which individual emancipations were being effected.
29. Clark, *The State Records*, XXIV, 964.

holders;[30] another was set free upon the request of Richard Dobbs Spaight, noted Revolutionary leader in North Carolina;[31] and a mother and daughter were set free upon the request of the free Negro husband and father.[32] The spirit of the Revolution had made itself felt; and even at the risk of increasing the group whose presence was feared to no small degree, the solons of North Carolina proceeded to carry the Revolutionary philosophy to its logical conclusion.

While the Constitution of North Carolina, which was completed on December 23, 1776, cannot be described as altogether liberal, so far as the free Negro was concerned it was about as liberal as he could have expected. His status was by no means degraded in this frame of government, and while the use of the term "freeman" was to be interpreted in a number of ways, there were times—down to 1835—when it was interpreted to the advantage of the free Negro. The franchise clauses provided:

> That all Freemen of the Age of twenty-one Years who have been Inhabitants of any one County within the State twelve months immediately preceding the Day of election and possessed of a Freehold within the same County of fifty Acres of Land for six months next before and at the day of Election, shall be entitled to vote for a member of the Senate. [Any free male adult who had been in the state twelve months and had paid public taxes could vote for members of the House of Commons for the county in which he resided.]
>
> That all persons possessed of a Freehold in any town in this State having a Right of Representation and also all Freemen who have been Inhabitants of any such Town twelve months next before and at the Day of Election, and shall have paid public taxes shall be entitled to vote for a member to represent such Town in the House of Commons. . . .[33]

In a document in which the makers were mindful to restrict the religion of its public officials to that of Protestantism and which was not ratified by the people of the State, it is significant that the term freeman was used unqualifiedly. The fact that it remained unchanged for two generations, moreover, is an indication of its acceptability to a majority of the people. Professor Bassett significantly observes:

> The Constitution of 1776 had made provisions by which it was not possible to keep any free Negro who could comply with the necessary conditions from voting for assemblymen as freely as

30. *Ibid.*, XXIV, 850, 859, 963. 31. *Ibid.*, XXIV, 929.
32. *Ibid.*, XXIV, 930. 33. *Ibid.*, XXIII, 981.

whites. What had been the actual intentions of the builders of the constitution was never satisfactorily known. In view of the fact that free Negroes were free men in 1776, it seems but fair to assume that they were not intended to be debarred of the franchise, there being no statement to that effect. At all events, they were allowed to vote.[34]

34. John S. Bassett, "Suffrage in the State of North Carolina, 1776-1861," American Historical Association, *Annual Report for the Year 1895*, pp. 276-277.

CHAPTER II

Growth of the Free Negro Population

We adhere to the Declaration made by our country Men in the year (1776) Viz, that all men are created equal ... that the human race however varied in color are Justly entituled to Freedom, and that it is the duty of Nations as well as Individuals, enjoying the blessings of freedom to remove this dishonor of Christian character from among them....

From the Constitution of the North Carolina
Manumission and Colonization Society, October, 1819.

NUMBERS AND DISTRIBUTION

THE COLONIAL period does not provide the student of the free Negro with any accurate information either as to the number of free Negroes in North Carolina or where they resided. Here and there one finds a remark about them which may shed light on the areas of concentration, but reliable information does not appear until the beginning of the national period.[1] At the time of the taking of the first census in 1790, there were 5,041 free Negroes in North Carolina.[2] This number compared favorably with the number in other Southern states. Virginia and Maryland had 12,866 and 8,043 respectively, while South Carolina had only 1,801.[3]

By 1800, the number of free Negroes had grown to 7,043, at which time the slave population was 133,296 and the total population 478,103. The majority of these free Negroes were concentrated in twenty-five coastal and piedmont counties. (See Map I.)[4] No county of the mountain region had as many as 100 free Negroes.[5] Already, certain

1. The number of free Negroes in Bladen County may have been sizable during the Revolution, for, in making a report concerning the King's land in Bladen County, the officer noted that more than a score of "free Negars and Mulattus" constituted a mob which "traitorously assembled together in Bladen County, October 3, 1773." Ms. in the County Records for Bladen County, 1773. The growing importance of free Negroes as subjects of taxation may be suggestive of their growth in number.

2. John Cummings, *Negro Population in the United States,* p. 57.

3. *Ibid.,* p. 57.

4. This and the succeeding maps were drawn by the writer from maps in the collection of the North Carolina Historical Commission. The information is taken from various volumes of the first seven census reports.

5. In the Morgan District, including six mountainous counties—Burke, Buncombe, Lincoln, Rutherford, Wilkes, and Ashe—there was a total of only 236 free Negroes!

—Less than 100
—Between 100 and 300
—Between 300 and 500
—Between 500 and 700

I. THE FREE NEGRO POPULATION IN 1800

tendencies toward concentration can be seen. Certain northeastern counties, notably Halifax and Northampton, are the areas of greatest free Negro population, each having more than 500 free Negroes in 1800. It is to be observed, however, that there were many eastern counties where the free Negro population remained small, and there were sixteen counties east of Wake County with less than 100 free Negroes each.

From the outset, free Negroes showed a tendency to concentrate in the towns. The difficulty, however, was that there were no sizable towns in North Carolina during the ante-bellum period. The fact that North Carolina was a *civitas sine urbibus* meant that the free Negro was, in the early period, and remained throughout the period essentially a rural group.[6] Of the 306 free Negroes that lived in Wake County in 1800, only eighteen were listed as residents of Raleigh. Twelve of Halifax County's 623 free Negroes lived in the town of Halifax. The leading towns, Wilmington, Fayetteville, and New Bern, had only nineteen, sixty-seven, and 144 respectively.[7]

The number of free Negroes continued to grow. Returns of the census for 1810 showed a total of 10,266 free Negroes out of a total population of 555,500. The slaves at that time numbered 168,824.[8] By 1820 the number of free Negroes had risen to 14,612 in a total population of 638,829.[9]

The year 1830 is an interesting point at which to study the growth of free Negroes in North Carolina. The number had increased by

6. Johnson, *Ante-bellum North Carolina*, p. 114.
7. U. S. Census Office, *Return of the Whole Number of Persons within the Several Districts of the United States.*
8. U. S. Census Office, *Aggregate Amount of Each Description within the United States of America*, pp. 75-76.
9. U. S. Census Office, *Census for 1820.*

almost 5,000 in the ten-year period just preceding the fifth enumeration, and the total had risen to 19,575.[10] The concentration follows the same lines that it followed in 1800. By 1830, five counties, all in the coastal area—with three of them bordering on Virginia[11]—had more than 900 free Negroes each. (See Map II.) Halifax, in the northeastern part

Legend:
—Less than 100
—Between 100 and 300
—Between 300 and 500
—Between 500 and 700
—Between 700 and 900
—More than 900

II. THE FREE NEGRO POPULATION IN 1830

of the State, had tripled its free Negro population since the beginning of the century, while Pasquotank, still farther east, had seen hers increase to four times its size in the early period.[12] Craven County, with its important town of New Bern, had slightly more than 1,000 free Negroes.

More than two thirds of the free Negroes were living in the area between Wake County and the coast in 1830, while only one piedmont county, Orange, had more than 500 free Negroes. Of the twelve counties having less than 100 free Negroes in 1830, seven were in the mountainous west, two were in the coastal area.[13] Free Negroes in North Carolina were decidedly rural in 1830. Nine leading towns of the State in this year had a total of only 963 free Negroes, which was scarcely 4 per cent of all the free Negroes in the State.[14] The free Negro population of Wilmington and Halifax, both in counties with a goodly

10. U. S. Census Office, *The Fifth Census,* pp. 91-93.

11. The overflow of free Negroes from Virginia to North Carolina is discussed below, pp. 42-46.

12. In 1830, Halifax County had 2,078 free Negroes; Pasquotank had 1,038.

13. It is interesting to observe that Pitt County, in the east, had only sixty-one free Negroes, while all the surrounding counties, Craven, Beaufort, Martin, Greene, and Edgecombe, were fairly densely populated with free Negroes. It may have been that Pitt County residents were peculiarly hostile to free Negroes. See below, pp. 211 ff.

14. The towns were New Bern, Fayetteville, Tarborough, Greensborough, Salisbury, Raleigh, Plymouth, and Warrenton. *Raleigh Register,* February 10, 1831.

number of free Negroes, seemed so relatively unimportant as not to be listed separately.[15]

The period 1830 to 1860 witnessed a growth of free Negroes by more than 50 per cent. The total free Negro population was 22,732 in 1840; in 1850 it was 27,463; and in 1860 it was 30,463.[16] Meanwhile, the slave population had grown from 245,601 in 1830 to 331,059 in 1860. Though slavery was becoming more widespread, as one historian has suggested,[17] it is interesting to observe that the rate of increase of free Negroes for the thirty-year period ending in 1860 was greater than that of slaves for the same period. (See Table II.)[18] By 1860, eight counties, all east of Moore and Chatham, had more than 900 free Negroes each,[19] while two other counties,[20] both in the coastal area, had more than 700 free Negroes each. (See Map III.) Halifax was still far ahead

□ —Less than 100

▨ —Between 100 and 300

▧ —Between 300 and 500

▨ —Between 500 and 700

▨ —Between 700 and 900

■ —More than 900

III. THE FREE NEGRO POPULATION IN 1860

of the other counties with a free Negro population of 2,452. Pasquotank was second with 1,507, and Robeson was third with a population of 1,462.[21] Four counties near the piedmont, Wake, Granville, Cumberland, and Robeson, were among the most populous, but they cannot be looked upon as piedmont counties in the same sense that Randolph and Guilford counties are. Sixteen counties still had less than

15. Census Office, *Fifth Census*, p. 90. *Cf. infra*, p. 19, note 24.

16. Cummings, *Negro Population*, p. 57.

17. Taylor, *Slaveholding*, p. 47.

18. The rate of increase of free Negroes in Maryland, however, was much more startling. See James M. Wright, *The Free Negro in Maryland*, pp. 84-93.

19. Wake, Granville, Cumberland, Robeson, Halifax, Hertford, Pasquotank, and Craven.

20. Beaufort and Wayne.

21. U. S. Census Office, *The Population of the United States in 1860*, pp. 350-351.

100 free Negroes.[22] All of these were either in the west or in the piedmont region.

TABLE II. POPULATION OF NORTH CAROLINA, 1790-1860

Year	White Population	Per cent of Increase	Per cent of Total Population	Slave Population	Per cent of Increase	Per cent of Total Population	Free Negro Population	Per cent of Increase	Per cent of Total Population
1790 ...	289,143	.....	73.2	102,726	.....	25.5	5,041	.....	1.27
1800 ...	337,764	17.19	70.6	133,296	32.53	27.8	7,043	39.71	1.49
1810 ...	376,410	11.44	67.6	168,824	26.65	30.3	10,266	45.76	1.84
1820 ...	419,200	11.36	65.6	205,017	21.43	32.1	14,712	45.35	2.3
1830 ...	472,823	12.79	64.1	245,601	19.79	33.1	19,543	32.15	2.61
1840 ...	484,870	2.54	64.3	245,817	.08	32.6	22,732	16.31	3.01
1850 ...	553,028	14.05	63.6	288,548	17.38	33.2	27,463	20.81	3.16
1860 ...	629,942	14.42	63.4	331,059	14.73	33.3	30,463	10.93	3.07

An examination of the census reports for the towns at the close of the period discloses the fact that free Negroes were still essentially a rural people in North Carolina. No town had as many as 700 free Negroes. Table III shows the extent to which there was a lack of concentration of free Negroes in the towns.

TABLE III. FREE NEGROES IN LEADING NORTH CAROLINA TOWNS—1860[23]

Town	Whites	Slaves	Free Negroes	Total
Elizabeth City........	952	620	217	1,798
Fayetteville...........	2,806	1,519	465	4,790
New Bern............	2,360	2,383	689	5,432
Raleigh..............	2,693	1,621	466	4,780
Wilmington...........	5,202	3,777	573	9,552
Total..........	13,913	9,920	2,409	26,342

Thus, it can be seen that less than 2,500 of the 30,000 free Negroes in North Carolina lived in towns of any size. It is interesting to observe, moreover, that the twenty other towns whose free Negro

22. The persistence of counties with less than 100 free Negroes is partially explained by the fact that in the west the counties were continuously in the process of reorganization. Thus, a county with more than 100 free Negroes may have found itself dismembered for the purpose of creating one or more counties. Consequently, a part of its free Negro population would, in the next census, be counted as that of the new county. Twenty-two new counties came into existence between 1830 and 1860. See David L. Corbitt, "North Carolina Counties and How They Got Their Names," *Raleigh News and Observer*, May 19, 1940.

23. From material found in Census Office, *Population for 1860*, pp. 350-359.

population was listed in 1860 would bring the urban free Negro population up to only 3,197.[24] This is scarcely 10 per cent of the total free Negro population of North Carolina in 1860.

This aspect of free Negro life in North Carolina—the tendency to live in the rural areas in a none-too-urban state—presents a marked contrast to the situation in other Southern states. In Virginia, which had a free Negro population of 58,042 in 1860, approximately 12,500, or 21 per cent, lived in the towns listed in the eighth census.[25] In Maryland, where there were 83,942 free Negroes at the time of the eighth census, 28,965, or more than 34 per cent, lived in towns. Baltimore alone had a free Negro population of 25,680![26] There were 9,914 free Negroes in South Carolina in 1860. Of these, 3,604, or 36 per cent, lived in the towns. Charleston had a free Negro population of 3,237.[27] The proportion was even greater in Louisiana, where there were 18,647 free Negroes. Approximately 14,000, or more than 75 per cent, lived in the towns.[28] At this time, New Orleans had a free Negro population of 10,689.

In no Southern state except Louisiana did the majority of free Negroes live in the towns, but a much greater proportion lived in the towns in most states than in North Carolina. And so, from beginning to end, the free Negroes of North Carolina were a rural people, as was an overwhelming majority of the inhabitants of the State. As a rural people, they were subject to all the limitations which circumstances usually fixed upon such a people in the ante-bellum South: isolation with its concomitants of social and economic backwardness; and inarticulateness, which brought in its wake political impotency and cultural sterility. There were, moreover, other limitations which society fixed on the free Negro. Of these, more will be said later.

MANUMISSION

The question may well be asked, "How is the increase of free Negroes in North Carolina to be explained?" The answer to such a query involves a rather detailed discussion of a number of social, political, and legal problems that arose in the period. By their very nature, these problems, even when they were not solved, contributed to the increase of free Negroes in North Carolina between 1790 and 1860.

24. *Ibid.*, p. 359. Halifax, North Carolina, the principal town of a county having 2,452 free Negroes, had only 192 free Negroes within its corporate limits.

25. *Ibid.*, pp. 518-520. There were more than 1,000 free Negroes in each of four cities: Alexandria, Norfolk, Petersburg, and Richmond.

26. *Ibid.*, p. 214.

27. *Ibid.*, p. 452.   28. *Ibid.*, p. 195.

The movement to manumit slaves, by will, deed, and legislative enactment, was well under way before the opening of the nineteenth century. The closing years of the colonial period witnessed the practice of freeing Negro slaves in the last will and testament of the slave-holder, as in the case of Mrs. Jean Corbin, who stated:

> It is my Will and desire, that my Negroe fellow Peter, who hath Long & faithfully Served me, be, at the time of my dēath Liberated & Set free, and it is my further Will and direction that my Executors herein named pay him Eleven pounds proc. money per Annum during his natural life, as a reward of his fidelity, and for his Support and Maintenance.[29]

Emancipation by legislative act continued as in the colonial and early national period, and in 1791 the General Assembly passed several acts in which slaves were given their freedom.[30]

Since the early colonial period, there had been laws in North Carolina which sought to regulate the manumission of slaves. The law of 1715 prevented the master from setting free any Negroes that had been "Runaways or Refractory." It pointed out, however, that this was not intended to prevent "any man from setting his Negro free as a Reward for his, or their honest and Faithful service, provided that such Negro depart the Government within six months after his freedom. . . ."[31] The manumission law of 1723 likewise made it compulsory for the newly freed Negro to abjure the State soon after manumission.[32] After admitting, in the preamble, that many free Negroes returned after being out of the State for a short time, the law stated that such offenders were to be sold into slavery to the highest bidder. In 1741, the Assembly passed an act which provided that "No Negro or Mulatto slaves shall be set free . . . except for meritorious Services, to be adjudged and allowed of by the County Court." The free Negro was still forced to leave within six months, violation of which involved being sold into slavery.[33] In 1777, this law was passed again, with slight revisions.[34]

In 1796, the General Assembly again turned its attention to the problem of the free Negro and specifically to that of manumission. In order to clear up any "doubts" that may have arisen "as to the extent

29. John Bryan Grimes, *North Carolina Wills and Inventories*, p. 135.

30. *Laws Passed by the General Assembly of North Carolina, 1790-1804* (Raleigh, 1805), p. 23.

31. Clark, *State Records of North Carolina*, XXIII, 65.

32. *Ibid.*, XXIII, 107.

33. *Ibid.*, XXIII, 203-204.

34. *Ibid.*, XXIV, 14.

of the liberation powers vested in the county courts" by previous acts, it stated the powers clearly:

> Be it . . . enacted . . . That no slave shall be set free in any case, or under any pretence whatever, except for meritorious services, to be adjudged of and allowed by the County Court, and license first had and obtained therefor; and that such liberation when entered of record, shall vest in the said slave, so as aforesaid liberated, all the right and privilege of a free born negro, anything in the said act to the contrary notwithstanding.[35]

The General Assembly and the county courts (the superior courts after 1830) were the media through which masters freed their slaves in North Carolina in the national period. Despite the fact that the General Assembly continued to place restrictions of various kinds on manumission, it continued to set slaves free by its own enactments. In 1812 the Assembly began the practice of requiring bond for every Negro set free. After stating in an act that a Negro girl named Violet "be and is hereby emancipated," the Assembly pointed out,

> That nothing in this act contained shall be so construed as to authorize the emancipation of the said Violet until Thomas Hamilton [the petitioner] shall have entered into bond with sufficient security in the sum of two hundred and fifty pounds, made payable to the chairman of the County Court of Nash . . . that the said Violet never become a charge or burthen to any counties in this State.[36]

Thus, the Assembly came to the conclusion that free Negroes were likely to be "burthens" to the community and that every precaution, short of preventing manumissions altogether, should be taken to guard against the prospect of having a burdensome element in the community. The Legislature declined to place many restrictions on itself with regard to manumission, and exercised a very wide latitude of discretion in the whole matter of setting Negro slaves free. The courts, however, were carefully regulated by the Assembly whenever that body felt that the courts were becoming too lax in their manumission policies.

The law of 1796 was left unchanged for a number of years. Meanwhile, county courts did their bit in setting Negroes free in North Carolina. Every term of the county courts was an occasion for the manumission of a number of slaves. The procedure seemed only

35. *Laws, 1790-1804*, p. 3. The law of 1796 had nothing to say about Negroes leaving the State upon emancipation.

36. *Laws Passed by the General Assembly, 1805-1816* (Raleigh, 1817), p. 24.

perfunctory, and the records give one the impression that slaves were manumitted with ease. The following is an example of the procedure which was followed in manumission cases:

> Read the petition of Mary Carter setting forth that she is the owner of a Negro man Slave named Anthony and is desirous of emancipating said slave for his meritorious Services—The Court ordered that the said Mary Carter have leave to emancipate and set free the said Slave and that he be entitled to all the privileges and immunities of a free Citizen agreeable to the Laws of this State.[37]

An examination of the county records of North Carolina for the first decade of the nineteenth century discloses the fact that many slaves were freed in this manner.[38] In no instance was there found any detailed discussion of the matter of "meritorious services." It is, therefore, difficult to make any statement as to the extent to which the performance of meritorious services had to be proved before the Court of Pleas and Quarter Sessions.

One case which came before the Supreme Court in 1838 sheds interesting light on the problem of meritorious services. The plaintiff had been emancipated in 1809 when two years old—at the same time that her mother was emancipated. A descendant of her former master contended that she was still a slave because at two years of age she could not have performed meritorious services as required by law. This, together with the fact that the petition could not be found, made the manumission void, he argued. After pointing out that the record of what the master said and did in court was sufficient evidence to demonstrate his desire to manumit the slave, Chief Justice Ruffin said,

> We are also of the opinion that its [the manumission's] efficacy is not impugned by its silence as to meritorious services, and that it cannot be impeached by presumption or evidence that the plaintiff had not, or could not, perform them. The acts of a court on a subject within its jurisdiction are presumed to be right, and that presumption cannot be contradicted when the court is one of exclusive jurisdiction, whose judgments are not subject to revision. Such was the County Court when this transaction took place. The law forbade it to allow emancipation except for meritorious

37. Ms. from the County Records of Craven County; Minutes of the Court of Pleas and Quarter Sessions, September, 1802.

38. A slightly different form reads, "A Petition was exhibited to the Court by Abraham Adams, Sr., requesting the emancipation of a mullattoe wench by the name of Rachel together with a Boy her son by the name of Joseph—The prayer of the petition granted." From the County Records of Beaufort County, Minutes of the Court of Pleas and Quarter Sessions, March, 1809.

services. If the court corruptly granted the license in an improper case, the judges were punishable, but the act was valid.[39]

The eminent jurist concluded by saying that the power of manumission, in the hands of county courts, was no doubt abused and gave this as a reason for the transfer of this power to the superior courts in 1830.

After the master had gone into court and received permission to emancipate his slave, he presented the slave with a deed of emancipation. Thus, in March, 1817, John C. Stanly was given leave to emancipate "Sally, a slave."[40] In September, 1817, the minutes show "A deed of emancipation from John C. Stanly to Sally was acknowledged by said John C. Stanly."[41]

The manumission of Negro slaves was increased considerably by the efforts of several organizations which gave their attention, in whole or in part, to the cause of the Negro. The avowed opposition of the Quakers to slavery was well known throughout the State during the entire national period. That they were active in trying to speed up manumission was equally well known. An act of 1796 made it unlawful for any "religious society or congregation in the state to elect any number of their body as trustees, which trustees . . . shall have full power to purchase and hold in trust for their society or congregation any real estate, and to receive donations of whatever kind, for the use and benefit of such society or congregation." The only limitation placed on religious societies was that no single congregation could hold more than 2,000 acres of land. In advising the Quakers concerning the manner in which the law affected them, William Gaston said in 1809 that,

> donations of personal property, such as money, slaves, etc. may be received to any amount—such donations can not be set aside by any persons claiming under the donors, nor can they be impaired by anyone, unless by the creditors who have made such gifts fraudulently to defeat the recovery of just debts. . . .[42]

Taking their cue from the advice given by the eminent attorney, the Quakers proceeded to buy up slaves and to emancipate them. The Quakers, moreover, may have had a great deal to do with the manner in which the "meritorious service" clause was disregarded by the county courts.[43] The Legislative Papers are filled with petitions

39. Sampson v. Burgwin, 20 N. C., 17.

40. County Records of Craven County: Minutes of the Court of Pleas and Quarter Sessions, March, 1817.

41. *Ibid.*, for September, 1817.   42. Sherrill, *Quakers*, p. 33.

43. Johnson, *Ante-bellum North Carolina*, p. 594.

from Quakers requesting more lenient laws on manumission and praying for the passage of individual acts emancipating certain slaves.[44] In 1826, they were feverishly working for manumission, as attested by the following newspaper report:

> At the annual meeting of the Society of Friends in this State, held last Fall, that respectable body came to the resolution of manumitting and removing all the coloured people held by them, that were willing to leave the country; and since that time they have been concerting their measures for carrying their intentions into effect.[45]

It was well that the Quakers were seeking some way in which to dispose of the slaves held by them, for the time was not far off when such tenure would be made impossible by the Supreme Court. In a ruling in 1827, the highest tribunal of the State ruled that Quakers could not hold slaves. In vivid and forceful language Chief Justice Taylor said:

> When Quakers hold slaves, nothing but the name is wanting to render it at once a complete emancipation; the trustees are but nominally the owners and it is merely colorable to talk of future emancipation by law, for as none can be set free but for meritorious services the idea that a collection of them will perform such services . . . is quite chimerical.
>
> The right of acquiring property and of disposing of it in any way consistently with law is one of the primary rights which every member of society enjoys. But when the law invests individuals or societies with a political character and personality entirely distinct from their natural capacity, it may also restrain them in the acquisition or use of property.[46]

The Chief Justice went on to describe the danger of having a group of slaves in the community that were slaves in name only. He expressed fear of a *bellum servile* if Quakers were allowed to purchase slaves and to hold them. In equally strong dissenting language, Justice Hall pointed out that there was nothing in the law of 1796 or in the Quaker creed that forbade them to hold title to slaves. He concluded by saying that the Court "ought not to take a step into the moral world and anticipate preventive remedies for possible infractions of the law."[47]

In 1833, Justice Ruffin reiterated the point of view of the majority

44. See Mss. in the Legislative Papers of North Carolina for 1809, 1811, and 1815.
45. *Raleigh Register,* May 30, 1826.
46. Trustees of the Quaker Society of Contentnea v. Dickenson, 12 N. C., 120.
47. *Ibid.,* p. 126.

of the Court in the above case.[48] It is interesting to observe, however, that at the same term the same Justice pointed out that after Quakers had held slaves for three years, a suit to recover them could not be successful, because the Statute of Limitations protected them.[49] Justice Gaston, who, as a young attorney, had advised the Quakers to buy up slaves and manumit them if they desired, had an opportunity to uphold his point of view in 1841, when he held that when a man and wife had agreed to the disposition of her personal property, she could leave her slaves to whomever she pleased, even though the recipient was a "steady old Quaker who would not own slaves."[50]

The Quakers worked not only through their Yearly Meetings but also organized a North Carolina Manumission Society. The stronghold of this society was in the Quaker counties of Guilford, Randolph, and Chatham. Mr. Sherrill attributes its organization to the great antislavery preacher, Charles Osborn.[51] At the first meeting, in July, 1816, Manumission Society chapters from Center, Caraway, Deep River, and New Garden were represented. The organization grew rapidly in the eighteen-twenties. By 1826, there were twenty-three branches, with more than a thousand members in Guilford, Chatham, Orange, Davidson, Randolph, and Forsyth counties. Female manumission societies were organized in 1825, five of which were in existence in 1827.[52] It had about forty branches before its decline in the early part of the next decade.[53]

As the name suggests, the organization was primarily interested in the emancipation of slaves in North Carolina. In its constitution it declared:

> The human race however varied in Color are Justly entituled to Freedom, and that it is the duty of Nations as well as Individuals, enjoying the blessings of freedom to remove this dishonor of Christian character from among them—But more especially in these United States where the principles of freedom are so highly professed.[54]

The Manumission Society proceeded to do everything possible to free the slaves and to alleviate suffering among free Negroes. At its Center House meeting in April, 1818, a proposition was introduced "to Search into the condition of the free people of color, and the expediency of

48. Redmond v. Coffin, Executor of Thomas Wright, et al., 17 N. C., 351.
49. White v. White, 18 N. C., 264.   50. Newlin v. Freeman, 23 N. C., 387.
51. Sherrill, *Quakers*, p. 38.   52. *Ibid.*, pp. 39 ff.
53. Hugh T. Lefler, ed., *North Carolina History Told by Contemporaries*, p. 268.
54. Henry M. Wagstaff, *Minutes of the North Carolina Manumission Society*, p. 39.

enforcing the law against Kidnapping."[55] The extent to which the Manumission Society was successful in its several undertakings is unknown. It is possible, however, to observe the ire which it provoked in some quarters. Charles Fisher, one of North Carolina's most articulate proslavery spokesmen, described the establishment of a "Manumition Society" as the most dangerous method adopted by the Quakers to carry their scheme into effect. Fisher said that there were more than 100 branches in 1829 and that no pains were spared "to extend them into every neighborhood. . . . The avowed object of the Societies is general emancipation. Each Society labors in its own sphere, in circulating pernicious doctrines and once in every year a general meeting of delegates is held, where Quakers and Manumitionists meet and consult on the progress of their work."[56] While these remarks were made by a fierce antagonist at the zenith of the influence of the Manumission Society, they do shed light on the activities of that body.

Fisher was not alone, however, in his castigation of the Manumission Society of North Carolina and its activities in enlarging the number of free Negroes in the State. The *North Carolina Standard,* one of the leading Democratic papers in the State, was violent in its attacks. In commenting on the society's alleged support of Garrison's abolitionist activities, the journal roundly condemned the organization and challenged the *Greensborough Patriot,* unofficial organ of the society, to tell where the society "holds forth" and "how many Democratic Republicans belong to it."[57]

It is difficult to estimate the influence of the North Carolina Manumission Society. The rise of the abolitionists, the growing unprofitableness of slavery in North Carolina, and the movement of the population south and west—out of the plantation stronghold in the State—all contributed to the increase in the number of free Negroes. It is interesting to note, however, that when the Manumission Society was at its height the emancipation of slaves proceeded with the greatest dispatch. Between 1824 and 1826, more than 2,000 slaves were freed in North Carolina.[58] The Manumission Society undoubtedly had a share in this rather wholesale emancipation.[59]

55. *Ibid.,* p. 27.

56. Charles Fisher, "Papers Relative to Slavery, Abolition, and the Colonization of Negroes." Ms. in the Charles Fisher Papers, University of North Carolina Library.

57. *North Carolina Standard* (Raleigh), January 15, 1830.

58. Alice D. Adams, *The Neglected Period of Anti-Slavery in America (1808-1831),* p. 34.

59. See William Birney, *James G. Birney and His Times,* p. 80.

By 1830, the laws concerning manumission had become something of a dead letter and were rather generally disregarded. The increase of free Negroes in every part of the State provoked so much unfavorable comment that the General Assembly was moved to strengthen its laws and to tighten its requirements. The directions for the manumission of slaves were made quite specific:

Any inhabitant of this State, desirous to emancipate a slave or slaves, shall file a petition in writing in some one of the Superior Courts of this State, setting forth . . . the name, sex and age of each slave intended to be emancipated, and praying permission to emancipate the same; and the Court . . . shall grant the prayer . . . on the following conditions, and not otherwise, viz, That the petitioner shall show that he has given public notice of his intention to file such petition at the court house of the county, and in the State Gazette for at least six weeks before the hearing of such petition; and that the petitioner shall enter into bond, with two securities . . . payable to the Governor . . . in the sum of one thousand dollars for each slave named in the petition, conditioned that the slave or slaves shall honestly and correctly demean him, her, or themselves . . . and that within ninety days shall leave the State of North Carolina and never afterwards come within the same.[60]

In this act, the Assembly sought to check quick decisions to emancipate slaves and to discourage manumission by requiring a bond of considerable size for good conduct and by forcing the newly freed Negroes to leave the State. In another section, the law made it valid, with certain qualifications, "for any person by his or her last will and testament to direct and authorize his or her executors to cause to be emancipated any slave or slaves, pursuant to this act."[61] It further provided that slaves over fifty years old could be emancipated for meritorious services which, incidentally, had to consist "in more than general performance of duty."[62]

The records of the courts and of the Legislature show that the law of 1830 did not hamper, to any great extent, the increase of free Negroes in the State. Masters continued to arrange for the emancipation of slaves. It seems that the forces, benevolent or otherwise, which motivated emancipation were much stronger than the barriers which

60. *Laws Passed by the General Assembly of North Carolina, 1823-1831* (Raleigh, 1832), p. 12.

61. *Ibid.*, p. 13.

62. *Ibid.*, p. 13. This part of the law was upheld by the Supreme Court of the State in 1859 in Abner Feinster, Executor, v. Tucker, et al., 58 N. C., 68.

were erected by the law of 1830. In October, 1837, Alfred Hatch deeded his slave Henry to his son with the instructions that, "as early as practicable after my decease, procure the emancipation of the said negro . . . to compensate his highly meritorious services rendered to me. . . ."[63] In her will of May, 1838, Mary McKinley specified that her eleven slaves should be emancipated.[64] Likewise, the county records show that slaveholders continued to free their slaves in their wills, by deed, and otherwise.[65]

The Supreme Court of North Carolina was always hostile to that part of the law of 1830 which permitted masters to free their slaves in their wills. In a case which came before the Court in 1848, that tribunal declared that the slave, George Washington, could not be emancipated by the will of his mistress.[66] Again, in 1860, the Court declared void that part of a will which sought to free the increase of slaves which were kept in the State.[67]

Meanwhile, considerable pressure was being brought to bear on the General Assembly to enact a law prohibiting the emancipation of slaves by wills. Toward the end of the period, several bills were proposed which sought to prevent emancipation by wills. In 1859 Mr. McDonnell proposed such a bill in the House of Commons.[68] It passed the Senate, but on the second reading in the House it failed to pass by a vote of thirty-five to fifty-eight.[69] Finally, in 1861, the Assembly passed "An Act to Prohibit the Emancipation of Slaves by Will." It provided that "No Slave in this State shall hereafter be emancipated by last will and testament, or deed, or other instrument or conveyance to take effect as to said emancipation after the death of the testator. . . ."[70]

Negroes were not altogether inactive in the movement to manumit slaves. It is practically impossible to ascertain the extent to which slaves purchased themselves. Because of the laws which required the performance of meritorious services as a prerequisite to manumission, the matter of a financial transaction between the slaves and the master

63. Alfred Hatch Will, October 25, 1837. In the James W. Bryan Papers, University of North Carolina Library.

64. Mss. in the Legislative Papers of North Carolina, 1840-41.

65. See the County Records of Wake, Craven, and Beaufort counties, 1836-40.

66. Creswell et al. v. Emberson, 41 N. C., 103.

67. Myers and wife, and the same administrator as John A. Lillington v. Williams et al., 58 N. C., 286. In 1816, when the Assembly passed an act of emancipation against the desire of the administrator of the deceased's estate, the Court held that the act was void. Allen's Administrator v. Peden, 4 N. C., 332.

68. A copy of the bill is in the Legislative Papers for 1858-1859.

69. *Journal of the House of Commons, 1858-1859* (Raleigh, 1860), p. 500.

70. *Laws Passed by the General Assembly, 1860-1861* (Raleigh, 1862), p. 69.

never found its way into the records. The law of 1830 sought to prevent the purchase by slaves of their own freedom when it provided that,

> The petitioner shall swear that he or she has not received in money or otherwise the price or value, or any part thereof, of said slave, or be induced to petition his or her emancipation in consideration for any price paid therefor or to be paid.[71]

Now and then, one finds evidence indicating that the Negro had purchased his own freedom. Isaac Hunter, free Negro shoemaker of Raleigh, said that "by the kindness of his . . . master he was permitted to do small jobs for himself and by great industry and saving he accumulated from his small gains a sum sufficient to buy himself from his master and so purchased and payd for himself."[72] In his memoirs, Lunsford Lane told how he saved the money which he made in the tobacco business until he had $1,000 at which time he successfully negotiated for his freedom.[73]

A sizable number of free Negroes was active in the effort to secure the freedom of their relatives or friends. The freedom of one's mate was zealously sought during the entire period, and in a majority of cases the efforts were successful. In 1795, the following act was passed by the General Assembly:

> Whereas, Lemuel Hall, a free man of mixed blood, hath represented to this General Assembly, that he hath purchased a certain Woman slave, called Jenny, for a valuable consideration, who hath since become his legal wife; and he hath had by his said wife Jenny three children . . . and whereas the said Lemuel Hall hath petitioned this General Assembly to emancipate and set free his wife and children. . . .
>
> Be it therefore enacted . . . That the aforesaid persons . . . shall henceforth be emancipated and set free . . . and the said persons of color to be liberated . . . are hereby declared to be entitled to all the privileges and immunities which free people of color enjoy and possess in this State, any law to the contrary notwithstanding.[74]

71. *Laws, 1823-31*, p. 13.

72. Ms. in the Legislative Papers for 1840-41.

73. William G. Hawkins, *Lunsford Lane; or Another Helper from North Carolina*, p. 49. Lane also told of another Raleigh slave whose master agreed to manumit him upon the payment of $800. When the slave had paid $400 the master said he had changed his mind about the price and he would have to pay $1200 in all. The slave did not choose to do this and with a free pass went to Boston to live.

74. *Laws, 1790-1804*, p. 28.

The County Court of Craven County was convinced that Sarah, the wife and property of Thomas Newton, a free Negro, had "rendered many and meritorious services and is a well disposed and orderly person. . . ." It was therefore ordered that Sarah be emancipated "upon complying with the directions of the Acts of the General Assembly in such cases provided."[75] At the same session, Robert Lisbon, a free Negro, secured the liberation of his wife.[76]

The effort of John Malone to emancipate his wife and son was an important matter before the General Assembly in 1846. In his petition, Malone said that his "industry, honesty, and sobriety" during thirty years of residence in Raleigh had won for him the "confidence and respect" which he enjoyed in his community. By hard work and economy, Malone had been "able to lay by a little money and property, and though a free Negro" he had done this "without exciting the suspicion of white gentlemen against his honesty." He then asked that his wife and son, whom he had purchased, be emancipated and be permitted to remain in the State, despite the law which required their removal within ninety days. A number of the leading citizens of Raleigh[77] signed a petition in behalf of Malone, in which they described him as sober, orderly, and prosperous.[78] Of great weight was another petition signed by the entire group of governing officers for the city of Raleigh in which the statement was made that John Malone was known for his "sobriety, order and integrity; and for a free Negro his character was extraordinarily good." There was also a petition from the Wake County Grand Jury.[79] As a result of the pressure, the Assembly passed an act in which the Malones were emancipated and permitted to remain in the State.[80]

Free Negroes were continuously seeking the freedom of their children. In 1801, Amelia Green presented a petition to the Craven County

75. Minutes of the Court of Pleas and Quarter Sessions of Craven County, March, 1811.

76. *Ibid.* See also the Minutes of the Court of Pleas and Quarter Sessions of Bertie County, 1811.

77. Among the signers were Will H. Haywood, Jr., George Badger, Joseph B. G. Roulhac, and George Settle.

78. A point made by both Malone and the citizens was that his wife was past the child-bearing age and that the number of free Negroes would not be indefinitely increased by her emancipation.

79. All of these manuscripts are in the Legislative Papers of North Carolina for 1846-47.

80. *Laws Passed by the General Assembly, 1844-1847* (Raleigh, 1848), pp. 297-298. In 1840, the Assembly had rejected the plea of a free Negro woman that her slave husband be set free. The petition of forty-two Fayetteville citizens was apparently of insufficient weight. Legislative Papers for 1840.

Court, praying for the emancipation of her daughter Nancy. After taking action, the court recorded the following minutes:

> On reading the petition . . . it being certified and satisfactorily made appear to the Court that the said Nancy is deserving of meritt —Ordered that the prayer of the said petition be granted.[81]

The Legislature of 1808 emancipated the two children of Rose, a free woman of color, of Chowan County.[82] Robert Lisbon purchased his daughter Myrtilla "from the fruits of hard labor and honest industry" and then secured her emancipation through the county court.[83] In 1855, the Reverend Robert Green, a free Negro preacher of New Bern, was in New York trying to raise $2,500 with which to purchase and free his five children.[84] The anti-free Negro sentiment which had reached its peak by 1856 perhaps prevented Lila Abshur from securing the emancipation of her father, whom she had owned for a number of years.[85]

The most influential free Negro in the manumission movement was John C. Stanly of New Bern. Having received his own freedom by an act of the Legislature in 1798, he proceeded to amass a fortune in farming in Craven County and by operating a barber shop in New Bern. By 1805, he had purchased his wife and two children, who were emancipated in that year by the Craven County Court.[86] In 1807, he was successful in obtaining leave of the county court to emancipate his wife's brother.[87] In 1812, he emancipated a Negro "woman slave called Rachel for long and meritorious services."[88] The next year Stanly obtained leave to emancipate another woman, Tempe.[89] In 1815, he emancipated a Negro woman and her five children, as well as a slave man.[90] In 1816, he set free a woman Rachel and her six children.[91] In

81. Minutes of the Court of Pleas and Quarter Sessions of Craven County, December, 1801.

82. *Laws, 1805-1816*, p. 40.

83. Minutes of the Court of Pleas and Quarter Sessions of Craven County, September, 1813. Later, Lisbon manumitted another slave. See Minutes for September, 1816.

84. *Newbern Journal*, September 19, 1855. Reprinted from the *New York Times*.

85. The petition for his emancipation is in the Legislative Papers for 1856. Every emancipation bill brought before this session was rejected.

86. Minutes of the Court of Pleas and Quarter Sessions of Craven County, March, 1805.

87. Minutes of the Court, December, 1807.

88. Minutes of the Court, December, 1812.

89. Minutes of the Court, December, 1813.

90. Minutes of the Court, March, 1815; June, 1815.

91. Minutes of the Court, June, 1816.

1817 and 1818, he set free three women.[92] A record such as that of John C. Stanly has few counterparts in the history of the free Negro.

Whenever it was difficult to emancipate the slave by following the procedure prescribed by law or whenever persons had more influence in the Legislature than in the courts, recourse was had to the former body for the emancipation of slaves. The Raleigh newspapers for the period 1830 to 1860 abound in notices indicating that the signer intended to ask leave of the next General Assembly to emancipate his slaves.[93] The petitions before each session of the General Assembly for the emancipation of slaves were numerous, and many were acted upon favorably.

The emancipation of Jerry, a slave belonging to Hon. D. M. Barringer, evoked state-wide comment. Mr. Barringer, a prominent lawyer, diplomat, and statesman, had carried Jerry to Europe during his fourteen years of service and in the petition described him as a "universal favorite." He further stated that Jerry was remarkable for his "honest, humility, and . . . was one of the best colored men living." One representative said,

> The very creditable manner in which Jerry conducted himself among the abolitionists of the North last summer ought to be of itself double inducement to every member of the House to liberate him. And when in New York once, meeting some North Carolina brokers, shaving the paper money of their State, he took gold from his pocket and redeemed the paper at its full value, for the honor of his native State.[94]

During the debate, Jerry's picture was passed around, and Zebulon B. Vance, serving his only term in the House of Commons, moved that it "be sent to the Senate with a proposition to print!"[95] Though several members of both houses spoke against the bill, it passed the second reading in the House of Commons by a vote of ninety-four to seventeen and became law before the end of that session.[96]

In 1855 the Assembly was literally swamped with petitions asking the emancipation of James Hostler of Wilmington. Hostler had saved

---

92. Minutes of the Court, June, 1817; March, 1818.

93. For example, the following notice was attached to an emancipation petition in the Legislative Papers for 1838: "Notice is hereby given that I shall apply to the next General Assembly . . . for an act to emancipate Caroline Cook She being born a Slave and her children to wit, Pamelia Cook, Archibald T. Cook, James Ellis Cook and Martha Jane Cook. *Signed*, Arch^d Lovelace." (Clipped from the *Raleigh Register*, September 29, 1838.) In the Archives of the N. C. Historical Commission.

94. *Greensborough Patriot*, December 23, 1854.

95. *Ibid.*   96. *Ibid.*, February 24, 1855.

the life of Thomas Hall Yates in 1846, and Yates showed his gratitude by sending a fervent plea for emancipation for the slave. In part, Yates said,

> Some time in the year 46 i was at work some 23 or 4 feet in hight from the floor and i was taken with a fitt standing in one plank 12 inches wide and with great risk he actively got where i was and there held me until the fitt left me. . . . And at another time i was attacted in the same way and when i came to myself i found myself in possession of my old Friend James with his wearied sympathy.[97]

In addition to this petition, there were several others: One told of the circumstances under which Hostler had been acquired; another, signed by thirty-nine citizens of Wilmington, told of his good character and conduct. The Assembly was evidently convinced. A bill was passed which set Hostler free and gave him "all the rights and privileges which are enjoyed by free persons of color" in North Carolina.[98]

In seeking to emancipate his slave, Sam Morphis, and to obtain permission for him to remain in the State, James Newlin of Alamance used a considerable amount of pressure on the General Assembly. Morphis, a hack driver and waiter at the University of North Carolina, had ingratiated himself into the favor of students and teachers alike. A student from Virginia told how Morphis had saved his life; President Swain of the University endorsed the letter of the student. Forty-three citizens of Chapel Hill, including President Swain and Thomas Ruffin, signed a plea that the petition in behalf of Morphis be given favorable consideration. A petition submitted by a group of students at the University had a number of interesting features. In addition to speaking well of Morphis, the petitioners took occasion to point out that this was "the first petition which has ever been presented to you from the students of your University." They asserted that a compliance with their wishes would not "as they humbly conceive, injuriously affect the good order of Society," and they entertained "high hopes that a consideration of the subject will prevail with the General Assembly to emancipate the aforesaid Sam Morphis." Of the 309 students who signed the petition, seventy-eight were from ten Southern states other than North Carolina. A bill to emancipate Morphis was introduced by Mr. Lynn of Orange, but its postponement prevented its being taken up at that session of the Legislature.[99]

97. Ms. in the Legislative Papers of North Carolina for 1855.   98. *Ibid.*
99. All of the manuscripts concerning the proposed emancipation of Sam Morphis are in the Legislative Papers for 1856.

Despite the pressure which was brought to bear from time to time on the General Assembly, it did not always comply with the request of the petitioners to emancipate their slaves.[100] By a vote of forty-one to seventy-one the Assembly refused to emancipate the wards of Polydore Johnston, a free Negro.[101] Likewise, they refused to set free a slave who was described in the petition as "so little distinguishable from white persons that it would shock our feelings that she would be compelled to remain in bondage."[102] Of course, there was pressure of another kind being brought to bear, namely by those who condemned the very principle of emancipation. In protest to a bill which sought to emancipate certain slaves in Wake County, 110 citizens of Raleigh signed a petition which read, in part, as follows:

> Your memorialists properly appreciate the *motives* of those who have . . . petitioned the Legislature, but they are forced to deprecate the policy of increasing the number of free negroes—already becoming a nuisance in the whole southern Country. . . . We cannot conceal from view the danger which *must* sooner or later result from the emancipation of slaves with the privilege of remaining in the State. They can visit at Pleasure any portion of the Northern States. When *there*, they will likely fall into the hands of those fanatics who are doing everything in their power to disturb our peace and destroy our happiness. . . . The emancipation of these negroes would be establishing an evil precedent—one calculated to produce dissatisfaction among our slaves. There are many others, who are no doubt looking forward for similar favours from the General Assembly. . . . Where will they stop? Emancipate all?[103]

Such a forceful argument could not be ignored altogether, and petitions such as this were undoubtedly responsible for some of the rejections voted by the Assembly. Despite pressure of this kind, however, the General Assembly of North Carolina, between 1791 and 1855,[104] passed thirty-seven acts of emancipation in which ninety-eight Negroes were set free.[105]

---

100. Nor did the Assembly always follow the advice of the committee assigned to look into the matter. In 1855, the Assembly passed two acts of emancipation which had been reported unfavorably by the Committee on Propositions and Grievances and the Committee on Private Bills. Ms. in the Legislative Papers for 1855.

101. *Journal of the House of Commons, 1827* (Raleigh, 1828), p. 180.

102. Ms. in the Legislative Papers for 1852.

103. Ms. in the Legislative Papers for 1840-41.

104. The Assembly passed no acts of emancipation after 1855.

105. The writer went through the private laws for the period and counted the number of acts and the number of Negroes set free.

Miscegenation

It is impossible to ascertain the extent to which miscegenation is practiced in any given society. The restraints placed upon the individual by the mores of the group and the legal restrictions imposed by the body politic act as devices which force much of the relationships underground. Only the obvious, the inevitable, results bespeak the existence of certain social relationships between the races; and the measurement of these relationships under such circumstances becomes extremely difficult.[106] Two types of race mixing directly affected the growth of the free Negro population: the relationship between white men and Negro women, and the relationship between white women and Negro men, slave or free.

The offspring of slave women by white men were slaves, according to the law, but it was not uncommon for their lot to be made easier by their fathers. Professor Johnston suggests that the mulatto was in most cases the descendant of white men and Negro women.[107] In 1860, this mixed group constituted more than 70 per cent of the free Negro population in North Carolina. The wills of some of the slaveholders show that they often displayed a considerable degree of benevolence by making provisions for their children by slave women. Here we are concerned with these provisions only when they included emancipation. A Wilmington farmer acknowledged his two children by one of his slaves, and before his death he emancipated them. In order that these children would not run into any difficulty later, the executors of the estate had them emancipated again, this time by the General Assembly.[108] In his will, made in 1814, another farmer made the following statement: "I give . . . unto my Mulatto Son Willie Abel one hundred acres of my swamp land . . . he having been free'd by the Court March term 1801."[109] These examples could be multiplied. They are sufficient to show that there were times when the free Negro population was increased as a result of the benevolent action of white fathers.

During the entire period, laws were in force which forbade the marrying of whites and blacks. The law of 1715 remained in effect until 1741, when the General Assembly for the Colony saw fit to strengthen it with a new enactment, which read:

For Prevention of that abominable Mixture and spurious issue, which hereafter may increase in this Government, by white Men

106. James Hugo Johnston, *Miscegenation in the Ante-Bellum South*, pp. 1 ff.
107. *Ibid.*, p. 1.   108. *Journal of the Senate, 1812* (Raleigh, 1813), p. 41.
109. Ms. in the Legislative Papers for 1814.

and women intermarrying with Indians, Negroes, Mustees, or Mulattoes, Be it enacted . . . That if any white Man or Woman, being free shall intermarry with an Indian, Negro, Mustee or Mulatto man or woman, or any Person of Mixed Blood, to the Third Generation, bond or free, he shall, by Judgment of the County Court, forfeit and pay the sum of Fifty Pounds, Proclamation Money, for the use of the Parish.[110]

The law then stated that if any minister or justice of the peace be found guilty of performing a ceremony in violation of the above provisions, he would also have to pay a fine of fifty pounds.

These laws of the colonial period did not, however, prevent an occasional union between whites and Negroes. When indicted on a charge of marrying a mulatto man to a white woman in 1725, John Cotten pleaded guilty and was "dismist without paying costs."[111] The following confession also provides interest:

> The Information of yᵉ Reverend Mʳ John Blacknall of Edenton . . . Taken before Christopher Gale, Esq: Chief Justice of the sayd Province this Second day of March 1725 who sayeth that upon the Sayd Second day of March he the sayd John Blacknall did joyn together in the holy estate of Matrimony according to the form of the Church of England . . . Thomas Spencer a White man and a molatto Woman named Martha paul both of Curratuck precinct contrary to an Act of Assembly . . . Whereby he the sayd John Blacknall hath incurrᵈ a penalty of fifty pounds the one half to the Informer which he therefore demands, the other to be lodged in the hands of the Governor.[112]

Obviously, the Reverend Mr. Blacknall had scruples neither against marrying whites and Negroes nor against breaking the law, so long as he coöperated with the court by acting as informer. One wonders if the twenty-five pound loss that he sustained in the transaction was made up by the couple which he was kind enough to "joyn together." That Negroes were still marrying whites toward the end of the colonial period can be seen by the statements of petitioners to the General Assembly, who in 1775 asked that the tax on interracial marriages be reduced.[113]

It was not until 1830 that the General Assembly declared that mar-

---

110. Clark, *State Records*, XXIII, 160.

111. Re Cotten (from the records of the General Court), Saunders, *Colonial Records*, II, 594, 602.

112. Re Blacknall; Saunders, *Colonial Records*, II, 672.

113. Saunders, *Colonial Records*, II, 295.

riages between free Negroes and whites were null and void.[114] The clerk of the county court was enjoined from issuing a license to a mixed couple, violation of which was punishable by fine and imprisonment. The same penalty was to be meted out to anyone celebrating such a marriage.[115] Although this law was omitted in the Revisal of 1836, it was re-enacted in 1839[116] and again in 1854.[117]

The clandestine relationships between Negro men, slave and free, and white women provided an interesting source by which the free Negro population was recruited. The number of instances in which such cases have come to the public eye bear testimony to their importance as a social problem in ante-bellum North Carolina. In arguing for a more satisfactory divorce law[118] in the columns of the *Raleigh Register,* "A Citizen of Richmond" pointed out that a man from Halifax had been denied a divorce although he proved that his wife left him "and attached herself to a free Negro, by whom she had several children." The same writer also gave an example of a white wife's delivering a mulatto child shortly after her marriage to a young white man of Wake County.[119] A few years later, a divorce was sought by a husband on the grounds that his wife claimed as her own "an infant bearing the most certain marks of a coloured Father."[120]

When slave Jim was convicted of having committed rape on the body of a white girl, a physician and several other citizens urged the governor to pardon the slave, contending that the child which was born subsequently was of mixed blood, but not a result of the relationship for which the slave was to be hanged.[121] In reviewing the case of a fight between a free Negro woman and a white woman, the governor received, from reliable witnesses, information that the white woman was one of infamous character, that her associates were Negroes, "and that her daughter . . . had a mulatto child."[122]

---

114. *Laws Passed by the General Assembly, 1823-31* (Raleigh, 1832), pp. 9 ff. It is to be observed here that this law affected the free Negro population adversely only so far as the marriages of free Negro men and white women were concerned. The free Negro woman gave her own status to her child regardless of who the father happened to be.

115. *Ibid.,* p. 10.

116. *Laws Passed by the General Assembly, 1835-1839* (Raleigh, 1840), p. 33.

117. *Revised Code of North Carolina,* Ch. 107.

118. At this time, all divorces were secured by legislative enactments, of which there were very few. See Johnson, *Ante-bellum North Carolina,* pp. 218 ff.

119. *Raleigh Register,* November 30, 1809.

120. Ms. in the Legislative Papers for 1813.

121. Legislative Papers for 1826-1827. See also the papers and letters of Governor Burton. This case is of interest here because it was established that the child was a free Negro.   122. Governor Burton's Papers, 1826-27.

The records seem to indicate that more free Negro children of white mothers were born after 1830 than before. Several cases which came to the Supreme Court bear upon this subject. In arguing for a divorce one petitioner had asserted that he knew that his wife had a child at the time of their marriage, but he thought it was his. After their marriage, he discovered that the child was a mulatto.[123] At the same time, another husband sought a divorce on the grounds that his wife became the mother of a mulatto child. In this case, the plaintiff was denied a divorce because, in marrying her because of pregnancy, he could not presume her to be chaste. Justice Ruffin pointed out that the petitioner was "criminally accessory to his own honor in marrying a woman whom he knew to be lewd."[124] Thus, the unfortunate husband had to go on acting as the father of this free Negro base-born child.

Among the charges that one husband made were that his wife had deserted his bed and board and had borne three illegitimate children, one of whom was colored. In this case, the husband was denied a divorce, because the Court said that his malicious desertion, the first infraction of the matrimonial contract, forced her to pursue the course brought out in the proceedings.[125] In another case, a white mother went into court and forced the Negro father of her child to support it.[126]

Two other cases bring out the fact that white mothers, at times, contributed to the increase of the free Negro population. When her husband died intestate, the widow, who was the mother of a free Negro child, went into court to secure her share of the deceased husband's estate. In ruling on the case, Chief Justice Ruffin said,

Whatever cause this women may have given her husband for taking steps to have their marriage dissolved, and thereby protect his estate from her claims, it is sufficient for this case that he did no such thing, but did leave her his widow and under no bar to her claims, as such, on his property.[127]

In another case, the white mother of two Negro children attempted to prevent the county court from binding them out under the law of 1826 on the grounds that she was white, and the law consequently did not apply to her base-born children.[128] The Court, speaking through

123. Borden v. Borden, 14 N. C., 436.
124. Scroggins v. Scroggins, 14 N. C., 430.
125. Whittington v. Whittington, 19 N. C., 65.
126. State v. Haithcock, 33 N. C., 34.
127. Walters v. Jordan, 34 N. C., 122.   128. See below, p. 123.

Justice Pearson, said that "the County Court has power to bind out *all* free base-born children of color without reference to the occupation or condition of the mother."[129]

Though the extent to which miscegenation was a factor in the growth of the free Negro population is indeterminable, there is no doubt as to its importance. The preponderance of mulattoes among free Negroes and the examples of free Negro children born of white mothers seem to establish its significance as a factor—indeed, an interesting one—in the growth of the free Negro population in North Carolina.[130]

RUNAWAY SLAVES AND IMMIGRANT FREE NEGROES

There was always the possibility, however slight, that a slave might escape from the bonds of his master and become accepted as a free Negro in another community. The number of runaways in any given year was fairly large, to which the advertisements in the newspapers will attest.[131] Since the treatment of free Negroes in North Carolina was as good as, and in many cases better than, that of any other Southern state, it is not unlikely that many of the runaway slaves of North Carolina remained within the State and that many from other states came into North Carolina.[132]

Often, the slaveholders suspected that their runaways were passing as free Negroes and expressed this view in their advertisements. In advertising for his runaway slave, John Jones said,

> Runaway from the Subscriber in August last, from Mrs. Webbs, in Franklin County, a Bright Mulatto Fellow, named Sion, about 22 years of age. . . . He has a white tall woman with him . . . and he passes for a free man. . . .[133]

Another owner offered a ten-dollar reward for his two runaways, "a fellow and a wench" who had left his plantation near the Alamance post office in Guilford County. He added, "It is supposed they will

129. Midgett v. McBryde, 48 N. C., 36.

130. Incidentally, several white prostitutes in 1860 were the mothers of free Negro children. See the unpublished census schedules for the eighth census (Wake County).

131. See, for example, the *Raleigh Register* for 1809.

132. It is interesting to observe, in this connection, that of the eight counties most densely populated with free Negroes in 1860, four were next to the Virginia border and one was on the South Carolina border. Two others were less than 100 miles from the state line.

133. *Raleigh Register,* February 23, 1802; and in subsequent issues for several months.

make for Edenton, as they were raised there, and it is expected they will pass for free."[134]

The Negro runaway described in the following advertisement must have given the owner a considerable amount of trouble, for there is a tone of exasperation even in the notice which offered a reward of $25:

> Ran away from the subscriber in Caswell Co., in the month of June, 1818, a Negro boy named Charles. He is black complected . . . and has an open, prepossessing countenance. The last time I heard of him was his having broken jail in Martin County . . . in April last, where he was apprehended. He had a free pass and had been passing as a free man for some time—there was another fellow in company with him who also had a free pass. It is more probable that they will remain together and obtain a new set of passes. . . .
>
> William Fuller.[135]

It is not difficult to find cases where the slave had been away for some length of time. One can be sure that in these instances the slaves were attempting to pass as free Negroes either within or without the State. Mr. Fuller's slave, in the preceding advertisement, had been away for more than two years. In 1803 the sheriff of Orange County had confined in the "Hillsborough Gaol" two Negro men from Georgia, one of whom had been absent from his master for nearly two years.[136] In advertising for his "bright mulatto woman, named Piety," Nathaniel Hunt indicated that she had been away for a year and that he supposed that "she passes for a free woman."[137] These slaves, moving about as they did for one, two, or more years, possessed most of the rights and privileges enjoyed by Negroes legally free.

The possession of an emancipation certificate was not always conclusive proof to the officials that the bearer was a free person. The jailer of Wake County saw fit to hold such an individual in 1807:

> Committed to Wake County Jail on the 18th Inst. a Negro man, of a yellowish complexion. . . . He calls himself Richard Freeman and has a certificate of Emancipation with him purporting to be from his late master Thomas Everitt of Northumberland County, Virginia, but which is suspected to be a forgery.
>
> The owner of said Negro is requested to come forward, prove his property, and take him away.[138]

134. *Raleigh Register*, August 12, 1805.   135. *Raleigh Register*, July 7, 1820.
136. *Raleigh Register*, December 5, 1803.
137. *Raleigh Register*, August 10, 1809. Piety was only sixteen years old.
138. *Raleigh Register*, March 2, 1807.

Enticing a slave to run away was a dangerous matter which carried with it a severe penalty under the law.[139] Yet, there are several cases on record in which free Negroes were brought into court on charges of enticing slaves to run away. In Pitt County, Dorset Wiggins was tried for his life on charges of "enticing Bill, a slave belonging to Isaiah Respess . . . to run away. . . ."[140] Although Wiggins won his case, many were satisfied that he was guilty and that his exoneration was the result of the unwillingness of the jury to send a man to the gallows short of murder. The editor of one paper remarked sententiously that the acquittal of Wiggins showed the need of a penitentiary. If North Carolina had a prison, the journalist asserted, Wiggins would not go unpunished.[141] In a case which reached the Supreme Court in 1855, two free Negroes were found not guilty of stealing a slave because the State had not proved that the slaveholder did not give consent, in writing, to the persons who carried the slave away.[142]

Ante-bellum North Carolina was the scene of much movement to and from plantations by runaway slaves. That many left never to return is an accepted fact. Many of those individuals who refused to accept slavery abjured the State and found a home in the North or in some other Southern state. That a sizable number remained in North Carolina and augmented the number of free Negroes already there is a conclusion that seems inescapable in the light of the facts.

The movement of free Negroes from other states into North Carolina was a matter which always plagued the citizens of the State. The increase of free Negroes within the State from causes over which the citizens in general had little or no control was more than sufficient for those who looked upon them as a menace to law and order and a drain on the community. But the point of view that Virginia, South Carolina, Tennessee, and other neighboring states would have to care for their own free Negroes gradually became a matter of public policy. The law of 1795 did not prevent free Negroes from entering North Carolina, but it sought to discourage them:

III. And be it further enacted, That if any free person of colour shall come into this State by land or water . . . he, she, or they shall

139. Under the law of 1779, it was a capital felony to steal or seduce away a slave. Clark, *State Records*, XXIII, 220.

140. *Newbern Journal*, April 11, 1855.   141. *Ibid.*

142. State v. Woodley, 47 N. C., 266. See also the *North Carolina Standard*, April 16, 1851. See State v. Martin, 34 N. C., 113, in which the Supreme Court reversed the lower court's conviction of a free Negro for stealing a slave. Justice Pearson said that "to constitute a felony in the case of stealing slaves, the taking of the slave must be from the *possession of the owner*," which was not proved in this case.

be compelled to give bond and security to the Sheriff . . . in the sum of two hundred pounds, for his, her or their good behaviour, during the time he, she or they may remain in this State; and it is hereby declared to be the duty of the Sheriff to apply to the above described persons, and take from them a bond as aforesaid; and if any person so applied to should refuse to give such a bond, the Sheriff . . . shall be and is hereby authorized . . . to take him, her or them into custody, and confine them . . . in the gaol of the county, until the ensuing court. . . . If the jury empanneled by the court shall find that such person does come within the meaning of this act, then . . . the court shall compel such person to give bond as aforesaid for his, her or their good behaviour, and upon failing so to do, the court shall order such person to be sold, for the benefit of the State, at public auction.[143]

As severe as the provisions of the act of 1795 may seem to be, it was not very discouraging to the Virginia free Negro, who was finding life in the Old Dominion more and more unbearable. Already it had become unlawful for free Negroes to migrate into Virginia except when traveling as servants to white persons.[144] In 1823 the Legislature of Virginia passed a law stating that free Negroes, previously punishable with imprisonment in the penitentiary for terms of more than two years, were thereafter to be whipped, transported, and sold into slavery beyond the United States.[145] At a time when free Negroes were under suspicion for all kinds of infractions of the law, this act loomed up as a threat to every free Negro that remained in the State. South Carolina prevented free Negroes from entering the State in 1800.[146] This law was reënacted and strengthened in 1821, an "accomplishment" which did not go unnoticed by the Raleigh papers.[147] After 1822, free Negroes in South Carolina were subject to a series of heavy taxes and were compelled to have white guardians.[148] Thus, the requirement of a two-hundred-pound bond in North Carolina was not severe when compared with the treatment they were receiving in neighboring states. It is small wonder, then, that the counties of the densest free Negro population in North Carolina were those adjacent to or near Virginia and South Carolina.

Incensed over a resolution of the Vermont Legislature in which

143. *Laws, 1790-1804*, pp. 10 ff.
144. Walter Hening, *Statutes at Large of Virginia*, XIII (Philadelphia, 1823), 239. This law was passed in 1792.
145. Russell, *Free Negro in Virginia*, p. 106.
146. John C. Hurd, *The Law of Freedom and Bondage in the United States*, II, 95.
147. *Raleigh Register*, January 26, 1821.
148. Hurd, *Law of Freedom and Bondage*, II, 97.

slavery was declared to be an evil and in which its abolition was advocated, Governor Burton brought the matter of slaves and free Negroes before the General Assembly of North Carolina in December, 1826. Among other things, he recommended a revision of the laws relative to calling out the militia to suppress insurrections, those for appointing and keeping patrols, and those in relation to the migration of free persons of color into the State. He raised the question "whether the policy of our sister States, prohibiting the migration of free persons of colour within their boundaries, should not be met by countervailing enactments. . . . "[149]

Early in 1827, the following law was passed:

> Be it enacted by the General Assembly of the State of North Carolina . . . That it shall not be lawful for any free negro or mulatto to migrate into this State; and if he or she shall do so contrary to the provisions of this act, and being thereof informed, shall not, within twenty days thereafter, remove out of the State, he or she . . . shall be liable to a penalty of five hundred dollars: and upon failure to pay the same, within the time prescribed in the judgment awarded against such person or persons, he or she shall be liable to be held in servitude, and at labor for a term not exceeding ten years, in such manner and upon such terms as may be prescribed by the court awarding such sentence. . . .[150]

In another section of the act, a fine of $500 was to be imposed on anyone found guilty of transporting free Negroes into the State.[151]

The act of 1827 did not pass the Assembly without some opposition. The journals of both houses make reference to a debate on the subject,[152] and when the vote was taken, it was passed in the House of Commons with seventy-five for and thirty-nine against the bill. In the Senate, forty-five voted for and fourteen voted against the bill. An analysis of the vote taken in the House of Commons is not very revealing for the reason that of the thirty-nine representatives who voted against the bill, twenty-three were from counties in which the other representative (most counties had two representatives) voted for the bill. In four counties, both representatives voted against the bill. These counties were Haywood, where the free Negro population was negli-

149. The Message of Governor H. G. Burton to the General Assembly, December 26, 1826. *Journal of the House of Commons, 1826-1829* (Raleigh, 1830), p. 117.

150. *Laws, 1825-1830*, p. 13.   151. *Ibid.*, p. 14.

152. The *Raleigh Register* for January 6, 1827, said, "The bill to prevent free persons of color from migrating into this State . . . has been, the bank bill excepted, the most fruitful theme of debate which has arisen during the session. It occupied two days in the House of Commons, in the Committee of the Whole. . . ."

gible;[153] Randolph, which was one of the Quaker strongholds; Wayne, an inland county which was not directly affected; and Craven, which had the densest free Negro population.[154] It can hardly be said that the motives for the vote in the House of Commons on the bill to prevent the immigration of free Negroes into North Carolina are easily discernible.

The Senate provides a more satisfactory situation for analysis for the reason that there was only one senator from each county and he could speak and vote with greater independence. Of the fourteen senators who voted against the immigration bill, five came from border counties that would be directly affected by the bill.[155] It may be added, however, that in 1820 only one of these counties, Brunswick, had as many as 200 free Negroes within its boundaries. It may also be said that the fourteen senators who voted against the immigration law represented a free Negro population of less than 3,000 (according to the census of 1820) at a time when the free Negro population of North Carolina numbered more than 14,000.[156] When one observes that the senators from the border counties where free Negroes were numerous[157] voted for the immigration law, it may be said that experience in their home counties had demonstrated the undesirability of large numbers of free Negroes.

The press heralded the law of 1827 as a real contribution to law and order in the State. The *Raleigh Register* said that expediency justified the measure. "Experience had shown that those free Negroes were at the bottom of all riots and rebellions among our slave population. It became them as representatives of the people, to check an evil so monstrous in its nature and so fatally calculated to subvert the foundation of our government."[158] In reviewing the work of the Legislature during the session just closed, a Fayetteville newspaper observed,

Of the few of the 150 acts passed . . . which can be regarded as generally useful or important in their provisions, there is none more so than that to prevent the migration of free people of color into this State, which, divested as it is of some features of doubtful expediency, with which it was originally reported, is an act called

153. There were only nineteen free Negroes in Haywood County in 1820.

154. There were 1,744 free Negroes in Craven County in 1820.

155. These counties were Stokes, Surry, and Wilkes on the Virginia border, and Brunswick and Richmond on the South Carolina border.

156. See the population census for North Carolina in United States Census Office, *The Census for 1820*. It may also be pointed out that in four counties, Montgomery, Randolph, Orange, and Guilford, there was a sizable amount of Quaker influence.

157. For example, Northampton, Gates, Warren, Granville, and Robeson.

158. *Raleigh Register*, January 23, 1827.

for by every consideration of convenience and safety. The laws of our sister States, Virginia on the one hand and South Carolina on the other, are such as to drive considerable numbers of this refuse species of population from both those States into this. They are as unwelcome here as there, and this Legislature will deserve the thanks of the people for giving an effectual check to their further ingress.[159]

Although the law was thus rather well received, not many years passed before exceptions were asked and in some cases granted. One of the outstanding examples is that of Aquilla Wilson Day, a free Negro woman of Halifax, Virginia. In 1829, she married Thomas Day, a free Negro cabinetmaker and man of considerable property, of Milton, North Carolina. When he threatened to leave the State if his wife was not permitted to come into North Carolina and live with him, sixty citizens of Milton sent an urgent plea to the Assembly in 1830 asking that she be allowed to remain in the State "free from the fines and penalties" of the act of 1827. Among the reasons given for wanting Thomas Day to remain was that he was a "first-rate workman, a remarkably sober, steady and industrious man, a high minded, good and valuable citizen, possessing a handsome property." One individual assured the Legislature "that in the event of any disturbance amongst the blacks, I should rely in confidence upon a disclosure from him as he is the owner of slaves as well as of real estate."[160] On December 24, 1830, the bill to authorize Aquilla Day to reside in the State was read and passed in the House of Commons. It passed the Senate the following week. Many of the men who sponsored the immigration law of 1827 were still in the General Assembly. It is interesting to observe that many who voted, in 1827, to keep free Negroes from migrating into the State were, in this case, to be found on the side that was willing to make an exception to the rule.[161]

Upon the advice of his friends in Raleigh, Isaac Hunter went to New York and under the laws of that State secured his manumission from his master, John Holloway of Raleigh. Upon returning to Raleigh, he continued to ply his trade as a boot and shoemaker until a process was served against him declaring that he was living in the State in violation of its laws. Hunter placed a petition before the Legis-

159. *Carolina Observer*, February 14, 1827.

160. *Journal of the House of Commons, 1830-1831* (Raleigh, 1832), p. 238.

161. For example, Bateman of Tyrrell, Foy of Jones, Gary of Northampton, J. A. Hill of Wilmington, Stedman of Gates, and Stockard of Orange all voted to prohibit the migration of free Negroes into North Carolina. In 1830, these men voted to permit Aquilla Day to remain in the State.

lature asking that he be permitted to remain long enough to· "wind up his business," which included the purchase of his wife and four children. Sixty-five citizens of Raleigh united "in praying of the Assembly to pass an act permitting him to remain" until he could settle his business and take his family away with him.[162] After pointing out that free Negroes could be of service to the community if they were honest, peaceable, and industrious, the Committee on Propositions and Grievances of the House of Commons, to which was referred the Hunter petition, observed,

> It will be wise and politic to take no step which may tend to drive from the State any single one of that portion of our free persons of color who have established a good character.[163]

The Committee recommended favorable consideration especially in view of the fact that Hunter only wanted to remain long enough to finish paying for his family.[164] In pursuance of this recommendation, the General Assembly passed a resolution allowing Isaac Hunter to remain in the State for twenty days. It provided that "after the expiration of the said twenty days the said Isaac Hunter, if he shall not be removed from this State, shall be subject to all the pains and penalties prescribed for free persons of color migrating into this State. . . ."[165]

Lunsford Lane, who, like Isaac Hunter, had secured his manumission in New York, found himself face to face with the problem of trying to circumvent the immigration law. He had lived unmolested for a number of years after returning from New York. During this time, he worked in the governor's office and for himself, trying to save enough money with which to purchase his family. In 1840, several "younger and adventurous whites" began to object to his presence, contending that he was living illegally in North Carolina.[166] Panic-stricken with the prospect of either leaving, paying a $500 fine, or being sold for ten years, he submitted a petition to the Legislature asking that he be allowed to remain for twelve months. A resolution, based on his petition, was reported favorably by the Committee, but it was killed in the House of Commons by an indefinite postponement.[167] After

162. Among the signers of the petition was William Boylan, the owner of Hunter's wife and children.

163. Ms. in the Legislative Papers for 1840-41.   164. *Ibid.*

165. *Laws Passed by the General Assembly, 1840-43* (Raleigh, 1844), 207. In the resolution as it was originally proposed, the limit for Hunter's sojourn in North Carolina was two years. On the manuscript, the two years was scratched out and twenty days substituted. Ms. in the Legislative Papers for 1840-41.

166. John S. Bassett, *Antislavery Leaders of North Carolina*, p. 67.

167. Ms. in the Legislative Papers for 1840-41.

lecturing in the East, Lane returned to Raleigh to purchase his family, much to the consternation of a number of the citizens of Raleigh. Only the protection of the governor and the mayor made it possible for him to get out of town with no more damage than being tarred and feathered.[168] The action taken on the petitions of several other free Negroes was similar to that taken on the Lane petition.[169]

The question that frequently arose was, "Does the Immigration Law of 1827 apply to a slave who leaves the State for a short period of time and returns with the status of a free Negro?" This question was settled by the Supreme Court in the decade before the Civil War and thus another blow was dealt to the forces that made for the increase of free Negroes in North Carolina. In 1851, the Court held that a testator's will could not be carried out when it provided for the removal of slaves to some state for the purpose of emancipation and the subsequent return of those individuals to North Carolina. The Court said that the proceedings were void and "were in fraud of the Laws of North Carolina."[170]

The law of 1827 was again brought to the front by the Court in 1853. In a case coming up from Richmond County, the Court upheld the decision of a lower court which convicted a free Negro for having migrated into the State and failing to depart within twenty days.[171] In the revisals of the next year, the law of 1827 was strengthened in the following manner:

> Free negroes not now lawful residents and inhabitants of the State, shall never hereafter become so by any length of time, neither they nor their issue; and in all cases where such free negroes are under the age of 16, it shall be the duty of the County Court of the County in which they reside, to remove them at the expense of the County; and all such as remain to that age, shall be deemed guilty of a misdemeanor, and on conviction shall be fined five hundred dollars.[172]

There can be no doubt that there were times when the immigration of free Negroes into North Carolina caused considerable anxiety on the part of its citizens. At such times, perhaps, "the strictest watches were kept and prompt measures taken to enforce the law," as a newspaper

---

168. See Hawkins, *Lunsford Lane,* and Bassett, *Antislavery Leaders,* for detailed accounts of Lane's interesting life.

169. See the Petition of Jacob, Mary, Patsey, Meriwether, and Matilda to the General Assembly in 1844. Ms. in the Legislative Papers for 1844.

170. Green et al. v. Lane et al., 43 N. C., 52.

171. State v. Jacobs, 44 N. C., 211.

172. *Revised Code of North Carolina,* p. 575.

advised in 1851.[173] Yet, one may be sure that there were long periods of time when the laxity of enforcement and the preoccupation of the citizens with other matters made it possible for free Negro immigrants to make their way into North Carolina. As long as they led a peaceable and humble life, there was little likelihood that they would be apprehended. Thus, they could remain for a number of census enumerations. In 1850—more than twenty years after the immigration law was passed—608 of the free Negroes of North Carolina had been born in other states of the United States, while sixteen had been born in foreign countries.[174]

MAINTAINING THE STATUS OF A FREE MAN

The maintenance of freedom, even in the limited sense in which it was applied to the free Negro, was something for which he had to make a continuous fight. It was by no means enough to have been manumitted, or even to have been born free. The free person of color had to maintain a strict vigil over his status lest it be reduced to that of a slave. The maintenance of this vigil constitutes an interesting page in the history of the free Negro in North Carolina and served, in a very real way, to bolster the number of free Negroes which were to be found there. Had they not struggled to keep what freedom they did have, the number of free Negroes in North Carolina would not have been as large as it was.

The loss of court records from time to time or the possibility of such a loss was a constant threat to the Negro's freedom. If his right to freedom was challenged and the court records revealed nothing in his favor, there was a great likelihood that he would lose his freedom altogether. Thus, he learned to have his right to freedom entered in various public records and to secure certificates or affidavits of his freedom. For example, Emanuel Hails went into the Craven County Court and had this affidavit filed after his freedom had been questioned:

> This is to certify that I have known a certain black man by the name of Emanuel Hails this ten or twelve years and he has always passed as free, and I have never known anything of him but that he has been an honest and hardworking person ever since he has been in this place; also I believe him to be as feasible a person as any whatsoever. Given from under my hand this 17th day of September, 1807.
>
> Thomas O. Bryan.[175]

173. *Fayetteville Observer,* November 11, 1851.
174. United States Census Office, *The Seventh Census,* p. 309.
175. Minutes of the Court of Pleas and Quarter Sessions for Craven County, 1807.

Sometimes the court, upon hearing testimony, would issue a certificate of freedom in the name of the court. The Beaufort County records for 1843 reveal a number of such certificates, one of which follows:

It appearing to the Court that Polly Titterton is and has always been known and reputed to be a free woman of colour, ordered that the Clerk of this Court give her a certificate to that effect containing a description of her person.[176]

The whole question of the status of the offspring of slaves and of free Negroes under certain circumstances was decided by the Supreme Court of North Carolina in a series of interesting cases. A slaveholder, residing in Virginia, made the following will concerning some slaves on his North Carolina plantation several years before his death:

My will and desire is that my negro woman "P" shall have her freedom immediately; and that all the rest of my black people should serve until my youngest shall be of the age of twenty-one years. . . . After my youngest is of age, my will is that all my negroes shall be free.[177]

Before the youngest child of the testator had reached his majority, one of the slaves gave birth to a daughter. The question was: Is the offspring of this slave, who is to be free at a later date, entitled to freedom also? In clear language, Justice Gaston held that the child, although born after the testator died and before his youngest child came of age, was entitled to freedom after the latter event.[178]

The decision in the above case did not remain in effect very long, however. Two years later, in 1842, a similar case came before the Court. Briefly, the facts are as follows: In 1805, a Virginia slaveholder manumitted his slave Polly, to take effect April 1, 1814. He moved to North Carolina and brought Polly with him. Before her manumission became effective, she gave birth to a daughter, who, in turn, was the mother of the plaintiff, William Mayho. Was Mayho entitled to freedom? Chief Justice Ruffin declared that any issue born to a slave before manumission became effective was a slave. He said, "The Court cannot . . . escape the conclusion that the plaintiff's mother was born a slave and so, consequently, was he. With this conviction it becomes

---

See also the affidavits to prove the freedom of Patsy Watkins of Guilford County, in the Legislative Papers for 1831-1832.

176. Minutes of the Court of Pleas and Quarter Sessions for Beaufort County, 1843. See also the certificates of Southey, Eliza, and Nancy Keas, in the same minute book.

177. Campbell v. Street, 23 N. C., 86.   178. *Ibid.*, p. 88.

our duty to affirm the judgment of the lower court consoling ourselves that the sentence is not ours, but that of the law, whose ministers only we are."[179]

One must not get the impression that all individuals who may have been entitled to the status of free Negro were anxious to be classified as such. The reluctance of individuals to fall into that category did not, however, cause the Court to hesitate when it seemed that they should be placed there. Facing a charge of fornication and adultery for marrying a white woman, William P. Watters contended that he was descended from Portuguese and not from Negro or Indian ancestors. One witness swore that he knew the grandparents of Watters and that they were "coal black" Negroes. The Court gave the following decision:

Although the act which annuls marriage between the two races, uses the words "persons of color" generally, we are of the opinion, that expression must be construed in reference to other disabilities imposed, for reasons of a similar nature upon persons of mixed blood. The Act of 1777 . . . and the Constitution . . . designate such persons as those descended from negro ancestors to the fourth generation inclusive, though one ancestor of each generation may have been a white person. And thus restricted, the act includes the defendant, who, at most, was only the third generation from a full Negro.[180]

When Whitmell Dempsey, as a free man of color, was indicted for carrying a gun without a license, he denied that he was a free Negro and therefore contended that he did not come under the act which was being enforced. By tracing his white ancestry, he attempted to show that he was not a free person of color within the meaning of the statute, but Chief Justice Ruffin disagreed. The eminent jurist said,

It is true that the defendant is not a negro who is a black person, entirely of the African race. Nor is he a mulatto, according to the proper original signification of the term. . . . And the court could hardly undertake of itself to construe the expression "free person of color" so as to bring one within the statutes creating felonies, or otherwise highly penal, merely because he derived from some remote ancestor a tinge of color that was not white. . . . But the legislature has shown clearly that in penal statutes free negroes, mulattoes, persons of mixed blood etc. come within the provisions of the acts.[181]

179. Mayho, by his Next Friend, v. Sears, 25 N. C., 159.
180. State v. Watters, 25 N. C., 308.
181. State v. Dempsey, 31 N. C., 265; see also State v. Chavers, 50 N. C., 25, for a similar case but a different ruling.

In the struggle to maintain the status of free men, those who were detained as slaves were perhaps the most numerous and, in some ways, had the greatest difficulty. In moving about from place to place, the free Negroes' right to such liberties was always subject to be questioned by whites. The mantle of suspicion was always around them. That they were runaway slaves or that they were convicts were presumptions that were all but conclusive in some quarters. Regardless of how long the individual had been accepted as a free Negro in the community in which he lived, there was always the possibility that descendants of his former master or of his ancestor's master might attempt to force him into the rank of slaves.

There are a number of cases which reached the Supreme Court in which the Negro's right to freedom even after the lapse of a long period of time was questioned. When the son of a slaveholder tried to force May Stringer into slavery after her family had enjoyed thirty years of freedom through the manumission of her grandmother, the Court, through Justice Nash, said:

> From 1807, the mother of the plaintiff and her descendants have been, in the community in which they live, considered and treated as free persons. After a period of thirty years, the defendant without pretense of right as far as we are informed, seized upon the plaintiff and questions her right of freedom. After so long an acquiescence by the public in her enjoyment of her freedom, every presumption is to be made in favor of her actual emancipation, especially against a tresspasser and wrongdoer.[182]

In another case in which the action was also one of trespass *vi et armis,* some interesting points of view were expressed by the Supreme Court. When the grandson of a master who had manumitted his slave woman questioned the right to freedom of the daughter, the Superior Court of New Hanover County decided against the alleged free Negro woman. The court said that the records did not show valid emancipation, and that, thirty years later, the descendants of the Negro who was illegally set free should be returned to slavery. When the case came to the Supreme Court, Justice Battle swept aside any errors in detail and procedure when he said for the Court,

> Surely, after such a distinct acknowledgement by the owner that he applied for and obtained from the Court a license to liberate his slave, and had from that time permitted her to go free, and he and all other persons had for more than thirty years treated her and

182. Stringer v. Burcham, 34 N. C., 40.

regarded her and her daughter as free, every presumption ought to be made in favor of her actual emancipation according to law.[183]

Thus, it became an accepted principle of law that after thirty years of unquestioned freedom the presumption that a person was free was all but conclusive.[184]

The presumption of one's status, whether slave or free, often depended on his color. In a series of cases, the Supreme Court established a set of principles that came to be the accepted law throughout the State. When the plaintiff in a case arising in 1802 was eight days of age, she was found in a barn by the defendant, who was then twelve years old. The plaintiff was of olive complexion, had long hair, and a prominent nose. The plaintiff's counsel insisted, therefore, that the defendant could not presume that the plaintiff was a slave. The majority opinion, read by Justice Taylor, merits extensive quotation.

> I acquiesce in the rule laid down by the defendant's counsel, with respect to the presumption of every black person being a slave. . . . If . . . a person of that description claims his freedom, he must establish his right to it by such evidence as will destroy the force of the presumption arising from his color. . . .
>
> But I am not aware that the doctrine of presumption against liberty has been urged in relation to persons of mixed blood, or to those of any color between the two extremes of black and white; and I do not think it is reasonable that such doctrine should receive the least countenance. Such persons may have descended from Indians in both lines, or at least in the maternal; they may have descended from a white parent in the maternal line or from mulatto parents originally free, in all which cases the offspring following the condition of the mother is entitled to freedom. Consider-

183. Allen v. Allen, 44 N. C., 71; see also Sampson v. Burgwin, 20 N. C., 17; and Mayo v. Whitson and Pearce, 47 N. C., 223.

184. See also Justice Battle's decision in Jarman v. Humphrey, 51 N. C., 41, in which he said that after an emancipation has been accepted for thirty years as valid, the "title of the former owner is divested and enures to the benefit of the colored persons," regardless of whether "such proceedings were regular or otherwise." See, also, the opinion of Justice Pearson in Cully v. Jones, 31 N. C., 126, in which he pointed out that when "more than 40 years have been allowed to pass from the act of emancipation and the birth of the plaintiff before any claim was made to hold her as a slave during all which time she passed as a free person . . . almost anything will be presumed in order to give effect to the act of emancipation." But see Brookfield v. Stanton, 51 N. C., 156, where the case was remanded to the lower court for a new trial. Brookfield was unsuccessful in this attempt to maintain his freedom for, although he was accepted as free for thirty years, the lower court would not permit the jury to consider evidence submitted to show that Brookfield's family had been enslaved less than thirty years prior to the plaintiff's birth. Therefore, the Supreme Court said that there had been an error in the trial before the lower court.

ing how many probabilities there are in favor of the liberty of these persons, they ought not to be deprived of it upon mere presumption, more especially as the right to hold them in slavery, if it exists at all, is in most instances, capable of being satisfactorily proved.[185]

This case, decided in 1802, gave the benefit of the doubt to persons of mixed blood, but made it clear that black persons were not to enjoy the benefit of that doubt. In 1828, this view was again expressed by the court in giving instructions to the jury. The judge told them that if the plaintiff was of "black African complexion, they might presume ... that she was a slave; if she was of yellow complexion, no presumption of slavery arose from her color."[186] From this time to the end of the period, mulattoes and persons of mixed blood had an excellent opportunity to establish their freedom if there was any doubt as to their status.[187]

Even when the question of color did not arise, there were instances in which a Negro's freedom was challenged; and he had to prove it to the satisfaction of the authorities. Sometimes, mere suspicion of being a slave was sufficient reason for one's detention, but subsequent release was often the reward—however questionable—for diligent contentions. In Beaufort County, the following case was recorded:

> Joshua Leigh, a man of Colour detained for more than twelve months in the Prison of the County of Beaufort under the supposition of his being a slave—and the Court deeming the circumstances of the case strongly presumptive that he is a free man and wrongly held in *duress vite*. It is ordered that on his coming into Court and taking the oath of Insolvency and giving the Bond for his good Behaviour, as required by law, that the Jailer set him at liberty, and he came here into Court, and took the oath of an Insolvent Debtor and was accordingly discharged.[188]

That many free Negroes were illegally held in bondage was generally known throughout the State, and it was viewed with considerable disfavor. The North Carolina Manumission Society had a committee which was to look into the matter of free Negroes who were

185. Gober v. Gober, 1 N. C., 166.   186. Scott v. Williams, 12 N. C., 236.

187. See Nichols v. Bell, 46 N. C., 44. In this case, the defendant asked the court to instruct the jury that "in case of persons of a shade of color darker than that of a mulatto, the law presumed that they were slaves." The court refused to give such instructions and remarked, "Let the presumption rest upon the African race—That is a decided mark; but to carry it into shades would lead us into darkness, doubt, and uncertainty, for they are as varied as the admixture of blood against the races, and against the rule that presumptions are always in favor of liberty."

188. Minutes of the Court of Pleas and Quarter Sessions for Beaufort County, 1824. See also Free Jack v. Woodruff, 10 N. C., 58.

being illegally held as slaves. At a meeting in 1825, the Deep Creek branch reported that a "number of colored people" were being "illegally held in bondage in Surry County and perhaps in some other Naboring County" and solicited advice. The Society dismissed the matter with the advice not to do anything in a "society capacity."[189]

Many of the free Negroes who were held as slaves had been stolen, either by the persons who held them or by individuals who subsequently sold them. The first law against the stealing of free Negroes was passed in 1779.[190] The weakness of that first law is revealed in the preamble of the law of 1801 which sought to put an end to the stealing of free Negroes:

> Whereas by the . . . Act [of 1779] no penalty is annexed to the stealing, carrying off, and selling free negroes and mulattoes within the limits of this State, for the remedy whereof,
> Be it enacted . . . That any person who shall hereafter steal or sell any free negro or free negroes, or persons of mixed blood, knowing the same to be free or stolen, or shall by violence, seduction, or any other means, take or convey any free negro or free negroes, or persons of mixed blood, or appropriate the same to his, her or their own use, and being thereof legally convicted, shall for every such offence be fined not less than fifty pounds, nor more than five hundred pounds and imprisoned not less than three months, nor more than eighteen months, anything in the before recited act to the contrary notwithstanding.[191]

Thus, the nineteenth century opened with a very strong legal denunciation of the stealing and selling of free Negroes. Despite this fact, the law was flagrantly violated before the end of the year. The *Raleigh Register* reported the following incident in the autumn of 1801:

> On the 29th Instant, about Midnight, four men came to the House of Valentine Locust, an aged free Negro, who resides on Leek Creek, in Wake County, and calling at the Door to gain admittance, as soon as the door was opened, two of them entered with clubs, and instantaneously knocked down the old man and his wife and beat them to such a Degree as scarcely to leave life, and whilst they were in that Situation the robbers carried off two of their children.[192]

189. Wagstaff, *Minutes*, p. 107.
190. Reported in the *Raleigh Register*, January 13, 1801.
191. James Iredell, *Laws of the State of North Carolina, 1715-1790* (Raleigh, n. d.), p. 378. The law of 1779 dealt only with the stealing of free Negroes and taking them *out* of the State.
192. *Raleigh Register*, October 6, 1801.

The Raleigh newspaper was incensed over the occurrence and called upon the community "to contribute everything in their powers . . . to the detecting and punishing such vile offenders" and asked other editors to give this item a place in their papers. The editor expressed much pleasure in another column, set up later, when it was learned that the free Negro children had escaped while their captors were asleep.[193] In December of the same year, another advertisement made known the fact that a free Negro girl had disappeared several months earlier, and it was supposed that she was stolen from her home in Wayne County.[194]

Before the end of the decade, another free Negro mother became alarmed over the disappearance of her children and placed the following advertisement in the newspaper:

Stolen
From the Subscriber, in Wake County . . . on Friday 21st Inst, three Girl children, of Colour, Free Born. [A description of Polly, Sukey, and Becky followed.]
   It is supposed that some dishonest Person has taken them off, for the purpose of selling them as Slaves. Any person that can give any information to the Printer hereof, so that I can get my children again, will be thankfully received, besides making any satisfaction I am able to do.

                                        Nancy Valentine.[195]

When a free Negro child was stolen from its mother in 1831, a newspaper carried an article which had as its caption, "An Atrocious Act." It said that suspicion was attached to "a certain individual, as the villain engaged in this business; but he will, in all probability, transfer the child to some accomplice, or sell it as soon as possible, as his property. . . . it is earnestly requested that any information which may lead to the discovery of the child may be communicated to the postmaster at Chapel Hill.[196]

That some free Negroes were actually sold as slaves can be seen in the convictions and liberations that are a matter of record. As early as 1789, the Craven County Court convicted one Stephen Tinker for bringing a free Negro woman and her two children from Connecticut and selling them to William Shepard as slaves. Tinker was placed

193. *Ibid.*, October 6, 1801.
194. *Ibid.*, December 15, 1801.
195. *Raleigh Register*, August 27, 1827.
196. News item from Chapel Hill, North Carolina, in the *Carolina Observer* (Fayetteville), March 10, 1831.

under a bond of £500 and required to carry the free Negro family back to Connecticut.[197]

The penalty for carrying a free Negro out of the State and selling him was death without benefit of clergy. Micajah Johnson of Fayetteville paid such a penalty in 1806 for taking a free Negro boy into Virginia and selling him as a slave.[198] Virginians, however, were selling their free Negroes into North Carolina in later years, as can be seen in an item taken from the *Fayetteville Observer* in 1855:

> Two men, Ruffin D. Freeman and William Freeman, father and son, of Brunswick County, Virginia, were arrested a few days ago for selling a free Negro as a slave to a gentleman in North Carolina (they having promised to divide the spoils with the Negro). The Negro ran away . . . was arrested in Petersburg, and then confessed the whole story. . . .[199]

The following item impresses one with the fact that the returns from trading in free Negroes were tempting even to those who should have had scruples against it:

> We learn from the Asheborough Bulletin that Lewis Parks and William Parks, brothers of Randolph County, were arrested a few days ago for selling a free Negro to Mr. March of Davie County for $650 and a carriage worth $450. The negro had previously, for the consideration of a gold watch, bound himself to Lewis Parks for 99 years. When March discovered the facts he went to Randolph and demanded repayment. Failing to refund, the brothers were committed to jail. After two days in jail they satisfied Mr. March and were discharged. They are still liable to criminal prosecution. Lewis Parks is a Baptist preacher, previously of fair reputation.[200]

The problem, then, of the Negro in ante-bellum North Carolina was twofold: There was the problem of *obtaining* freedom. It was one which was before a large number of the Negroes, consciously or unconsciously, throughout the ante-bellum period. Circumstances over which they oftentimes had little or no control threw many of them into the unique type of freedom that is to be described later. Through manumission, circumstances of birth, running away, and migration they arrived at the status in which their legal connotations of free Negro, free person of color, mulatto, person of mixed blood, etc. were almost

197. Ms. in the County Records of Craven County, 1789.
198. *Raleigh Register*, May 12, 1806.
199. *Fayetteville Observer*, July 30, 1855.
200. *Ibid.*, July 21, 1856.

as numerous as the shades of their complexions. Having arrived at that status, they found themselves face to face with the second problem: that of *maintaining* the status of free people. In danger almost every moment of having their right to freedom questioned, theirs was a difficult struggle. Certificates of freedom were often inadequate; and all too seldom did their ignorance of the procedures by which freedom was maintained elicit sympathy from a society that looked upon them as a "growing menace." The danger of being stolen, moreover, and sold back into slavery hung over the heads of adults and children alike. The fact that, by 1860, 30,000 Negroes in North Carolina had been able not only to obtain freedom but to maintain it is a fact more fully appreciated when viewed in the light of existing circumstances.

CHAPTER III

Legal Status of the Free Negro

I do not acknowledge any equality between the white man and the free negro, in the enjoyment of political rights—the free negro is a *citizen of necessity*, and must, as long as he abides among us, submit to the laws which necessity and the peculiarity of his situation compel us to adopt.

> Remarks of James W. Bryan on the disfranchisement of the free Negro at the North Carolina Constitutional Convention, June 13, 1835.

THE PROBLEM OF DISCIPLINE

THE GROWTH OF FREE Negroes in the State of North Carolina was most clearly manifested in the increasing concern of the citizens in general over the presence of this group. The alarm shown by an editor who queried, "What is to be done with this class of our population?"[1] had its counterpart in any period when the reports showed a substantial increase in the free Negro population. The legal status of the free Negro in North Carolina depended in a large measure on the attitude of the citizens, which was reflected in the laws which they passed affecting the free Negro. These laws were prompted by various forebodings which the citizenry entertained with regard to this anomalous group. If there was peace in the community and if the slave system seemed unchallenged, the legal status of the free Negro was raised considerably, not only because of a cessation of legislation restricting his activities, but also because of a relaxation in the enforcement of those laws which were on the statute books. Sensitive and delicate as the "peculiar institution" was, however, the least disturbance was amplified into an alarming situation which was the occasion for the further circumscription of the free Negroes. Thus, an important aspect of the legal status of the free Negro turns on the problem of disciplinary measures taken in time of panic, usually following rumors or fears of a servile insurrection.[2]

1. *North Carolina Standard,* October 16, 1850.
2. See Clement Eaton, *Freedom of Thought in the Old South,* Ch. IV, for a new treatment of the fear of servile insurrections.

The conspiracies of the slaves to revolt in North Carolina in the eighteenth century never reached the point of fruition, and the citizens did not reach a state of panic as a result of the rumors. The reports in 1775 that the blacks were going to revolt against their masters evoked no more than a comment by the North Carolina delegates to the Continental Congress that the State had taken necessary precautions to guard against such a possibility.[3]

No small part of the precaution was the development of a black code which sought carefully to regulate the various activities of the slaves and, to a less degree, of the free Negro. Beginning in 1715, the Lords Proprietors and the General Assembly had begun to establish rules governing the slaves within the Colony, and by the time of the Revolution the set of laws had been completed. The injunction against slaves traveling without passes,[4] the laws concerning the places and conditions under which Negroes could have meetings,[5] the severe penalties attached to the laws against enticing slaves to leave their masters[6] were all safeguards against possible insurrections. Even more effective precautions were the laws against the possession of weapons by Negroes,[7] and the penalty of death for consulting, advising, or conspiring "to rebel, or make insurrection."[8] The establishment of patrols from the very beginning, moreover, served to insure the enforcement, at times at least, of the laws that were being passed.

In the eighteenth century the free Negro was not the subject of legislation with regard to insurrections. To be sure, he was disciplined, but there seemed to be little connection in the minds of the legislators between slave insurrections and free Negroes. The laws regulating the manumission of slaves, the one against the intermarriage of free Negroes with whites, and the one to "discourage" the practice of perjury were the principal acts which directly touched on the activities of the free Negroes.

In the early years of the national period, the free Negroes of North Carolina were brought under closer surveillance of the law in a series of enactments by the General Assembly. In 1785, that body passed an act to "Restrain the conduct of slaves and others" in the towns of Wilmington, Washington, Edenton, and Fayetteville. After making further provisions for regulating the movements and activities of slaves, the law stated,

3. Saunders, *Colonial Records*, X, xxviii.
4. Clark, *State Records*, XXIII, 63.
5. *Ibid.*, XXIII, 65.
6. *Ibid.*, XXIII, 197.
7. *Ibid.*, XXIII, 201.
8. *Ibid.*, XXIII, 202.

And in order to discriminate between free negroes, mulattoes, and other persons of mixed blood and slaves:

X. Be it enacted . . . That all persons of the above mentioned description who are or shall be free on or before the said first day of May next, apply to the commissioners, trustees or directors of the respective towns aforesaid, in order to have their names registered; and every such person coming into the said towns . . . to reside, shall within three days . . . make like application; and the commissioners, trustees, or directors are hereby authorized to give every such free person a badge of cloth . . . to be fixed on the left shoulder, and to have thereon wrought in legible capital letters the word FREE.[9]

The registrant was required to pay two shillings to the town clerk for his services and eight shillings to the town officials for the use of their respective towns. No such registration law was passed for free Negroes living in the country. It was aimed at those areas where a number of free Negroes might take advantage of their color and make contact with the slaves for the purpose of "inciting them to revolt."

In 1795, a law was passed concerning the conduct of free Negroes throughout the State. There is little doubt that the activities of the Negroes in the West Indies during that "woeful decade" had a great deal to do with the enactment of these new measures,[10] for there were no events in North Carolina that could have given impetus to such regulations:

be it . . . enacted, That it shall be the duty of the several county courts in the state, to charge the grand juries of the respective counties to make presentments of all such free persons of colour as conduct themselves so as to become dangerous to the peace and good order of the state and county, upon which said presentment it shall be the duty of the court . . . to issue an order to the Sheriff to take into custody the person so presented and him safely keep until the next county court, when a jury shall be empanuled, as before directed in this act, and a trial agreeably thereto had; and if any person shall be found guilty . . . he shall be compelled to give bond and security as in case of persons coming into this state . . . ; and in case of failure . . . he, she or they shall be sold. . . .[11]

The law thus far constituted the most complete system of regulation that had surrounded the free Negro to date and harked back to twelfth-

9. Clark, *State Records*, XXIV, 727-728.
10. See Rosser H. Taylor, "Slave Conspiracies in North Carolina," *North Carolina Historical Review*, V (January, 1928), 25.
11. *Laws, 1790-1804*, p. 11.

century England, when Henry II created juries of presentment to examine certain individuals who might not be keeping the peace. This, however, was not enough for the North Carolina legislators, and in the next section they turned directly to the problem of insurrection:

> V. *And be it further enacted,* That when any number of negroes, or other slaves, or free people of color shall collect together in arms and be going about the country, committing thefts and alarming the inhabitants of any county, it shall be the duty of the commanding officer of such county, or captain of a troop of horse, upon three or more Justices of the Peace requiring the same, immediately to call out a sufficient number to suppress such depredations and insurrections. . . .[12]

Thus, the legislators of 1795 had improved considerably on the "precautions" taken by the officials of 1775. They had not only strengthened the laws regulating the activities of slaves, but they had also brought under the law the various movements of the free Negro, who conceivably might follow the example of his brethren in the not-too-distant West Indies.

In a letter to his son in June, 1802, Charles Pettigrew made the following remarks:

> We have a rumpus in the upper end of this [Beaufort] County with the negroes. Whether there are any of the conspirators among us I know not. No Discovery has been made nor anyone implicated that we hear of. I wish that when the [illegible] enter upon the tryal of the Edenton boys, the Examiners would be very particular in regard to the negroes at the Lake whether any of them have joined, for it is extraordinary if every other place abound so with conspirators and there should be none there or among us.[13]

In this letter, Pettigrew was referring to the trial of persons connected with the abortive insurrections in Bertie, Halifax, Jones, Martin, and other northeastern counties. On the next day after Pettigrew wrote to his son, a Raleigh newspaper reported that the Negroes "in and about the town of Windsor . . . had committed great havock."[14]

In the trials at Edenton, two Negroes were convicted and executed.[15] The "Lenity" which Pettigrew had condemned had not been followed,[16] because public opinion would not stand for it. This atti-

---

12. *Ibid.*, p. 12.

13. Pettigrew Family Papers, Charles Pettigrew to Ebenezer Pettigrew, June 21, 1802.

14. *Raleigh Register*, June 22, 1802. In a subsequent issue the editor admitted that the early reports had been somewhat exaggerated. July 6, 1802.

15. William K. Boyd, *History of North Carolina*, II, 218.

16. Pettigrew Family Papers, Charles Pettigrew to Ebenezer Pettigrew, May 10, 1802.

tude was likewise reflected in the legislation which was passed in the autumn of the same year. The new law contained a restriction on free persons as well as on slaves:

Be it ... enacted, That if any free person shall join in any conspiracy, rebellion or insurrection of the slaves, or shall agree to join in any such conspiracy, rebellion or insurrection, or shall procure or persuade others to join or enlist for that purpose or shall ... aid or assist any slave or slaves in a state of rebellion ... as by furnishing, or agreeing to promise to furnish such slaves with arms, ammunition or any other articles for their aid and support, every free person so offending and being thereof legally convicted, shall be adjudged guilty of felony, and shall suffer death without benefit of clergy.[17]

Although the Denmark Vesey insurrection of 1822 in Charleston, South Carolina, was directed by a free Negro and although the press of North Carolina gave considerable attention to this incident, the General Assembly did not see fit to pass any further measures restricting the activities of free Negroes. It was not until 1825 that any new regulations appeared, and these were only local. In that year, the Commissioners of Raleigh required registration of all free persons of color within its limits. These individuals were obliged to "produce satisfactory testimonials of good character," for which, in exchange, they were given permits of residence. A date, March 7, was set as the deadline for registration, after which time "such as claim to be free persons of colour and have no permits, will be rigorously dealt with."[18]

An event which occurred in far-away New England on November 15, 1825, had serious repercussions in North Carolina. It served in a material way to curtail the liberties of the free Negro. On that day, the legislature of Vermont passed the following resolution:

Resolved by the General Assembly of the State of Vermont, That slavery is an evil to be deprecated by a free and enlightened people, and that this General Assembly will accord in any measures which may be adopted by the general government for its abolition in the United States. ...

Resolved, that ... the Governor be requested to transmit a copy of the foregoing resolution to the Executives of the several States, to be laid before their several legislatures. ...[19]

When the General Assembly of North Carolina met in 1826, Governor Burton transmitted the resolution to that body with the comment that

17. Laws, 1790-1804, p. 12.   18. Raleigh Register, February 18, 1825.
19. Printed copy in the Legislative Papers for North Carolina for 1826-27.

this was an instance indicating that states, "like individuals, may fall into the common error of believing that they better understand, and with more skill . . . could manage the concerns of others, than they display in their own transactions. . . ." The Governor warned the Assembly that such meddling was a substantial threat to the independence of the State and urged that body to "provide every precaution against any emergency to which they may be exposed." He further stated that the frequent and misguided proceedings of people in other sections of the country in connection with slavery demanded from North Carolina a "sleepless vigilance." It was unfortunate, the chief magistrate of the State asserted, that other states undertook such interference, because it necessarily resulted in increasing the severity of the law toward Negroes. He then asked the Assembly to look into the matter of revising the laws respecting slaves and free Negroes.[20]

The Legislature accepted the challenge of Governor Burton and proceeded to answer the Vermont resolution. The North Carolina Assembly said,

> the Legislature of this State are at all times competent to regulate and control its internal concerns, nor will it permit an interference with them from any quarter whatever.[21]

The Senate proceeded to appoint a committee on free Negroes headed by Henry Seawell of Wake County. Before the session was over in January, 1827, a number of new laws had been passed which vitally affected the status of the free Negro. In addition to the law against free Negroes migrating into the State, which has already been discussed,[22] there was one which provided that certain free Negro children should be bound out, so as more effectively to teach them an honest and industrious occupation.[23] There was also a law against vagrancy which sought to force all able-bodied free Negroes to work. In part, it provided,

> That if any free negro or mulatto in any county in this State, who is able to labor, shall be found spending his or her time in idleness and dissipation, or who has no regular or honest employment or occupation . . . it shall and may be lawful for any citizen to apply to a justice of the peace . . . and upon affidavit obtain a warrant to arrest such persons and bring him or her before some

20. *Journal of the House*, 1826-1829, 117 ff. *Cf. supra*, p. 43.
21. Ms. in the Legislative Papers for 1826-27.
22. *Laws Passed by the General Assembly*, 1825-1830 (Raleigh, 1831), p. 13. *Cf. supra*, p. 43.
23. *Ibid.*, p. 15. *Cf. infra*, Ch. IV.

justice of said county; and if . . . it should appear to the said justice that . . . the free negro or mulatto comes within the provisions of this act, the . . . justice shall bind him or her with reasonable security to appear at the next court of said county.

The act further provided that if the free Negro could not provide the necessary security, he was to be detained in the county jail until the next session of court. If at the next court he was found guilty, he was to give bond for "good behavior and industrious peaceable deportment for one year." If the free Negro could not give the security and pay the court costs, the court was required to hire him out "for a term of service and labor which to them seem reasonable and just, and calculated to reform him . . . to habits of industry and morality, not exceeding three years for any one offense."[24]

In language more vivid than was contained in the resolution forwarded to the several state legislatures, North Carolina showed Vermont that it was "competent to control its own internal concerns." It had more carefully regulated its militia and patrols, it had circumscribed the activities of slaves, and it had gone far in proscribing the activities of free Negroes. These persons were now at the mercy of justices of the peace, and it is needless to say that at times extremely personal and petty considerations determined whether or not the free Negro was to provide a bond for his good conduct and pay the costs of the court, which he not infrequently lacked.

In the autumn of 1829, there appeared on the horizon an individual who created more fear in the hearts of the Southern slaveholders than any insurrection had done in previous years. This was David Walker, author of *Walker's Appeal in Four Articles*.[25] Walker was born in Wilmington, North Carolina, in 1785, the son of a slave father and a free mother.[26] As a youth he traveled all over the South and developed a deep and bitter sympathy for his slave brethren. In 1827 or 1828 he moved to Boston and opened a secondhand clothing shop. In September, 1829, the first edition of his *Appeal* appeared.

In the preamble of his essay, Walker asserted that the Negro in the United States was the "most degraded, wretched, and abject set of beings that ever lived since the world began."[27] This conclusion was

24. *Laws for 1825-30*, p. 15.

25. The complete title is *Walker's Appeal in Four Articles Together with a Preamble to the Colored Citizens of the World But in Particular and very Expressly to those of the United States of America.*

26. For a sketch of Walker's life, see Martha Gruening, "David Walker," *Dictionary of American Biography*, XIX, 340.

27. Walker, *Walker's Appeal*, p. 3. The writer's discussion is based on the second

based upon an extensive—and unfavorable—comparison of the Negro in the United States with the Israelites in Egypt and the Helots of Sparta. The first article was entitled, "Our Wretchedness in Consequence of Slavery," in which he described the manner in which Negroes were treated and the low regard in which they were held by whites. He asked his brethren,

> Are we men!! I ask you . . . are we MEN? Did our creator make us to be slaves to dust and ashes like ourselves? Are they not dying worms as well as we? . . . How we could be so *submissive* to a gang of men, whom we cannot tell whether they are as good as ourselves or not, I never conceive.[28]

The second article, "Our Wretchedness in Consequence of Ignorance," predicted the rise of a great Negro leader to guide the way to freedom and independence. He said, "As true as the sun ever shone in its meridian splendor, my colour will root some of them [the whites] out of the very face of the earth. . . . Ignorance as it now exists among us, produces a state of things, Oh my Lord! too horrible to present to the world."[29] So moved was Walker in observing the conditions that existed that at one point he exclaimed, "Oh Heaven! I am full!!! I can hardly move my pen!!!"[30] Jefferson did not escape the calumny of Walker for his remarks in his *Notes on Virginia* that he suspected that blacks were inferior to whites in the endowments both of body and mind. Walker said that the Negro's submissiveness and abject ignorance tended to confirm this point of view.

Walker condemned ministers and colonizationists in his last two articles, "Our Wretchedness in Consequence of the Preachers of the Religion of Jesus Christ," and "Our Wretchedness in Consequence of the Colonizing Plan." One excerpt from each will suffice:

> Can anything be a greater mockery of religion than the way it is conducted by the Americans? It appears as though they are bent only on daring Almighty God to do his best—they chain and handcuff us . . . and drive us around the country like brutes and go into the house of the God of Justice to return him thanks for having aided them in their infernal cruelties inflicted upon us.[31]

of three editions. The last two editions appeared close together in 1830. All of these editions are rare, but the first is extremely rare. See Clement Eaton, "A Dangerous Pamphlet in the Old South," *Journal of Southern History*, II (August, 1936), 322n.

28. *Ibid.*, pp. 10-11. 29. *Ibid.*, p. 25.
30. *Ibid.*, p. 25. 31. *Ibid.*, p. 49.

In protesting against all colonization plans, he said,

> America is more our country than it is the whites—we have enriched it with our *blood and tears*. The greatest riches in all America have arisen from our blood and tears: And they will drive us from our property and homes, which we have earned with our blood.[32]

Walker closed by quoting the Declaration of Independence to show that Negroes were justified in resisting, with force if necessary, the oppression of white masters.

Walker's Appeal stands preëminent among the antislavery writings of the militant period. That it would be most unwelcome in the slaveholding states goes without saying. In December, 1829, the mayor of Savannah learned that slaves in the city had copies in their possession. The governor of the State asked the legislature to pass strong measures against incendiary publications. "The legislature responded by passing several severe laws in regard to the colored population."[33]

These events in Georgia did not go unnoticed in North Carolina, and the Raleigh newspapers reprinted the items which were found in the Georgia papers.[34] It was not long, moreover, before North Carolina found herself face to face with the problem. In August, 1830, the Magistrate of the Wilmington police informed Governor Owens that a "well-disposed free person of Colour" had put a copy of Walker's pamphlet into his hands. In a somewhat alarmed tone he said that Walker had treated "in most inflammatory terms . . . the conditions of the slaves in the southern States, exaggerating their sufferings, magnifying their physical strength, and underrating the power of the whites; containing also an open appeal to the natural love of liberty." The official said that an investigation in his city disclosed the fact that a number of free Negroes and slaves "have for the few months past frequently discussed the subject of a conspiracy to effect the emancipation of the slaves of this place."[35] The magistrate of the Fayetteville police also showed some concern about the Walker pamphlet in his town and expressed fear of an insurrection there.[36]

Governor Owen responded to the excitement by writing a letter to the police of the principal towns in the State and to the senators of the

---

32. *Ibid.*, p. 73.

33. See Eaton, "Dangerous Pamphlet," *loc. cit.*, p. 328, and Eaton, *Freedom of Thought*, p. 122.

34. *Raleigh Star*, March 4, 1830.

35. Governor Owen's Letter Book, 1828-1830. James F. McRee to Governor John Owen, August 7, 1830, pp. 218-219.

36. *Ibid.*, L. D. Henry to Governor John Owen, September 3, 1830, p. 232.

thirty-two eastern counties calling their attention to the circulation of the pamphlet and the rumors of insurrection.[37] He said,

I beg you will lay this matter before the police of your town and invite their prompt attention to the necessity of arresting the circulation of the book alluded to; I would suggest the necessity of the most vigilant execution of your police laws and the laws of the State; and if, in the course of the investigation anything should transpire by which it may reasonably be believed that an Agent or Agents, have been employed in your neighborhood, I should be glad to have this Department informed of it with as little delay as possible.[38]

In his message to the General Assembly in November, the Governor transmitted a copy of the pamphlet by the former Wilmington free Negro with some animadversions on the subject. He said that the publication had been circulated extensively in the South and had been discovered in the five Southern states of Virginia, South Carolina, Georgia, Louisiana, and North Carolina. He said that the volume artfully distorted the "peaceful doctrines of the Bible" and was "intended and well calculated to prepare the minds of . . . [the] slave portion of our population for any measure, however desperate."[39] In speaking of the free Negro's part in the creation of the fear currently felt, the Governor said:

As it has been satisfactorily ascertained that some of the free persons of colour in this State have permitted themselves to be used as agents, for the distribution of seditious publications, it is respectfully recommended that all this class of persons residing within the State, be required to give security for the faithful discharge of those duties which they owe, in return for the protection they receive, from the laws of the State.[40]

Governor Owen pointed out that such a regulation could not prove onerous to the free Negroes of good character, "for the ease with which they will be enabled to give the security required, will serve as an exemption to them from any unpleasant operations of the law."

When the Assembly settled down to work the following week, a

37. Letters were addressed to the senators of the following counties: Bertie, Beaufort, Currituck, Carteret, Chowan, Cumberland, Camden, Craven, Duplin, Edgecombe, Franklin, Granville, Gates, Greene, Halifax, Hertford, Hyde, Johnston, Jones, Lenoir, Martin, Nash, Northampton, Onslow, Pasquotank, Perquimans, Pitt, Sampson, Tyrrell, Washington, Warren, and Wayne.
38. Governor Owen's Letter Book, 1828-1830. Circular Letter, August 19, 1830.
39. *Journal of the House of Commons, 1830-1831* (Raleigh, 1831), p. 161.
40. *Ibid.*, p. 161.

joint committee was appointed to look into so much of the Governor's message as dealt with slaves and free Negroes. Such prominent men as Richard D. Spaight of Craven County and David M. Barringer of Cabarrus County served on the committee.[41] This committee, with the coöperation of a large number of senators and representatives, rounded out the "Free Negro Code" which curtailed still further the immunities and privileges of that unfortunate group.

Naturally one of the first matters to come before the committee and before the Assembly was the question of enacting some law to put an effective check on David Walker and others of his ilk. It was absolutely necessary that this be done if the South was to maintain the *status quo*. Freedom of thought could not go unbridled in a society where critics of the system were becoming more active.[42] The "gradualist" period in the antislavery movement was rapidly drawing to a close[43] and rumblings of the militant period to come could already be heard. North Carolina was not to be caught unawares. The antislavery sentiment that had been in her midst for years had taught her what it could be like. How else could North Carolina reply to *Walker's Appeal* than by refusing to let it be circulated? The Assembly, therefore, passed "An Act to prevent the circulation of seditious publications." It made unlawful the circulation of any books and papers that tended to "excite insurrection, conspiracy or resistance in the slaves or free Negroes and persons of colour within the State."[44]

Closely connected with the law against seditious publications was another which prevented "all persons from teaching slaves to read and write, the use of figures excepted." The law explained that such teaching had a tendency to excite dissatisfaction in the minds of the slaves and produce insurrection. If a free Negro violated this act, he was to be "fined, imprisoned, or whipped, at the discretion of the court, not exceeding thirty-nine lashes, nor less than twenty lashes."[45] Contact of free Negroes with slaves was further regulated by the act which prevented free Negroes from gaming with slaves or suffering them to game in their houses, under penalty of a whipping "not to exceed thirty-nine lashes on his or her bare back."[46]

The Legislature of 1830-31 saw fit, moreover, to circumscribe more carefully the movement of free Negroes. The act against peddling wares out of one's county had motives that were more regulatory in the sense of discipline than in the economic sense. It provided,

41. *Journal of the House of Commons, 1830-1831* (Raleigh, 1832), pp. 9, 15.
42. Eaton, *Freedom of Thought*, pp. 124 ff.
43. Adams, *Neglected Period*, pp. 249 ff.   44. *Laws, 1823-31*, p. 10.
45. *Ibid.*, p. 11.   46. *Ibid.*, pp. 11-15.

That . . . it shall not be lawful for any free person or persons of colour to hawk or peddle any goods, wares or commodities whatsoever out of the limits of the county in which they reside, unless he or she has a license to do so, granted annually by the county court of the county where he or she resides; which license shall be granted only when seven or more justices are present, and upon satisfactory or good evidence of the good character of the applicant; and for issuing such license the clerk shall be entitled to eighty cents.[47]

Free Negroes found guilty of moving out of the county in violation of this act were to "forfit and pay the sum of fifty dollars for each and every offence" and were "liable to indictment in either County or Superior Court and upon conviction . . . [to] be fined or imprisoned at the discretion of the court" not to exceed six months.[48]

In order to prevent free Negroes from going out of the State and returning at will, the immigration law was amended in the following manner:

Be it enacted . . . That if at any time hereafter any free negro or person of colour, who may be a resident of this State, shall migrate from this State . . . and shall be absent for the space of ninety days or more, it shall not be lawful for such free negro or free person of colour to return to this State. . . .[49]

The penalties for the violation of this amendment were to be the same as those imposed by the original act. Exceptions were to be made only when the free Negro had been prevented from returning "by sickness or other unavoidable occurrence."[50] Thus, the energetic and enterprising free Negroes found themselves bound to the communities in which they resided, so that there was little likelihood that they would have an opportunity to get in league with the abolitionists of the North and to spread their "pernicious doctrines" about the State.

The Assembly did not stop there. It sought to regulate the activities of free Negroes even more completely, and to prevent the infiltration of new ideas from any source whatsoever. The preamble and a part of the quarantine act of 1830 describe the motives more vividly than any present-day writer could possibly do:

Whereas it has been highly necessary and essential to the welfare and safety of the good people of this State that merchant vessels, or ships coming by sea from other States or countries, with free persons of colour, acting as mariners . . . or in any other . . .

47. *Ibid.*, p. 11.
48. *Ibid.*, p. 12.
49. *Ibid.*, p. 18.
50. *Ibid.*, p. 18.

capacity, on board such vessel or vessels, should perform quarantine, and that means be adopted to prevent such free persons of
colour from coming into this State, or from communicating with
the coloured people of this State:

Be it enacted . . . That all ships or vessels coming into any port
of this State by sea from any port or place in any other State or
country, having on board any free negro or free person of colour
not being an inhabitant or inhabitants of this State employed as a
steward . . . or in any other capacity, or as a passenger, shall be
subject to quarantine for a space of thirty days.[51]

The act further provided that it was not lawful "for free negroes of
North Carolina to go on board such vessels or to have communication
with any free negroes on board such vessel" for any purpose whatsoever while it was riding in quarantine. Captains of vessels which carried free Negroes violating this act were to pay a fine of $50; and any
free Negroes caught ashore from quarantined vessels were to be imprisoned until the vessel left.[52]

The "Free Negro Code" was thus just about complete. The legal
status of the free Negro had been reduced considerably by the legislation of 1830. It had regulated their movements and activities more
than had ever been attempted in North Carolina before this time. Ingress to and egress from the State were extremely difficult. Movement
from place to place within the State had become well-nigh impossible,
and the least possible contact of free Negroes with slaves was a further
aim of the Assembly. Further safeguards were erected by new acts for
the regulation of the patrol and the distribution of public arms in case
of insurrection.[53] Indeed, North Carolina had little to fear from slaves
or free Negroes if fears could be allayed by legislative enactments.[54]
David Walker's *Appeal* had done more than any other single thing to
reduce the legal status of free Negroes in North Carolina.

The late summer and autumn of 1831 was a period in which events
occurred that caused fear to well up in the heart of every slaveholder.
In August, 1831, the insurrection of the "Black Prophet," Nat Turner,

51. *Ibid.*, p. 29.

52. *Ibid.*, p. 30. This act was to have some important economic consequences. See
below, p. 141.   53. *Ibid.*, pp. 16, 22.

54. The same Assembly passed an act requiring the free Negroes of Wilmington and
Elizabeth City to give annual bonds of $100 for good behavior. Ms. in Legislative
Papers for 1830-1831. There was also proposed a bill to prevent free Negroes from
preaching in certain counties, but it was indefinitely postponed by the House of Commons. *Journal of the Senate, 1830-1831* (Raleigh, 1832), pp. 139, 149. Fully one
fourth of the acts of this Assembly directly or indirectly affected the legal status of the
free Negro. *Cf. supra*, pp. 27-28, for the laws of 1830 regulating emancipation.

stirred not only the area around Southampton County, Virginia, but had immediate and far-reaching effects upon the entire South.[55] Perhaps typical of the reactions of whites were the words of William Pettigrew, a student at Hillsborough Academy, who wrote his father that "the negrows have been rising down in South Hampton, and have killed seventy white familys" and exclaimed, "Oh my Dear father, I hope that God will keep us in his ways forever."[56] The fear in the Southern states was a contagious germ that spread rapidly in all directions. It provoked a variety of reactions from persons in public and private life, and caused a number of Southern states to examine more carefully their "precautions" to see if they could withstand the onslaught of a "Black Prophet."[57]

North Carolina, of course, did not escape the effects of the Virginia uprising. The proximity of the tragic scene to her densest slave and free Negro population certainly did not serve to calm her fears. The excitement displayed in some of the most conservative quarters helped to enlarge still further the already exaggerated reports of the insurrection and the rumors of still more to come.[58] Nor did events themselves contribute toward calm and deliberate contemplations of the problems before North Carolinians. In early September, there were rumors of an insurrection south of Fayetteville.[59] On September 15, the *Register* carried news of a rebellion of the slaves in Duplin and Sampson counties.[60] Although a great deal of the killing attributed to the Negroes was denied the following week, the news had already had the effect of exciting the people further.[61]

No less a person than Governor Montfort Stokes was visibly alarmed by the Virginia insurrection and the events in North Carolina which followed. In his message to the Assembly he said that the slaves and free Negroes had become more discontented and ungovernable. He pointed out that "crimes committed in a late insurrection in an adjoining state, would seem to require further and early attention" to legislation on the activities of slaves and free Negroes.[62] Other Southern states were already putting their houses in order. Governor Roman of Louisiana called a special session of the Legislature on November

55. Joseph C. Carroll, *Slave Insurrections in the United States, 1800-1865,* chapter entitled, "Age of the Black Prophet" and succeeding chapters.

56. Pettigrew Family Papers, William Pettigrew to Ebenezer Pettigrew, September 3, 1831.

57. Eaton, *Freedom of Thought,* p. 93.   58. *Ibid.,* pp. 93, 94.

59. D. F. Caldwell Papers, John C. Latta to Robert C. Caldwell, September 14, 1831.

60. *Raleigh Register,* September 15, 1831.

61. *Raleigh Register,* September 22, 1831.

62. *Journal of the House of Commons,* 1831 (Raleigh, 1832), p. 145.

14, to "consider preventive measures against slave plots and insurrections."[63] The governor of South Carolina was likewise looking into
the matter of restrictive legislation.

Governor Stokes was not in favor of "multiplying severe and san-
guinary laws to operate upon those who know little and care less about
them." He thought it more advisable to establish "a more efficient and
accountable police, and to arm and equip one or more companies of
volunteers or detached militia, in each county, to be called out when
required and to be paid while in actual service."[64] What the Governor
was recognizing was that North Carolina had passed all the restrictive
measures necessary in the Legislatures of 1826-27 and 1830-31. Enforcement and patrol were the only needs at this time.

The apathy of the General Assembly of 1831-32 on legislation concerning slaves and free Negroes was not due to lack of interest in the
subject. They believed, moreover, that there were dangers arising out
of the presence of the free blacks within the State. The small amount
of free Negro legislation in 1831-32 was due to the already rather complete code covering the subject, on the one hand, and to recognition that
enforcement comes not so much from legislation as from the pressure
of public opinion, on the other. It is true that the Assembly passed a
few acts affecting slaves and free Negroes. There was one prohibiting
free Negroes from preaching,[65] one against slaves conducting themselves as free men,[66] and one concerning the collection of fines of free
Negroes.[67] But it would not be accurate to conclude that the Nat
Turner insurrection had an important effect upon the legislative policy
concerning free Negroes in North Carolina.[68]

After 1831, North Carolina experienced no nightmares of fear similar to those of 1826, 1830, and 1831. Now and then some incendiary
publications arrived from the North, but the suppression of them was
so complete that they could hardly have had any effect upon either the
slave or the free Negro population.[69] The two Methodist preachers
who denounced slavery in Guilford County in 1854 were summarily

63. Eaton, *Freedom of Thought*, p. 94.
64. *Journal of the House, 1831*, p. 145.   65. *Laws, 1831-1835*, p. 7.
66. *Ibid.*, p. 7.   67. *Ibid.*, p. 10.
68. Mr. Carroll, in his *Slave Insurrections* (p. 168), gives one the impression that
the development of the "Free Negro Code" in North Carolina came *after* the Nat Turner
insurrection. He credits the Assembly of 1831-32 with passing the measures against
free Negroes exciting slaves to rebel and teaching slaves to read and write, and with
passing the emancipation law removing manumission cases from the county courts to
the superior courts. As a matter of fact, these laws were passed in the *preceding* Assembly. *Cf. supra*, pp. 68 ff. Mr. Carroll's chapter references on p. 184 support this fact.
69. *Raleigh Register*, August 6, 1835.

arrested and instructed to desist.[70] The conspiracy of 1854 in the Chowan River section was so short-lived that few people other than the students at the Chowan Female College became disturbed.[71] In fact, there were almost no real causes for nightmares after 1831.[72]

Thus, it can be seen that the development of the "Free Negro Code" in North Carolina was a direct result of the apprehensions of whites concerning the duplicity of the free Negro. It was feared that he would be an important factor in any movement for a general liberation of the slaves. This fear, as Professor Taylor has suggested, "does not appear to have been well-founded."[73] Certainly, the free Negro of means entertained no ideas looking toward general emancipation. It will be remembered that a white citizen of Caswell County spoke of Thomas Day, the wealthiest free Negro in that part of the State, as one on whom he could rely "in the event of any disturbance amongst the blacks."[74] John Chavis, the most prominent free Negro in North Carolina, said that "immediate emancipation would be to entail the greatest earthly curse upon my brethren . . . that could be conferred. . . . I suppose if they knew I said this they would be ready to take my life, but as I wish them well I feel no disposition to see them any more miserable than they are."[75]

It was never proved that free Negroes had any connection with the slave conspiracies in North Carolina. In the abortive uprising in 1831 in eastern North Carolina, it was proved to the satisfaction of the Superior Court of Sampson County that the free Negroes who were indicted—Billy Baldwin, Archy Freeman, and Morris Cheves—were in no way implicated, and they were accordingly acquitted.[76] At the same time, it was reported that every free Negro in Raleigh was arrested and those who could not show that they were of good character were asked to leave the town.[77] It seems to the observer that there were more free Negro informers than there were conspirators. It was a free Negro who first told the Magistrate of the Wilmington

70. *North Carolina Standard,* October 2, 1850.

71. Christian Bell wrote her parents that she was "afraid to go to sleep" at night and that most of the girls were "excited . . . about the Negroes." Major Bell Papers, Christian Bell to her mother and father, June 20, 1854.

72. Taylor, "Conspiracies," *loc. cit.,* p. 34.

73. *Ibid.,* p. 27.

74. Affidavit signed by R. M. Saunders. *Journal of the House, 1830-1831,* p. 238.

75. John Chavis to Willie P. Mangum, April 4, 1836. Typescript in the Willie P. Mangum Papers; Archives of the North Carolina Historical Commission.

76. *Carolina Observer,* November 16, 1831.

77. Stephen B. Weeks, "The Slave Insurrection in Virginia in 1831," *The Magazine of American History,* XXV (1891), 451.

police about David Walker's *Appeal*.[78] When the slaves of Sampson and Duplin counties conspired to rebel in 1831, "the existence of the conspiracy was disclosed to a respectable gentleman, by *a free person of color*."[79] A bill was introduced in the Assembly asking that the free Negro, Levin Armwood, be given a reward of $250 for his "signal services to the State" in saving the white people from the "most brutal murders" by his timely information. Although the bill passed the House of Commons, the Senators did not feel disposed to spend the public funds in such a manner, and on January 12, 1832, they rejected the bill.[80] The free Negro's coöperation went unrewarded. More than that, however, he was made the victim of the panic-stricken population in its effort to destroy movements in which he had little or no part.

There were no more counterparts to the Assemblies of 1826 and 1830 so far as free Negro legislation was concerned. The laws passed during the last thirty years of the slave period were apparently afterthoughts in the establishment of a "Free Negro Code," or were measures which experience dictated in order more effectively to circumscribe the activities of the group. Some of the later laws dealt with the conduct of free Negroes in certain localities, as in the case of the act which set up rules for free Negroes working in the Dismal Swamp, in the northeastern part of the State. The act, passed in 1847, provided, in part,

> That no free person of color shall work . . . in the said swamp without having gone before the clerk of the proper court and caused a description of himself . . . and keeping and having ready to produce the copy of such description certified by the clerk [of the county court] . . . and any free person of color found employed . . . in the said swamp without such copy, shall be deemed guilty of a misdemeanor, may be arrested and committed, or bound over to the next court of the county . . . and on conviction may be punished by fine, imprisonment and whipping, all or any of them at the discretion of the court.[81]

By this act, the Assembly hoped to see to it that no free Negroes came into the Swamp without having first been approved of by the county authorities. The presence of a large number of slaves in the area and

78. See above, p. 66.

79. *Raleigh Register*, September 15, 1831. The italics are the editor's. See, also, Ulrich B. Phillips, ed., *Plantation and Frontier Documents, 1649-1863*, I, 101, for an account of the same incident, taken from the *Federal Union* (Milledgeville, Georgia), October 6, 1831.

80. Ms. in the Legislative Papers for 1831-1832. The petition was recommended by the justices of the peace of the County of Duplin.

81. *Laws Passed by the General Assembly, 1846-1847* (Raleigh, 1848), p. 110.

the difficulties in superintending their movements made such an enactment highly desirable. The legislators had received information that free persons of color and white men were aiding slaves to escape. The presence of undesirable free Negroes, moreover, served to undermine the morale of the slaves, who, in turn, engaged in "corrupting and seducing other slaves, and by their evil examples and evil practices, lessening the due subordination, and greatly impairing the value of slaves. . . ."[82]

In compliance with the provisions of this act, the clerks of the county courts of Gates, Pasquotank, Camden, and Currituck counties busied themselves with registering and certifying all the free Negroes working in the Dismal Swamp area. A form used by the clerks follows:

State of North Carolina ⎱   County Clerk's Office
Gates County   ⎰   May 14, 1853.

Edmond Boothe, said to be a free man, is hired the present year by William B. Whitehead of Suffolk, Virginia, and by him registered as one of his hands employed in the Great Dismal Swamp in the County of Gates aforesaid.

Said Edmond is about forty-eight years of age, of black complexion, is stoutly built, has a scar on his right hand, one on his breast, one on the left side of his face below the eye, and stands without shoes five feet eight inches high.

> In Testimony, etc.
> N. J. Riddick.[83]

Raleigh had its own set of laws which applied to free Negroes living within its limits. No free Negroes could reside there without first having obtained a permit from the Board of Commissioners, which was granted after the Board had been satisfied "that the applicant supports an honest, industrious, and peaceable character." The permit was to be forfeited upon misbehavior, and the offender was to pay a fine of $4. The ordinance provided further that,

It shall be held to be a violation of the good order of the Sabbath, for any free persons of colour to be loitering in any public streets of the city; and it shall be the duty of the city constables to take up such persons of colour so offending, and if no responsible white person will give a verbal pledge to the officer, that the offenders shall appear before the Intendant of Police . . . the follow-

82. *Laws, 1846-1847,* p. 109.
83. Ms. in the County Records for Gates County, 1853.

ing morning, he, she or they shall be whipped or otherwise dealt with, at the discretion of the Intendant or Magistrate.[84]

The possession of firearms and the use of spirituous liquors by free Negroes were two matters that were regulated throughout the State in the later period. Before 1840, there was no restriction on the possession of firearms by free Negroes, though slaves had been forbidden this privilege during the entire period. A slave, however, could carry arms if the master gave him the permission and gave a bond for his good behavior. In 1809, John C. Stanly, a free Negro of Craven County, granted such a privilege to one of his slaves, and it is so recorded in the minutes of the county court:

Upon application of John C. Stanly, ordered that his Negro man Abraham have permission to carry a gun upon the lands and plantations of the said John C. Stanly, the said John entering into the bonds required by law.[85]

In 1840, the restriction on the possession and use of arms was extended to free Negroes. The law provided:

That if any free Negro, Mulatto or free Person of Colour, shall wear or carry about his or her person, or keep in his or her house, any Shot-gun, Musket, Rifle, Pistol, Sword, Dagger or Bowie-knife, unless he or she shall have obtained a license therefor from the Court of Pleas and Quarter Sessions of his or her county, within one year preceding the wearing, keeping or carrying thereof, he or she shall be guilty of a misdemeanor, and may be indicted therefor.[86]

It is to be noted that the law did not forbid the possession and carrying of guns altogether, but restricted it to those free Negroes who had satisfied the county authorities that they were capable of handling such weapons with propriety. The county officials proceeded to grant licenses under the act.

After favorable consideration of a free Negro's application, a permit like the following was granted:

Ezekiel Moore, a free person of Collour, has permission to carry fire arms for the next twelve months.[87]

84. *Ordinances and By-Laws of the Board of Commissioners* (Raleigh, 1854), pp. 64, 69.

85. Minutes of the Court of Pleas and Quarter Sessions of Craven County, September, 1809.

86. *Laws Passed by the General Assembly, 1840-1843* (Raleigh, 1844), pp. 61-62.

87. Minutes of the Court of Pleas and Quarter Sessions of Beaufort County, 1843. Sometimes, the particular weapon was specified as in the court order "that Abram Allen

It was not long before this law was tested in the courts. In 1843, Elijah Newsom of Cumberland County was indicted for carrying a shotgun without a license. Although Newsom was found guilty, the court arrested the judgment upon the motion of the defendant's counsel. Thereupon, the solicitor for the State appealed. Before the Supreme Court, the defendant's counsel argued that the Act of 1840 was unconstitutional because it violated "Article II of the Amended Federal Constitution and Articles II and XVII of the Bill of Rights of North Carolina."[88] Judge Nash, speaking for the Court said, "This is not so." The judge suggested by interrogation that if the Act of 1840, which imposed a restriction on free Negroes from which white men are exempt, is void, all the legislation on the subject of free Negroes may be void. He continued,

> From the earliest period of our history free people of color have been among us as a separate and distinct class requiring from necessity in many cases, separate and distinct legislation. . . .
> The act of 1840 is one of police regulation. It does not deprive the free man of color of the right to carry arms . . . but subjects it to the control of the county court, giving them power to say . . . who of this class of persons shall have a right to the license, or whether any shall.[89]

After dismissing Article XVII of the North Carolina Bill of Rights as having no bearing on the case before the Court, the judge concluded by pointing out that by disfranchising the free Negro in 1835, the people—

---

have leave to carry and keep in his house a shotgun for the space of twelve months." Minutes of the Court, Beaufort County, December, 1841. See also the Minutes of the Court, Alamance County, 1850. Sometimes, moreover, the permit specified just where the free Negro could carry the weapon. In 1858, John Harris' permit said that he could "keep about his person and carry on his own land a shot gun." When Harris went hunting with some white men and carried his gun off his own land, he was indicted. The judge of the county court said that Harris had violated no law because the county court could not limit the license in such a manner. Judge Battle of the Supreme Court reversed the decision, contending that the limitations placed by the county were valid. State v. Harris, 51 N. C., 436.

88. The second amendment to the Federal Constitution states: "A well regulated Militia, being necessary to the security of a Free State, the right of the people to keep and bear Arms, shall not be infringed."

Article III of the North Carolina Bill of Rights provides: "That no Man or set of Men are entitled to Exclusive or separate Emoluments or Privileges from the Community but in Consideration of Public Services."

Article XVII of the North Carolina Bill of Rights provides: "That the People have a right to bear Arms for the Defence of the State; and as standing Armies in Time of Peace are dangerous to liberty, they ought not to be kept up; and that the military should be kept under strict subordination to, and governed by, the civil Power."

89. State v. Newsom, 27 N. C., 183.

the "highest . . . of authority"—demonstrated the point of view "that free persons of color cannot be considered as citizens in the largest sense of the term."[90]

Later on, the question arose as to whether a free Negro, if hired by a white person to carry a gun, needed to obtain a license from the county court. In 1847, a free Negro of Perquimans County was hired by a white man to get shingles from Pasquotank County and was given a pistol to carry back and forth. When the free Negro was indicted on a charge of violating the Act of 1840, the county court exonerated him, but the State appealed the case to the Supreme Court. In affirming the decision of the lower court Judge Nash, who had upheld the act four years earlier, said that since the defendant was merely hired to carry the pistol and claimed no right to use it, he did not come within the provisions of the Act of 1840.[91] He further stated that, "Degraded as these individuals are, as a class . . . it is certain that among them are many worthy of all confidence and into whose hands these weapons can be safely trusted, either for their own protection or for the protection of the property of others confided in them."[92]

Toward the end of the period, there was considerable agitation to place even greater restrictions on the free Negro's privilege of owning and using weapons. In 1856, a group of citizens of Robeson County asked the Assembly to pass an act providing that no free Negro be permitted to have a gun "unless he is a free holder and give bond with good security and then not be allowed to carry it off the land."[93] These petitioners also wanted the Assembly to regulate the possession of dogs by free Negroes.[94]

In 1859, a bill was proposed in which no free Negroes were to be permitted to carry the arms named in the Act of 1840 and enjoining the county courts against issuing licenses to free Negroes. This bill was rejected on January 21, 1857.[95] Finally, in 1861, a law was passed which made the possession of arms by Negroes a misdemeanor, punishable by a fine of not less than fifty dollars.[96] Nothing less than the imminence of a civil war could force the representatives to take so drastic a move as to forbid free Negroes to possess arms of any kind.

It can hardly be said that the movement to prevent the use of ardent

90. *Ibid.*, p. 185.   91. State v. Lane, 30 N. C., 188.
92. *Ibid.*, p. 189.   93. Ms. in the Legislative Papers for 1856.
94. They wanted a law passed to prevent free Negroes from owning more than one dog. But 69 citizens of Northampton County wanted to forbid the possession of dogs by free Negroes altogether. Ms. in the Legislative Papers for 1857.
95. Ms. in the Legislative Papers for 1859.
96. *Laws Passed by the General Assembly, 1860-1861* (Raleigh, 1862), p. 69.

spirits by free Negroes had any visible connection with the temperance movement in North Carolina, though the former may have been an outgrowth of the latter. By 1830 the general movement against the intemperate use of alcoholic beverages was well under way. At that time, no audible objections to their use by free Negroes was made. In 1840, thirty-six citizens of Robeson County asked that the Assembly pass laws regulating the sale of spirituous liquors to free Negroes. In showing the need for such an enactment, the citizens spared no language in describing the evils flowing from the unrestricted use of liquor by free Negroes:

> The County of Robeson is cursed with a free-coloured population that migrated originally from the districts round about the Roanoke and Neuse Rivers. They are generally indolent, roguish, improvident, and dissipated. Having no regard for character, they are under no restraint but what the law imposes. They are great topers, and so long as they can procure the exhilarating draught seem to forget entirely the comfort of their families. All that has been written against the use of ardent spirits will apply with all its force to them. . . . All the evils accompanying an excessive use of it afflict that population.[97]

The petition was turned over to the Committee on Propositions and Grievances, and after some deliberation that body expressed a disinclination to endorse the petition. The committee deeply lamented "the fatal effects of intemperance," but believed that there was no remedy in legislation. A general law would punish the innocent as well as the guilty. "This would be pronouncedly unjust if not unwise. And if such a law be devised who or what tribunal shall be clothed with such discriminating power." The committee cited the ineffectiveness of the general laws of Massachusetts, South Carolina, and Georgia. The report concluded by saying that good results may come from a strict observance of the laws already in force and the setting of "a proper example on the part of the more reflecting and patriotic."[98]

The Robeson County petitioners did not receive such slight attention for long. In 1844, the General Assembly took the first step in the direction of regulating the use of spirituous liquors by free Negroes. In that year, the following act was passed:

> Be it enacted . . . That it shall not be lawful for any free negro or mulatto in this State, to sell, either directly or indirectly, any ardent spirits to any person whatever: *provided,* that any free negro or

97. Ms. in the Legislative Papers for 1840-1841.
98. *Ibid.*

mulatto shall be permitted to sell any ardent spirits that may have been made by him or her.[99]

This law did not make it impossible for free Negroes to obtain alcoholic drinks. They could make all they wanted to drink and sell. If they were not so enterprising, they could secure it from white persons. Perhaps the Robeson County citizens were still dissatisfied.

The general dissatisfaction with the law of 1844 can be easily seen. Almost every meeting of the Legislature in subsequent years was the occasion for the proposal of a new law on the use of liquors by free Negroes. In 1850, it was proposed that it be unlawful "for any person . . . to buy of, Trafick with or sell to any Indian, free Negro or person of mixed blood . . . any spirituous liquors, wine or cider."[100] This bill passed the House of Commons, but failed in the Senate. A similar law was proposed in 1852, but it also failed to pass the Senate.[101]

Meanwhile, Raleigh was undertaking to deal with her problem without the help of the Assembly. The town ordinances of 1854 contain the following provision:

If any person shall at any time be found in a state of intoxication in the Market House, or having been in a disorderly Manner therein, or idly lying on the benches thereof, if a white or a colored free person, he shall be subject to a fine not exceeding ten dollars nor less than four dollars.[102]

When the Assembly met in the autumn of 1854, a bill was proposed to prohibit the sale of intoxicating liquors to free Negroes, making it a penal offense at the pleasure of the court.[103] There was considerable opposition to the bill. One representative said that there were many honorable free Negroes and it would be wrong to prohibit them from purchasing liquor. Another argued that "if a free Negro was to be engaged in ditching with water up to his knees, it would be morally wrong to prohibit him from obtaining the necessary stimulation, and he might die for want of it."[104] On the following day, the bill was rejected by the House of Commons by a vote of 68 to 54. Similar bills were proposed in 1856 and 1857, but both were lost because of indefinite postponement.[105]

99. *Laws Passed by the General Assembly, 1844-1847* (Raleigh, 1848), p. 123.

100. Ms. in the Legislative Papers for 1850.

101. Ms. in the Legislative Papers for 1852.

102. *Ordinances*, p. 71.

103. Ms. in the Legislative Papers for 1854.

104. Reported by "Q in the Corner" and printed in the *Fayetteville Observer*, January 22, 1855.

105. Mss. in the Legislative Papers for 1856 and 1857. The bill in 1856 forbade the

In the autumn of 1858, William Green of Franklin County proposed a bill that became law on February 16, 1859.[106] It provided,

That no person shall sell, or deliver to or buy for, or be instrumental . . . in procuring for any free person of color, for cash, or in exchange for articles delivered, or upon any consideration whatever, or as a gift, any spirituous liquors, or liquor of which alcohol is an ingredient, except upon the written certificate of some practicing physician or magistrate stating that the same is necessary for medicinal purposes.[107]

The passage of this sumptuary legislation marks the climax of the legal restrictions on the free Negro in ante-bellum North Carolina. By 1859, the discipline was as complete as could have been desired by the most fiery antagonists of this portion of the population. Fears entertained by whites of what the free Negroes would or could possibly do to the order of things invoked more response from the legislators than any other force. These fears, regardless of whether they were ill-founded or based upon a reasonable assumption of possible occurrences, were extremely potent in providing a stimulus for the reduction of the legal status of the free Negro to a negligible level. Only in the courts and in the general enforcement of the laws could he have hoped to salvage some of the "privileges and immunities" that free men enjoyed.

The Free Negro in Court

It was one thing to have a very elaborate set of statutes defining the legal status of the free Negro and quite another to see that they were interpreted in the interest of the legislators and stringently enforced. Besides, there were important privileges and immunities that were never denied him, and he could secure a great deal of protection by pointing to these guarantees. They were the same as those granted to all citizens of North Carolina in the "Declaration of Rights" drawn up by the "Representatives of the Free Men of the State," at Halifax on December 7, 1776.[108] Among them were the "privilege of habeas corpus, trial by jury, right of challenge, ownership of property, and the privilege of transfer, devise, and descent."[109]

Though the free Negro enjoyed the right to sue during the entire national period, this right was seriously hampered at a very early date.

---

sale of liquor to free Negroes except for medicinal purposes, while the one in 1857 required that the free Negro receive permission from a justice of the peace.

106. It was Mr. Green who proposed the bill in 1856.

107. *Laws Passed by the General Assembly, 1857-1858* (Raleigh, 1859).

108. Clark, *State Records*, XXIII, 977.

109. Johnson, *Ante-bellum North Carolina*, p. 601.

Naturally a right such as this is valuable only when there are certain other accompanying guarantees. Among them are the right to secure witnesses among lawful and truthful men, the right to offer testimony in one's behalf, and a guarantee of immunity against incompetent witnesses. The national period had hardly opened before the first two of these guarantees were denied. In 1777, the General Assembly passed an act which established the incompetency of free Negroes as witnesses, once and for all:

> All Negroes, Indians, Mulattoes, and all Persons of Mixed Blood descended from Negro and Indian Ancestors, to the Fourth Generation inclusive (though one Ancestor of each Generation may have been a white Person) whether Bond or free, shall be deemed and taken to be incapable in Law to be Witnesses in any Case whatsoever, except against each other.[110]

The passage of this act prevented the free Negro from testifying in any case against a white man and made it impossible for him to gather testimony in such a case other than from white persons. Thus, if no white witnesses were present at a particular transaction between a white person and a free Negro, or if they were present but did not choose to testify in his favor, the free Negro's opportunity for justice was not very great. He could enjoy the rather empty consolation, however, that he could offer testimony against a slave.

That the testimony of a slave was to be rejected in a trial of free men was a point of view for which free Negroes contended from the very beginning. The first test came in 1794, when a free Negro was indicted for burglary. His counsel objected to the competence of one of the State's witnesses who was a slave. The judge ruled, "If there be anything in the objection the Court will attend to it at the trial." Before the trial, however, the prisoner had escaped, and the question of the competence of the slave as a witness was left undecided.[111] In 1796, Judge Williams refused to admit the testimony of a slave against a free Negro.[112]

There were those, however, who were dissatisfied with the ruling of 1796 and sought to make admissible the testimony of a slave against a free Negro. In 1821, an act was passed which validated such testimony. The language of the statute is significant.

110. Clark, *State Records*, XXIV, 61. A similar act was passed sixty years earlier in Maryland; *cf.* Wright, *Free Negro in Maryland*, p. 118.

111. State v. George, a Free Negro, 1 N. C., 68.

112. Cox v. Dove, a Free Negro, 1 N. C., 76.

In all pleas of the State, where the defendant may be a negro, Indian, or person of mixed blood . . . whether such person be bond or free, the evidence of a negro or negroes, Indian or Indians, mulatto or mulattoes, and of all persons of mixed blood . . . whether the person or persons whose evidence is offered be bond or free, shall be admissible and the witnesses competent; subject nevertheless to be excluded upon any grounds of incompetency which may exist.[113]

By the act of 1821, North Carolina fell into line with the action that was being taken in other parts of the South. In 1801, Maryland passed a law in which slaves were permitted to testify against free Negroes who were charged either with stealing or receiving stolen articles from others. In 1808, the restrictions upon the use of Negro evidence in criminal prosecutions were removed entirely.[114] In 1801, the Virginia laws of evidence were changed "so that a slave was a good witness in pleas of the Commonwealth against a free Negro."[115] The obvious objection to such a law was that persons with so little responsibility could, upon their oath, offer testimony against a free Negro that might lead to the latter's conviction by the State. That this law was subject to abuse by slaveholders who wanted to rid their communities of free Negroes is seen by the proposal which came before the Legislature in 1830 to "inquire into the expediency of altering or amending the law . . . so as more effectually to prevent a future *abuse* of the same." The Committee on the Judiciary, however, felt it "inexpedient to pass any law upon the subject," and the report was concurred in.[116] For the remainder of the period, slaves were allowed to offer testimony against free Negroes in prosecutions by the State.[117]

Although the law of 1777 provided that Negroes were incapable to offer testimony except in cases against each other, it was possible for whites to suffer as a result of the testimony of a free Negro. When the validity of the will of a free man of color was contested on the grounds that the testator was *non compos mentis,* the co-plaintiff of the widow, a free woman of color, was a white woman. The plaintiffs argued that the defendants, free persons of color, could not testify because it would be against a white woman and therefore inadmissible. In ruling on

113. *The Revised Statutes of the State of North Carolina Passed by the General Assembly at the Session of 1836-1837* (Raleigh, 1837), I, 583.

114. Wright, *Free Negro in Maryland,* p. 119.

115. Russell, *Free Negro in Virginia,* p. 66.

116. *Journal of the House of Commons, 1830-1831,* p. 232.

117. See *The Revised Code of North Carolina Enacted by the General Assembly at the Session of 1854,* Ch. 107, Sec. 71.

that point, Judge Daniel said that the fact that one of the co-plaintiffs was white was not enough to exclude the testimony of free persons of color. It was the admissions and declarations of the widow, a free Negro, concerning her husband's state of mind that were under scrutiny, and free Negroes could defend or dispute them.[118]

The inadmissibility of the testimony of a free Negro jeopardized his opportunity to establish a good case for himself, of course. But it did not mean that he could not be successful before the bar. Two white men evicted by force a free Negro and his family from their home. When indicted, the white men said that Fuller, the free Negro, had agreed to the eviction. Nevertheless, they were found guilty before the Granville County Court and appealed to the Supreme Court. In a decision, interesting for its phraseology as well as for its reasoning, Chief Justice Pearson said,

> Fuller, being a free negro, was not competent as a witness and could not have been heard *on oath* to prove the fact alleged, to-wit, that he had agreed that Emory might take possession. We are unable to see any principle upon which *his* naked statement, on the day after the matter occurred, is admissible to prove the fact. His statement is certainly no more to be relied on than his oath. There was no error in the decision of the court below.[119]

The right of the free Negro to trial by jury was never denied. During the early period, he enjoyed that right under the guarantee of the Declaration of Rights and the Constitution of 1776 just as all North Carolinians did. Even when the repressive acts of 1826-27 were passed, a respectable deference to the principle of "due process" was made when the legislators stated:

> That in all cases arising under this act, the free negro or mulatto, who is charged with an offence, upon application to the court for that purpose, shall have a right to have the facts of his or her case tried by a jury upon an issue or issues made up under the direction of the court for that purpose.[120]

When the free Negro appeared before the jury, he had certain rights that had to be respected. When Asa Jacobs was indicted by the Brunswick County Court for carrying firearms in violation of the Act of 1840, he denied that he was a free Negro. Although the jury inspected him in the effort to ascertain the veracity of his contention he

118. Ragland et al. v. Huntingdon et al., 23 N. C., 421.
119. State v. Emory and another, 51 N. C., 142.
120. *Laws, 1825-1830*, p. 16.

objected but was overruled by the court. The jury rendered a verdict for the State. Jacobs appealed to the Supreme Court. Judge Battle said that the State could not compel a man to be inspected against his wishes, "because it was compelling him to furnish evidence against himself in a criminal prosecution." He pointed out that it would have been all right if Jacobs had volunteered to have the jury inspect him:

In the present case we know that the presiding Judge did not intend to compel the defendant to offer himself to the inspection of the jury by an act of arbitrary power, but he did it in what he deemed to be the exercise of a rightful authority; if in that he erred, as we think he did, his error may have prejudiced the cause of the defendant, and for that the defendant is entitled to another trial.[121]

It is difficult to ascertain the extent to which free Negroes enjoyed the benefit of counsel in the lower courts. The impecunious state of a large number of them made the employment of counsel a difficult matter. The pettiness of many of their offenses, moreover, often made the use of counsel unnecessary. The records of the county courts do not shed any light on the extent to which free Negroes were represented by men trained in the law. The minutes give very little of the details of trials and the personnel of the principals. Usually, only the decision of the court is recorded. The beginning of most of the items, "It appearing to the satisfaction of the Court," is not very revealing.[122] No information is given as to how the court became satisfied. Naturally, one wonders if able counsel was on the free Negro's side at the time.

In the superior courts, free Negroes usually had counsel. Not infrequently they were represented by two members of the bar. In 1836, James T. Morehead, brother of Governor Morehead, collaborated with John W. Norwood to defend Henry Harris, a free Negro, before the Caswell Superior Court on a charge of arson.[123] In 1851, Messrs. French and McNeil successfully defended a free Negro who was charged with murdering a slave. The case was tried before the Robeson Superior Court.[124] The free Negro woman who was merely branded for killing her husband would not have escaped with so light a punishment had not it been for her counsel, Wm. B. Wright and

121. State v. Jacobs, 50 N. C., 256. See the decision in State v. Chavers, 50 N. C., 11, where the defendant offered himself for inspection by the jury.

122. See, for example, the Minutes of the Court of Pleas and Quarter Sessions for Alamance County, 1854, and Beaufort County, 1847.

123. *Raleigh Register*, May 24, 1826.   124. *Fayetteville Observer*, April 1, 1851.

C. G. Wright. These prominent members of the Fayetteville bar were successful in getting the charge of murder changed to manslaughter and thereupon advised her to plead guilty.[125]

In cases before the Supreme Court, the free Negro was often quite ably represented. After returning from his duties in the United States Senate in 1837, Robert Strange represented a free Negro, Charles Oxendine, in his appeal from an adverse decision in the Robeson County Court.[126] Associated with him was Hon. George E. Badger, later Secretary of the Navy and Whig United States Senator.[127] The Bryan brothers of New Bern were among eastern North Carolina's most prominent attorneys. Even after J. H. Bryan moved to Raleigh, he and his brother collaborated in winning Augustine Cully's freedom when a white man insisted that he was a slave.[128] During the time that Jesse G. Shepherd was Speaker of the House of Commons, he defended William Chavers on the charge of carrying a gun without the proper license.[129] When Duncan McRae was running for governor in 1858, he found the time to represent William Brookfield in his effort to secure his freedom.[130]

There can be little doubt that all free Negroes whose cases reached the Supreme Court did not have the funds to employ able counsel. Doubtless, many legal questions arose which excited the interest of judges and attorneys alike, and they were interested in having them settled. There were also instances, one can be sure, where some of the attorneys were acting as *amici curiae;* and the free Negro thus became the recipient of wise and able counsel. That the free Negroes were represented ably and with a considerable amount of success can be seen by observing the number of instances in which they won their freedom in cases coming before the Supreme Court.[131]

If the free Negro was unsuccessful in defending himself against criminal prosecutions by the State, he might expect punishment ranging from whipping, to death without benefit of clergy. The severity of the punishment depended, of course, upon the seriousness of the crime. Whipping was the most common type of punishment, and was used to chastise most of the petty offenders. Free Negroes who preached or exhorted in public were to receive "upon conviction before a single magistrate . . . not exceeding thirty-nine lashes on his bare back."[132]

125. *Fayetteville Observer,* May 21, 1855.
126. State v. Oxendine, 19 N. C., 417.   127. *Ibid.,* p. 417.
128. Cully v. Jones, 31 N. C., 126. *Cf. supra,* p. 52, n. 184.
129. State v. Chavers, 50 N. C., 25.   130. Brookfield v. Stanton, 51 N. C., 156.
131. See Chapter 2, the section on "Maintaining the Status of a Free Man."
132. *Laws, 1831-1835,* p. 7.

So were free Negroes who were found guilty of gaming with slaves.[133] After 1826, free Negroes who sold firearms to slaves were guilty of a misdemeanor and were to receive thirty-nine lashes.[134]

Maiming, during the colonial period, was not an unusual form of punishment for what were considered serious crimes. Perjury was disdained by the citizens of colonial North Carolina, and they sought to discourage it in every possible way. Any Negro, bond or free, who gave false testimony against a slave who was charged with committing a capital crime was rigorously dealt with. The law of 1741 said,

> Every such Offender shall, without further Tryal, be ordered by the said Court to have one Ear nailed to the Pillory, and there stand for the Space of one Hour, and the said Ear to be cut off, and thereafter the other ear, nailed in like manner and cut off. . . . And moreover . . . to order every such offender Thirty Nine lashes well laid on, on his bare Back, at the common whipping Post.[135]

No offense was punishable by such maiming in the national period. In the early part of the nineteenth century, the criminal code underwent a gradual reform, and maiming disappeared as a form of punishment.[136] Branding and burning, however, seem to have been practiced by the courts throughout the period, apparently without legislative sanction. In the Superior Court of Raleigh, the following incident was reported in 1807:

> A free youth of colour who calls himself Isaac Watson, was tried on a charge of Grand Larceny, for breaking open the desk of Dr. Calvin Jones . . . whilst in his service . . . and stealing thereout a pocket Book of the value of five shillings. . . . The Jury returned a verdict of *guilty*.
>
> The benefit of clergy having been prayed in his favor and granted, the judge sentenced him to be burnt in the hand, and the sentence was immediatly carried into effect in the presence of the Court.[137]

In 1830, a free Negro was found guilty of manslaughter and was accordingly "burnt in the hand."[138] When Sylvester Chavers, a free woman of color, was found guilty of fatally stabbing her husband with a "dirk knife," she was sentenced to be branded, and "after the punishment was inflicted, she was discharged."[139] When Joe Manly, a free

133. *Laws, 1823-1831*, p. 14.   134. *Laws, 1825-1830*, p. 19.
135. Clark, *State Records*, XXIII, 202-203.
136. Johnson, *Ante-bellum North Carolina*, pp. 650 ff.
137. *Raleigh Register*, April 6, 1807.   138. *Raleigh Register*, May 17, 1830.
139. *Fayetteville Observer*, May 21, 1855.

Negro of Franklin County, was found guilty of murdering his brother, he was not only given a prison sentence of twelve months, but was branded as well.[140]

Owing to the lack of money of free Negroes, fines were often an ineffective punishment. Nevertheless, a number of offenses carried with them a penalty of fines. In 1785, the General Assembly, in seeking to regulate the relations between slaves and free Negroes, said that if a free Negro was found guilty of entertaining slaves, he was to be fined ten pounds. The second offense carried with it a fine of twenty pounds with the proviso, "that when the offender shall be unable to pay the forfeiture, he or she may be whipped for the first or second offense or both of them."[141] It will be remembered, also, that in the act of 1830 to prevent free Negroes from peddling outside the county in which they lived, a fine of fifty dollars was to be paid by the offenders.[142] After 1844, free Negroes found guilty of selling spirituous liquors were to "forfeit and pay the sum of ten dollars."[143] A fine of from ten to fifty dollars was to be paid by free Negroes found guilty of buying ardent spirits after 1858.[144]

Some of the laws which imposed fines on free Negroes stated that an alternative of whipping or imprisonment could be meted out, at the discretion of the court.[145] Many of them did not, however, and the difficulty of the judges in punishing impecunious free Negro offenders in such instances was obvious to everyone. In 1831, the matter was brought to the attention of the Assembly by a group of citizens of Guilford County. Apparently, they had reached their wits' end in dealing with this group. Their assertions reveal their exasperation:

> They are generally thievish, drunken, Idle, disorderly people, committing riots, affrays, Sabbath breaking, and Committing all manners of illegal and immoral acts. And they are generally poor and Insolvent, and when convicted of crimes, they take an Oath of Insolvency and the County is then compelled to pay the State's costs. And owing to the above consideration they go often unprosecuted for fear of incurring expence to the County. We therefore Petition your Honorable body to . . . pass a special law for Guilford County, that whenever a free negro or mulatto shall be convicted of any crime if they are unable to pay the costs

140. *North Carolina Standard*, April 14, 1858.
141. Clark, *State Records*, XXIV, 729.   142. *Laws, 1823-1831*, p. 12.
143. *Laws, 1844-1847*, p. 124.   144. *Laws, 1858-1859*, p. 76.
145. See the law forbidding free persons of color to teach slaves to read and write: *Laws, 1823-31*, p. 11.

of prosecution that they shall be sold to him who will take them for the shortest time and pay the cost of the prosecution.[146]

When the Assembly met in November, 1831, it took up this matter and enacted a measure not only to satisfy the petitioners from Guilford County, but to alleviate similar conditions all over the State. The law provided,

That when any free negro or free person of colour shall be hereafter convicted of any offence against the criminal laws of the State, and sentenced to pay a fine, and it shall appear to the satisfaction of the Court that the free negro . . . so convicted is unable to pay the fine imposed, the court shall direct the sheriff . . . to hire out the free negro . . . so convicted to any person who will pay the fine for his services for the shortest space of time.[147]

Not many years passed before this law was tested before the Supreme Court. When a free Negro of Sampson County was unable to pay a fine of $200 for assault and battery, it was ordered that the sheriff hire him out according to the law of 1831. The defendant appealed his case to the Supreme Court. He contended that the law of 1831 conflicted with that part of the State Constitution which protected the person of a debtor after ascertained insolvency from imprisonment for debt.[148] The defendant further contended that the law conflicted with "those sections in our Declaration of Rights which prohibit the imposition of excessive fines and the infliction of cruel punishments and destruction of the property of a free man other than by the law of the land."[149] The Attorney General insisted that Manuel, the free Negro, was not a beneficiary of these provisions because he was not a citizen of North Carolina.

Judge Gaston, speaking for the Court, denied the contention of the Attorney General. He said that slaves manumitted in North Carolina became free men and therefore "if born within North Carolina are citizens of North Carolina." The eminent judge went on to explain,

146. Ms. in the Legislative Papers for 1831-1832. The petition was signed by seventy-four citizens of Guilford County.

147. Laws, 1831-1835, p. 10.

148. Section XXXIX of the Constitution provided, "That the Person of a Debtor, where there is not a strong Presumption of Fraud, shall not be confined in Prison after delivering up, bona fide, all his Estate, real and personal, for the Use of his Creditors, in such Manner as shall be hereafter regulated by Law." Clark, State Records, XXIII, 984.

149. Section XII of the Declaration of Rights provided, "That no Freeman ought so be taken, imprisoned, or disseissed of his Freehold, Liberties or Privileges, or outlawed or exiled, or any Manner destroyed or deprived of his Life, Liberty or Property, but by the Law of the Land."

however, that a fine is a punishment and not a debt within the meaning of Section 39 of the State Constitution. In upholding the Act of 1831, he said,

Whatever might be thought of a penal statute which in its enactments makes distinctions between one part of the community and another capriciously and by way of favoritism, it cannot be denied that in the exercise of the great powers confided to the Legislature for the suppression and punishment of crime, they may rightfully apportion punishments according to the condition, temptations to crime, and ability to suffer, of those who are likely to offend as to produce in effect that reasonable and practical equality in the administration of justice which it is the object of all free government to establish.[150]

At the very moment that Judge Gaston was writing the decision in State v. Manuel, the General Assembly was busy revising its laws on insolvent debtors. As ratified in January, 1839, the law provided that after an insolvent person convicted of a crime had remained in prison for twenty days, he should be discharged.[151] Since the act did not specifically exclude free Negroes, the immunities granted in it were temporarily construed to include free Negroes. This construction was quite short-lived, however, for in 1841 the law of insolvent debtors underwent further revision. It provided that the Act of 1839 "shall be, and the same is hereby repealed, so far as it extends, or may be construed to extend to free Negroes or free persons of Colour."[152]

The lack of housing facilities for criminals made imprisonment an unpopular method of punishing free Negroes in ante-bellum North Carolina. An alternative was usually given to a prison sentence. Thus, the offenders of the law prohibiting peddlers from going outside their county were to be fined or imprisoned "at the discretion of the court: *Provided,* however, that the imprisonment shall not exceed the term of six months."[153] The crime of circulating incendiary and seditious publications was a felony, punishable by a year's imprisonment and whipping at the pillory.[154] It will be remembered that free Negroes leaving quarantined vessels were to be imprisoned until time for the boat to leave the port.[155]

The lack of a state penitentiary mitigated against long terms of imprisonment. Instead of a long term, some additional punishment was meted out. When Frederick Matthews, a free Negro, was found guilty

150. State v. Manuel, 20 N. C., 116.   151. *Laws, 1835-1839,* p. 32.
152. *Laws, 1840-1843,* p. 61.   153. *Laws, 1823-1831,* p. 11.
154. *Laws, 1823-1831,* p. 10.   155. *Cf. supra,* p. 70.

of assaulting a white man with a deadly weapon he was "sentenced to three months imprisonment, to stand two hours in the stocks on two different days and to give bond, with good security, in the sum of 18 pounds."[156]

The crimes for which a free Negro might suffer death were crimes which were everywhere considered felonious. If he was found guilty of inciting slaves to rebellion or insurrection, he was to suffer death without benefit of clergy.[157] Upon conviction the second time for circulating seditious publications, the free Negro was to suffer death.[158] Death without benefit of clergy was the penalty which Henry Harris received for setting fire to the Orange County jail.[159] Free Negroes found guilty of murder or rape were to be hanged, of course.

As may be suspected, there were some crimes the punishment for which was different for white offenders and free Negro offenders. White persons found guilty of gaming with slaves were to be fined or imprisoned, while free Negroes were to be whipped.[160] The fine for white persons found guilty of teaching slaves to read and write was from $100 to $200, while free Negroes guilty of the same offense were to be fined, imprisoned, or whipped.[161] Similar differences existed in almost every law which applied to whites and free Negroes. One has to go no further than an examination of the resources of the group to understand why one was usually fined while the other received "thirty-nine lashes well laid on." The point of view of Judge Gaston on the need for establishing "practical equality in the administration of justice" was being put into practice by the members of the General Assembly, in this connection.

Once the free Negro was convicted of a crime, he could entertain little hope of escaping punishment. Since the governor had the power to grant reprieve and to pardon, however, the free Negro could look to the Chief Executive of the State for clemency. That this was not an impossible procedure can be seen upon an examination of the record of Governor Montfort Stokes. On September 20, 1832, he granted a reprieve to Washington Taburn, a free Negro. The Superior Court of Granville County had found Taburn guilty of burglary and had sentenced him to hang in October. Owing to the petitions of "many respectable citizens of Granville" who promised to send Taburn to Haiti upon pardon, the Governor granted a reprieve of six months.

156. *Raleigh Star and Gazette*, October 13, 1826.
157. *Laws, 1790-1804*, p. 12.
158. *Laws, 1823-1831*, p. 10.   159. *Raleigh Register*, May 24, 1836.
160. *Laws, 1823-1831*, pp. 14-15.   161. *Laws, 1823-1831*, p. 11.

This would give the citizens an opportunity to raise money for Taburn's deportation.[162] In the same year, the Governor granted a pardon to Abednego Valentine, "a free person of colour." Valentine had received a sentence of six months' imprisonment for forcibly entering a dwelling house. The Governor said that Valentine had no felonious intention, "but was seeking an interview with a female slave who slept in the house." The Governor's action was further prompted by the fact that Valentine had a wife and six children dependent on his labor for support.[163]

That justice was sometimes miscarried or that justice was sometimes totally absent from proceedings involving free Negroes may be surmised merely from their degraded position. In October, 1842, Allen Jones, a free Negro blacksmith of Raleigh, was dragged from his home and was "shockingly whipped." In reporting the incident, the *Register* said,

> No cause is assigned for the act, but if we recollect aright, it was this Allen Jones, who, with his wife and several children whom he had purchased and emancipated, some months ago appeared before the Anti-Slavery Convention in New York and made a speech, in which he spoke of a coat of tar and feathers he had received from a certain class of persons in Raleigh. Having imprudently returned to Raleigh, we suppose these persons have thus revenged themselves on him.[164]

Raleigh was aflame over the beating of Allen Jones. A majority of the citizens looked upon the incident as most unfortunate. An indignation meeting, "one of the biggest town meetings ever held," condemned the outrage. Many prominent citizens spoke, including T. P. Devereux, one of North Carolina's largest slaveholders. The editor of the *Register* showed no sympathy whatever with those who took the law in their own hands. He said,

> We hope that the good people of Raleigh will not stop short of the most condign punishment of this outrage, not because of the individual against whom it was perpetrated (for we suspect that he is deserving of no sympathy) but for the sake of LAW, which we desire to be upheld against all infractions.[165]

162. Letter Book of Governor Montfort Stokes, No. 29, p. 125.

163. Letter Book of Governor Stokes, No. 29, p. 125.

164. The recollections of the editor in this case are strikingly similar to the facts in the Lunsford Lane case, but Lane did not return to Raleigh after being tarred and feathered. It is difficult to believe, however, that the editor could have confused the well-known Lunsford Lane with anyone else. Cf. Hawkins, *Lunsford Lane*, pp. 155, 175.   165. *Raleigh Register*, October 26, 1842.

By no means did all North Carolinians share the views of the citizens of Raleigh with regard to mob action against free Negroes. When a free Negro sailor was found on the streets of Wilmington using "impertinent, if not seditious language," the patrol of the city "chastised him, jailed him, and when let out, chastised him again." The *Wilmington Aurora* said,

> The flogging was inflicted in both cases by a slave and witnesses assert that it was never better done. This may be Judge Lynch's Law, but we think it a very good one. Nor has the patrol stopped here. They have extended their services into the tribe of free Negroes who have swarmed here from other sections and squatted in the perlieus of the city, and already have and now are in the act of abating much of that nuisance. The thanks of the public are due to them.[166]

It is difficult to believe that such action would have been condoned by the Supreme Court of North Carolina. Intimidations and questionable methods of punishments were usually condemned by that body. Had the free Negro sailor pressed his case against the Wilmington patrol, he might have recovered damages. Even at the close of the period, the Supreme Court stood out against intimidation of the free Negro. When a free Negro in the employ of a white man was whipped in the effort to get him to confess to a murder, the Court convicted the assailant on a charge of assault and battery. In his remarks, Judge Manly said,

> The battery was committed to compel Fisher to furnish evidence of his own guilt, upon the accusation of homicide.
> No free person, of whatsoever color, can, according to law, be thus coerced.[167]

That the Supreme Court was the greatest protector of the rights of free Negroes can be seen by the decision it made in several important cases. The manner in which it upheld the Negro's right to freedom has already been discussed.[168] The Court, however, did not stop there. In 1838, it held that a white man could not use violence to eject a free Negro from his property, regardless of his right to the property. The fact that the free Negro "had in fact the *possession* thereof" when it was invaded "with such lawless violence," was sufficient to convict the invaders.[169] The Court also upheld the right of a free Negro to strike

166. Reprinted in the *North Carolina Standard*, October 30, 1850.
167. State v. Norman, 53 N. C., 200.
168. *Cf. supra*, pp. 51 ff.   169. State v. Bennett, 20 N. C., 135.

a white man in self-defense. In New Bern, Lawrence Davis was arrested for violating the town ordinance requiring all free Negroes who were delinquent in their taxes to work on the streets "two days for each and every dollar of tax due the town by them." The officer who arrested Davis attempted to tie him when the latter struck him. In denying that the free Negro was guilty of assault and battery, Chief Justice Pearson said,

> Self-defense is a *natural* right, and although the social relation of this *third class* of our population, and a regard for its proper subordination, requires that the right should be restricted, yet nothing short of manifest public necessity can furnish a ground for taking it away absolutely; because a free negro, however lowly his condition, is in the "peace of the State," and to deprive him of this right would be to put him on the footing of an outlaw.[170]

Justice Pearson admitted that the law would not allow a free Negro to return blow for blow and engage in a fight with a white man.[171] He insisted, however, that if the free Negro could prove that it became necessary to strike a white man to protect himself from great bodily harm and grievous oppression he was justified in doing so.

> An officer of the town having a *notice to serve on the defendant* without any authority whatever, *arrests him and attempts to tie him!* Is not this gross oppression. . . . What degree of cruelty might not the defendant reasonably apprehend after he should be entirely in the power of one who had set upon him in so highhanded and lawless a manner? Was he to submit tamely? or was he not excusable in resorting to the natural right of self-defense.[172]

Thus, it can be seen that the seeming harsh and illiberal laws of North Carolina were often softened by those who interpreted and administered them. One cannot say, however, that the citizens of Raleigh indignant over the beating of a free Negro, represented the views of a majority of the people of North Carolina. The reactions of

170. State v. Davis, 52 N. C., 42.

171. In 1850, the Court said that it was quite all right for a white man to strike a free Negro for insolence. In this case, Atlas Jowers, a free Negro, had called a white man a liar, whereupon the white man struck Jowers. Justice Pearson said, "The same reasons by which a blow from a white man upon a slave is excusable on account of insolent language, apply to the free negro who is insolent. . . . If a slave is insolent, he may be whipped by his master . . . but a free negro has no master . . . and unless a white man, to whom the insolence is given, has a right to put a stop to it in an extrajudicial way, there is no remedy for it. . . . Hence, we infer from the principles of the common law that this extrajudicial remedy is excusable, provided the words or acts of the free negro be in law insolent." State v. Jowers, 33 N. C., 379.

172. State v. Davis, 52 N. C., 43.

the people of the State toward free Negroes depended upon the social, economic, and political conditions which existed in the several communities. Nor can it be said that the somewhat liberal interpretations of the Supreme Court received the approbation of the bench and bar throughout the State. But these conflicts of ideas, these differences in points of view, were the atmosphere in which the concept of the legal status of the free Negro in North Carolina developed. That it represented liberalism in some respects, extreme conservatism in others, and contradictions in many may be explained by these conditions.

The observation of a Wilmington editor in 1850 that the laws were "stringent enough against free negroes generally" was a sound and accurate one.[173] If one could have relied on legislation alone, he would have been reasonably certain that the strait jacket "Free Negro Code" would have all but prevented the free Negro from committing unlawful acts. If one could have had confidence even in a half-hearted enforcement of the law, he would have been fairly certain that the free Negro would have been a relatively harmless creature in the community. It will be interesting, therefore, to examine the conduct of the free Negro in ante-bellum North Carolina with a view to seeing whether or not the hopes and expectations of the North Carolina legislators were realized.

A recitation of the crimes in which free Negroes were implicated would require a disproportionate amount of space in so general a study. Samples drawn at random will be sufficient to study the conduct of the free Negro. Fighting with fists and with weapons was the result of arguments over various issues; and the outcome was not always fortunate for one or both parties. When John Gragson, white, and Frederick Matthews, a free Negro, engaged in a fight which followed an argument, the free Negro shot Gragson and "then struck him over the head with the but end of the musket."[174] In 1830, Cordy Hammonds, a free Negro, was indicted in the Wake Superior Court for shooting William Holmes, another free Negro, with intent to kill. He was found guilty and sentenced to three months' imprisonment.[175] Twice within two years William Holmes was shot. The last time his

173. From the *Wilmington Aurora,* reprinted in the *North Carolina Standard,* October 30, 1850.

174. *Raleigh Star and Gazette,* April 14, 1826. In a petition asking for a pardon for Matthews, eleven citizens of Raleigh described Gragson as a "man of low and lawless character" and said that "Matthews has supported and does support a very fair character as an honest and peaceable citizen—as much or more so than any man of his color in the city." Although Matthews had been in jail for six months (waiting for the next session of the county court) the plea was rejected. Ms. in the papers of Governor H. G. Burton, October 23, 1826.   175. *Raleigh Star,* October 14, 1830.

assailant was a white man who was sentenced to an imprisonment of twelve months.[176] That stabbing one's victim was a form of assault indulged in by free Negroes is seen in the example of one Mitchell, free Negro of Raleigh, who slashed another free Negro in Fayetteville so viciously that physicians feared for his life.[177]

From the beginning of the national period, there were stringent laws against thefts and robberies committed by free Negroes.[178] Nevertheless, the press of the period gives one the impression that free Negroes were in the vanguard in the taking of other persons' properties. The mantle of suspicion often fell on free Negroes when anything came up missing. In 1802, Wayne County officials took up Benny Grimson, free Negro of Person County, because he carried with him a "middling large sorrel Horse. . . . It is supposed from the suspicious Manner in which the . . . Fellow made his appearance . . . that he came by the property dishonestly." Grimson, however, broke prison, and when a horse of Mr. William Dickins was missing the same morning, it was supposed that the free Negro had stolen it.[179]

Grimson was only one of a number of free Negroes who were suspected of horse stealing during the early part of the nineteenth century. Note the following advertisement:

> There is great cause to suppose (says one of our correspondents) that a combination has taken place between a free mulatto man by the name of Cullen, who lately lived on South Dividing Creek, Beaufort County, and some of his white neighbors. He left the neighborhood about the first of November last, and a few days afterwards one of his white neighbors went off and soon returned with a large young sorrel stud Horse. . . . [180]

In 1807, a very light free mulatto was described as having committed "a singular piece of villainy." When his employer sent him into the country from Raleigh to secure a load of corn, "he drove the team into the woods, took off the best horse and rode off, leaving the [illegible] . . . remaining horses tied, at a distance from any road, and where they had nearly perished before they were found, having stood in the snow

---

176. *Carolina Observer*, March 10, 1831. On January 2, 1832, Governor Stokes pardoned the white assailant, William Spivey, with the expectation that he would "leave the State or give the Security for good behaviour as required by the Sentence. . . ." Letter Book of Governor Montfort Stokes, No. 29, p. 97.

177. *Carolina Observer*, August 24, 1831; also reported in the *Raleigh Register*, September 1, 1831.

178. See the enactment of 1787 in Clark, *State Records*, XXIV, 890.

179. *Raleigh Register*, April 6, 1802.   180. *Ibid.*, December 31, 1804.

two days and three nights without food!"[181] A reward of $50 was offered for the apprehension of the free mulatto.[182]

The case against many free Negroes went further than suspicion, and the records reveal that a number of them were convicted of theft, robbery, burglary, etc. In 1807, the Superior Court of Wake County found Isaac Watson guilty of grand larceny, having broken into his employer's desk and stolen a purse.[183] When the Warren Superior Court met in May, 1827, "William Hansell, a free lad of color . . . was convicted of burglary on the dwelling House of a lady of great respectability . . . and stealing $5 worth of Sugar Candy and other articles." It was pointed out that this was only one of many offenses which the lad had committed. The editor observed that "altho' young, he is considered a most consummate and hardened villain." The Court sentenced him to die on the third Friday in May "by hanging at the gallows near Warrenton."[184]

In 1830, Salisbury Mainer, a free Negro, received fifteen stripes after having been found guilty of petty larceny by the Wake Superior Court.[185] In 1852, "At Sampson Court . . . William Boon, Alias William Hussey, a free mulatto, was convicted of Burglary with intent to commit a Rape." Boon's sentence was not given in the report.[186] In 1859, Benjamin Small was convicted of grand larceny by the Superior Court of Pasquotank County.[187]

The refusal, or, more properly, the inability, of some free Negroes to adjust themselves to conditions in North Carolina can be seen in the commitment of the more serious crimes. Benny Grimson, the individual suspected of horse stealing in 1802, was by no means the only free Negro who refused to remain in prison to await trial. In 1822, Jack Harris, held in the Wake County jail under suspicion, escaped with several other prisoners, all white.[188] In 1831, Governor Stokes was seeking to extradite London Pollock from New York, where he

181. *Ibid.*, January 26, 1807.

182. *Ibid.*, February 2, 1807. On two occasions, when trunks were cut from the Fayetteville stage, free Negroes were immediately suspected. See *Raleigh Register*, May 22, 1826, and January 21, 1830.

183. *Raleigh Register*, April 6, 1807.

184. *Warrenton Reporter*, reprinted in the *Raleigh Star*, May 3, 1827.

185. *Raleigh Star*, October 14, 1830.   186. *Fayetteville Observer*, May 4, 1854.

187. *Greensborough Patriot*, November 11, 1854. Notice also the conviction of Robert George, a free Negro, who with several white persons was found guilty of passing counterfeit money on the bank of Georgetown, South Carolina. State v. Cheek, 35 N. C., 114. Undoubtedly, there were many other types of theft and burglary involving free Negroes that have not come to the writer's attention.

188. *Raleigh Register*, July 12, 1822.

had gone after breaking out of the Craven County jail.[189] When Henry Patrick could find no other way of escaping from the Brunswick County jail, he burned it to the ground. A reward of $25 was offered for his capture.[190]

Despite the fact that arson was an extremely serious crime, punishable by death without benefit of clergy, other free Negroes were found guilty of committing such a crime. The motives for the action of Henry Harris are not discussed, but the Caswell Superior Court found him guilty of setting fire to the Orange County jail in 1836.[191] In 1855, the Cumberland Superior Court found Rachel Freeman guilty of "setting fire to the dwelling of Mr. A. H. Whitfield" of Fayetteville.[192] Upon appeal, the Supreme Court remanded the case for a new trial because "the jury was misled by much irrelevant testimony which the court allowed to be submitted."[193] In the second trial, however, she was again found guilty.[194]

The General Assembly passed the following act in 1823:

> Be it enacted . . . That any person of colour, convicted by due course of law, of assault with intent to commit a rape upon the body of a white female, shall suffer death without benefit of clergy.[195]

This was merely a reinforcement of the general law against rape that had always been on the statute books. Despite the indignation which was aroused at the report of any relations between white women and Negro men, several free Negroes placed themselves in this position; or at least they were found to be so by the juries. In 1831, Henry Carroll, a free boy of color, was indicted for an attempt to commit a rape upon a young white woman of Johnston County. He was defended by "Messrs. Manley and George W. Haywood, with great ingenuity, considering the utter hopelessness of the task assigned them by the court." It took the jury but a few minutes to find him guilty of the same offense for which his brother was hanged during the previous year.[196] A number of respectable citizens, dissatisfied with the conviction, asked the Governor to stay the execution.[197] The Governor complied with

189. Letter Book of Governor Montfort Stokes, No. 29. Montfort Stokes to the Governor of New York, May 24, 1831.

190. *Fayetteville Observer*, January 29, 1850.

191. *Raleigh Register*, May 24, 1836.

192. *Fayetteville Observer*, May 19, 1855.

193. State v. Freeman, 49 N. C., 5.

194. *Fayetteville Observer*, November 13, 1856.

195. *Laws, 1823-1831*, p. 42.

196. *Raleigh Register*, April 14, 1831.   197. *Ibid.*, May 12, 1831.

their request to stay the execution until September 2, and at a later date he extended the reprieve for another two months.[198]

Free Negroes were also tried for committing rape upon the bodies of women of their own color. In 1836, Jones Kiff was tried on an indictment of rape committed on a free Negro woman "supposed to be 80 years of age." William Haywood, Jr., counsel for the defendant, secured a verdict of acquittal.[199] Whether this case was taken more lightly by the court than other rape cases is not revealed in the report.

The taking of life was a crime of which many free Negroes were accused. Anthony Wiggins, a free mulatto, had indentured himself to James Hayes for life. When Hayes did not return from the field where his slaves and Wiggins were working, a search was made. Hayes' body was found half buried. The slaves testified that Wiggins had murdered their master in order to recover his freedom.[200] The Bertie Superior Court found him guilty, and he was hanged November 9, 1810.[201] In 1859, Joe Mills was found guilty of murdering eighty-year-old Betsy Williams. He had confessed the deed, and a "desire to hang him on the spot was manifested by the crowd. Law prevailed, however, and he was sent on to the Enfield jail. His plea of idiocy was disregarded, and he was sentenced to be hanged on November 18."[202]

Mere accusation, however, was not enough to convict a free Negro of murdering a white person. When the fall term of the Cumberland Superior Court opened in 1851, Dave Jones was on the criminal docket for the murder of a white woman in Campbellton in August.[203] "The Jury, after a few minutes consultation, returned a verdict of *not guilty*."[204] The circumstances are not discussed in the report of the case.

Nor did the free Negro always suffer conviction when indicted for the murder of a slave. In a fit of jealousy "a negro fellow named Jacob, the property of Mr. William Lightfoot," attacked Trueman Goode when he found the latter, a free Negro, visiting his wife. Goode, however, got the better of the fight and stabbed Jacob in the

---

198. Letter Book of Governor Montfort Stokes, No. 29, pp. 22 and 45. The writer was unable to find out the final disposition of Carroll. See also the *Greensborough Patriot*, October 24, 1856, for a report on the holding of Henry Pittman on a charge of rape.

199. *Raleigh Register*, April 12, 1836.

200. *Ibid.*, June 7, 1810.   201. *Ibid.*, November 29, 1810.

202. From the *Newbern Delta*, reprinted in the *Western Democrat* (Charlotte), September 13, 1859.

203. *Fayetteville Observer*, November 11, 1851.

204. *Ibid.*, November 18, 1851. The italics are the editor's.

heart, causing instant death.[205] After Goode was turned over to the sheriff by his own father, he was tried and acquitted. The jury took the point of view that Goode killed the slave in self-defense.[206] In 1851, the Robeson Superior Court likewise found Louis Hunt not guilty of murdering "Silas, a slave, the property of Mr. McClean."[207]

An examination of the records for the last decade of the ante-bellum period seems to suggest that free Negroes had their greatest difficulty in getting along with each other. Northampton County was the scene of an exciting fight between two free Negroes in a boat on the Roanoke River in 1854. One was killed in the affray, and the other was indicted for murder. Although he was found guilty by the Superior Court, the Supreme Court could not agree with the conviction. The higher court felt that the greatness of the provocation ensuing from the quarrel and the passion naturally produced by the conflict could have resulted in nothing more than manslaughter.[208] The strife among free Negroes is further seen in the murder of Gilbert Chavis by a free Negro man and woman on the Fayetteville road, about two miles from Raleigh.[209]

Cumberland County had its share of altercations involving free Negroes. In 1855, Roland Lomax was killed by his father during a drunken brawl. The Superior Court found the free Negro guilty of manslaughter and sentenced him to whipping and six months' imprisonment.[210] It was in this year that the court found Sylvester Chavers guilty of manslaughter for killing her free Negro husband.[211] Two free Negroes, both of whom were said to have been drinking, engaged in a fight in Fayetteville in October, 1851, in which one was stabbed to death.[212] The assailant was found guilty of manslaughter and sentenced to receive thirty-nine lashes and to pay a fine of $100.[213]

The Franklin Superior Court had on its criminal docket for April, 1858, a charge of manslaughter against Joe Manly for killing his brother Bill, both free Negroes. The jury remained out all night and returned a verdict of guilty the next morning at eleven o'clock. The defendant was sentenced to be imprisoned for twelve months and to be branded.[214] In the following year, two free Negroes of Hertford

---

205. *Raleigh Register*, May 2, 1826.   206. *Ibid.*, October 10, 1826.
207. *Fayetteville Observer*, April 1, 1851.
208. State v. Curry, 46 N. C., 260.
209. *Greensborough Patriot*, November 11, 1854.
210. *Fayetteville Observer*, May 19, 1855.
211. *Cf. supra*, p. 87.
212. *Fayetteville Observer*, November 3, 1856.
213. *Ibid.*, November 17, 1856.
214. *North Carolina Standard*, April 14, 1858.

County engaged in a fight in which one was stabbed to death.[215] Governor Ellis offered a reward of $100 for the assailant, who was believed to have left the State.[216]

Legislation, therefore, did not prevent free Negroes from running the entire gamut of criminal offenses against the State. It cannot be said with any degree of certainty, moreover, that legislation even checked their criminal offenses. In the year after the largest number of repressive measures was passed, free Negroes were described by a group of citizens of Caswell County as having become "so ungovernable that it is thought you [the representatives from Caswell County] should take into consideration the subject ... and introduce before the legislature now in session some bill as in your judgments will be best calculated to suppress them." The citizens said that the free Negroes had done considerable injury "by killing cattle, cutting our horses throats, and cutting two other horses ears."[217]

The *North Carolina Standard,* in its issue of November 6, 1850, described the free Negroes as "vicious, idle, and disorderly, and therefore a deadweight on the body politic." While these utterances were made by individuals who were as remote from dispassion as one can imagine, there is little doubt that some of their assertions were true. Interestingly enough, both these statements were made by individuals who were asking for more repressive legislation. It seems that nothing should have been clearer to these persons than the fact that all their legislation up to that point had been of little avail, although it had been quite extensive. They failed completely to realize that the free Negro criminal could not be legislated out of existence by repressive measures. The free Negro's social and economic difficulties were so great that crime was often merely the reaction to his dilemmas. It is in these difficulties that the explanations can be found for the development and growth of the free Negro criminal.

Citizenship in the Larger Sense

As citizens of North Carolina, free Negroes were expected to share in the support of the government. In return for the protection which it offered them, the authorities thought it no more than just that these individuals render support to the armed forces of the State, that they contribute financially to the maintenance of government, and that they render other various services to the State when called upon to do so.

215. *Wilmington New Era,* March 8, 1859.
216. *North Carolina Standard,* March 30, 1859.
217. Ms. in Legislative Papers for 1831-1832.

In the colonial period, free Negroes served in the militia of North Carolina with no apparent discrimination against them.[218] The muster roll of the regiment of Granville County for 1754 listed five free Negroes belonging to Captain Osborn Jeffry's company.[219]

The problem of defending North Carolina against the British became so great in 1779 that the Assembly promised freedom to all slaves who served in the army with the impression that they were to receive freedom.[220] At no time did a large number of Negroes of North Carolina serve in the Revolutionary Army. The return of the North Carolina Brigade showed that there were only fifty-eight Negroes enlisted, forty-two of whom were in service on August 24, 1778.[221] That some received their freedom as a result of service in the army is seen by the Act of 1784 "for Enfranchising Ned Griffin, Late the property of William Kitchen." Griffin was described in the act as having faithfully served as a soldier in the continental line of North Carolina for twelve months. He was therefore "enfranchised and forever delivered and discharged from the yoke of slavery. . . ."[222] In 1849, the *Edenton Whig* gave an account of the death of a 101-year-old free Negro soldier. He had served under Washington at Yorktown at the close of the war.[223]

After the Revolution, little interest was manifested in having Negroes, bond or free, serve in the armed forces of North Carolina. With the philosophy of the Revolution becoming less and less potent as the nineteenth century opened, free Negroes came to be regarded as unfit for service in the State militia. The adjutant-general of the militia said in 1819 that "it lessens the respectability of a military company to have men of colour in the ranks, and prevents many from mustering who would otherwise do so."[224] This apparently was the point of view of more individuals than the adjutant-general, for in 1812 the General Assembly passed the following act:

> Be it enacted . . . That it shall not be lawful for the Captain or Commanding Officer of any company of militia to enroll any free Negro or Mulatto in his company; *Provided always,* that it shall

218. Walter Clark, "Negro Soldiers," *North Carolina Booklet*, XVIII (1918), 57.
219. Clark, *State Records*, XXII, 372.   220. Clark, *State Records*, XXIV, 221.
221. W. B. Hartgrove, "The Negro Soldier in the American Revolution," *Journal of Negro History*, I (1916), 127.
222. Clark, *State Records*, XXIV, 639. The writer did not discuss service in the army as a factor in the growth of the free Negro population for the reason that the records suggest that it was negligible.
223. Laura Wilkes, *Missing Pages in American History*, p. 51.
224. *Journal of the House of Commons, 1809* (Raleigh, 1810), p. 15.

and may be lawful at all times to enroll a sufficient number of such in any Militia Company as Musicians.[225]

Thus, free Negroes were excluded from the militia of North Carolina for the remainder of the period.[226]

The exclusion of free Negroes from the militia, except as musicians, did not mean that their manual labor was spurned. In 1847, it was proposed that they be pressed into the service to work in the quartermaster's department. The proposed law provided,

> That the Quarter Master of Each Regiment of Militia or Volunteers, shall have authority to order out, as many free male persons of color, between the ages of eighteen and forty-five—within the bounds of his Regiment, as he may deem necessary, for the purpose of clearing off parade grounds. . . .[227]

If any free Negro refused or neglected to obey such an order he was to be fined "two dollars per day, for each and every day on which, he or they has or have, refused or neglected to obey such order."[228] The bill did not pass the House, although there was much sentiment in favor of it. Even though free Negroes served the militia as musicians and, perhaps, as manual laborers between 1812 and 1860, it can hardly be said that the free Negroes contributed a great deal toward the defense of the State during the ante-bellum period.

Despite the fact that free Negroes were regarded as "an idle, indolent, and thriftless people," they were called upon from time to time to assist in bearing the financial burdens of the State. The difficulty of distinguishing between taxation as a form of discipline on the free Negro and taxation as a means of more closely incorporating him into the body politic becomes clear upon an examination of the records. Regardless of the motives, the fact remains that the free Negro was a subject of taxation down to the close of the period.

In 1723, the colonial assembly passed an act which provided that all free Negroes over twelve years of age who were inhabitants of North Carolina were to be "deemed and taken for Tithables" and were to pay the "same Levies and Taxes as the other Tithable Inhabitants. . . ."[229] It was possible, however, to obtain an exemption from this law. The Assembly, in 1775, decided that Dorothy Stringer, a free

---

225. *Laws Passed by the General Assembly, 1805-1816* (Raleigh, 1817), p. 1.

226. This law was reënacted in 1836, *Revised Statutes*, I, 171; and in 1854, *Revised Code, 1854*, p. 399; and in 1861, *Laws, 1860-1861*, p. 24.

227. Ms. in the Legislative Papers for 1846-1847.

228. *Ibid.*   229. Clark, *State Records*, XXIII, 106.

Negro woman of Craven County, was an "object proper to be exempted from paying Levies and Taxes," and she was accordingly exempted.[230]

The national period opened with the same taxation laws applying to free Negroes that applied to the other citizens of North Carolina. That many free Negroes were often delinquent in the payment of their taxes is to be expected. In the preamble of an act of 1827, it was complained that they frequently neglected to pay their taxes. After observing further that "from the small value of their chattels and from other causes, it has been found impracticable to enforce the collection thereof," the law provided,

> That, hereafter, when any free negro or mulatto, liable to pay a public tax shall reside on the land of another person, with his or her consent, the person on whose land such free negro or mulatto may reside, shall include each and every such free negro or mulatto, as a free poll, in his or her list of taxable property, and be liable to pay all public, county and parish taxes on every such free negro or mulatto.[231]

Naturally, this law discouraged white persons from permitting thriftless and impecunious free Negroes to remain on their land. Nevertheless, a number of whites kept free Negroes on their plantations and listed them as free black polls in the returns.[232] The number of free Negroes living on the land of white persons in 1860 suggests the extent to which whites had to pay taxes on free Negroes.[233]

Free Negroes, excluded as they were from the common schools of the State, were not expected to contribute to the support of those schools. In order that there should be no misunderstanding on the subject, the Assembly provided in 1843,

> That it shall not be lawful for any County Court in this State, to tax any free person of color, for the support and maintenance of any common School or Schools in this State.[234]

A discriminatory capitation tax on free Negroes was proposed in 1857. All white persons were to be exempt, but all "free colored males over the age of twenty-one years and under the age of sixty years, and all slaves over the age of twelve years shall be subject to a capitation tax." In recommending that this amendment to the Constitution be rejected,

230. *Ibid.*, V, 529.
231. *Laws, 1825-1830*, p. 21. This law was reënacted in 1861. *Laws, 1860-1861,* Second Extra Session, p. 72.
232. See, for example, the tax lists of Beaufort County, 1847.
233. *Cf. infra*, pp. 149 ff.   234. *Laws, 1840-1843*, p. 92.

the Committee on Constitutional Reform said that it would "violate the compromises of the Constitution, encourage the spirit of hostility to slavery, divide the citizens of the State into two parties . . . a slavery and abolition party, and will inevitably tend to array the East against the West and defeat the suffrage." The bill was laid on the table February 2, 1857, and was not taken up again.[235] In the light of the facts, it would be safe to say that the free Negroes of North Carolina did not bear a great part of the taxes of the State.

Free Negroes could not vote in North Carolina during the early colonial period. It had not been intended that they should vote. This could be seen in the complaint made to the Lords Proprietors concerning the situation in 1701.[236] The law of 1715 provided that "no Negro, Mullatto or Indians shall be capable of voting for Members of the Assembly."[237] When the election laws were revised in 1734 and again in 1743, no disability was placed on the eligibility of free Negroes to vote. The act of 1743 set up with considerable care the machinery for electing members of the General Assembly. In the section which defined who shall be qualified as electors, the following statement was inserted:

And for the Prevention of Disputes which may hereafter arise in Election of Burgesses, concerning who shall be understood to be a Freeholder: Be it enacted, That every Person who hath an Estate Real, for his own Life, or the Life of another, or any estate of greater Dignity, of a sufficient Number of Acres, in the County which by this Law enables him to vote . . . shall be accounted a Freeholder.

And be it further Enacted . . . That no Person hereafter, shall be admitted to give his Vote in any Election of Burgesses in any County . . . unless he hath been an Inhabitant of this Province Six Months, and hath been possessed of a Freehold . . . of Fifty Acres of Land at least Three Months before he offers to give his Vote, and is also of the full Age of Twenty One Years. . . .[238]

Thus, the qualification for voting was based upon property, residence, and age rather than upon race after 1743. There is no conclusive evidence, however, that Negroes voted during the colonial period.

When the State Constitution was adopted in 1776, no discrimination was made among the races of men residing in North Carolina.[239] Enfranchisement was looked upon as a right of all free men, and for a time the law enforcement officers failed to show that they saw any

235. Ms. in the Legislative Papers for 1856-57.
236. Cf. supra, p. 9.
237. Saunders, Colonial Records, II, 215.
238. Clark, State Records, XXIII, 208.   239. Cf. supra, p. 12.

difference between free white men and free Negroes. It is difficult to ascertain the extent to which free Negroes were a factor in politics during the national period. That they voted in certain communities is a matter of record; and that their vote was feared in certain quarters has also been established as a fact. Judge Buxton, in his *Reminiscences of the Bench and Fayetteville Bar*, said that the vote of the free Negro was eagerly sought. "The opposing candidates, for the nonce oblivious of social distinction and intent only on catching votes, hobnobbed with the men and swung corners all with dusky damsels at election balls."[240] Professor Shugg describes the free Negro as having the balance of power in certain North Carolina elections. At one time there were 300 colored voters in Halifax County and 150 in Hertford County.[241]

John Chavis was active in politics all during the 1820's. He took special pride in having Willie P. Mangum, a former student, in the Federal Congress. Without solicitation, Chavis offered advice to Mangum on every conceivable public question. During one campaign, he wrote Mangum,

> There is much rumour abroad that you will not be elected again because you support the election of Mr. Crawford [for the Presidency]. It is supposed Mr. Crudup will oppose you, and if he does, your election will be doubtful. If you offer and I am alive I will vote for you.[242]

Later, Chavis wrote Mangum that he had fought for him as uniformly since he had been in Congress as he did before the election.[243] The type of advice that Chavis could offer on public questions can be seen in the following letters:

> I disapprove of three of your votes—Van Buren, the Bank, and the fast day, but my greatest grief is that you should be in favor of the reelection of General Jackson for the presidency. . . . Let G. J. be elected and our Government is gone and even in its present situation it would require a Hamilton, a Jay, and an old Adams bottomed upon G. Washington to repair its ruins.[244]

240. Quoted in Stephen B. Weeks, "The History of Negro Suffrage in the South," *Political Science Quarterly*, IX (1894), 676.

241. Roger W. Shugg, "Negro Voting in the Antebellum South," *Journal of Negro History*, XXI (1936), 358. In the Convention of 1835, Mr. Branch of Halifax said that there were two or three hundred free Negro voters in his county. *Proceedings and Debates of the Constitutional Convention of 1835* (Raleigh, 1835), p. 70.

242. John Chavis to Willie P. Mangum, January 28, 1825.

243. Chavis to Mangum, May 24, 1826.

244. Chavis to Mangum, July 21, 1832.

I believe him to be an honest man, but there is no trait in his character . . . that qualifies him for the seat of a chief magistrate. . . .
I appeal to you as a gentleman of candour and penetrating understanding to begin at his cradle, and point out . . . the regular traits
in his character up to the seat he now fills and shew me what it is
that constitutes him a dignified Character and one who is fitly
qualified to fill the seat of a chief magistrate.[245]

Chavis wrote Mangum frequently. His knowledge of political
affairs in and around Raleigh was remarkable.[246] During his last
years, he continued to manifest a great interest in politics and in his
protégé. When Mangum was opposed by W. H. Haywood in 1836,
Chavis said that it would kill him if Haywood won. He offered to
leave his home in the country and go to Raleigh to find out what he
could. The guise of trying to open a school for free Negroes would
shield the real motives for his visit to Raleigh, he asserted.[247]

Chavis had no counterparts during the ante-bellum period, it is
true; but in other sections of North Carolina free Negroes were active
in politics. The activity of free Negroes in New Bern aroused the ire
of a number of the citizens of that town, and they moved to check
their influence. In a communication to the General Assembly they
said that "many of the free negroes residing in . . . Newbern, claim the
right of voting for a Representative of said town in the House of Commons and that fifty or more actually exercise that right." The petitioners insisted that the term, freemen, as used in the franchise clauses
of the Constitution, was inapplicable to free Negroes. A freeman, the
memorialists asserted, "is by the standard a lawful man—*Homo liber
et legalis*—one who is not restrained from making contracts of any
kind, except such as are forbidden to all citizens generally, one who
can sit on juries and can participate in the Administration of the law."
They said that it was well known that free Negroes did not possess
these rights and had not the capacity to acquire them. The New Bern
citizens appealed directly to the fears and passions of the representatives
when they said,

A very large portion of our own population are slaves and recent
occurrences must deeply impress on your Honorable Body the
vital necessity of keeping them in a state of discipline and subordination. Your Memorialists believe they hazard nothing, in saying
that permitting free negroes to vote at elections, contributes to

245. Chavis to Mangum, August 8, 1832.
246. Chavis to Mangum, June 27, 1836.
247. Chavis to Mangum, November 17, 1836, and February 1, 1837.

excite and cherish a spirit of discontent and disorder among the slaves. During the heat of party contest, they are courted and caressed by both parties and treated apparently with respect and attention. When the slave sees him whom he regards as his associate and equal . . . thus respectfully treated by men of high character . . . we respectfully ask . . . if the barrier of opinion which alone keeps him in subjection is not effectively undermined?[248]

The memorialists concluded by asking the Assembly to ascertain and determine the true construction of the Constitution on the matter of free Negro voting. There were 164 signers of this petition, and many were representative of the best that New Bern had to offer. Both the Bryan brothers signed, as well as the very prominent James Haywood, William Russell, and Oliver J. Dewey.

That free Negroes were a factor in the political life of New Bern is further seen by a comment which John H. Bryan made to his brother-in-law in the summer of 1832:

Charles [Shepard] as you know is a candidate again and is violently opposed by the free negroes, and Messrs. Alfred and Edward Stanly—They have been very anxious to bring out Mr. Manly in opposition and I think it is probable they will vote for him, whether he is a declared candidate or not.[249]

While the number of free Negroes who voted may not have been very large, it was of sufficient size in some localities to cause considerable concern. Those who viewed the free Negro vote as inimical to the best interests of the State—and to their candidate—were exceedingly hostile to free Negro voting.

The dissatisfaction of many citizens with free Negro voting coincided with some other grievances which they harbored against the machinery of government which functioned under the Constitution of 1776. Professor Boyd points out the most important grievance when he observes,

Prior to 1835 representation was divided equally among the counties; consequently the eastern counties, larger in number but inferior to western counties in population, had a majority in the legislature and controlled its work. This inequality in representation was the principal issue in local politics for many years and colored almost every issue.[250]

248. Ms. in the Legislative Papers for 1831-1832.

249. Pettigrew Family Papers, John H. Bryan to Ebenezer Pettigrew, July 27, 1832.

250. William K. Boyd, "The Antecedents of the North Carolina Convention of 1835," reprinted from the *South Atlantic Quarterly* (1910), p. 3.

As the population moved westward and as the demand for greater representation became more audible there, the East held on to her advantage with even fiercer tenacity. This intensified the sectional struggle that had gone on for almost a half-century.[251]

In 1822, a group of citizens calling themselves "Friends of Convention" met at Raleigh and declared that the principle of representation as established in the Constitution was "anti-republican, unjust, and oppressive and ought . . . to be so altered and amended, as to secure to every freeman . . . an equality of privileges and influence in the government. . . ."[252] They urged the calling of a convention to rectify this evil. Thirty-one men accordingly met in Raleigh on November 10, 1823, to consider ways of getting the Constitution amended. A cleavage among the reform leaders, however, prevented the consummation of a workable plan.[253] The agitation for a constitutional convention continued, and finally, in 1834, one was called to meet in June, 1835.

According to the act of the General Assembly which provided for the convention, free Negroes were not excluded from voting for delegates to the convention. All persons qualified to vote for members of the House of Commons were entitled to vote for delegates.[254] The act, in defining the powers of the convention, said that, among other things, it could consider "equalizing and reducing the representation in the legislature, making provision for the Assembly to meet biennially instead of annually, and abrogating or restricting the right of free negroes or mulattoes to vote for members of the Senate or House of Commons."[255]

When the convention met on June 4, 1835, some of North Carolina's most distinguished citizens were among its members. Nathaniel Macon, for years a Representative and Senator in the Federal Congress, was chosen president. Governor D. L. Swain, former Governor John Branch, Judge William Gaston, Richard D. Spaight, and John M. Morehead were only a few of the dignitaries present.[256] Committees were assigned to consider various proposed amendments. The reports of these committees were to be considered by the convention in the

251. Henry G. Connor, "The Convention of 1835," *North Carolina Booklet*, VIII (1908), 89 ff.

252. *Proceedings of the Friends of Convention*, p. 3.

253. *Journal of a Convention Assembled at . . . Raleigh . . . to Adopt . . . Measures . . . to procure an Amendment to the Constitution. . . .* pp. 3 ff.; and Boyd, "Antecedents," *loc. cit.*, pp. 22-23.

254. *Laws, 1831-1835*, p. 4.   255. *Raleigh Register*, May 19, 1835.

256. For a discussion on the personnel of the convention, see Connor, "Convention of 1835," *loc. cit.*, p. 96.

committee of the whole. The first question discussed was a proposition
to abolish borough representation.[257] The western part of the State
scored its first victory by securing a majority to vote for the adoption
of the amendment abolishing borough representation.

The second matter before the convention was the question of abrogating or restricting the privilege of free Negroes to vote. As soon as
the proposal to abrogate the privilege of free Negroes to vote was introduced, a lively debate ensued. There were those who supported disfranchisement, those who opposed it, and those who favored certain
property qualifications for free Negro voting. The first to speak was
Judge Joseph Daniel of Halifax. He offered a resolution that all free
Negroes possessing a freehold estate of $250 should be entitled to vote
for members of the House of Commons.[258] Judge Daniel felt that the
door should be open to "all colored men of good character and industrious habits." He believed it would be good policy to "adopt such a
course as would have a tendency to conciliate the most respectable
portion of the colored population, and thereby give them a standing
distinct from the slave population, and afford them an opportunity of
some intercourse with the whites."[259]

Weldon Edwards of Warren County said that "if the Bill of Rights
which said that people of North Carolina ought not to be taxed without their consent freely given, bears upon negroes equally with whites,
it would appear wrong to deny them a vote for members of the Assembly." Judge Daniel replied that the Bill of Rights did not apply to men
of color, but he was willing to allow colored men of property and
standing to vote for members. "From an observance of their conduct
for the past thirty years he could say that they uniformly voted for
men to represent them of the best character and talents."[260]

One of the ablest spokesman for those who favored the disfranchisement of free Negroes was James W. Bryan of Carteret County.
In a lengthy speech, he contended that Negroes did not vote in the
colonial period, had no part in drawing up the Constitution and Bill
of Rights, and therefore had no standing in the State so far as the
privilege of voting was concerned.[261] In a moving, if not convincing,
peroration Mr. Bryan concluded:

257. Six towns, Wilmington, New Bern, Edenton, Halifax, Hillsboro, and Salisbury,
had sent representatives to the House of Commons since 1776. In 1789, Fayetteville was
granted this privilege.
258. *Proceedings and Debates*, p. 60.
259. *Ibid.*, p. 61. His colleague, Mr. Branch, supported him. p. 70.
260. *Ibid.*, p. 62.   261. *Ibid.*, p. 66.

North Carolina is the only Southern State . . . that has *per-mitted* them to enjoy this privilege; and so far as my experience and observation extends, her interests have not been promoted by the concession of the privilege. . . . This is a nation of white people —its offices, honors, dignities and privileges, are alone open to, and to be enjoyed by, white people. I am for no amalgamation of colors. . . .[262]

Mr. Bryan then stated that to give the free Negro the privilege of voting would be to "make him the tool of the ambitious and designing demagogue and subject him to a slavery *ten times* more ignominious than that of the disfranchised private citizen—You increase the sources of corruption for your own citizen, without conferring any benefit on the free Negro."[263]

Many others spoke for and against the disfranchisement of the free Negro. Nathaniel Macon, the venerable president of the convention, spoke in favor of disfranchisement. He said that free Negroes never were considered as citizens and no one had the privilege of voting but citizens. He was in favor of treating them well, but "was opposed to any of them being allowed the right of suffrage."[264] Wilson of Perquimans County alarmed the convention by pointing out that "there are already 300 colored voters in Halifax, 150 in Hertford, 50 in Chowan, 75 in Pasquotank, etc., and if we foster and raise them up, they will soon become a majority—and we shall next have negro justices, negro sheriffs, etc."[265]

Among the most articulate opponents of disfranchisement of free Negroes were Emanuel Shober of Stokes, John Giles of Rowan, and Judge William Gaston of Craven.[266] It was sufficient for Mr. Shober that they were human beings, were free agents, and had a free will. "We have always considered them as subjects fit for taxation and certain public duties. If fit for these purposes, they ought to be allowed some privileges."[267] Mr. Giles said that even if free Negroes did have some influence in elections, he was not disturbed unless it could be proved that they gave such elections a bad direction. He said that if the free Negro sold his vote, it was to a white purchaser, who by his actions was setting a very poor example:

262. *Ibid.*, p. 67.
263. *Ibid.*, p. 68; *Raleigh Register*, July 7, 1835.
264. *Proceedings and Debates*, p. 70.   265. *Ibid.*, p. 80.
266. Connor, "Convention of 1835," *loc. cit.*, p. 99, says, "The western men took no part in the discussion. . . ." This statement seems to be in error, in view of the fact that Giles and Shober were both from western counties.
267. *Proceedings and Debates*, pp. 72-73.

The people, by their own free will sent us here, and when this sound principle is acted upon in our elections, we shall hear no more of free negroes' votes being purchased. No free negro would ever think of offering his vote in the market. Do we owe these people nothing? . . . We have the power and ought to devise some mode of raising them from their present degradation.[268]

Mr. Gaston denied that the question was whether or not the right of suffrage should be granted to free Negroes. He insisted that it was whether it should be taken away. He said that the free Negro should not be politically excommunicated. "Let them know they are a part of the body politic, and they will feel an attachment to the form of Government, and have a fixed interest in the prosperity of the community, and will exercise an important influence over the slaves."[269]

For the better part of two days the debate continued. Each side could claim, with some reason, that it had made the better argument. Those who wanted a limited franchise had a weighty argument when they contended that it would put a premium on the progress of the free Negro and conciliate the most respectable of that class. Those who opposed disfranchisement argued with force that the services of free Negroes in the formative years of the State ought to be recognized. The proponents of disfranchisement were at least not without consistency when they contended that the laws of North Carolina and of other states which restricted the activities of the free Negro showed clearly that he was not a citizen in the larger sense and should not enjoy so high a privilege as voting. In summing up the arguments, Professor Bassett says,

> It must be confessed that the friends of the free negro had made the weaker argument. The natural strength of their position lay along the lines of the natural rights of man. They had confined themselves almost solely to the question of expediency. In ignoring the real strength of the negro's cause they perhaps acted wisely![270]

The question on which the convention took the vote was whether the report of the committee on the disfranchisement of free Negroes should be adopted. The committee had reported,

> That free negroes and mulattoes within four degrees inclusive, be deprived of the privilege of voting for members of the Senate and House of Commons in this State.[271]

268. *Ibid.*, p. 74.   269. *Ibid.*, p. 79.
270. Bassett, "Suffrage in North Carolina," *loc. cit.*, p. 278. The exclamation mark is that of the present writer.
271. *Journal of the Convention of 1835* (Raleigh, 1835), p. 22.

The report was adopted by a vote of sixty-six to sixty-one.[272] An examination of the votes cast on either side discloses some points that are of unusual interest to the student of ante-bellum North Carolina. (See Map IV.) Of the counties that can be described as distinctly

—Counties voting for disfranchisement
—Against disfranchisement
—Divided

IV. THE VOTE TO DISFRANCHISE FREE NEGROES IN THE CONVENTION OF 1835

eastern, only eight voted against the disfranchisement of the free Negro. The fact that Halifax County, with more than 2,000 free Negroes, should be found on this side is interesting indeed. The presence of such a large number of free Negroes seems to suggest a rather tolerant attitude on the part of the county. Her two representatives at the convention, former Governor John Branch and Judge Joseph Daniel, were among the most liberal men of the East. They saw no justice in complete disfranchisement and therefore voted against it.[273] The vote of the other eastern counties against disfranchisement is perhaps a reflection either of happy relations between the races or the nonexistence of a problem, due to the scarcity of free Negroes.[274]

The vote to disfranchise free Negroes appears quite sectional in character when one begins to examine the votes of the West. Of the twenty-six counties voting solidly against disfranchisement, eighteen were west of a line drawn on the eastern border of Cumberland County. Only seven distinctly western counties voted with the majority in disfranchising the free Negro.

Every question that came before the convention was colored by the sectional strife between the East and the West. The question of abol-

272. *Proceedings and Debates*, p. 80.

273. Governor Branch's liberalism is seen in his attitude toward the religious tests in the Constitution. He declared that nothing short of a complete abolition of the test would cure the evil which such a requirement created. Johnson, *Ante-bellum North Carolina*, p. 428.

274. Neither Camden nor Columbus had 100 free Negroes in 1830.

ishing borough representation resolved itself into an East-West dispute. A cursory glance at the map on the vote to disfranchise free Negroes shows one section lined up against the other. When the most important question of the convention arose—that of giving the West more representation—the sectional character of the vote is more apparent. (See Map V.) Not one western county voted against the

—Counties opposing equalization

—Supporting equalization

—Divided

V. THE VOTE TO EQUALIZE REPRESENTATION IN THE HOUSE OF
COMMONS, IN THE CONVENTION OF 1835

equalization, and only four distinctly eastern counties voted for it. The correlation between the votes on the disfranchisement of the free Negro and those on equalization of representation is rather high. Had there not been local factors which determined the disfranchisement vote of some of the delegates, the correlation would be still higher, no doubt. Nineteen counties that had voted against the disfranchisement of the free Negro voted for the equalization. The East-West antipathy had gone to a dangerous extreme. In the clash, "the slaveholding element of the east had worked the disfranchisement of the free negro."[275]

The matter of disfranchising free Negroes did not come up again until late in the convention, when the amendment was up for the second reading on July 6. Judge Gaston of Craven could not let the matter go by without reiterating and extending his remarks. He said that the majority of free Negroes in North Carolina in the colonial period were the offspring of white women and were "therefore entitled to all the rights of free men." He contended that disfranchisement would be forcing free Negroes "down yet lower in the scale of degradation, and encouraging ill-disposed white men to trample upon and abuse them as beings without a political existence and scarcely

275. Bassett, "Suffrage in North Carolina," *loc. cit.*, p. 280.

different from slaves."[276] In order not to disfranchise free Negroes altogether, Judge Gaston offered an amendment which made it possible for free Negroes to vote if they possesed over $500 worth of property. Samuel King of Iredell, Charles Fisher of Rowan, Owen Holmes of New Hanover, and Henry Seawell of Wake all spoke in favor of a property qualification for voting, but to no avail.[277] When the vote was taken, there were fifty-five for and sixty-four against Gaston's amendment.[278] On July 6, 1835, the original amendment to the Constitution was adopted, and free Negroes were thus disfranchised.[279]

The correspondent who wrote that "The poor free negroes have gone by the board" described vividly just what had happened in the convention of 1835.[280] This correspondent appeared quite sympathetic with the cause of the free Negro and said that certain free Negroes like John C. Stanly of New Bern "should have plead trumpet-tongued in behalf of the more respectable of this degraded class." Nor was the Raleigh correspondent of the Fayetteville paper alone in his sympathy for the free Negro. The editor of the *Observer* remarked,

> There is, so far as we can learn, a general feeling of regret in this community to the total disfranchisement of the free coloured people. There are a few . . . of that class in Fayetteville, who have every qualification of intelligence, respectability, usefulness, and property, to entitle them, fairly, to exercise this high privilege.[281]

When the constitution was up for ratification, the editor of the *Observer* spoke for its adoption, although he had "serious objections to certain sections."[282]

The *Raleigh Register* likewise voiced disapproval of the disfranchisement of free Negroes. Although it asked that its readers vote for the adoption of the amended Constitution, its reservations were pronounced on the matter of the disfranchisement of the free Negro:

> That the right of suffrage, on the part of the free people of color, was totally abrogated, is to us a source of regret. We hoped that it would have been continued to those of this class who have

276. *Proceedings*, p. 351.

277. *Ibid.*, pp. 352-354.   278. *Ibid.*, p. 357.

279. In its final form the amendment read: "No free negro, free mulatto, or free person of mixed blood, descended from negro ancestors to the fourth generation inclusive (though one ancestor of each generation may have been a white person), shall vote for members of the senate or house of commons."

280. To the editor of the *Observer*, June 14, 1835. Printed in the *Carolina Observer*, June 16, 1835.

281. *Carolina Observer*, June 16, 1835.   282. *Ibid.*, October 27, 1835.

an interest at stake in the country, and a character to entitle them to the privilege."[283]

The *Newbern Specator* also voiced disapproval of the disfranchisement clause. The editor said that he was always in favor of modifying free Negro suffrage and saw no reason to change his opinion. He concluded by pointing out that justice demanded "that this class of people should be exempted from taxation, if denied a voice in elections."[284]

In abrogating the privilege of the free Negro to vote, North Carolina was not acting apart from the other states of the South. It was merely catching up with the other Southern states. At no time during the national period could free Negroes vote in Virginia[285] or South Carolina.[286] After 1789, Negroes in Georgia were excluded from the suffrage by understanding,[287] and, in 1799, Kentucky introduced "free white men" into its franchise clause.[288] In the nineteenth century, other Southern states fell into line, including Maryland in 1809,[289] and Florida, Alabama, Mississippi, and Louisiana as they came into the Union. In 1834, Tennessee restricted the suffrage to white men.[290] Indeed, North Carolina found herself lagging behind certain Northern states. By 1818, Connecticut had disfranchised the free Negro, as had New Jersey and Pennsylvania in 1820 and 1830 respectively.[291] In waiting until 1835 to disfranchise the free Negro and then by a majority of only five votes, North Carolina placed itself among the most liberal states in its attitude toward free Negroes.

The free Negro did not cease to be a factor in elections with his disfranchisement in 1835. The delegates had hardly arrived at their respective homes in July when a group of citizens of Rowan County held a meeting in which they resolved to oppose the election of Van Buren to the presidency. They declared that "his vote in the New York Convention to place *free negroes* as regards the right of suffrage, on an equal footing with white men, is another evidence of what his principles are on this subject, so important to the people of the slaveholding states." The presence of Charles Fisher and John Giles, Rowan County's delegates to the late convention, did not go unnoticed

283. *Raleigh Register*, September 29, 1835.

284. Reprinted in the *Raleigh Register*, September 29, 1835.

285. Russell, *Free Negro in Virginia*, p. 120.

286. Weeks, "History of Negro Suffrage," *loc. cit.*, p. 672.

287. *Ibid.*, p. 674.   288. *Ibid.*, p. 678.

289. Wright, *Free Negro in Maryland*, p. 119; a law of 1783, moreover, denied to persons manumitted thereafter the privilege of voting.

290. Weeks, "History of Negro Suffrage," *loc. cit.*, p. 675.

291. *Ibid.*, p. 678.

by the Democratic press. After pointing out that both Giles and Fisher spoke and voted against the disfranchisement of free Negroes, the *North Carolina Standard* remarked, "Oh Consistency, where is thy virtue? Oh Shame! Where is thy blush."[292] The *Register,* Whig in politics, rejoined that the *Standard* had hopelessly distorted the facts of the Rowan meeting.[293] When William H. Haywood said in a speech in 1840 that John M. Morehead, Whig candidate for governor, was too liberal in his attitude toward free Negroes, "One of the People" reminded Haywood that he, too, had a record of leniency toward the free Negro. The anonymous writer quoted Haywood as having spoken and voted for a number of emancipation bills in the Assembly of 1834-1835.[294]

When Van Buren was running for reëlection in 1840, his vote for the free Negro franchise was still being condemned in North Carolina.[295] Since the New York convention, however, Van Buren had committed an act even more unforgivable in the eyes of the *Raleigh Register.* He had sanctioned a proceeding by which a naval officer was convicted upon the testimony of two Negroes! No explanation that Van Buren gave as to the abundance of evidence from numerous sources against the naval officer could absolve the President from the "crime" of accepting collaborative testimony from Negroes. During the entire summer of 1840, the Raleigh newspaper made much of the fact that "Mr. Van Buren considers the negro as good as the white man."[296]

The extent to which the presidential campaign of 1840 was a heated one is well known to all students of history. The Whigs were more determined than ever to come out victorious, but in North Carolina their candidate, General Harrison, was no more free from some connection with Negroes than was Van Buren. "A Southern Man" from Nash County wrote a letter to the editor of the *Raleigh Register* in which he discussed the circulation of a paper "calculated to alarm a most daring and fearless spirit." The publication contained a print representing General Harrison, as President of the United States, "hav-

292. Reprinted in the *Raleigh Register,* July 14, 1835.

293. *Raleigh Register,* July 14, 1835.

294. *Raleigh Register,* June 26, 1840. It is worthy of note that the same issue carries the news that President Van Buren had just appointed William H. Haywood, Jr., United States Attorney for the district of North Carolina.

295. *Raleigh Register,* February 21, 1840.

296. *Raleigh Register,* June 23, 1840. When one recalls the *Register's* attitude toward the free Negro, one wonders if the objections which it had to Van Buren were based more on the fact that he was a Democrat than that he voted for Negro suffrage. See the *North Carolina Standard,* September 9, 1840, for Van Buren's letter defending his actions.

ing a poor one-leg Soldier, not only sold because he is poor, but sold to a free negro." It also contained a description of the sale of the Honorable Kenneth Rayner, planter and prominent Whig politician, to a Negro, "expressed in such language as is most revolting to every honorable and high minded man." One of the planters of Nash County had an occasion to discuss the pamphlet with a free Negro, and the former went into great detail in describing the contents to the latter.

A short time after, the free negro went over to a poor widow woman's, close by, and addressed himself to her and her daughter, telling them all he had just learned about the print. He told them that when General Harrison was elected President all the negroes would be set free, and that all the poor white people would have to be sold. Now, said he, (speaking to the widow) you know you are in debt, and will have to be sold, and I will buy you and treat you as good as James Battle would.[297]

"A Southern Man" considered this as an incendiary publication and that, as such, it ought to have been suppressed. He apparently overlooked the fact that the Whigs' stories about the consequences of a Democratic victory were perhaps equally exaggerated.

No less heated was the gubernatorial campaign between John M. Morehead and Judge Romulus Saunders. Morehead was well known for his liberalism, and had voted against the disfranchisement of free Negroes in the convention of 1835. The *Standard,* which had vigorously supported Judge Saunders, was mortified over reports that free Negroes had voted the Whig ticket in certain parts of North Carolina. Its mortification is seen at best advantage in its own language:

A writer in the last Western Carolinian states that "at one of the precincts in *Wilkes* County, the two judges who presided over the ballot box, in which the votes for Governor were deposited, *did permit* Free Negroes *to vote;* and the list of voters officially returned to the Sheriff, is darkened by the Name of almost as black a negro as there is in the county." The same writer states "if law and justice could have prevailed at the different precincts in Wilkes, the majority for *Morehead* would have fallen off at least 300 votes." We hope some friend in Wilkes will investigate this matter—give us the names of the judges, and have the fact verified that Free Negroes were allowed to vote. This thing is worthy of being exposed. Let us see what the hypocritical party, who are making a noise about *negro testimony* will say to negro votes.[298]

297. *Raleigh Register,* August 18, 1840.
298. *North Carolina Standard,* September 9, 1840.

When General Alfred Dockery was running for governor on the Whig ticket in 1854, the *Asheville News* took pleasure in attacking him for his vote against the disfranchisement of free Negroes in 1835. The *News* said that when the question of popular election of governor was up, Governor Dockery dodged the issue by finding business away from the convention. But when the proposition to allow free Negroes to vote for members of the Assembly was up, "the General's business all seems to have centred in the Convention, and he there devoted his time and energies to putting free negroes in an equality with white men...."

It will thus be perceived what sort of a candidate the Whig party have put before the people. A man who is in favor of extending greater privileges to free negroes than that class exercise in any *Abolition State*. Almost all the free States have excluded free negroes from voting, and some have prohibited them from coming into their limits, yet the Whig party of North Carolina have selected as their strongest man Gen. Dockery whose course in the convention shows very plainly that he thinks a free negro ought to exercise all the privileges that a white man does. . . . The General, on this negro equality platform would run well in Burke and McDowell, for there are a great many worthless and trifling free negroes there who would stick to him like a brother, on account of his friendship for them in the convention.[299]

In succeeding issues, the editor of the *News* renewed his attack on General Dockery. They were variations on the theme that had been enunciated at the opening of the campaign.[300] In one issue, the *News* ventured to predict that, if elected, General Dockery might recommend a change in the Constitution permitting free Negroes to vote and at the same time prohibiting illiterate white men from voting.[301]

General Dockery was not without his articulate supporters, however. The *Fayetteville Argus* said that in voting against the disfranchisement of free Negroes in 1835, General Dockery identified himself with those who believed that *"taxation without representation was tyranny."*[302] He thought that if free Negroes were taxed for the support of the government, they ought, "under proper restrictions, to be allowed to vote."[303] Even after General Dockery had lost the election

---

299. *Asheville News*, May 11, 1854.

300. See the *Asheville News*, May 25, 1854.

301. This comment was made in connection with an observation that the Connecticut House of Representatives had just passed a resolution to amend the State Constitution permitting Negroes to vote but setting up a literacy test for all persons seeking to vote. *Asheville News*, July 6, 1854.

302. The italics are the editor's.

303. Reprinted in the *Greensborough Patriot*, May 20, 1854.

to Thomas Bragg, the *Greensborough Patriot* had an opportunity to defend the loser and at the same time to castigate the Locofocos of the State. The latter, while vehemently attacking the General for his vote in 1835, had elected a man to the United States Senate that voted the same way. The *Patriot* asked those who pretended to see the danger to the South in General Dockery's vote if the election of Asa Biggs to the Senate proved that they were sound or that they were guilty of "hypocritical demagoguery."

Among the fiercest papers in opposing General Dockery for his vote just referred to was the *Asheville News*. It usually designated General D. as the Free Negro candidate. Will it be so clever as to inform the public what it thinks of the election of Mr. Asa Biggs. Speak out; don't be afraid.[304]

Thus, even though the free Negro was disfranchised in 1835, he was not void of political influence in North Carolina down to the close of the period. He may even have voted in local elections after 1835. In the heated state and national elections after the disfranchisement, the free Negro may have voted more than the records reveal. That he was a factor in almost every election is a matter of record, for the votes in the convention of 1835 haunted every aspirant to public office from that time on. When the issues were slim and the aspirants of small stature, the electioneers pulled the free Negro vote out of the proverbial closet and not infrequently assisted in sounding the death knell of this or that candidate.

304. *Greensborough Patriot*, December 2, 1854.

CHAPTER IV

The Free Negro in the Economic Life of North Carolina

Free negroes are with us a degraded class of men, living in a condition but little better than that of the brute creation and having no regard for an honest name, and fair reputation, can procure such a living by pilfering and theft. As a general rule, they idle away their time and only labor when more dishonest means fail them and hunger oppresses them. . . .

From petition by the mechanics of Rowan County to the North Carolina General Assembly, 1851.

THE FREE NEGRO WORKER

A CONSIDERATION of the free Negro in the economic life of North Carolina presents a number of serious problems to the student. The scarcity of town directories and other town records makes it difficult to obtain information concerning the free Negro in the skilled and unskilled activities in the urban areas. The failure of the county records to give detailed accounts of activities in the rural areas and to make regular distinctions between free Negroes and other free persons prevents the observations concerning the rural free Negro from being as conclusive as one would desire. Not until 1850, when the federal census schedules were enlarged to include information on occupations and real and personal property, does one find adequate information on the free Negro in the economic life of North Carolina.

There are, however, various valuable sources that may be explored and exploited with some degree of success by the student of the free Negro. Petitions and letters in the legislative papers, though often biased and subjective, yield a considerable amount of information on the subject. With regard to certain aspects of the problem, the county records are of great importance. Newspapers, travelers' accounts, and private letters often give one a fair idea of the place of the free Negro in the economic life of the State. By careful observations, considered analyses, and reasonable inferences, one can draw an adequate picture of this phase of the free Negro problem.

As one may well expect, a large number of free Negroes earned their living at the unskilled types of labor. Without any training whatever, the more ambitious free Negroes could find opportunities for work in the rural areas and in the towns if sentiment against their presence was not too hostile. Circumstances which presented themselves in the colonial period, however, made it possible for free Negroes to prepare for the more skilled occupations and thus to raise their earning power to a considerably higher level.

As early as 1733, the children of free Negro parents were being bound out as apprentices. In that year it was reported to the Upper House of the General Assembly that "divers free people, Negroes and Mulattoes were bound out until they came to 31 years of age, contrary to the consent of the Parties bound out." The Upper House was informed that these practices were frequent and well known and it was thought that "divers persons will desert the settlement of these parts fearing to be used in like manner so unlawfully."[1] On July 12, 1773, the General Assembly passed an act declaring that the binding out of free Negroes against their consent was an illegal act, in the courts of the State.[2]

As the years went by, several acts were passed which brought a larger and larger number of free Negro children within the scope of the apprenticeship laws and made periods of service compulsory under certain circumstances. In 1741, the Assembly passed the following act:

> If any White Servant Woman shall, during the time of her Servitude, be delivered of a child begotten by any Negro, Mulatto or Indian, such Servant, over and above the Time she is . . . to serve her Master . . . for such offense shall be sold by the Church Wardens of the Parish for two years after the time by Indenture . . . is expired . . . and such Mulatto child or Children of such Servants, to be bound by the County Court until he or she arrive at the age of thirty one years.[3]

The act of 1741 thus dealt rigorously with the white servant mother of free Negroes. At the same time, it provided for a sound training of the child by requiring the master to teach him the art and mysteries of some recognized trade. There is no way of knowing, however, the extent to which white servants became the mothers of free Negroes. In an inventory of the estate of Mr. James Wright in 1745, the following item was in the list: "one mulatto Wench Judy bound until she be 30 years old."[4] It may be that Judy was bound out under the law

1. Saunders, *Colonial Records*, III, 556.
2. *Ibid.*, III, 585.   3. Clark, *State Records*, XXIII, 195.
4. J. B. Grimes, *North Carolina Wills and Inventories*, p. 574.

of 1741; but her case, like the others for which there are only meager records, remains problematical.

The law which brought under the control of the authorities a much larger number of free Negro children was passed by the Colonial Assembly in 1762. All free base-born children were to be bound out until they reached twenty-one years of age, "and the Master or Mistress of every such Apprentice, shall find and provide for him or her Diet, clothes, Lodging, Accommodations, fit and necessary; and shall teach or cause him or her to be taught, to read and Write, and at the Expiration of his or her Apprenticeship, shall pay every such Apprentice the like allowance as by law appointed, for Servants by Indenture or custom."[5] By including all free base-born children, the act of 1762 broadened considerably the scope of the earlier act. By implication, the law also included children whose parents were unable to care for them.[6] Any doubt that may have arisen in this connection was cleared up in 1826 when the Assembly passed an act empowering the justices of the county court "to bind out the children of free Negroes or mulattoes, where the parent, with whom such children may live, does or shall not habitually employ his or her time in some honest industrious occupation."[7]

When the national period opened, free Negro children were being apprenticed in large numbers. They were brought before the county court, and if it was found that they were base-born or that their parents were unable to provide for them, they were bound out. These apprentice records, of which the following is an example, were entered in the minutes of the county courts:

Ordered that Hannah aged 13 years and a boy aged 11 years children of old Brandum a free negro—a girl aged 14 years and two twin boys aged 7 years children of Aaron Spellman—Hezekiah a boy aged 7 years son of Kesiah Stringer—John aged 9 years, Dale aged 8 years children of Hezekiah Stringer—two girls aged 10 and 12 years children of Emanuel Hails and Ellen Hails all of whom are free persons of color be taken by Thomas Patridge One of the constables attending this court and brought before the court now sitting to be bound out agreeably to the acts of the General Assembly.[8]

5. Clark, *State Records*, XXIII, 581.
6. *Revised Statutes*, Chapter on Apprenticeship.
7. *Laws, 1825-1830*, p. 15.
8. Minutes of the Court of Pleas and Quarter Sessions for Craven County, September, 1807.

This binding out of groups of free Negro children did not seem to be the rule, however. Usually, a single free Negro child was bound out to an individual for the purpose of learning a specific trade. The following seems to be typical of the proceedings entered in the county court records:

> Ordered that Polly—a mulattoe, of the age of Four years of age be bound an apprentice to Dan Wallard to learn the trade of a Seamstress. (The daughter of Mona White.)[9]

On the basis of the court order, an indenture was executed by the court and the prospective master.

In some counties, a printed form of indenture was used for both white and free Negro apprentices. One used in Bertie County vividly illustrates the obligations of the master and the apprentice to each other:

> This Indenture made the 11th day of November in year of our Lord one thousand eight hundred and eleven—between George Outlaw Esq, chairman of the County Court of Bertie, and the rest of the Justices of said court, of the one part, and Samuel Sharrock of the other part, Witnesseth, that the said George Outlaw—in pursuance of an order of said Court made this day, doth put, place and bind unto the said Samuel—Solomon Wiggins an orphan of color—seven years—with the said Samuel Sharrock to live after the manner of an apprentice and servant, until the said apprentice shall attain the age of twenty-one years, during all which time the said apprentice faithfully shall serve, his lawful commands everywhere gladly obey, he shall not at any time absent himself from his said master's service without leave, but in all things as a good and faithful servant shall behave towards his said master.

The obligations of the apprentice were no more exacting than those imposed on his master:

> And the said Samuel doth covenant, promise and agree to and with the said Chairman and Justices that he will teach and instruct, or cause to be taught or instructed, the said Solomon Wiggins in the art and mystery of a Cooper and also to read, write, and cypher agreeable to law; and that he will constantly find and provide for said apprentice, during the term aforesaid, sufficient diet, washing, lodging, and apparel fitting for an apprentice; and also all other things necessary, both in sickness and in health. In Witness whereof, the parties to these presents have hereunto inter-

9. Minutes of the Court of Pleas and Quarter Sessions for Beaufort County, June, 1810.

changeably set their hands and seals the day and year first above written.

George Outlaw
Sam Sharrock[10]

An observation of the occupations to be learned by free Negro apprentices provides an interesting preliminary study of the avenues of economic activity that may have been pursued by adult free Negroes. The records for Craven County seem to be fairly complete; and Table IV is a picture of the apprenticeship system in that county for the period. The thirty-two occupations to which free Negro children were

TABLE IV. FREE NEGRO APPRENTICES IN CRAVEN COUNTY, 1800-1860[11]

Occupation	1800-1824	1825-1860	Occupation	1800-1824	1825-1860
Baker	1	..	House Servant	..	2
Barber	2	..	Mariner	3	..
Blacksmith	3	4	Mason	..	2
Boatbuilder	1	..	Merchant	1	..
Body Servant	..	1	Milliner	..	1
Bricklayer	1	..	Painter	..	1
Brick Maker	1	2	Plasterer	5	1
Carpenter	6	14	Seamstress	1	2
Carriage Maker	..	2	Shipbuilder	2	..
Caulker	..	2	Ship Carpenter	4	1
Cook	..	1	Shoemaker	5	8
Cooper	27	14	Spinner	23	32
Distiller	..	1	Tailor	2	..
Farmer	2	24	Tanner	2	..
Harness Maker	..	1	Trunk Maker	1	..
House Carpenter	4	..	Waiter	..	1

apprenticed in Craven County were representative of the conditions in other counties. Naturally, the occupations of the apprentices depended upon the occupations of the masters. One can be sure that the master more often instructed than he caused to be instructed. If, therefore, the larger number of men of standing in the community were farmers, the majority of the apprentices were engaged in learning the art and mysteries of farming. In some counties, apprentices were learning to be weavers, gardeners, and wheelwrights.[12]

10. Apprenticeship certificates, 1811-1826. Mss. in the County Records for Bertie County. In 1820, this free Negro orphan was bound to Mary Sharrock. Some counties had special printed forms for free Negro apprentices. They were the same as those used for white apprentices; see County Records for Halifax County, 1828, Apprenticeship Bonds of Free Negro children; and those for Pasquotank County, 1842-61, Apprenticeship Bonds of Free Negro children.

11. From the County Records for Craven County, 1800-1860.

12. "On motion ordered that Patsy Brown a free mustee aged five years old in April next be bound an apprentice to Sarah Mouseau until she arrives at the age of 18 years

The trades which free Negro girls could learn were rather limited, and only a few can be classified as skilled. They could become spinners, weavers, cooks, house servants, body servants, milliners, and seamstresses. Boys, however, had a relatively large number of occupations open to them. During their term of apprenticeship, it is quite likely that boys would be of greater service, as far as general usefulness was concerned, than girls. The apprentice records for Pasquotank County seem to bear out the point of view that girls were less desirable as apprentices than boys. In the last eighteen years of the period, ninety-five free Negro girls were bound out as apprentices; but during the same period 168 free Negro boys were placed under the tutelage of masters.[13]

Not infrequently, free Negro children were bound out to free Negro masters. It may have been that the more affluent free Negroes took over the children of their less fortunate brethren to prevent their being bound by the county court to some person with whom they were not acquainted. The records of Craven County show that John C. Stanly, a wealthy free Negro, was continuously binding free Negro children to himself; and the benevolent nature of that individual may have been asserting itself in these cases.[14] Other free Negroes were binding free Negro children, for benevolent or other motives. In 1842, two free Negro boys were bound to Asa Tetterton to learn the trade of a cooper. It was entered in the minutes that the mother consented to the binding.[15] In 1847, Southey Kease, well-to-do free Negro of Beaufort County, agreed to teach the eight-year-old free Negro son of Lovey Moore the trade of a caulker.[16] In 1850, Hosea Blango was bound to John Moore to learn the trade of a cooper, "the mother of said Hosea being in Court and assenting to the same."[17]

All parents, however, did not consent to the loss of the services and the company of their children. Indeed, some vigorously protested the actions of the county courts in executing indentures of apprenticeship

---

she to learn the trade of a weaver." Minutes of the Court of Pleas and Quarter Sessions for Beaufort County, March, 1810.

13. Apprentice Bonds of Free Negro children 1842-1860, County Records of Pasquotank County.

14. See the Minutes of the Court of Pleas and Quarter Sessions of Craven County, 1810-1820.

15. Minutes of the Court of Pleas and Quarter Sessions of Beaufort County, September, 1842.

16. Minutes of the Court of Pleas and Quarter Sessions of Beaufort County, February, 1847.

17. Minutes of the Court of Pleas and Quarter Sessions of Beaufort County, March, 1850.

without their knowledge and consent. Martin Black displayed much exasperation in the Craven County Court, in 1811, when he

> appeared and stated that during the present term two of his children had without his knowledge and consent been bound to Benjamin Borden, that said children were free and born in lawful wedlock. Whereupon it was ordered that said order be suspended and that a notice issue to said Benjamin to appear at next term and shew cause if any he has wherefore the said order should not be rescinded.[18]

There was no mention of the case in the next sessions of the county court, and it may be that the case was settled satisfactorily out of court.

Elizabeth Keese of Beaufort County was notified to appear at the next court in 1837 "to show cause why her two children—Mary and Henry Keese should not be bound apprentices."[19] This case did not come up at the later sessions of the court in December, 1837, and March, 1838. The same may also be said of the case of Levin Powers, who was required to show why his son should not be bound as an apprentice "to some discreet and suitable person until said Sylvester arrive at the age of twenty-one years."[20] When Price Laughton and his wife went into the county court and sought to have the indenture of their son rescinded, the court, upon hearing the whole case, refused to rescind the indenture.[21]

Several of the cases went to the Supreme Court, but unless it was clear that the free Negro child was illegally bound out, that body refused to release him. In a case that came up from Moore County in 1833, the plaintiff charged the defendant with harboring a girl apprentice. The girl had left her master after the county court ruled that since the indenture did not specify the trade she was to learn it was not binding. Judge Gaston pointed out that in so ruling the judge of the lower court was in error. He said that under the act of 1762 an indenture which neither binds the master to teach his ward to read and write nor to learn a certain trade is valid as between the master and the apprentice.[22]

Alfred Prue, a free boy of color, was bound by the Franklin County Court to one Fuller, who left the State in 1849, and turned his apprentice over to one Hight of Franklin County, who in turn gave him to

18. Minutes of the Court of Pleas and Quarter Sessions of Craven County, March, 1811.

19. Minutes of the Court of Pleas and Quarter Sessions of Beaufort County, September, 1837.   20. *Ibid.*, December, 1843.

21. *Ibid.*, June, 1852.   22. Dowd v. Davis, 15 N. C., 51.

his son-in-law in Granville County. In 1857, Prue left the son-in-law's home and went at large in Granville County until March, 1858, when he was brought to the Franklin County Court and bound to Hight. The boy contended that he was a resident of Granville County and consequently the Franklin County Court had no jurisdiction over him. In upholding the action of the Franklin County Court, Judge Ruffin said,

> A free boy of color, rightfully bound as an apprentice, remains subject to the jurisdiction of the County Court wherein he was bound until discharged in the mode provided by law.[23]

If a master desired to give up his apprentice, he was required by law to appear in the county court and surrender the indenture. In June, 1807, John Dove was apprenticed to John C. Stanly, and in September of the same year the master appeared in the Craven County Court and gave up the indenture. The boy was then apprenticed to William Jones to learn the trade of a cooper.[24] The November term of the Beaufort County Court records the following proceeding:

> John Watson Esq., to whom a free boy of color, named John Camper was heretofore bound an apprentice came here into Court and resigned his Indentures and the same accepted.[25]

If the master did not observe the requirements of good treatment of the apprentice which were imposed upon him by law, it was possible for the apprentice or the parents to enter a complaint, and upon proof the indenture would be revoked. In 1834, Diana Keas was released from her apprenticeship to Samuel Dean "on account of maltreatment of said Dean towards her."[26] In 1843, Sidney White was released from Bennett Gaskill when the court found that he was unfit to be her master. The same day the court "ordered that the said girl Sidney be bound apprentice to Mrs. Sarah Woolard to learn the trade of a seamstress."[27] After John Peartree had committed homicide and had escaped, the Beaufort County Court rescinded the indenture of Bill Mackie to him and ordered that he be bound to Henry R. Paul to learn the occupation of a farmer.[28]

Neglect was ample grounds for rescinding an indenture, the Supreme Court decided in 1858. When Fred Owens of Currituck went

---

23. Prue v. Hight, 51 N. C., 265.

24. Minutes of the Court of Pleas and Quarter Sessions of Craven County, September, 1807.

25. Minutes of the Court of Pleas and Quarter Sessions of Beaufort County, November, 1824.　　26. *Ibid.,* May, 1834.

27. *Ibid.,* March, 1843.　　28. *Ibid.,* March, 1854.

to the West Indies and left his ward Polly Gordon with his wife, Jasper Chaplain sought to break the indenture and secure Polly as his apprentice. The Court decided that in leaving his ward for seven months, Fred Owens had shown that he was unfit to be her master. The wife, the Court said, had no legal interest in the transaction and could not act for her husband.[29]

The system of apprenticing free Negro children was not modified extensively after 1826. After 1838, the master was not required to teach the free Negro apprentice to read and write,[30] but in many instances the master continued to agree to observe the mandate of the earlier law.[31] In 1851, it was made unlawful for a master to carry his free Negro apprentice outside the limits of the county without first obtaining the permission of the county court. Under no circumstances could he take the ward beyond the limits of the adjoining county.[32] In 1860, a group of citizens asked the Legislature to pass an act "requiring masters to pay the parents of apprentices such sum annually as the County Court may direct until the apprenticeship period was ended." Because of indefinite postponement, this proposition was not voted upon.[33]

Although the apprenticeship system in North Carolina had as its primary function the care of poor children, it is interesting to observe that there existed some differences in the administration of the system as it applied to white and free Negro children. White girls were to be released at eighteen years of age, but free Negro girls had to remain with their masters until they were twenty-one.[34] After 1838, it was still incumbent upon the masters to teach their white wards to read and write, but they were no longer obliged to teach their free Negro wards. While the longer apprenticeship period required for free Negro girls may have reflected the greater difficulty which free Negro girls experienced in finding a place for themselves in society, there can be little doubt that the discrimination in literacy requirements was a clear effort on the part of the legislators to prevent free Negroes from rising out of the low intellectual attainments which characterized the group.

As an effective method of training free Negro children to become proficient workers and intelligent citizens, much could be said for the

29. Owens v. Chaplain, 48 N. C., 325.   30. *Laws, 1838-1839.*

31. See, for example, the bond of James Suydem whose ward, Thomas Hendrick, was to be taught to read and write. Minutes of the Court of Pleas and Quarter Session for Craven County, 1839. See, also, the minutes for 1840, 1841, and 1844.

32. *Laws, 1850-1851,* pp. 176-177.

33. Ms. in the Legislative Papers for 1860-1861.

34. *Revised Statutes,* VI, 68.

apprenticeship system. If, in addition to giving his ward a "suit of clothes worth ten dollars and fifty dollars . . . in money" when he arrived at the age of twenty-one years, Robert Pickard had taught him to be a good farmer, his ward had much for which to thank him.[35] If, in addition to teaching Clarissa Cannon to be a good spinster, Rigdon Griffin also taught her to read and write—as he promised to do, even in 1846—he had performed a great service for her.[36] If the masters were instrumental in raising the moral life of their free Negro apprentices and refrained from crushing the spirit of these youths they were transforming a disciplinary system into an effective training period which could contribute a great deal to the growth and development of this group.

As a method of controlling and training free Negro youth the apprenticeship system was in the ascendancy between 1800 and 1860. The young people of Craven County who learned to farm, to make shoes, and to weave in the first two decades of the nineteenth century were ready to work and earn their living as artisans in the next two or three decades. Naturally more free Negroes learned to be farmers than anything else. Nevertheless, the whole occupational picture of free Negroes in North Carolina must be viewed with the apprenticeship system in mind. The fact that there were almost 2,000 free Negro children in the homes of white people at the close of the period suggests the extent to which the system of apprenticing was still an important factor in the economic life of the free Negro.[37]

The opportunity of free Negroes to earn a living by working for themselves or for others was limited by a number of circumstances which vitally affected their status in the community. The apprehension with which their presence was viewed served to restrain many prospective employers from using them. The fear of the consequences that would arise from the use of free and slave labor on one job often resulted in the refusal to hire free Negroes. The hostility which grew to considerable proportions between the free Negro and the white worker erected an unbridgeable chasm between these groups that had more in common than they realized. The insistence of those who "knew" the free Negro—that he was lazy, indolent, and thievish—engendered more consternation than sympathy; and the free Negro worker had to overcome this before he could receive favorable con-

35. Minutes of the Court of Pleas and Quarter Sessions of Alamance County, November, 1852.
36. Minutes of the Court of Pleas and Quarter Sessions of Craven County, 1846.
37. Appendix I gives the number of free Negro apprentices by counties in 1860.

sideration. Fear and apprehension, hostility and consternation—these were only a few of the obstacles in the way of the free Negro worker.

The construction of disciplinary devices often hampered the free Negro's opportunity to make a living. When fears and apprehensions arose, the legislators would not stop short of depriving the free Negro of any opportunity to make a livelihood if such action would bring about a more peaceable free Negro group. Thus, although a large number of free Negroes made their living peddling their wares from place to place, the Legislature did not hesitate to put an effective check to it. In 1830, an act was passed making it unlawful "for any free person or persons of colour to hawk or peddle any goods, wares or commodities whatsoever out of the limits of the county in which they reside, unless he or she has license to do so, granted annually by the County Court."[38] It was more than a difficult task to get seven justices to agree on a free Negro's good character as the law required, and not a very easy one for some of the free Negro peddlers to spare the eighty cents for the license. It is therefore understandable why none of Pasquotank County's more than 1,000 free Negroes was able to secure a license to peddle in 1834.[39]

The memorial of a number of the citizens of Lenoir County to the Assembly in which they asked the prohibition of "all colored traders of spirituous liquors, or other articles of Merchandize, except such as shall procure from the said county court a license," was typical of the restrictions sought by various groups of citizens.[40] The petitioners said that free Negroes from New Bern brought in cakes, tobacco, and spirituous liquors to sell; and while in Lenoir County these free Negroes, the citizens declared, urged the slaves to steal pigs, lamb, and poultry, and this had a most disastrous effect on the morale of the slave population.[41]

Although the memorial was laid on the table for the remainder of the session, it undoubtedly had the effect, in 1831, of increasing the concern for the free Negroes who moved about the State. It also contributed toward the passage of a law at the same session requiring all free Negro peddlers to obtain a license to sell goods within the limits of their resident county.[42] This carried the law of 1830 a step further.

38. *Laws, 1823-1831*, p. 11. *Cf. supra*, p. 69 for an extensive quotation from this enactment.

39. See the Minutes of the Court of Pleas and Quarter Sessions of Pasquotank County, 1834.

40. *Journal of the Senate*, 1831-32, p. 9.

41. Ms. in the Legislative Papers for 1831-32.

42. *Laws, 1831-1835*, p. 24.

In 1852 a bill was proposed to prohibit free Negroes from peddling anywhere within the State. The offender was subject to a ten-dollar fine, to be collected either by the seizure of his property or by the hiring out of his time. Although the House of Commons passed the bill at its second reading, upon the recommendation of the committee considering it, the Senate rejected it.[43] Thus, free Negroes could peddle, with the limitations imposed in 1830 and 1831, until the end of the period.

The discrimination against free Negro peddlers is quite apparent when one examines the law as it affected white peddlers. Free Negro peddlers had difficulty in obtaining permission to peddle any kind of goods within the State. They had to secure the approval of seven justices, in addition to paying an annual license fee of eighty cents. In the case of white peddlers, the State, in an effort to encourage the use of the products made at home, required that peddlers having or selling goods "not of growth, produce, or manufacture of this state" secure license at an annual cost of $20.00.[44] As long as they sold products made or grown within the State, they did not have to obtain a license.

For the free Negro who had received no special training in a given field, only the unskilled types of labor were open to him. The free Negro who told Frederick Olmsted that any one of his group could get good wages "if he's a mind to be industrious, no matter wedder he's slave or free" suggested that the enterprising unskilled free Negro could find work with comparative ease.[45] In view of the sentiment against free Negroes, it is difficult to agree with one of the more fortunate of the group. The use of Negro stevedores, for example, had been vigorously protested just four years before the conversation between the free Negro and Olmsted. Negro stevedores were said to be helping slaves escape. Writing in the *Wilmington Journal* a slaveholder said that in order to protect the white interests of the slaveholding communities, "we must have *White* men in the place of *negroes* engaged in that business, who shall be under the obligations to inspect the stowage of vessels.[46] Toward the end of the period, fewer and fewer free Negroes were used as stevedores in the seaport towns.

In the northeastern part of the State, a considerable number of free Negroes secured work in the Great Dismal Swamp. The regulations with regard to work in that area, however, certainly erected obstacles

43. Ms. in the Legislative Papers for 1852.
44. *Laws, 1835-1836*, p. 13.
45. Frederick Law Olmsted, *Journey Through the Seaboard Slave States*, I, 210.
46. *Wilmington Journal*, October 19, 1849.

of considerable magnitude in the way of some free Negroes.[47] Mere presentation of one's self did not always secure one a job in the Swamp. The employers wanted to be certain that their free Negro workers were harmless and amenable. A recommendation from a respectable white citizen naturally made things much easier. Jacob Skeeter and his brother were, therefore, fortunate in having a personal letter from J. B. Norfleet to present to the officials of the Cherry and McPherson Swamps in 1855. In requesting Colonel I. W. Worrell to employ these free Negroes, Norfleet said he would appreciate any assistance that could be given them.[48] Despite the fact that improvements were being made in the swamp lands down to the close of the period, only two counties—Martin and Tyrrell—had any free Negro swamp hands in 1860.[49] (See Table V.)

There were other unskilled occupations which free Negroes could pursue in ante-bellum North Carolina. They could be common laborers, ditchers, farm hands, fishermen, gardeners, miners, railroad hands, servants, timber hewers, turpentine hands, washerwomen, or watermen. These individuals had to compete in the open market for the sale of their labor. There were white men who did not object to this type of employment and the census of 1860 shows that many were engaged in some of these pursuits.[50]

There were serious objections to the hiring out of slave labor. Slaves hired out, it was said, were in a state of semi-freedom, and the development of the concomitant habits made them difficult to control. Slaves hired out, moreover, might take advantage of the opportunity to participate in conspiracies and insurrections.[51] Finally, there were those who thought that the hiring out of slaves was the preliminary step and, therefore, a bad one, to emancipation.[52] Wherever these objections were voiced, the hated free Negro actually might have had a better opportunity than the slave to hire himself out.

The great competition, nevertheless, came from slave labor. From the very beginning, the practice of hiring out slaves was a common thing in North Carolina. The newspapers carried advertisements of

47. Cf. supra, pp. 74-75.

48. Ms. in the County Records of Gates County, J. B. Norfleet to Col. I. W. Worrell, May 2, 1855.

49. Some of the other counties, however, may have listed their free Negro swamp hands as common laborers, ditchers, or timber hewers.

50. See, for example, the population schedule for New Hanover, 1860. In the Bureau of the Census.

51. Taylor, Slaveholding in North Carolina, p. 75.

52. Olmsted, Journey into Seaboard States, I, 210.

TABLE V. OCCUPATIONS OF FREE NEGROES IN NORTH CAROLINA IN 1860

County	Baker	Barber	Bartender	Blacksmith	Boatman	Brick Maker	Butcher	Cabinetmaker	Cake Peddler	Carpenter	Chair Maker	Coach Maker	Common Laborer	Confectioner	Cook	Cooper	Distiller	Ditcher	Engineer	Factory Worker	Farm Hand	Farmer	Fireman	Fisherman	Gardener	Hack Driver	Hammer Man	Harness Maker	Hatter	Hostler	Iron Moulder	Mason	Mattress Maker	Mechanic	Midwife	Miller	Miner	Musician	Nurse	Painter	Plasterer	Prostitute	Railroad Hand	Saddler	Seaman	Seamstress	Servant	Sexton	Shoemaker	Spinner	Swamp Hand	Tailor	Tanner	Tenant	Timber Hewer	Tobacco Hand	Turpentine Hand	Washerwoman	Waiter	Waggoner	Waterman	Weaver	Well Digger	Wheelwright	Miscellaneous
Alamance				4				1				2	42						1			14	10								1					3		1		2	2								2																1
Alexander													5									1																											1																3
Alleghany	1			2						2			5		2	1						4										1		2						1	1						1		1	1								2							
Anson	1			2	2								5			1	2					3	4									6		1	2					1					7	1	1					1						1			1			
Ashe	1			2						10			67								9	13																														1														
Beaufort										2			35		2	16	2				5	20	1			2				1															7	1	11											5			1				
Bertie		1						2		4			41		1	1	2				14	22			1			1						1	2	1				1									1							20	3			1	1	1		2	
Bladen				3									13									6																															1										1		
Brunswick				1						5			2									7																																										
Buncombe										1			18			2						4		2	1							2			2					2						3	13		1		2						1	2							
Burke							1			1			7		1	1						4																										9		9	2								1							
Cabarrus										4							1					6						1				1								2							1										1		1	1					
Caldwell																					3	1																		2			2				9			1							1								
Camden																						11													2									1		1	1					1					55							
Carteret										3												18										2															23											21							
Caswell								2					20									6																		1										1		1													
Catawba										1												6										1			1	1																												
Chatham										4			7			2					7	10													2					2							1					2					1								
Cherokee	1																1																				1																												
Chowan										3			18						2			5																										9											1							
Cleveland										1											3	3										2																		1								1							
Columbus				2	8												1				37	5										1			1																														
Craven	5			2	52		3			1			1	1	4	26	1		1		39	4						2		1	7	11		4						2	1					13	58		9			2						55			1	1		3	4
Cumberland		2		5	22			3	6	16			87			26	3		5		37	29				9					7				2					5	2					13	58		9							6	55			1	1		3	4
Currituck				4									9			10					39	13	1									6			2	1				1					1	13	19		1								8							7
Davidson				3						1			11				2				9	9																										23																	
Davie													16								4	3															1																											
Duplin					1					1			29	1	4				2		5	8		2		1						2			1					1			2		1	2	1										1	8							
Edgecombe				1	1								11			2			1			10													1								2													1		7							1
Forsyth				2	2			1		6			16				1		1	1	31	1						1				1				1				1			2			2						1					2	8							4
Franklin				1									29									8										3																										2	7							
Gaston				1	1								11		1					3		2				1											1									2																			
Gates	3			5	2					2			38	1	1	2						23		2		1						1		3						2	2								2			1				1	2	8						1	4
Granville				8						4			78		1	2	1			3	70	10						1		3		3		1		8	1			3							20		5			1						7				3			1
Greene				2	6								90		1	5			2		18														1		4			3													1			5		8						1	2
Guilford				9					2	13			23		2		1		2		384	175	3	5								15								1			2			34	13		4	1193		1	1		5			35				22	2	2	
Halifax				3	3					1																1											1																													
Harnett																						3																																											

County	1	2	3	4	5	6	7	8	9	10	11	12	13	14	15	16	17	18	19	20	21	22	23	24	25	26	27	28	29	30	31	32	33	34	35	36	37	38	39	40	41	42	43	44	45	46	47	48	49	50	51	52	53	54	55	56	57	58	59	60	61	62	63	64	65	66
Henderson				3				1			12								2	2												1																															
Hertford			3				6		144				2		70	35					5	1	1				9	1		4	3	19	2				5		1																					1
Hyde								9							12																																														
Iredell								1							2															4	1				1																									
Jackson															1															4	1		1																										
Johnston			6					11			1	3		5	8					1																																						
Jones							1	10	1	2				2																2		1					1																						
Lenoir		2					3	6	1				21	2				1		1							1			1	1				1																								
Lincoln		2					1	2					3	2	1				1							3	1						1																									
Macon		1					1	15						9																								1				2																	
Martin														13																																											
McDowell								2			23				2			1	1	2		9							5					1	1																							
Mecklenburg	2	3				1		86					1	2					2		3								6																							1	1
Montgomery		1					1	2						2					1				1						1					1																1	1
Moore		3		1	5	1		2	1	2	4	5	8	61	11	19			1				8			1			1																			14					1	
Nash	4		1	5	1	1	31	29	2	6		8		8	11	6	2	6		10	5		2	1	5		2	41	3	2		17	1			14		51	1			6	2
New Hanover	1	4		3			4	23	6	6	1	14		104	30				4	3	1		1	2	7		1	5		17	1		1		1			1					6	2
Northampton			3			1		15	6	3			1	15	9	2			4	3	1					1	13		4													2	1
Onslow	4		8			1	22	4	1	7	1			240	47		3	1	7		1	1		4	4		27	13	30		2				1		71					
Orange/Pasquotank							2	13	1					54	12					2	1						4	15	1	2				17									
Perquimans		1						20						24	8													1															
Person		1					4	16			2			2	1													2				1	3									
Pitt/Polk								1							7													9	6	1											4	
Randolph		4				1	1	24		1				62	10				1									9	2	1				1				1				4	
Richmond		3		1	1	2		5						40	23																								12				1
Robeson		3				5		73	1	1	1			28	86				1				2		1		3		1									1	1		2	
Rockingham		2	1		1			16		1	1	12		16	2				2				2	2		3		1	1		1							6		1	3	7
Rowan	2	1					2	7						2	1				1	2			2	2		7		1	1			1		1					1			2
Rutherford	1	2						5						2	1				1	2									1									19				1
Sampson		2					2	3		6		1		68	9				2										2													1	1
Stanly		2						5							3																								11	1			1
Stokes		1						1							2																												
Surry		4						12				1	1	10	3						1							4						5								1
Tyrrell		2					6	2			1			19	3				1	1			1					13														
Union							1					1		6	2								3			5		11		1												
Wake	5		10	1	1		19	106	2	3		14		51	32	10	1	1		13	2	1			5	6	4	3		9	6	6		1		37	2	1		1	1
Warren	1	6					6	2	1					30	17				2	1			5		2	1		2		4	4	6	1			10	2			2	1	5
Washington	1	1					4	45	1		6			5	3				1							2		3		2	3	4	4		1	23			6	3
Watauga								5		2				3	5				1	2																			
Wayne	1	1	7				10	11	1	3	2	3		23	28					1	2	1		1	2	3		3	1			1				2		3	8	
Wilkes		1					3	27						27	10				1	2		1						3	1			1						6	5
Wilson	2	1					3	13	3		1			34	9			2			2	2	3	1			2					5	6	22	3				9	5	6	3			1	1
Yadkin		5						15						7	2																			3				1				1
Yancey								2							8													1														
TOTAL	16	25	3	155	43	2	6	10	9	257	3	8	1587	1	54	101	19	136	8	17	1716	1048	24	20	6	24	2	5	2	16	9	120	12	24	18	21	14	5	8	66	24	5	37	6	61	175	413	2	59	244	2	7	8	9	29	7	98	412	6	21	11	44	5	23	42

slaves for hire, and not infrequently the masters sent the slave worker into town to earn money during the dull seasons.[53]

The direct information concerning the wages of unskilled free Negro laborers is almost nonexistent. Since they competed with slave labor that was hired out and since plantation books and newspapers spoke from time to time of the returns from such hiring out, it is possible to reach some tentative conclusions concerning the wages of the unskilled free Negroes. The Negro servant whom Olmsted observed helping the white retailer of tobacco thought that $10.00 per month for himself and $5.00 for his son were good wages.[54] This is just about the same as the wages that James Clark was receiving for the slaves he hired out in 1853.[55] As the period drew to a close the wages of Negroes steadily rose. Speaking of Negro hire in 1854, the *Fayetteville Observer* said,

At Raleigh, hands to work on the railroad are hiring at $250. In this part of North Carolina, turpentine hands bring about $200.[56]

This may not have been the amount that the average Negroes were getting, for the Clark slaves received $180 per year as late as 1858, though there was a considerable amount of fluctuation.[57] The *North Carolina Standard* pointed out that Negro men for ordinary farm and railroad work were hired in Raleigh in 1860 for from $100 to $125 per year. Good cooks hired for $75 and $100, house servants from $60 to $80, and turpentine hands from $160 to $175 per year.[58]

The free Negro artisan experienced greater opposition than did his unskilled fellows. This was due largely to the fact that in plying his trade he came into direct competition with a more energetic and articulate class of whites. The ante-bellum period was a period of unremitting effort on the part of whites to curtail or completely prevent the activities of free Negro artisans. Of course there were slave artisans who seriously hampered the opportunities of the free white skilled worker, but the latter viewed that situation with some degree of resignation. But no such apathy characterized his attitude toward the free Negro artisan. At times, however, both slave labor and free Negro labor were the target of his vehement outbursts. As early as 1773, the

53. *Fayetteville Observer*, December 23, 1840.

54. Olmsted, *Journey into Seaboard States*, I, 210.

55. Taylor, *Slaveholding in North Carolina*, p. 79. Clark's slaves were receiving $128 per year.

56. *Fayetteville Observer*, January 2, 1854.

57. Taylor, *Slaveholding in North Carolina*, p. 79.

58. *North Carolina Standard*, January 11, 1860.

legal pilots of Oacock Bar, in a communication to the Assembly, described their plight as a result of free Negro and slave competition. They said,

> Sundry Negroes as well free men as slaves to a considerable number by unjust and unlawful means take upon themselves to pilot Vessels from Oacock Bar up the several rivers to Bath, Edenton, and New Bern and Back again—to the Great prejudice and Injury of your Petitioners.
>
> Your Petitioners therefore humbly begg leave to observe to your Excellency that the pilotage at the said Barr at present noways answers the solitary Ends Intended by Law as Great Confusion and Irregularity daily Insue from the Insolent and Turbilent disposition and behavior of such free Negroes and Slaves.
>
> Under these circumstances your Petitioners humbly Pray your Excellency would please take this matter into Consideration and Prevent the like for the future by denying License or Branch to any free Negro or Slave Whatsoever.[59]

Not infrequently, the violent objections which whites had to the influx of free Negroes into the State were based on the disturbing fear that the labor market would thus be flooded. This was especially true in the western counties where slavery was not deeply entrenched. The antagonism of Asheville citizens to free Negroes throughout the period doubtless had an economic as well as a social basis. In 1824, a group of Asheville citizens asked the Assembly to pass an act to impose a $50 poll tax on the migration into the State of free Negroes, whom they described as a public nuisance.[60] The general hostility of the *Asheville News* has already been observed.[61] The plan to enslave free Negroes, moreover, received its heartiest support from citizens in the vicinity of Asheville.[62]

Free Negro mechanics were especially irritating to the white artisans. As North Carolina began to develop a program of internal improvements during the late ante-bellum period, free Negro mechanics found opportunities to work in the railroad construction programs and in the erection of public buildings and the like. This created so much ire in the eastern part of the State that the white mechanics began a concerted action to prevent the use of free Negroes.

59. Saunders, *Colonial Records,* IX, 803-804.
60. Ms. in the Legislative Papers for 1824.
61. *Cf. supra,* pp. 119 ff.
62. See Petition of Asheville Citizens to the General Assembly, November 29, 1858, and the letter from James A. Patton to S. T. Baird, December 1, 1858. Mss. in the Legislative Papers for 1858.

Printed petitions were circulated, signed, and sent by citizens of Beaufort and Craven counties to the Legislature for the purpose of airing their grievances. They viewed the increase of the free Negro population with much alarm, and they deprecated the weakness of North Carolina's "Free Negro Code" in comparison with that of Virginia's. They requested the Assembly to lay a tax on free Negro mechanics for the purpose of colonizing them in Liberia.[63] There is no record of the petition's having received any consideration by the Assembly.

In protesting the presence of free Negroes in their county, the mechanics of Rowan County "and others friendly to the industrial pursuits of the people of North Carolina" stated the problem even more clearly. They said,

> All the mechanical arts are greatly depressed in North Carolina by an undue competition arising, First from free negro mechanicks, and Second from mechanicks both white and black in the non-slaveholding States. The first species of competition is unfair for the following reasons:
> Free negroes are with us a degraded class of men, living in a condition but little better than that of the brute creation and having no regard for an honest name, and fair reputation, can procure a living by pilfering and theft. They idle away their time and only labour when more dishonest means fail them and hunger oppresses them, and then, at necessity. They are never governed in fixing the prices for their labor by consideration of a fair compensation for the services rendered, but only by the causes above set forth.[64]

Back of the Rowan County mechanics' general indictment of the free Negro mechanics was the desire to bring them completely under the control of the white group. In language interesting for its sheer presumptuousness, the petitioners said,

> With respectful deference your petitioners would suggest that free Negro Mechanicks should by law be bound to an apprenticeship so long as they pursue their trade within the limits of this State and that they should only be permitted to work at such trade under the direction and controul of the master to whom they are bound, and that they should furthermore be required to take out a license annually upon proof of good moral character only and paying therefor a reasonable fee to the State.[65]

In trying to justify the need for a license, the petitioners pointed out that the prerequisites of such a certificate "would exclude all dishonest

63. Ms. in the Legislative Papers for 1850.
64. Ms. in the Legislative Papers for 1851.   65. *Ibid*.

and idle free Negroes from the mechanical pursuits." With such an exclusion, it would seem that the need for an apprentice relationship would have been removed. Despite the fervent plea of more than 100 citizens of Rowan County the petition was laid on the table, where it remained until the close of the session.[66]

It was unfortunate for the free Negro artisan that he was the object of such contempt and distrust. In a world that was none too friendly, this attitude on the part of his white competitors made his lot immeasurably more difficult. For the better part of the period, the white artisan failed to see any wisdom in developing a close relationship between himself and the free Negro. When he came to desire a relationship with the free Negro artisan it was based on the principle of domination instead of coöperation. In the absence of an abundance of materials of various kinds bearing on the activities of the free Negro, it is not possible to support the sweeping generalizations and indictments made by the whites that the free Negro artisan was content to "procure a living by pilfering and theft." Doubtless, many free Negroes, trained while slaves to perform certain skilled tasks, were shiftless and were not interested in advancing their position and thought little of the comfort of their families. They could little appreciate the opportunities which were theirs to contribute to the growth and development of their group. Just as visionless, however, was a considerable portion of the white artisans, who, down to the close of the period, failed to understand their function in society and the importance of their relationship to other groups as well as to their own.

Regardless of what may be said for the case set up by those who condemned the free Negro artisan, nothing is more certain than that the citizens of Rowan and Beaufort counties had overstated their cases. Free Negro artisanry was not nearly so degraded as they would have the Assembly and the general public believe. Just as yeomanry and artisanry had been the most important element in building up the State of North Carolina, so had the free Negroes who belonged to these groups done the most for the constructive development of their class. Among them were bakers, barbers, bartenders, blacksmiths, boatmen, butchers, cabinetmakers, carpenters, caulkers, cooks, coopers, distillers, engineers, drivers, hostlers, iron moulders, mariners, masons, millers, painters, plasterers, saddlers, seamstresses, shoemakers, spinners, tailors, tanners, wagoners, weavers and wheelwrights. (See Table V.)

66. See the endorsement on the petition. See also the assertion of the mechanics of Concord, N. C., in 1856 that free Negroes took away the business that belonged to white laborers. Charles Wesley, *Negro Labor in the United States*, p. 71.

When Thomas Buchanan, agent of the American Colonization Society, went to Wilmington to fit out an expedition for Bassa Cove, Liberia, in 1838, he took that opportunity to interest the free Negroes there in colonization, "explaining carefully the difficulties to be encountered as well as the advantages to be gained by their removal to Liberia." In talking with individual free Negroes at the close of the meeting, Buchanan encountered one, "a very respectable mechanic of considerable property and great influence," who was interested in going. He expressed much regret that he was prevented from making the trip "by a large job of work on hand."[67] Here is one free Negro mechanic who does not very well fit the description made by the Rowan County petitioners. By 1860, there were twenty-four free Negro mechanics plying their trade in North Carolina.[68]

Few of the skilled occupations were without some free Negroes, and many came to be looked upon as efficient and dependable. Joseph Dennis, a free Negro of Fayetteville, was described by a white citizen as "a mechanic of considerable skill and has frequently been in my employ."[69] John C. Stanly, of New Bern, was one of the leading barbers of the community and used the money which he earned at this occupation as his initial investment in plantations and town property that made him one of the wealthiest men of Craven County.[70] Known as "Barber Jack," Stanly was said at one time to be worth more than $40,000.[71] John Good, another free Negro barber of New Bern, was so successful in his trade as a barber that he was able to support his two half sisters after his white father had died.[72] For economic or other reasons, however, John Revels, a free Negro barber of Salisbury, was

67. "Report of Thomas Buchanan," *African Repository* (February, 1838), XIV, 53-54.

68. Here the term "mechanic" is used in the sense that it was used in the census of 1860. This usage of the term is quite vague since it did not include such workers as cabinetmakers, factory workers, wheelwrights, and the like. It is conceivable, therefore, that there were more than twenty-four free Negroes who were mechanics in 1860. In view of the fact that occupational designations were used carelessly during the period, it is most difficult to get an accurate picture of free Negroes in certain types of work.

69. Ms. in the Legislative Papers for 1840.

70. See James B. Browning, "The Free Negro in Ante-bellum North Carolina," *North Carolina Historical Review*, XV (January, 1938), 29, in which the writer says, "The existence today of Negro barber shops which cater exclusively to a white clientele is but a faint reminder of the pre-war days when free Negro barbers had a veritable monopoly in this type of business." In view of the fact that there were only 24 free Negro barbers in North Carolina in 1860, it can hardly be said that they had a monopoly in that business. (See Table V.)

71. Bassett, *Slavery in North Carolina*, p. 44.

72. *Ibid.*, p. 45.

extremely unhappy and "put an end to his existence" by committing suicide in 1833.[73]

A goodly number of free Negroes made a living in various maritime occupations. As boatmen, pilots, seamen, stewards, and cooks they could often find employment in seaport or river towns. That they were an important group in these occupations around the middle of the period is seen by the attitude of the merchants and shippers in Wilmington. When the Legislature passed an act in 1830 to quarantine vessels hiring free Negroes,[74] a great howl went up from employers in the seaport towns in North Carolina. Their attitude was expressed in an article which appeared in the *Wilmington Recorder* the following spring. In regard to the effects of the quarantine act, the writer said,

> In nine cases out of ten, no white sailor can be employed as cook or steward; and in such case, a captain would either have to go without either of these necessary adjuncts or sail to some other state. At present, we understand the merchants of Wilmington are in want of vessels to carry away the produce lying on their wharves. But few vessels are owned in the port, and they must have cooks at least, yet if they carry a free coloured man out in that capacity they cannot bring him back, and but few will engage on these terms.[75]

The writer then added that "a string may *be stretched till it breaks!*"[76] Thus it can be seen that legislation for the purpose of disciplining free Negroes worked considerable hardship on the merchants and shippers of North Carolina. Others must have also felt that the string was about to break. In 1831, the Assembly was convinced of the absence of wisdom in the quarantine act and passed the following:

> *Be it enacted.* That so much of an act, passed at the last session of the General Assembly, as subjects ships or vessels coming into ports of this state with free persons of colour on board to thirty days' quarantine, be, and the same is hereby repealed.[77]

Free Negroes experienced little difficulty in securing employment in North Carolina in the building trades. Masons, brick makers, and stone dressers were in demand in North Carolina's growing towns, and the protestations of white workers were not strong enough to cause a

73. *Raleigh Register*, November 12, 1833.

74. *Cf. supra*, p. 70.

75. Reprinted in the *Raleigh Register*, August 28, 1831.

76. The italics are the editor's.

77. *Laws, 1831-1835*, pp. 14-15. More than 100 free Negroes were employed in the maritime occupations in 1860.

ban to be placed on the use of free Negro workers in these trades. John Y. Green was a well-to-do free Negro carpenter and contractor in New Bern who amassed a considerable fortune by securing big jobs in connection with the building programs of his home town.[78] It was largely through his own industry as a carpenter that James D. Sampson was able to become a respected and wealthy citizen of Wilmington.[79] There were always free Negro plasterers and painters, such as Hillard Dunstan, John Pettiford, and Eaton Bowser of Franklin County.[80] Almost 500 free Negroes made their living in the building trades in 1860.[81]

Many free Negroes made their living as blacksmiths, cabinet and chair makers, harness and carriage makers, and as boot and shoe-makers. Many villages and towns of ante-bellum North Carolina had their free Negro blacksmiths and not infrequently these individuals were men of considerable wealth and influence. Thomas Blackwell, who lived in what is now Vance County, was considered one of the best blacksmiths in his county and accumulated a sizable fortune, in-cluding several slaves.[82] Thomas Day of Milton was a leading cabinet-maker whose work was highly praised by many of his customers and friends. When his friends described him as a first-rate workman and an excellent mechanic, they were recalling his accomplishments in making many of their own beds, chairs, and cabinets.[83] The pew which he made for his family at the white church in Milton is still there, a monument to his skill as a worker in wood. By 1860, Thomas Day not only owned a considerable amount of property including several slaves, but also employed a white journeyman cabinetmaker as well.[84]

It will be remembered that Isaac Hunter, who had so much diffi-culty in purchasing his wife and children and getting them out of the State,[85] had made the bulk of his money as a boot and shoemaker in Raleigh.[86] Henry Evans, in addition to being a Methodist preacher, was a shoemaker of some ability.[87]

78. Bassett, *Slavery in North Carolina*, p. 45.

79. James B. Browning, "James D. Sampson," *Negro History Bulletin* (January, 1940), p. 56; and Browning, "Free Negro in Ante-bellum North Carolina," *loc. cit.*, p. 28.

80. See Table V and the unpublished census schedule of 1860, Vol. 16.

81. See Table V.

82. C. D. Wilson, "Negroes Who Owned Slaves," *Popular Science Monthly*, LXXXI (1912), 491; and George C. Shaw, *John Chavis*, p. 34.

83. *Journal of the House*, 1830-31, pp. 238 ff.

84. See the unpublished census schedule of 1860 for Caswell County, Vol. 6.

85. *Cf. supra*, p. 45.   86. Ms. in the Legislative Papers for 1840.

87. John S. Bassett, "North Carolina Methodism and Slavery," *Trinity College His-torical Society Papers*, IV (1900), 8.

Coopers and turpentine distillers were important workers in eastern North Carolina, where the pine forests afforded a lucrative livelihood in the extractive industries. That there were more than a hundred free Negroes engaged in these activities in 1860 shows that they did not neglect this field altogether. There were not many large factories in North Carolina during the period. The reluctance of employers to have Negroes and whites working side by side in the new mechanical industries worked a hardship on the free Negro, for he was usually the one stricken from the picture when doubts arose as to the feasibility of such a setup. Nevertheless, there was a goodly number of free Negroes employed as factory hands, iron moulders, and firemen during the period. In 1860 there were seventeen factory hands, twenty-four firemen, and nine iron moulders who were free Negroes.[88]

There were few skilled occupations which free Negro women could enter. The most important were those of spinning, weaving, and dress-making. The number of free Negro girls who were apprenticed in these fields suggests that a sizable number would be capable of engaging in these occupations upon coming of age. Catherine Stanly augmented the financial resources which her father left her by making dresses for white women in New Bern.[89] A number of free Negro women increased the family income by spinning and weaving the clothes for their own family and for others. In 1860, there were almost 300 free Negro spinners and weavers in North Carolina, of whom women comprised a considerable majority. At the same time, 175 free Negro women were engaged in the occupation of dressmaking. Free Negro women also secured considerable employment as midwives and nurses. Here and there, free Negro women branched out into other lines. For example, Mary A. Lee conducted a profitable bakery shop in Plymouth, Washington County, and in 1860 she was worth $2,750.[90]

There is no evidence other than that of the Rowan County mechanics that free Negro artisans were employed at wages lower than those paid to white artisans. Doubtless, there were times when competition between the free Negro and white artisan caused the former to underbid for a particular job, which he may have been able to do because of the lower standard of living which usually prevailed. Competition, however, was never so keen among the artisans as to cause a prostration of wages. It is not difficult to believe, therefore, that if there was any difference between the wages of white and free Negro

88. See Table V.
89. Unpublished population schedule of the census for 1860, Vol. 10.
90. U. S. Census office, unpublished population schedule of North Carolina, Vol. 16, at the Bureau of the Census.

artisans it was not very considerable. In 1860, the average annual wages of a selected number of artisans in North Carolina were as follows:[91]

Blacksmith	$222	Cabinetmaker	$323
Brickmaker	164	Iron moulder	202
Carpenter	403	Harness maker	302
Carriage maker	285	Shoemaker	316
Cooper	306	Wagoner	261

The wages, of course, varied in different localities. Where the supply of labor was inadequate to perform the desired tasks, wages were relatively high. Thus, in busy Craven and Cumberland counties, coopers received an annual wage of $317 and $318 respectively, when the average wage for that occupation was $306. In the same way, one can be certain that the wages of the free Negro artisan varied from place to place. His wages were affected to some extent by the attitude of the community toward persons of his kind. If he were a Thomas Day, his color had little to do with his wages. But if he were less desirable and therefore less welcome in the community, he could not command the highest wages—if he had the good fortune to obtain employment at all.

Some free Negroes were able to make a living in a variety of other ways. The amassing of a small fortune by Louis Sheridan of Bladen County illustrates what can be done under adverse circumstances. Starting with a small store in Bladen County in the early years of the nineteenth century, he soon developed a business that was among the largest in his section of the State. His business connections with leading New York merchants were extensive, and through John Owen, former Governor of North Carolina, he met other influential men, including Arthur Tappan. At one time Sheridan purchased on credit goods worth $12,000 for which he paid with "honorable fidelity."[92] When he left for Liberia in 1837, Thomas Buchanan, of the Pennsylvania Society for the Colonization of Free People of Color, described him in the following language:

For energy of mind, firmness of purpose, and variety of knowledge, he has no superior. He is emphatically a self-made man, who has fought his way through adverse and depressing circumstances, to an eminence seldom, if ever attained by any of his color in this country. He has been for years engaged in an extensive and successful business, and is worth fifteen or twenty thousand

91. *Census Office,* Population in 1860, III (Manufactures), 437-438.
92. Eugene P. Southall, "Arthur Tappan and the Antislavery Movement," *Journal of Negro History,* XV (1930), 170.

dollars. Throughout his native state he is honored and esteemed by all who know him, and he leaves this country with the best wishes of every class of the community.[93]

Even though this may be an overly enthusiastic account of Louis Sheridan, there is little doubt that he possessed many of the qualifications mentioned in Buchanan's report. That the circumstances were not quite so "adverse and depressing" can be seen in the ease with which he secured the New York connections through his influential friends in North Carolina. That he had the firmness of purpose and energy of mind, however, is seen in his activities after reaching Liberia. When he was offered the position of storekeeper and general superintendent, the economizing Governor of Liberia lamented that $1200 was the "lowest for which he would engage."[94] His outspoken opposition to the tyrannical, shortsighted rule of the governor and to the unfair advantage taken of the colonists demonstrates, moreover, his independence of mind and spirit. In writing to Lewis Tappan about the governor, Sheridan said:

See him without the smallest degree of mercantile knowledge, laying on and charging enormous advances, say one or two hundred per cent, on the very necessaries procured by voluntary contributions, gotten together under the pretense of benefitting the colored man in Africa, and of which he receives not one iota beyond what he buys at enormous advances charged on their original cost in the United States. You may fancy this a distorted picture of affairs in Liberia, but Sir, I would rather that my right hand should perish from my body than pen a lie.[95]

Some free Negroes engaged in several different occupations in the effort to obtain a living for themselves and their families. It was not uncommon to meet with a painter and plasterer, a cabinetmaker and cooper, and a hostler and porter. Lunsford Lane is a good example of how an individual could pursue several lines of endeavor with some degree of success. Before Lane obtained his freedom he had gained some experience in performing a variety of tasks. He made most of the purchases for the household and carried this out with considerable ingenuity:

93. Colonization Society of the City of New York, *Sixth Annual Report* (New York, 1838), p. 11.
94. American Colonization Society, *Twenty-Third Annual Report* (Washington, 1840), p. 29.
95. Quoted in Southall, "Arthur Tappan," *loc. cit.*, p. 171.

He would meet the poor farmers long before sunrise, and make his purchases—if chickens were wanted, he ordered them by the dozen—Sometimes he purchased on his own account when salable articles were offered at low prices, these he stored in cellars of merchants of his acquaintance, and furnished to the families of the town as they were needed.[96]

Lane was often called upon to attend evening parties as the head waiter, and for his valuable services on such occasions he was liberally compensated. Returns were especially good when the Legislature was in session. Not only did he wait on tables, but also acted as bootblack, valet, and bartender.[97]

Before and after his freedom Lane furnished the members of the Legislature with their smoking tobacco. His father had taught him a way of preparing the weed that was quite agreeable to a large number of smokers. He put his tobacco up in fifteen-cent packages, and while serving as messenger in the Governor's office, he always carried tobacco on his rounds through the offices.[98]

Lane told in his own words how he conceived the idea of also making a pipe:

It occurred to me that I might so construct a pipe as to cool the smoke in passing through it, and thus meet the wishes of those who are more fond of smoke than heat. This I effected by means of a reed which grows plentifully in that region. I made a passage through the reed with a hot wire, polished it, and attached a clay-pipe to the end, so that the smoke should be cooled in flowing through the stem.[99]

In the following statement, Lane described his continued prosperity and the expansion of his business:

My customers were not only among the slaves and free people of color, but many of my friends among the White population sent to my shop for articles needed. As my little means increased, I entered into a considerable business in firewood, which I purchased by the acre standing, cut it, hauled it into the city and de-

96. Hawkins, *Lunsford Lane*, pp. 23-24.

97. *Ibid.*, p. 24.

98. The following resolution suggests the salary which Lane received as the Governor's messenger: "Resolved that the Public Treasurer pay to *Lunsford Lane*, a free man of Colour, twenty-four dollars, for six months attendance on the Executive office, from the first of July, one thousand eight hundred and forty to the first day of January, one thousand eight hundred and forty-one." *Laws, 1840-1843*, p. 204. The original Ms. of the resolution, endorsed by Mendenhall of Guilford County, is in the Legislative Papers for 1841.

99. Hawkins, *Lunsford Lane*, p. 26.

posited it in a yard, and sold it out as I advantageously could. To facilitate this increasing business, I kept one or two horses and various vehicles, by which I was enabled to do a variety of work at trucking about town—In the manufacture I met with considerable competition, but none that materially injured me—Those who undertook the manufacture could neither give the article a flavor as pleasant as ours, nor manufacture it so cheaply; so they either failed in it, or succeeded but poorly.[100]

In a state that was always as decidedly rural as North Carolina, and where a large majority of the free Negroes lived in the rural areas,[101] it is not difficult to understand why most of the free Negroes made their living from the soil. The majority of the free Negro children who were apprenticed were bound out to learn the trade of a farmer, and upon coming to manhood they expected to pursue this occupation.[102] Since, moreover, it was extremely difficult for free Negroes to secure training in the skilled trades and in the more literary pursuits, they were not found in large numbers in these activities. But they *had* to make a living. Tradition and what little training they had compelled the free Negroes to seek their living from the soil.

North Carolina was never one of the chief slaveholding states. The slaves numbered less than those of her neighbor states of Virginia, South Carolina, and Georgia. As a matter of fact, 67 per cent of the slaveholding families held fewer than ten slaves in 1860, while 72 per cent of North Carolina's families had no slaves at all. This suggests that in a state where the plantation system was fairly well entrenched the supply of slave labor was definitely limited. The farm labor in North Carolina was done not only by the slave but, in some areas, by the members of the white farming family, by white farm laborers, and by free Negro farm laborers. In finding this opportunity for work, the free Negro was extremely fortunate, and his labor was not as frequently rejected as it was in the more skilled occupations. Naturally, there were objections to his presence on plantations where there were slaves, but these objections were more likely to be raised to the hiring of free Negroes on the neighbor's plantation than on one's own. Though there may have been fears that the free Negro's presence on a slave plantation might cause insolence among the slaves as well as inspire desires of freedom among them, this did not prevent the white slaveholders from hiring free Negroes to perform some of the tasks from time to time.[103]

100. *Ibid.*, p. 82.
101. *Cf. supra*, p. 19.
102. *Cf. supra*, pp. 130 ff.
103. See the unpublished census schedules for 1850.

There was, moreover, an opportunity for the free Negro to secure seasonal work on the farms of North Carolinians who had no slaves at all. The yeoman frequently harbored violent antipathies for the slave system and would refuse to hire slave labor even when it was available. He was more likely to look for assistance, during rush seasons, among the poor landless whites or among the free Negroes. The large number of free Negro farm laborers in counties where there was little or no slaveholding seems to support this point of view. In Cabarrus County, for example, there were fourteen free Negro farm laborers and only four free Negro farmers.[104]

Naturally, there were more free Negro farm hands in counties where the free Negro population was large. These counties, incidentally, usually had a large number of slaves. As field hands, drivers, and all-round laborers, free Negroes found opportunities for work on the larger plantations. It was not unusual for free Negroes to live on slave plantations. Some of them had slave wives or husbands, and the benevolent master often permitted them to live there together, hiring the services of the free person.[105] Thomas Newton of Craven County secured his freedom from his master, Benjamin Woods, and, by continuing to work on the place, was able to purchase his wife, who had been the slave of the same Benjamin Woods.[106]

Of course the number of free Negro farm laborers varied from county to county. The number to be found in any particular county depended not only upon the scarcity or abundance of farm labor, slave and free, and the attitude of the whites toward free Negro labor, skilled and unskilled, but also upon the mobility of the landless free Negro population. It was extremely difficult for free Negroes, although without the trappings which usually tie people to a particular location, to move from one place to another. The reluctance of those in authority to grant passes permitting free Negroes to move about and the impecunious state of a majority of the free Negroes made it difficult for free Negro farm laborers to migrate even to the adjoining county. It was possible, therefore, for a newly freed slave, trained in a skilled occupation, to live and die in an area that was least suited for his advancement.

104. See Table V, "The Occupations of Free Negroes in North Carolina in 1860." It is quite likely, moreover, that a sizable number of the free Negroes who gave their occupation as "common laborer" found work on the farms and may have been, more properly, "farm hands."

105. See, for example, the unpublished population schedules for the census of 1860.

106. Minutes of the Court of Pleas and Quarter Sessions for Craven County, March, 1811. See, also, in the minutes for March, 1815, the case of Reuben Calloway.

With these facts in mind, it is interesting to observe the location of the bulk of the free Negro farm hands in North Carolina. Of the 1,746 free Negro farm hands in North Carolina in 1860, more than 1,000 were located in the seven eastern counties which constituted the stronghold of the slave system.[107] Halifax County alone had 384 free Negro farm hands, while Pasquotank County had 284. Thirty-one counties were without any free Negro farm hands at all, while 700 were scattered among the remaining forty-eight counties.[108]

A more interesting group of free Negroes who made their living from the soil were those who either rented land or owned land and planted their own crops. They may properly be called the free Negro yeomanry. It was possible for a free Negro to obtain permission from a white landowner to live on the latter's land and to cultivate a portion of it and share in the returns from his labor. This, however, was looked upon with disfavor, and whites were discouraged in the practice. It may be recalled that the law of 1827 required each white person to list all free Negroes living on his land and to be responsible for the taxes which might be levied on such free Negroes.[109] Free Negro tenants who showed a disposition to work and to bear their responsibilities could still convince landowners that they would not be a burden to them. The tax lists of various counties and the census reports bear witness to the fact that there were free Negro tenants on the lands of white persons down to the end of the period. In the tax list for Beaufort County in 1850, for example, A. Eborn, free Negro, was listed as the tenant of John Cutter, white.[110] In the same list, F. Hackey was the tenant of Samuel Swan, white.[111] One wealthy white farmer, R. H. Reddick of Lower Broad Creek, had fourteen free Negro tenants on his land and was responsible for $143.93 in taxes for them.[112] At the end of the period many free Negro tenants were still living on the land of white landowners.[113]

That the number of free Negroes who owned their own farms was considerable can be seen from the table on free Negro owners of real and personal property in the appendix. Many of these individuals, like John C. Stanly, had started with small holdings, and by thrift and

107. Granville, Halifax, Hertford, Northampton, Pasquotank, Perquimans, and Sampson.

108. It is interesting to observe that the majority of the counties with no free Negro farm hands was located in the western part of the State. See Table V.

109. Cf. supra, p. 104.

110. Ms. in the County Records for Beaufort County, 1850.

111. Ibid.   112. Ibid.

113. See, for example, the unpublished census schedules for Wake and Halifax counties.

business acumen had accumulated large holdings. They usually engaged in tobacco and cotton farming and marketed their crops in the same manner as other farmers in the State. By far the majority of the property owned by free Negroes was in the rural areas and was, of course, in the possession of free Negro farmers.

The free Negro farmer was generally in better circumstances than free Negroes in other economic pursuits. In 1860, there were 1,048 free Negro farmers in North Carolina.[114] Of this number, approximately 50 per cent possessed some real property.[115] In some cases they did not own a sufficient amount, but the figures seem to suggest that the free Negro farmer was becoming a landowner. David Reynolds, a farmer of Halifax County, owned $3,000 worth of land.[116] J. A. Collins of Hyde County had $1,000 worth of real property by 1860.[117] The well-known Thomas Blacknall of Franklin County owned $6,000 worth of land.[118] Of the fifty-three free Negroes worth more than $2,500 in 1860, thirty-one were farmers.[119] In North Carolina, then, the free Negroes who made their living from the soil numbered approximately 3,000. Doubtless this number could be augmented considerably when one takes into account the numbers of minors and housewives who assisted their fathers and husbands in the fields. That they constituted the most important element in the economic life of the free Negro in North Carolina in terms of numbers and holdings is clearly shown by the facts. For the most part they went their way unnoticed. The disproportionate part of the stage occupied by the free Negroes in other pursuits was the result of the focus of light upon them in the more thickly settled communities. Meanwhile, the free Negro farmer, living in the inarticulate and relatively sparsely settled countryside, steadily rose in economic independence and, consequently, in the respect—somewhat disquieted, perhaps—of his fellows.

THE FREE NEGRO PROPERTY OWNER

At no time during the period before the Civil War was the free Negro's right to own real property questioned. He enjoyed all the protection in the matter of acquisition, transfer, devise, and descent that other citizens of North Carolina enjoyed. The records of the county courts indicate that free Negroes used them regularly for the purpose of recording changes in ownership of real and personal property. The

114. See Table V.   115. See Appendix II, No. 3.
116. Ms. in population schedules for 1860, Vol. 19.
117. *Ibid.*
118. *Ibid.*, Vol. 16.   119. See Appendix II, No. 1.

following record is typical of many that were found in the minutes of the county court:

A deed from Ezra F. Holmes to Southey Kaeise (free Negro) was proved in open court by the oath of Wm. T. Bryan a witness thereto ordered to be registered.[120]

Having once acquired land, the free Negro could be fairly sure that the courts would stand by him during his period of possession. In 1838, Benjamin Curry, a free Negro of Guilford County, was driven off the property which he had owned for twelve years by four white men. One of them claimed that Curry had sold him his house, land, and five slave children and the transaction had been executed in a deed of trust between the two parties. At the trial, the solicitor for the State objected to the deed as evidence, contending that it was a slick piece of extortion and that the free Negro never intended to give up his land. The lower court convicted the defendants of having "riotously and routously" assembled to disturb the peace of the State and with force of arms trespassed upon the property of Benjamin Curry.

The defendants appealed the case to the Supreme Court. After making a thorough review of the facts in the case and after listening to lengthy arguments from both sides, Judge Gaston, speaking for the Court, said:

We are of the opinion that there was no error in the conviction of which the defendant complains. In cases where the law gives to the judges a discretion over the quantum of punishment, they may, with propriety, suspend the sentence [in this case it was a fine of $100 for the principal defendant] for the avowed purpose of affording the convicted an opportunity to make restitution to the person peculiarly aggrieved by his offense.

The judgment against the defendant is, therefore, reversed, and this opinion is to be certified to the Superior Court—for the county of Guilford, with directions to award sentence of fine and imprisonment against the defendant agreeably thereto and to the laws of the state.[121]

The leniency of Judge Gaston was inspired by the defendant's having already restored the property to the free Negro. Though there was a reversal of the conviction, the case remains significant in that the

120. Minutes of the Court of Pleas and Quarter Sessions of Beaufort County for December, 1843.

121. State v. John H. Bennett, 20 N. C., 135 ff.

Supreme Court goes on record as being vigorously opposed to the infringement of property rights even in the case of a free Negro.[122]

Free Negroes could sell or transfer their land at will as long as it was for a legal consideration. In 1833, for example, Benjamin Neale of Craven County sold 100 acres of land, and the following indenture makes known the transaction:

February 4, 1833 ⎫
State of N. C.   ⎬
County of Craven ⎭

Be it known that Benjamin Neal (coloured man) for and in consideration of the sum of fifty dollars to me paid in hand by William B. Masters of the same State and County aforesaid, have bargained sold enfeoffed and confirmed unto the said Wm. B. Masters his heirs and assigns forever a certain parcel of land. [A description of the land follows.] The said Benjamin Neale purchased of Thomas Cooke dec. containing by estimation one hundred acres be the same more or less. To have and to hold the said piece or parcel of land with all woods ways waters and every other appurtenances thereunto belonging against the lawful claims of all and every person.

Benjamin Neale[123]

The right of a free Negro to sell his property was confirmed by the Supreme Court in a case that came before it in 1843. A white man, Pearson, rented a small tract of land for one year to Elijah Powell, a free Negro, who promised to give him one-half the corn crop. The justice of the peace gave Pearson permission to sell Powell's crop. Powell asked that the sale be postponed until after it was gathered. When the corn was sold, one Hare objected, saying that he had already bought Powell's share, after the corn was dried. Pearson denied that Powell could sell his share, contending that he was only a servant. The Nash Superior Court said that Powell was a tenant and could therefore dispose of his property as he pleased. In upholding this view, the Supreme Court, through Judge Daniel, said:

Even if Powell was a servant, the division had given him a share which all would have to admit. The corn had been placed in the defendant's barn upon a naked bailment for safe-keeping. The

122. See also the case of State v. Emory, 51 N. C., 142, in which the Supreme Court held that a free Negro could not be forcibly ejected from the possession of a house.

123. Ms. in the James W. Bryan Papers. See also the deed from Jno. and Rebecca Hambleton, free Negroes, to Churchill Moore, in the Minutes of the Court of Pleas and Quarter Sessions of Beaufort County for December, 1842.

sale of it and the demand by the purchaser put an end to the bailment.[124]

It was not at all unusual for free Negroes to direct the disposition of their property through wills. Upon the death of the testator, the will was recorded in the minutes of the county court and an executor was appointed by the court. The minutes of the Beaufort County Court for 1843 give a typical example:

State of North Carolina ⎱
Beaufort County ⎰

A paper writing purporting to be the last will and testament of John Hambleton deceased (free Negro) was duly proved in open court to be the last will and testament of said John Hambleton and duly executed so as to pass seal on personal estate by the oath of John W. Latham the subscribing witness thereto and ordered to be recorded and Edward Hyman the Executor named therein was qualified as Executor.[125]

An interesting case involving the will of a free Negro woman was that of the aged Mary Green of Wilmington, who left all her property to a white attorney. She looked to him not only for counsel, but also for protection and occasionally for small sums of money. In addition to these favors, he also collected rent on the property that had been accumulated by the testator's deceased free Negro husband. The only relative, a niece, had received a house and lot from her aunt before she died. Upon the advice of the free Negro husband, all the property was left to the lawyer. The niece contended that her aunt had been under "undue influence" and sought to have the will invalidated. Upon losing the case in the New Hanover Superior Court, the niece appealed to the Supreme Court. In upholding the decision of the lower court, Judge Manly said:

It seems that the legatee [Joshua Wright] and the decedent [Mary Green] stood in relation of client and attorney, *patron* and *dependent,* and the court below—informs the jury that persons bearing these relations—are to be suspected and scrutinized more closely and carefully than dealings between others. These relations, as facts pertinent to the issue—were submitted to the jury with

124. Hare v. Pearson, 26 N. C., 62.

125. Minutes of the Court of Pleas and Quarter Sessions of Beaufort County for June, 1843. Free Negroes were sometimes appointed Executors, as in the case of Southey Keis, of Beaufort County, who in March, 1856, appeared in court and qualified as the executor of the estate of Mary Keis. Minutes of the Court of Pleas and Quarter Sessions of Beaufort County for March, 1856.

proper instructions. That was all, we think, the court was authorized to do by the law of the land.

We concur with the court below—that undue influence must be fraudulent and controlling and must be shown to the satisfaction of a jury, in a court of law, upon an issue of *devisavit vel nom*.[126]

Free Negroes, as other individuals, sometimes had difficulty in establishing their rightful claim to property left them in a will. If, however, their freedom could be established and if the circumstances under which the will was made were valid, the free Negro could secure the necessary protection in the courts of the State. In 1851, one Benjamin Dicken of Edgecombe County died. His will directed his executor to free all his slaves and send them to some free state and divide $12,000 among them. All except one woman, who died soon after, left the State. Her daughter, who had gone to Canada, claimed her mother's share of the estate for her and the other children. The executor claimed that the mother had not complied with the will since she had not left the State and, therefore, her heirs could claim no part of the money intended for her. Judge Pearson of the Supreme Court said that the removing of Negroes was not a condition precedent to emancipation, but a condition subsequent, "by the non-performance of which they may forfeit their newly acquired freedom." The judge was satisfied that the deceased free Negro woman had good intentions:

1. We are satisfied that Mariah, [the mother of the plaintiff] at the time of her death—was to all intents and purposes, a free woman, and had the capacity to take property and transmit it by succession to her personal representative.
2. We are also satisfied that the children of Mariah were entitled to call upon her administrator to make distribution among them, as her next of kin—and we think it clear that all of her children are to be considered distributees.[127]

In one case, several technicalities arose which made it difficult for a free Negro devisee to retain the town property that had been left her by a wealthy white man of Tarboro. In his will he said, "I give and devise to Mary Ann Jones, a free colored woman of the town of Tarboro and to her heirs and assigns forever, the lot of ground and the house thereon erected on which she now lives." Since two lots adjoined each other, the testator's executor interpreted the will literally and proceeded to take possession of the lot next to the one on which the devisee's house stood. Before his death, the testator had fenced in both

126. Wright v. Howe, 20 N. C., 318.
127. Alvany, a free woman of color, v. Powell, 54 N. C., 34.

lots together, and the free Negro woman used both lots for a garden and for other purposes. In 1860, Judge Manly of the Supreme Court awarded both lots to the estate of the free Negro woman, by that time deceased. He took the point of view that the gift to the free Negro woman "is not confined to the fifty yards square called a lot in the plan of the town, but extends at least to the lands enclosed and used in connection with the house." In the will, the testator used *lot* to mean *parcel* or piece.[128]

Perhaps the most interesting case of the period involving the inheritance of property by free Negroes arose in 1857. While a slave, one Miles married another slave. Afterwards, he was freed and subsequently purchased his wife. They had one child; then, the wife was set free, and they had several other children. After this wife died, Miles married a free Negro woman by whom he had three children. When he died intestate, in 1857, a contest arose between the two sets of children over the division of the property. The children by the first wife claimed tenancy in common with the children by the second wife. When the case came before the Supreme Court, that body denied that the children by the first wife had any valid claims:

A slave cannot make a contract. Therefore, he cannot marry legally. Marriage is based upon contract. Consequently, the relation of "man and wife" cannot exist among slaves. Neither the first nor the others of the children by the first wife were legitimate. The parties after being freed ought to have married according to law; it is the misfortune of their children that they neglected or refused to do so, for no court can avert the consequences.[129]

The possession of slaves by free Negroes was the only type of personal property that was ever questioned during the ante-bellum period. There may not have been much objection to the ownership of one's own family by a free Negro; but when one undertook to acquire slaves to improve his economic status, there were those who looked upon it as a dangerous trend, the legality of which was seriously questioned. If the free Negro was not a full citizen, could he enjoy the same privileges of ownership and the protection of certain types of property that other citizens enjoyed? Around this question revolved a great deal of discussion at the beginning of the militant period of the anti-slavery movement.

When a slave was found guilty of concealing a slave on board a

128. Doe on the demise of Mary Ann Jones v. Norfleet, 20 N. C., 365. A plan of the lots was included in the court report.
129. Doe on the demise of Francis Howard v. Sarah Howard, 51 N. C., 238 ff.

vessel, in violation of the act of 1825, it was contended by his owner that the prisoner, a slave, was not a person or mariner within the meaning of the act and that Green, the owner of the concealed slave, was a mulatto and hence not a citizen of the State and could not own slaves. The decision of the Supreme Court handed down in 1833 by Judge Daniel established once and for all the rights of the free Negro in the matter of ownership of slaves. He said,

> By the laws of this State, a free man of color may own land and hold lands and personal property including slaves. Without therefore stopping to inquire into the extent of the political rights and privileges of a free man of color, I am very well satisfied from the words of the act of the General Assembly that the Legislature meant to protect the slave property of every person who by the laws of the state are entitled to hold such property. I am, therefore, of the opinion that the owner is a citizen within the meaning of the act of Assembly, and it appearing he was a mulatto is not a reason to grant a new trial to the person who concealed his slave.[130]

The decision of Judge Daniel remained the accepted point of view until the very end of the period. When the hostility between the sections was developing into open conflict, the free Negro in the South witnessed an almost complete abrogation of his rights. One of the most significant laws passed during the momentous session of 1860-1861 was the act "to prevent free Negroes from having the control of slaves." While it did not affect a large number of free Negroes within the State,[131] it showed the extent to which the North Carolina solons were willing to go in order to combat the forces that were striking at the very heart of their long-cherished system. Among other things, the law provided,

> That no free Negro, or free person of color shall be permitted or allowed to buy, purchase, or hire for any length of time any slave or slaves, or to have any slave or slaves bound as apprentice or apprentices to him, her, or them, or in any other wise to have the control, management or services of any slave or slaves, under the penalty of one hundred dollars for each offence, and shall further be guilty of a misdemeanor, and liable to indictment for the same.[132]

130. State v. Edmund, a slave, 15 N. C., 278.
131. The number of free Negroes who owned slaves was steadily decreasing. *Cf. infra*, p. 160.
132. *Laws, 1860-1861*, p. 69.

Another section of the law provided that free Negroes already possessing slave property would not be affected by the enactment.[133]

Despite the innumerable obstacles that stood in the way of the accumulation of property by free Negroes, several amassed a considerable amount of property during their lifetime. Of course, the case of Louis Sheridan[134] cannot be duplicated many times, but he was by no means the only free Negro who could be considered wealthy in ante-bellum North Carolina. The life of Julius Melbourn is about as interesting as one can find in the period. Born a slave on a plantation near Raleigh in 1790, he was bought, at five years of age, by the wealthy widow of a British army official, who lived in Raleigh. When her only son was slain in a duel—said to have been fought because of some derogatory remarks concerning his mother having reared Melbourn as a gentleman—the slave was emancipated and made sole heir to the estate of $20,000. By the time Melbourn was twenty-five years old his estate was worth about $30,000. By careful saving and shrewd investment, he was soon worth $50,000. When he decided that he could not live and die in a country "where the laws sustained and justified such disregard to individual rights and tolerated such inhumanity" as was manifested in the treatment of free Negroes, he sailed for England, where he spent the remainder of his life. That he was still wealthy is attested by the fact that he set his son up in a $20,000 mercantile business in London.[135]

The census for 1860 lists fifty-three free Negroes who possessed more than $2,500 worth of property. Among these was Jesse Freeman of Richmond County, who was worth $20,300;[136] James D. Sampson, a carpenter of New Hanover County, who was worth $36,000;[137] Hardy Bell, a farmer and merchant of Robeson County, whose property had a value of $14,000;[138] and Lydia Mangum, whose Wake County property was worth $20,816.[139]

The bulk of the free Negroes who owned property, however, were possessors of small estates worth a few hundred dollars or less. These, moreover, comprised only a small percentage of the total free Negro population. The great majority of free Negroes in North Carolina were, during the entire period, propertyless. At the end of the period, only 3,659, or slightly more than 10 per cent, owned any property. Of

133. *Ibid.*, Section 2. 134. *Cf. supra*, pp. 144 ff.
135. Julius Melbourn, *Life and Opinions of Julius Melbourn, passim.*
136. Unpublished schedules of the eighth census, Vol. 13.
137. *Ibid.*, Vol. 11. 138. *Ibid.*, Vol. 13.
139. *Ibid*, Vol. 16. For a list of the free Negroes possessing more than $2,500 worth of property in 1860, see Appendix II, No. 1.

this number, only 1,211 owned real estate.[140] In few counties did more than 10 per cent of the free Negroes own property. Craven County, with 1,332 free Negroes in 1860, had only 179 free Negro property owners. Cabarrus County, with 115 free Negroes, had twelve free Negro owners of property. Halifax County, with its 2,452 free Negroes, however, had 463 free Negroes who owned property.[141]

In some counties, free Negroes owned no real estate. There were six such counties in 1860.[142] While each county listed some personal property held by free Negroes, eight counties listed only one such person each.[143] Perhaps nothing is a more striking commentary on the plight of the free Negro in North Carolina than his inability to acquire property, both real and personal.

A study of the value of the property which free Negroes did possess will shed further light on the economic status of the free Negro in ante-bellum North Carolina. Of course it is difficult for one living in the fifth decade of the twentieth century to appreciate the figures which reveal the value of property owned by free Negroes in ante-bellum North Carolina. Land values were so much lower at the time that it was quite possible for a free Negro with 100 dollars' worth of real property to have an adequate amount for farming purposes, and with a few hundred dollars he could erect a house that would be about as modern as the age could provide. There was a likelihood, however, that the land of the free Negro would be the least desirable in a given area. Since the majority of them were small farmers, they faced the same difficulty that other North Carolina yeomen faced: that of trying to obtain satisfactory property in the same market where the more resourceful plantation owner was making his purchases. It is a point of interest, therefore, that some free Negroes, like John C. Stanly and James D. Sampson, were able to acquire some of the most desirable land in their respective communities.

New Hanover County was first in free Negro real property with a value of $37,720, which included some rather valuable town property in Wilmington. Robeson was second, with a value of $37,555. Halifax was third, with real property owned by free Negroes valued at $30,948.

140. The figures were compiled from a study of the property holdings of free Negroes as given in unpublished population schedules of the eighth census (1860). For a complete list of the number of holdings, by counties, see Appendix II, No. 2.

141. See Appendix II, No. 2.

142. They were Alleghany, Davie, Harnett, Haywood, Jackson, and Madison. Interestingly enough, none of these counties is in the eastern part of the State.

143. They were Catawba, Haywood, Henderson, Hyde, Jackson, Martin, McDowell, and Rutherford.

Three counties had real property owned by free Negroes with values ranging from $20,000 to $30,000. The value of free Negro real property in other counties ranged from the $15,987 of Granville to the $50 of Catawba. The total value of real property owned by free Negroes in 1860 was $480,986.

On the whole, a large number of free Negroes possessed some type of personal property, ranging from silver watches to farming tools. Thus, in the larger number of counties, the value of personal property was higher than the value of real property. Martin, Mecklenburg, and Sampson counties are among the interesting exceptions, however. Wake County, with personal property valued at $45,362, led the field. Incidentally, this amount was twice the value of real property in the same county. Robeson, New Hanover, and Pasquotank followed in that order. The total value of personal property owned by free Negroes in 1860 was $564,657.

The poverty of the free Negro group can be seen clearly through this study of the value of the property of the group. They possessed an aggregate wealth of $1,045,643. When one considers that more than 30,000 people had to share in this wealth of slightly more than a million dollars, the realization of their plight is inescapable. The per capita wealth of the free Negroes of North Carolina was only $34.00 in 1860. Thousands of these were landless and without any kind of property. Even when one ascertains the per capita wealth of the free Negro property owners in North Carolina, the picture remains gloomy. The free Negro property owners had a per capita wealth of $287.00. It must be remembered that fifty-three of these owners were worth more than $2,500 each, while several in this number were worth more than $15,000 each. This means that Margaret Reid of Mecklenburg County, with $75 worth of realty and $10 worth of personal property, was more nearly the rule than the exception.[144]

One subject in which considerable interest has always been manifested is the ownership of slaves by free Negroes. At no time during the ante-bellum period were free Negroes in North Carolina without some slaves. The motives for such ownership were perhaps as benevolent as they were in other groups. Without doubt, there were those who possessed slaves for the purpose of advancing their economic well-being. With such a view in mind, these free Negro slaveholders were more interested in making their farms or carpenter-shops "pay"

144. See the unpublished schedules of the eighth census, Vol. 11. For the table of the value of real and personal property owned by free Negroes in 1860, see Appendix II, No. 4.

than they were in treating their slaves humanely. The capitalistic-minded free Negro owners of slaves can usually be identified because of their extensive holdings of realty and personalty and because of their inactivity in the manumission movement. For thirty years, Thomas Day used slaves to help him in his cabinetmaking business. In 1830, he had two;[145] by 1860 he had three.[146] For thirty years, Thomas Blacknall of Franklin County kept slaves, though the number fell from seven to three between 1830 and 1860.[147]

It seems that by far the larger portion of free Negro owners of slaves were the possessors of this human chattel for benevolent reasons. There are numerous examples of free Negroes having purchased relatives or friends to ease their lot. Many of them manumitted such slaves,[148] while others held title to slaves who were virtually free. An examination of slaveholding by free Negroes seems to bear out this point. Slave Richard Gaston ran away from his master and remained in the woods until his free Negro wife had saved the necessary funds for his purchase.[149] Lila Abshur continued to hold title to her father when the Legislature acted unfavorably on her petition to emancipate him.[150] While John Stanly undoubtedly held some slaves with the view to increasing his wealth,[151] he held others purely out of benevolence.[152]

The fluctuation in the number of free Negro owners of slaves during the period under observation is an interesting development. At the time of the taking of the first census in 1790, twenty-five free Negroes in eleven counties owned seventy-three slaves.[153] In 1830, the number of free Negro slaveholders had increased to 191, distributed in 37 counties, while their human chattel numbered 620.[154] Interestingly enough, by 1860 there were only eight free Negro owners of slaves, the latter numbering 25.[155]

145. C. G. Woodson, *Free Negro Owners of Slaves in 1830*, p. 24.

146. See the list of free Negro owners of slaves for 1790, 1830, and 1860 in Appendix III.

147. Woodson, *Free Negro Owners*, p. 25, and the unpublished population schedules for the census of 1860.   148. *Cf. supra*, pp. 29 ff.

149. C. D. Wilson, "Negroes Who Owned Slaves," *Popular Science Monthly*, LXXXI (1912), 485.

150. Ms. in the Legislative Papers for 1856.

151. In 1830, John Stanly held 18 slaves. Meanwhile, he had emancipated a considerable number. In 1860 his daughter held seven slaves.

152. *Cf. supra*, p. 31.

153. *Heads of Families in the United States in 1790, passim.* The census reports for Caswell, Granville, and Orange counties were destroyed before the publication of this volume.

154. The unpublished population schedules for 1830 in the Bureau of the Census; and Woodson, *Free Negro Owners*, pp. 24-26.   155. See Appendix III.

After a careful examination of the records, one can make several interesting observations. In the first place, the number of slaves held by free Negroes was usually small. Notable exceptions are the eleven slaves held by Samuel Johnston of Bertie County in 1790;[156] the 44 slaves each owned by Gooden Bowen of Bladen County and John Walker of New Hanover County in 1830;[157] and the 24 slaves owned by John Crichlon of Martin County in 1830.[158] Free Negroes usually held one, two, or three slaves, and the petitions of free Negroes to manumit relatives suggest that a sizable number of slaves had been acquired as a result of benevolent motives.

In the second place, the increase in the number of free Negroes with an accompanying increase in economic independence on the part of some caused a larger number of Negro slaves to be acquired by free Negroes. No doubt, moreover, there was some effort to conform to the pattern established by the dominant slaveholding group within the State in the effort to elevate themselves to a position of respect and privilege. Thus, by 1830, more than 600 slaves were held by free Negroes. Finally, the remarkable decline both in the number of free Negro slave owners and in the number of slaves held toward the end of the period suggests the increasing economic and political difficulty that the free Negro was encountering. Many of those held in 1830 had been manumitted, according to the plans of the free Negro owners. Other slaves had been lost in the maze of economic setbacks that many free Negroes experienced.[159] Perhaps, also, the fervor to acquire slave relatives and set them free was waning as the free Negro himself began to doubt the blessings of freedom.[160] Thus, even before it became illegal for free Negroes to acquire slaves in 1861, the group had ceased to make such acquisitions. In this case, the enactment merely made legally impossible that which the free Negro had already ceased to do.

The economic plight of the free Negro was seen in difficulties which he had with his creditors. Even John C. Stanly, the wealthy free Negro of Craven County, was hard pressed for cash at times. The Bryan papers, which abound in materials concerning his numerous transactions (the Bryans were his lawyers), contain this item, which is a case in point:

156. Clark, *State Records*, XXVI, 278.   157. Woodson, *Free Negro Owners*, p. 24.
158. *Ibid.*, p. 25.

159. In such case, the free Negro was losing his slaves in much the same way that the white slaveholder was losing his slaves. By 1860, the rate of increase of slaves in North Carolina was noticeably declining. *Cf.* Taylor, *Slaveholding in North Carolina*, *passim*.   160. *Cf. infra*, Ch. VI.

Ninety days after date I promise to pay Nathan G. Blount on order one hundred and thirteen dollars and fifty cents for value received with interest. March 26th, 1829, $113.50.

John C. Stanly

Though Stanly lost heavily in later years, he never became completely impoverished.

Free Negroes were likely to receive harsh treatment from those to whom they owed or had owed money. In Charlotte, Mice Taylor, a free Negro, was killed by a white man when he refused to pay for some lumber which he was said to have received from the white man. When the free Negro denied the debt, a fight ensued in which the free Negro received three fatal stabs.[161] When the Superior Court met, it found the white assailant guilty of manslaughter, and he was branded.[162]

By 1832, the State had solved its problem of insolvent free Negro debtors by requiring them to be hired out to pay their fines, taxes, etc.[163] The private creditor, however, received no relief from the enactment of 1832; and he found himself faced with the problem of trying to collect debts from insolvent free Negroes. In 1859, an effort was made to extend the bill to include free Negroes who were unable to pay their private debts.[164] "After a considerable discussion in the House in which Messrs. Outlaw, McKay, and Norwood spoke against it," the bill passed by a vote of 55 to 33. The Senate, however, refused to approve it, and it never became a law.

Surrounded on all sides by a legal system which denied them the opportunity to seek a livelihood where they could and by a hostile community that often made them as unwelcome as a contagious disease, the free Negroes tried to find their place in the economic life of North Carolina. If they were "idle, thievish, roguish, and indolent" they merely reflected the restraints and stigmata that society had placed upon them, and their reactions were no more than natural. In view of the circumstances, it is not surprising that they were not a more powerful economic force than they were. The amazing thing is that in such circumstances they were able to acquire more than a million dollars worth of property by the end of the period and to have had several hundred slaves in their possession during the seventy-year period ending in 1860.

161. *Western Democrat*, February 5, 1856.

162. *Western Democrat*, May 20, 1856.   163. *Cf. supra*, p. 89.

164. Ms. in the Legislative Papers for 1859. The bill was endorsed by Representative Pritchard of Mecklenburg County.

CHAPTER V

Social Life of the Free Negro

Be it enacted . . . That it shall not be lawful under any pretense for any free negro, slave or free person of colour to preach or exhort in public, or in any manner to officiate as a preacher or teacher in any prayer meeting or other association where slaves of different families are collected together.

Laws passed by the General Assembly of
North Carolina, 1831.

As a group in the society of ante-bellum North Carolina, the free Negroes found themselves literally encircled by a number of laws and practices that forced upon them an extremely limited compass in which to live. Although they were within physical proximity to whatever social, political, and economic developments were taking place, they were only to a very limited extent participants in those developments. They were as good an example as could be found in the national period of our history to substantiate the point of view of John Dewey that "persons do not become a society by living in proximity any more than a man ceases to be influenced by being so many feet or miles from others."[1] The integration of a group into the society of a particular community depends largely upon the extent to which there is communication between the group and the community. The lines of communication between the free Negro and the remainder of the people of North Carolina were very few, and these few were being "cut down" as rapidly as they could be discovered. This was particularly true in the spheres of social and intellectual relationships, although it was also true in the political and economic fields as well.[2]

Despised and viewed with contempt by a majority of the whites and looked down upon by many of the Negro slaves, whose social and economic position gave them some degree of security, the free Negro found himself forced into a group—caste-like in its attributes—from which there was almost no escape. If the relegation of the Negro in the ante-bellum South to an inferior status can be regarded as an

1. John Dewey, *Democracy and Education* (New York, 1928), pp. 1-7.
2. *Cf. supra*, Chs. 3 and 4.

accommodation through which the race problem found a natural solution,[3] it can be said with some degree of confidence that the free Negro was a caste within a caste. As a result of birth, education—or lack of it—and social status, the free Negro found himself forced to seek the majority of his associations and social experiences within his relatively small group. As a member of this group he was, of course, under the influence of the *esprit de corps*.[4] His actions and reactions were generally representative of those of the group.

For the free Negro in ante-bellum North Carolina, this social condition had untold implications. His forced status had the effect of developing habits of thought and modes of action that at once reflected his despised position and his efforts to compensate for it. The society of North Carolina offered to the free Negro ideas already molded, rules of conduct already approved. These ideas and rules of conduct changed from time to time, of course, but not at the behest or solicitation of the group which they most seriously affected. Now and then a rebel appeared within the group, but the social control was so vigorous, so complete, that he was soon brought into the line of conformity. The laws affecting the movements from place to place, education, and social intercourse of the free Negro were designed to develop and maintain a prescribed pattern of action. In addition to the laws, moreover, the mores of the community compelled it to object vigorously to any real social or intellectual advancement of this "caste within a caste." These conditions must be kept in mind in making an inquiry into the social status of the free Negro in ante-bellum North Carolina.

EDUCATION

In speaking of the wretchedness of the free Negro in consequence of his ignorance, David Walker said, "Ignorance as it now exists among us, produces a state of things, oh my Lord! too horrible to present to the world . . . and when my Curious observer [who is desirous of seeing the full force of ignorance developed among the colored people of the United States] comes to take notice of those who are said to be free (which assertion I deny) and who are making some frivolous pretentions to common sense, he will see that branch of ignorance among the slaves assuming a more cunning and deceitful course of procedure."[5] The extremely limited opportunities for the

3. *Cf.* R. E. Park, "Introduction" to J. Steiner, *The Japanese Invasion* (Chicago, 1917), p. xii.

4. S. Sighele, *Psychologie des sectes,* translated in R. E. Park and E. W. Burgess, *Introduction to the Science of Sociology* (Chicago, 1930), p. 205.

5. Walker, *Appeal*, pp. 24-25.

development of their mental faculties were viewed by Walker as largely responsible for the wretched plight of the free Negro in the ante-bellum South.

It goes without saying that the educational opportunities of free Negroes in ante-bellum North Carolina were few. Had it not been for the apprenticeship system, it is safe to say that the educational achievement of the free Negroes would have been far below the level that was attained. This system was by and large a functional one. The free Negro apprentice was schooled in the art of making a living.[6] Under the law of 1762 it was compulsory, moreover, for every master to teach or cause his ward to be taught to read and to write. Under this system, the literacy of the free Negro group increased considerably, though it is difficult to believe that each master observed the law to the letter. Even after the law of 1838 relieved the master of the obligation of teaching free Negro apprentices to read and write, many agreed to teach their wards these fundamentals.[7] Indeed, most·of the free Negro apprentices of Craven County in the 1850's were under indentures which specified that they were to be taught to read and write.[8]

As a method of educating free Negroes, the apprenticeship system in North Carolina was very important. In addition to teaching the free Negro how to make a living, it placed him in a position where he could come in contact with the literary activities of the white children and their fathers. If the apprenticeship system was responsible for the majority of the skilled free Negroes in the later period, it was responsible also for a large number of the literate free Negroes in the census of North Carolina in 1850.[9]

Much of the training given to free Negro apprentices was undoubtedly imparted begrudgingly or unconsciously by the white masters. The movement to curtail the teaching of free Negro wards suggests the apprehension with which the whites viewed the prospects of an "educated free Negro caste."[10] Some whites in ante-bellum North Carolina, however, deliberately undertook to provide education for slaves and free Negroes. As early as 1763, the members of the Anglican faith were promoting educational institutions for Indians and Negroes.

6. *Cf. supra*, p. 129. 7. *Cf. supra*, p. 129.
8. This conclusion is reached after a careful examination of the apprenticeship bonds for Craven County from 1850 to 1860. Mss. in the County Records of Craven County.
9. *Cf. infra*, p. 169.
10. *Cf. The Journal of the House, 1826-1827*, in which Joel King of Franklin sought to "repeal so much of the act of 1762, as requires the Master or Mistress to teach or cause to be taught colored apprentices to read and write." On February 3, after debate, the bill was postponed indefinitely.

From Globe, North Carolina, an agent of the Society for the Propagation of the Gospel made the following report of his activities to the secretary of the organization:

> A society called Dr. Bray's associates have done me the Honor of making me Superintendent of their schools in this Province, have fixed a school mistress among them, to teach 4 Indian and 2 Negro boys and 4 Indian girls to read and to work and have supplied them with books for that purpose. . . .[11]

The Presbyterians and Methodists were actively engaged in the education of the slaves and free Negroes of western North Carolina in the early years of the nineteenth century. At that time, they were also actively engaged in the movement to abolish slavery. Although they ceased to have a major role in the antislavery movement after 1835, Woodson says that "There continued still . . . a goodly number of these churchmen who suffered no diminution of interest in the enlightenment of Negroes."[12] The minutes of the Presbyterian Synod of North Carolina for 1851 contain the following observation on Negro education:

> We are encouraged by the good attendance on the means of grace generally reported; by the fact that prayer-meetings are generally kept up in our congregations; that Sabbath Schools and Bible classes are sustained in most of our churches; . . . that increased attention is given to the instruction; that opposition, to a considerable extent successful, is maintained against intemperance, and against the causes tending to its prevalence.[13]

Perhaps the Quakers accomplished more than any other sect in the task of educating the Negroes of ante-bellum North Carolina. As early as 1771 they were teaching slaves to read and write.[14] Toward the end of the eighteenth century, the Quakers entered into the task of educating the free Negroes with such zeal that one authority credits them with having been largely responsible for the free Negroes of North Carolina entering the ranks of the most enlightened of ante-bellum free Negroes.[15] In 1816, a school for Negroes was opened to run two days a week for three months. The boys were to attend until they were able to "read, write and cipher as far as the rule of three," and the girls were to attend until they were able to read and write.[16]

---

11. Saunders, *Colonial Records*, VI, 995.
12. C. G. Woodson, *The Education of the Negro Prior to 1861*, p. 182.
13. *Minutes of the 38th Session of the Presbyterian Synod of North Carolina, 1851*, p. 21.
14. Woodson, *Education of the Negro*, p. 46.
15. *Ibid.*, p. 113.
16. Wagstaff, *Minutes*, p. 59.

In 1821, Baron Coffin, a leading Quaker of the Deep-River district, made a recommendation for the establishment of a separate school for free Negroes.[17] In commenting on such a prospect, Coffin said "It seems from the experiment made [in 1816] that a considerable part of the expense might, probably, be paid by those who would send. Such an establishment would have a tendency to do away with that delicate feeling, or squeamishness, which seems to pervade the white population with regard to mixing, whites and blacks in the same school."[18] After considering the matter, the acting committee of the Deep-River Meeting House made the following report on September 24, 1821:

> That taking the subject of educating the people of Colour under consideration, they think proper to propose that the General Association make such addition to the fund already on hand, as it may think proper, and appropriate the interest thereof to the exclusive purpose of educating the people of Colour; and that said fund be still increased as the Association gains ability, and that the number of pupils be increased in proportion to the increase of interest.[19]

Nothing more was said about these proposals in the minutes of the Manumission Society, but there is every reason to believe they were carried out, in part at least. In traveling through North Carolina in 1825, William Forster, the noted English Missionary for the Society of Friends, was greatly encouraged by the way in which the Quakers were undertaking to educate the free Negroes. He said that they had no less than 500 under their care and that most of them were being educated and given an opportunity to hear the Scriptures.[20]

The continued interest of Quakers in the education and general welfare of the free Negroes of North Carolina was observed by Thomas Shillitoe, who visited in North Carolina in 1829. In part, he said:

> June 1, 1829—attended the Narrows meeting, after which we attended a Committee of Friends, who have the charge of a considerable number of free coloured people some of whom have been freed by Friends, and others have been willed to Friends by persons not in profession with our Society, in order to their becoming freed; the great load of care that has developed on this committee,

17. S. B. Weeks, *Southern Quakers and Slavery*, p. 231.

18. Coffin used the term "coloured children" which was never used in connection with slave children. The later recommendations, using the term "people of color," show clearly that the Quakers were here concerned with free Negroes.

19. Wagstaff, *Minutes*, p. 62.

20. William Forster, *Memoirs of William Forster*, II, 31.

calls for the near sympathy of their absent friends, from the ignorance and untowardness of those they have to do with, in addition to the severity of the laws of the state relative to free coloured
people.[21]

Certainly the laws with regard to the free Negro were severe
enough in 1829, when Shillitoe made the above statement. But the
next decade was to see them become increasingly severe, not only in
connection with their legal and economic well-being, but also in the
field of education. The laws against the teaching of slaves, which were
passed in 1831 and 1832,[22] had an adverse effect on the future generations of free Negroes in that it meant that the recruits from the slave
ranks had received almost no opportunity to become literate. The
implications are that Negroes who became free after 1832 were, for
the most part, illiterate and certainly added nothing to the intellectual
development of the free Negro in North Carolina.

In the Legislature of 1834-35, a bill was introduced to prohibit a free
Negro from teaching his own children or causing them to be educated.
The bill, however, did not pass.[23] Even at a time when North Carolina was taking measures to protect itself against possible encroach-
ments of the free Negro populace, it felt that it could not go that far.
It was reported in the Brooklyn, New York, *Advertiser* that the bill
actually became law. This inaccurate statement brought an immediate
denial from the *Raleigh Register,* which commented,

> It is an old saying, that the D——l is not as black as he is
> painted, and so it is with our legislature. Some of their doings
> were outrageous enough in all conscience, but they exhibited no
> such symptoms of barbarity as the above extract would indicate.[24]

Despite the sentiment against the education of free Negroes and
despite the fact that there was no provision by the State for their education, free Negroes continued to learn to read and write. It is to be
remembered that some Negro apprentices were still being taught to
read and write.[25] There were, moreover, some schools which were
giving considerable attention to the education of free Negroes. In 1854,
the *New Bern Atlantic* complained that it was a "notorious fact" that

21. Thomas Shillitoe, *Journal of Thomas Shillitoe,* II, 365.
22. *Cf.* Woodson, *Education of the Negro,* p. 168. Woodson says that the law prohibiting the teaching of Negroes was passed in 1835. As a matter of fact, it was passed
in 1831. See *Laws, 1831-35,* p. 7.
23. Ms. in the Legislative Papers for 1834-35.
24. *Raleigh Register,* January 7, 1835.
25. Ms. in the County Records of Craven County, 1849.

day schools were being maintained for the enlightenment of the people of color of the town.[26]

The education of free Negroes in North Carolina after the eighteen thirties is one of the most puzzling problems in the history of ante-bellum North Carolina. Complaints such as the one registered by the New Bern paper were few; but there is no doubt that there was a considerable amount of clandestine teaching of free Negroes. There was actually no State law against the private teaching of free Negroes, but public opinion refused to countenance any such procedure. Nevertheless, free Negroes were learning—and were in schools! The census of 1850 reported 100,591 whites and 217 free Negroes in school.[27] In twenty-five counties, free Negroes were in school. Wake County led with 52 free Negroes in school, Robeson County was second with 47, and Craven County third with 46.[28] While the number of free Negroes in school in 1850 is relatively small, the implications are significant. If 217 free Negroes were admittedly in school in North Carolina in 1850, there were undoubtedly many others who were receiving their training privately, indeed, secretly. The literacy figures indicate that a goodly number of free Negroes received the rudiments of education in North Carolina as late as 1850. One county historian has pointed out that although there were no records of any schools for the free Negroes of Gates County, over half the male free Negroes could read and write in 1850.[29] For the whole State, there are some interesting figures. Of the 12,048 free Negro adults, 5,191 (or 43 per cent) were literate.[30] In the light of this evidence, the suggestion that a considerable number of free Negroes received training in the fundamentals takes on some degree of reality.

The most important individual associated with the education of free

26. *Atlantic (New Bern)*, October 25, 1854.

27. Reported in the *Fayetteville Observer*, November 28, 1853, without editorial comment.

28. The following is a complete list of the number of free Negroes in schools in 1850, by counties:

Alamance	5	Columbus	1	Macon	12	Wake	52
Anson	2	Craven	46	Montgomery	7	Warren	2
Ashe	1	Davidson	4	Randolph	6	Watauga	4
Beaufort	2	Duplin	3	Richmond	1	Wilkes	3
Caswell	1	Gates	3	Robeson	47	Wayne	1
Chowan	1	Halifax	5	Surry	1		217
Cleveland	3	Hyde	4				

United States Census Bureau, *Seventh Census of the United States*, p. 315. These reports were made by families and not by the boards of education.

29. Isaac Harrell, *Gates County to 1860*, p. 66.

30. Census Bureau, *Seventh Census*, p. 317.

Negroes in North Carolina was John Chavis.[31] Chavis showed, at an early age, a predilection for rhetoric and the classics. Concerning his supposed attendance at Princeton University, Professor Knight says,

> There is no clear proof . . . that Chavis was ever a student at Princeton. Beyond the known fact that he was not graduated the institution has no genuine record of the man. . . . Although there are no known official records which verify his attendance there, the tradition or belief that Chavis was a student at Princeton is so well-founded that he is listed among the non-graduates of the institution. His presence at Princeton would not have been extraordinary because one or two Negro students and several Delaware Indians were there under [President] Witherspoon.[32]

Although some mystery surrounds Chavis' attendance at Princeton, there is little doubt that at one time he was a regularly enrolled student at Washington Academy, now Washington and Lee University, at Lexington, Virginia. In 1802, a motion in the Rockbridge County Court asserted that the court had known Chavis for a number of years and "that he had always conducted himself in a decent, orderly and respectable manner, and also that he has been a student at Washington Academy where they believe he went through a regular course of Academical studies."[33]

After a brief period of religious activity in Virginia as a "riding missionary" at the Hanover Presbytery in 1805, Chavis came to North Carolina, where he spent the remainder of his life. By that time he was fairly well prepared in rhetoric and the classics and well versed in the Scriptures. A lawyer of Granville County, George Wortham, said, "His English was remarkably pure, containing no 'Negroisms'; his manner impressive, his explanations clear and concise. . . ."[34] Indeed, Chavis himself thought well of his own accomplishments. In a letter to a former student, Willie P. Mangum, he remarked,

> Please give my best respects to Mrs. Mangum and tell her that I am the same old two and sixpence towards her and her children, and that she need not think it strange that I should say that her children will never be taught the theory of the English Language

31. A great deal has been written about John Chavis. Concerning the controversy among historians with regard to his training, see E. W. Knight, "Notes on John Chavis," *North Carolina Historical Review*, VII (1930), 326-345. For a list of the articles and books about Chavis, see the Bibliography.

32. Knight, "Notes on Chavis," *loc. cit.*, pp. 328-329. Several historians, including Bassett, believe that Chavis was a private pupil of Dr. Witherspoon in the Classics. Bassett, *Slavery in North Carolina*, p. 78.

33. Bassett, *Slavery in North Carolina*, p. 75.

34. Knight, "Notes on Chavis," *loc. cit.*, p. 320.

unless I teach them. I say so still. I learnt my Theory from Lind-
ley Murray's spelling book which no other Teacher in this part of
the Country Teaches but myself and I think it preferable to the
English Grammar.[35]

It seems that at first Chavis undertook to teach the children of both
races together, but there was some objection to this plan. Practical man
that he was, he soon altered this plan to comply with the wishes of his
white patrons. The following announcement is of interest not only because it presents the new plan but also because it reveals other facts
concerning his school—the tuition, the coöperation with the banking
officials of Raleigh, and the things which were stressed by him as a
teacher:

John Chavis takes this method of informing his employers, and
the Citizens of Raleigh in general, that the present Quarter of his
school will end on the 15th of September, and the next will commence on the 18th. He will, at the same time, open an *Evening
School*[36] for the purpose of instructing children of Colour, as he
intends, for the accommodation of some of his employers, to exclude all children of Colour from his Day School.
The Evening School will commence at an hour by Sun. When
the white children leave the House, those of Colour will take their
places and continue until ten o'clock.
The terms of teaching the white children will be as usual, two
and a half dollars per quarter; those of Colour, one dollar and
three quarters. In both cases, the whole of the money to be paid
in advance to Benjamin S. King.[37] Those who produce certificates
from him of their having paid the money will be admitted.
Those who think proper to put their children under his care,
may rely upon the strictest attention being paid not only to their
Education, but to their morals, which he deems an *important* part
of Education.
He hopes to have a better School House by the commencement
of the next quarter.[38]

There is no way of knowing how many free Negro children were
taught by John Chavis between 1808 and some date in the 1830's when
he retired from active teaching.[39] His teaching must have touched

35. John Chavis to Willie P. Mangum, September 3, 1831.
36. The italics are those of Chavis.
37. In 1808, King was a banker in Raleigh. Two years later, he was elected a city
commissioner of Raleigh. *Raleigh Register,* January 18, 1810.
38. *Raleigh Register,* August 25, 1808. Also in the issue for September 1, 1808.
39. Knight believes that Chavis conducted separate schools from 1808 until the
1830's. Knight, "Notes on Chavis," *loc. cit.,* p. 339.

many, in view of the fact that his school for free Negroes was conducted for almost thirty years. That his teaching of the free Negroes was effective and praiseworthy is illustrated in an editorial comment which appeared in a Raleigh newspaper in 1830:

On Friday last, we attended an examination of the free children of color, attached to the school of *John Chavis,* also colored, but a regularly educated Presbyterian Minister, and we have seldom received more gratification from an exhibition of a similar character. To witness a well regulated school, composed of this class of persons—to see them setting an example both in behavior and scholarship, which their *white* superiors might take pride in imitating, was a cheering spectacle to the philanthropist. The exercises throughout, evinced a degree of attention and assiduous care on the part of the instructor, highly creditable, and of attainment on the part of his scholars almost incredible. We were also much pleased with the sensible address which closed the examination. The object of the respectable teacher, was to impress on the scholars, the fact, that they occupied an inferior and subordinate status in society and were possessed of but limited privileges; but that even *they* might become useful in their particular sphere, by making a proper improvement of the advantages offered them.[40]

It is impossible, moreover, to make an estimate of the effect of the teachings of John Chavis on the social status of the free Negro in antebellum North Carolina. This status was doubtless raised through the efforts of his free Negro students, who, for more than a generation, were inspired by his lofty idealism and his insistence on the possibility that every individual might better his own condition. Perhaps it was elevated even more by the figure of John Chavis, teacher not only of free Negro children, but also of white children! As a teacher of such persons as Willie and Preston Mangum (whom he affectionately called "My Sons"), Archibald and John Henderson, Charles Manly, and James Wortham, he was a negation of much for which the white community stood in its attitude toward the free Negro. Intellectually, he was inferior to few North Carolinians. The lively interest which he displayed in all public questions was equal to that manifested by most leaders within the State.[41] He was, indeed, a citizen of North Carolina and a participant in its intellectual as well as its political developments.

40. *Raleigh Register,* April 19, 1830. The italics are those of the editor.
41. *Cf. supra,* pp. 106 ff. The letters of Chavis to Mangum abound in interesting comments on various public questions. Concerning the proposal to amend the Constitution regarding the election of the President, Chavis wrote Mangum, "I was pleased that you voted for the amendment . . . but for no other reason than I did not wish you to

Nor did the people of the State look with disfavor upon the several activities of John Chavis. On many occasions several substantial citizens of the State came to his rescue when he was in financial straits. The correspondence between Chavis and Willie P. Mangum reveals that the latter often assisted him in his business transactions. In 1825 Mangum assisted Chavis in getting a renewal of a note for $270 in a Raleigh bank, and Chavis expressed the hope that Mangum would see fit to pay the interest of $30.[42] On another occasion, he requested Mangum to get some money for him from his (Chavis') friend Judge George E. Badger.[43] In 1827, Benjamin Rogers of Raleigh gave Chavis a tract of land in Wake County.[44] The white people had done so much for Chavis that he came to expect assistance in various forms. His pride did not prevent his making solicitations wherever he thought they could be effective; and when there was no response he sometimes became indignant. After receiving no response to certain letters which he had written, he wrote Mangum,

> Please give my respects to my son Abraham Rencher and to General Barringer and tell them I would be glad to receive a letter from them. Tell them if I am Black I am free born American and a revolutionary soldier and therefore ought not to be thrown entirely out of the scale of notice.[45]

The greatest assistance to Chavis came in 1832 when the Orange Presbytery voted to support him and his wife for life. Coming, as it did, when Chavis was an old man without a substantial income from his school, the offer was extremely welcome and immediately accepted. Commenting upon the offer, Chavis said, "I view this Presbyterial arrangement as a merciful providence for which I am thankful."[46]

When the life of John Chavis came to a close sometime late in the 1830's he could look back on more than a generation of active service to various communities within the State of North Carolina. The effect which he had upon its intellectual development was far reaching, and was doubtless salutary on both whites and free Negroes. Posterity has

discover a disposition to trample upon the will of the people; but as to its actual amendment in that case, I am opposed because once a beginning is made to amend the constitution, away goes the best of human compacts. The truth is the constitution as it now stands places the people on firm ground, that they cannot sink or stop for, not so much so as to strain their joints much, and therefore I say let us move on as we have done." Chavis to Mangum, May 24, 1826.

42. Chavis to Mangum, January 28, 1825, and July 3, 1825.
43. Chavis to Mangum, November 16, 1827.
44. Chavis to Mangum, December 15, 1827.
45. Chavis to Mangum, March 10, 1832.
46. Chavis to Mangum, October 16, 1832.

been kind to John Chavis. A Federal Housing Project for Negroes in Raleigh has been named for him. The commissioners of the city of Raleigh have named a recreation park for him. In 1938, the North Carolina Historical Commission placed a marker near the park bearing the following inscription:

JOHN CHAVIS

Early 19th Century Free Negro preacher and teacher of both races in North Carolina. Memorial Park 200 yards east.

RELIGION

The Wayne County slave who remonstrated with the white preacher for his attitude toward the spiritual lives of the black creatures could doubtless have been speaking for the free Negroes as well as for the slaves. In part, he wrote,

> Master John, I want permition if you pleas to speak a word to you ... in the first place I want you to tell me the reson you always preach to the white folks and keep your back to us. is it because they sit upon the hill. we have no chance among them. then must we be forgotten because we cant get near nough without geting in the edg of the swamp behind you ... if I should ask you what must I do to be saved perhaps you would tell me pray let the bible be my gide, this would do very well if we could read. I do not think there is one in fifty that can read. I have been more fortunate than the most of the black people. I can read and write in my way as to be understood. ... If God sent you to preach to siners did he direct you to keep your face to the white peoples constantly or is it because they give you money ... did God tell you to have your meeting houses just larg enought to hold the white folks and let the black people stand in the sone and rain as the brooks in the field. ...[47]

Indeed, little attention was generally given by the whites to the spiritual life of the free Negroes. Here and there it was possible for slaves and free Negroes to enjoy separate religious instruction under the leadership of slaves or free Negroes. More often, however, provision was made to incorporate the free Negro as well as the slave into the religious activities of the whites. This was done either by giving them a special section in which to sit at the regular services or providing them with special services at the end of the regular services.[48]

47. This was written on the bottom of a letter from John Fort, Jr., to Hugh Brown of Robeson County, June 26, 1821. It is believed, therefore, that one of Fort's slaves was writing to Brown instead of to Fort. Perhaps the letter should have been addressed to Master Hugh. Ms. in the Neill Brown papers.

48. *Cf.* the unpublished autobiography of Brantley York, p. 55.

In the eighteenth century, various missionaries were willing to minister to the free Negroes and the slaves. They were usually the agents of liberal and benevolent organizations whose program was sufficiently comprehensive to include persons of all races and castes. When John Macdowell, a missionary for the Society for the Propagation of the Gospel, went into North Carolina, he took pride in relating his experiences with free Negroes. On one occasion he said, "I had so great a number of people . . . that we were obliged to assemble under the shady trees. I baptized one day . . . 32 children and adults among whom were 5 free mulattoes."[49]

Although the Quakers were actively engaged in alleviating the conditions among slaves and free Negroes, the question of the membership of free Negroes in the Society of Friends was a problem which caused considerable concern. In June, 1798, Isaac Linegar, a free Negro, requested membership in the Deep River Monthly Meeting. The matter was referred to the New Garden Quarterly Meeting held the same month. "This in turn referred it to the Yearly Meeting, which meeting at Little River in Perquimans County on 10 month 30th, 1798, referred it to the consideration of the committee appointed to consider the state of the society. This committee recommended the following day that it be recommended to said Quarterly Meeting to attend to the Discipline in that respect without distinction of color."[50]

In 1800, the matter was still before the Yearly Meeting. On this occasion, the New Garden Quarterly Meeting requested a ruling in the matter of receiving persons of color into membership. Apparently, there had been some opposition to Linegar's membership. After some discussion, the Yearly Meeting decided, "It is the Judgment of this meeting that the Discipline is fully sufficient in respect of receiving members and Friends recommended to strictly attend thereto."[51] Opposition was thus broken down by the firm refusal of the Yearly Meeting to discriminate against free Negroes. Accordingly, Isaac Linegar was accepted as a member of the Deep River Monthly Meeting on June 6, 1801.[52] There are no figures on the number of free Negro Quakers, but with the Linegar case as a precedent, it is reasonable to expect that other free Negroes were taken into membership.

Wherever free Negroes were permitted to participate in the religious life of the community, the records seem to suggest that they entered

49. Macdowell to the Secretary, February 9, 1760. Saunders, *Colonial Records*, VI, 225.

50. Henry J. Cadbury, "Negro Membership in the Society of Friends," *Journal of Negro History*, XXI (1936), 177.

51. *Ibid.*, p. 177.   52. *Ibid.*, p. 177.

with enthusiasm and sincerity. Thomas Blacknall, the well-to-do free Negro of the town of Franklin, was first a Presbyterian and later a Baptist. As a deacon in the Baptist Church of Franklin, he frequently led the congregation, composed largely of white men and women, in the prayer services.[53] Thomas Day, a prominent free Negro citizen of Milton, was an active leader in his local church.[54]

Toward the end of the period, despite the fact that free Negro preachers had been silenced,[55] some improvement can be discerned in the religious life of free Negroes in some sections of the State. The minutes of the Presbyterian Synod of 1858 contain some interesting observations with regard to the activities of that denomination in connection with the Negroes of North Carolina:

> It is worthy of special mention that increasing attention is given to the religious interests of the colored population. This is apparent in the special provision for their accommodation in the erection of places of public worship, in the frequency of preaching expressly to them, and in the oral instruction given them in the families.[56]

In Gates County, a great deal was done for the free Negro Baptists. One prominent citizen, who kept Negro concubines, built at his own expense a church for the free Negroes. The church, known as New Hope Baptist Church, had a free Negro preacher part of the time by the name of William Reid. No slaves were admitted, and for a long time after the war the church would not admit any Negroes who had been slaves, "the line always being drawn between those born free and those shot free."[57]

The improvement in the religious activities among the slaves during the nineteenth century may have had some salutary effect on the religious life of the free Negroes. In the search for devices that would maintain the status quo, the slaveholders of North Carolina, as in other states, turned to religion and set the church up as an institution which looked with approbation on the "peculiar institution."[58] In order that the free Negroes would not become a deterrent force in the social order, concessions were made to that element in society, with the result that they were accepted as members not only in white churches, but

53. Joseph Lacy Seawell, *Law Tales for Laymen*, p. 210.

54. *Cf. supra*, p. 45.

55. *Cf. supra*, p. 72 and *infra*, p. 179.

56. Presbyterian Synod of North Carolina, *Minutes of the Forty-Fifth Session, 1858* (Raleigh, 1859), p. 18.

57. Harrell, *Gates County*, p. 67.

58. W. S. Jenkins, *Pro-Slavery Thought in the Old South*, pp. 207 ff.

also in churches established for the exclusive use of the slaves.[59] While accurate and complete statistics are not available, there can be no doubt that a considerable number of free Negroes belonged to the organized religious life of North Carolina. In 1860, over one third of the members of the Chowan Baptist Association were Negroes. In 1830, one third of the Methodists of North Carolina were Negroes.[60] There can be no doubt, therefore, that these denominations, both of which boasted of having capable free Negro preachers, had free Negro members.

Free Negro preachers did more to elevate the religious life of the free Negroes than any other force. The several free Negro preachers who received state-wide recognition for their spiritual leadership of both races would have been a credit to any community. Before John Chavis became a teacher, he was an ordained minister of the Presbyterian faith. In 1801, the General Assembly of that denomination appointed him, "a black man of prudence and piety, as a missionary among people of his own Colour" in Virginia and North Carolina. As a missionary he executed his mission with diligence, fidelity, and prudence. Though his term ended in 1805, he served as a missionary intermittently until 1832, when the stringent laws of that year prohibited free Negroes from preaching.[61]

Chavis' acquaintance with the Scriptures can be seen in his writings, which were done in the later years of his life. After the laws of North Carolina silenced him, he wrote an exegesis on the doctrine of atonement, entitled "The Extent of Atonement." This publication was circulated widely and received favorable comment.[62] In 1837 he published a vigorous argument against the popular conception of Calvinism entitled, "Chavis Letter on the Doctrine of the Atonement of Christ," which was also widely circulated. The points of view expressed by Chavis in this work were the subject of discussion at the Orange Presbytery, to which he belonged, as early as 1833. The respect and admiration which the members had for him was best expressed in their decision to care for him and his wife for the remainder of their lives.[63]

Chavis was in a class by himself as far as the education of whites and free Negroes was concerned. This was not true, however, in the field of religion. Perhaps he surpassed the other free Negro ministers in formal training, but many of their contributions to the religious life

59. Cf. the unpublished manuscript of Fannie O'Kelly Peace, "History of the St. Paul A. M. E. Church of Raleigh, 1848-1940"; in the possession of the deceased author's family.

60. William K. Boyd, History of North Carolina, II, 209.

61. Knight, "Notes on Chavis," loc. cit., pp. 331-334.

62. Ibid., p. 337.   63. Cf. supra, p. 173.

of ante-bellum North Carolina were just as significant and lasting. Henry Evans, a free Negro shoemaker from Stokes County, had more to do with the establishment of Methodism in Cumberland County than any other one individual. As he passed through Fayetteville, en route to Charleston, where he proposed to locate, he made some observations of conditions among his people there. He was impressed with the fact that the Negroes were "wholly given to profanity and lewdness, Never hearing preaching of any denomination."[64] He decided to settle there and to make an effort to elevate the tone of life among the Negroes. Before many weeks had passed, he found much opposition to his presence. A town ordinance was passed which forbade his preaching within the corporate limits. He then moved to the "Sandhills," just outside Fayetteville. In this new location he reached a large number of Negroes and whites. His popularity grew so rapidly that he was invited to return to town. His services were by this time enjoyed by the more respectable whites. Opposition thus "melted like wax before a flame."[65]

Within a few years he had leased a lot for seven years and began building a church "20 by 30 feet out of rough edge materials. This was the first Methodist Church in the place. In a short time an addition of 10 feet was made to it."[66] At first, the organization was an independent one, but in time it was taken into regular connection, and Fayetteville became an appointment on an established circuit. In 1806, Bishop Asbury preached to the Evans congregation and entered the following remark in his diary: "Tuesday, January 15, Fayetteville. At the African Meeting House I preached at eleven o'clock . . . Fayetteville, Sunday 12, unwell—nevertheless I took the PULPIT."[67]

When the work became so heavy that Evans, in his old age, felt that he could no longer serve his congregation efficiently, he asked to be relieved. Accordingly, the Reverend Thomas Mason was assigned to the post in 1808 by Bishop Asbury.[68] A room for Evans was built in the back of the church, and he lived there for the remainder of his life. On the Sunday before he died in 1810, he tottered into the church and at the end of the sermon, he arose to speak:

> I have come to say my last word to you. It is this: None but Christ. Three times I have had my life in jeopardy for preaching

64. John S. Bassett, *North Carolina Methodism and Slavery* (Durham, 1900), p. 8.
65. Johnson, *Ante-bellum North Carolina*, p. 344.
66. Elizabeth Lamb, *Historical Sketch of the Hay Street Methodist Church, South*, p. 7.
67. Lamb, *Sketch of Hay Street Church*, p. 7.
68. *Ibid.*, p. 7.

the gospel to you. Three times I have broken the ice on the edge of the water and swam across the Cape Fear to preach the gospel to you, and if in my last hour I could trust to that or to anything but Christ Crucified, for my salvation, all should be lost, and my soul perish forever.[69]

Upon his death, Evans was buried under the church that today stands on the site of the First Methodist Church of Fayetteville.[70] No less a person than Bishop William Capers of the Methodist Episcopal Church paid him the following tribute at his death:

I have known not many preachers who appeared more conversant with the Scriptures than Evans, nor whose conversation was more instructive as to the things of God. He seemed always deeply impressed with the responsibility of his position. . . . The humility of the man, we must think, was praiseworthy. It was necessary under the circumstances. But what shall we say of a system that demanded a prostration of self-respect from a man of the Christly courage of Henry Evans! He did a great work, but might it not have been greater had he been untrammeled by the sense of his subordination?[71]

Up to 1831, free Negro preachers suffered no restraints placed on them by the State Legislature. If any legal disabilities existed, they were created by the local authorities, as in the case of Henry Evans of Fayetteville.[72] In that year, however, the growing concern of the populace for their slaves and the increasing disapproval with which the very presence of free Negroes in the State was viewed caused the General Assembly to take action on the matter of the preaching of free Negroes. On January 5, 1831, a bill was introduced in the Senate which prohibited slaves from meeting at night. At the third reading, Senator William B. Meares of New Hanover introduced an amendment which prohibited free Negroes from preaching in the presence of any slaves.[73] This bill was passed by the Senate in the amended form, but was indefinitely postponed by the House. When it finally emerged from the House, it was amended in such a way as to restrain the activities of free Negro preachers considerably more than the original amendment proposed to do. In its final form, the law read:

69. Bassett, *North Carolina Methodism*, p. 10. Bassett reports that of these words "Bishop Capers said simply and justly they were worthy of St. Paul."

70. Lamb, *Sketch of Hay Street Church*, p. 7.

71. Bassett, *North Carolina Methodism*, p. 9, quoted from the autobiography of Bishop Capers.

72. *Cf. supra*, p. 178.

73. *Journal of the Senate, 1830-1831*, p. 139.

Be it enacted ... that it shall not be lawful under any pretence for any free Negro, slave or free person of color to preach or exhort in public, or in any manner to officiate as a preacher or teacher in any prayer meeting or other association where slaves of different families are collected together.[74]

Chavis, who was still preaching, was thus almost completely silenced by the enactment of 1831. Other free Negro ministers were also prevented by the law from carrying on their religious activities. It is interesting to observe, moreover, that the Legislature was determined to make no exceptions to the rule, though several applications for lenience in specific cases were made. The case of Ralph Freeman was one of the most interesting to come before the Legislature. "Elder Ralph," as he was called, had received his freedom from his Anson County master soon after he displayed an inclination to preach. He was ordained as a Baptist minister and traveled as a missionary in Anson, Montgomery, Moore, Randolph, and Davidson counties. "He was considered an able preacher, was frequently called upon to preach on funeral occasions, was appointed to preach on Sabboth at the [Sandy Creek] Association, and frequently administered the ordinance of baptism and the Lord's Supper."[75]

The esteem in which he was held by his white colleagues is best demonstrated by his association with the Reverend Joseph Magee. For years they traveled and preached together. Upon the death of the Reverend Mr. Magee, who had died in the West, it was revealed that Freeman was to receive his riding horse, coat, Bible, and fifty dollars. The family requested Freeman to come and speak at the bier of his deceased friend. When he had finished, a collection was taken up for him. "A Methodist came up and handed Ralph one dollar. A Presbyterian, who observed it, said to him, you ought not to give Ralph anything ... because ... he has torn your system all to pieces. The Methodist replied, 'I believe he has preached the truth, and I will give him the dollar.'"[76]

When the law preventing free Negroes from preaching was passed Freeman was greatly mortified and had the sympathy of many whites. There is some evidence, moreover, that he was determined to preach in spite of the law. In the autumn of 1831, the following resolution, adopted by the Pee Dee Baptist Association, was published in a Fayetteville newspaper:

74. *Laws, 1831-1835*, p. 7.
75. George W. Purefoy, *Sandy Creek Association, 1758-1858*, p. 328.
76. Purefoy, *Sandy Creek Association*, p. 329.

Resolved, that from our long acquaintance with Elder *R. Freeman* and knowledge of his good deportment, and confidence in him as a preacher of the Gospel, *we recommend him as a preacher;* but we advise him to refrain from making evening appointments of his own, but to associate with and accompany his brethren in preaching as formerly.

J. Culpepper, Moderator.[77]

It is not known whether Freeman continued to preach during the following year. Doubtless, an effective check had been put on his exhortations; for a petition of seventy-two citizens asked the Assembly in 1832 to permit him to preach. In part, the petition said,

The prayers of your petitioners humbly sheweth that Ralph Freeman, a free man of colour, of the county of Anson, has been previously to the last session of the Legislature, for many years, a faithful and acceptable preacher of the gospel; that by an act passed at that Session, he was deprived of the exercise of that gift which he and his brethren believe that God had bestowed upon him; and that it is the earnest desire of the undersigned that he be allowed to preach as formerly. We therefore, pray you, that a special act of Assembly be passed granting him that privilege.[78]

When the Committee on Propositions and Grievances took up the matter, they could not escape the feeling that the various activities of free Negro preachers might result in another Nat Turner insurrection. That they were influenced by this possibility more than any other, perhaps, can clearly be seen in their report. The committee was satisfied with the respectability of the petitioners and with the reputation of Ralph Freeman as a preacher, but they deprecated the consequences that might ensue from his activities:

it would be the means of collecting large assemblages of Negroes together and thereby afford them greater facilities for the execution of their Nefarious designs. The law of the last session . . . has confined their clerical operations to individual families of Negroes . . . and does not prohibit him from exercising their gifts in complyance of their supposed call by the head of the Church to expound the misteries of the Sacred wrightings except as there specified.[79]

The Committee feared that a favorable consideration of this request would cause hundreds of other free Negroes to request similar consideration, thereby virtually repealing the act. It therefore reported the

77. *Fayetteville Observer,* November 30, 1831.
78. Ms. in the Legislative Papers for 1832-33.
79. Ms. in the Legislative Papers for 1832-1833.

bill unfavorably and asked to be discharged from further consideration of the subject.[80] No further action was taken on the Freeman petition at this and succeeding sessions of the Assembly.[81]

For the most part, free Negro preachers were effectively silenced by the law of 1831. The spheres in which they could act after that time were so small that it was impossible for a free Negro minister to live by devoting the major portion of his time and energy to his profession. The fear of insurrection, moreover, became so great after 1831 that the communities looked with absolute disfavor upon a free Negro who was engaged in any activity which would bring a large number of Negroes together. It was not difficult to enforce this law, for a large majority of the white citizens doubtless favored it. Despite the fact that in 1855 a New York paper described the Reverend Robert Green of New Bern as a free Negro preacher in good standing with the Episcopal church, it can be said with some degree of accuracy that the period of free Negro preachers in North Carolina came to a close in 1831.

SOCIAL RELATIONSHIPS

The various activities of the free Negroes of ante-bellum North Carolina encompassed considerably more than the matters of making a living, securing some kind of training, and seeking an opportunity to worship God. There were many hours when they were occupied with none of these pursuits, important though they were; and during these times, they, just as any other group of normal human beings, sought companionship and association with their fellows. Set apart as they were into a caste marked with a definite stigma, they were still free, of course, to seek association with their fellow free Negroes.

At no time during the period were there any restrictions on the relations of free Negroes with each other. Although the white citizens were willing to make distinctions among free Negroes in private or semiprivate association,[82] there was never a legal or official acknowl-

80. *Ibid.*

81. Likewise, the petition of thirty-one citizens of Buncombe County, including three ministers, to permit W. B. Hammonds, a "free cullard man," to preach was rejected in 1840. The legislators were apparently unimpressed with the petitioners' assertion that Hammonds "keeps company with no Negroes and all his associations is with white people and no person that knows him doubts his sincerity as a religious carracter but with a consciousness of obeying the laws of his Country goes with his head bowed down like a bull rush loaded with a burden too intolerable to be born." Ms. in the Legislative Papers for 1840-1841.

82. In his speech supporting the proposal to disfranchise free Negroes in the Constitutional Convention of 1835, Mr. Crudup of Granville admitted that "there were many individuals amongst the free people of color, who were virtuous and exemplary in their

edgment of the differences that must have existed among the free Negroes. Thus, they were all thrown into the same morass together, to sink or swim out of the mire that tended to hold back even the most able of them. Since they were forced to associate with each other, many free Negroes married within their own circle. Thomas Day of Milton[83] and Thomas Blacknall of Franklin[84] are examples of better known free Negroes who married free Negro women. There is no way of knowing the extent to which free Negroes married other free Negroes. The restrictions placed on their relations with individuals outside their group forced many of them to be content with their free Negro associates, even when they did not prefer them. The consequences of such forced associations were most unfortunate upon the development of a virile and energetic free Negro group.[85]

That some of the free Negroes objected vigorously to the limited opportunities afforded them for social intercourse is seen in the remarks that some of them made regarding their fellows. Julius Melbourn, who had been exposed to the best that white society could offer, described his fellow free Negroes in the most disparaging language. In the story of his own life, he said,

> The manners of this latter class [the free Negroes] were rude and vulgar, and most of them were licentious and vicious in their habits.[86]

Since social and intellectual development depends, in a large measure, on the contact of a particular group with forces and personalities outside the group, it is not surprising that many free Negroes sought contact with other social or racial groups. They may not have been conscious of the general stagnation and debility that would have resulted from any attempt at self-sufficiency. Perhaps they were attracted to other groups because of the fascination that many individuals experience merely from contact with things unfamiliar. Perhaps they

conduct; but he did not think it would be good policy to attempt to draw a line of distinction amongst them." *Proceedings of the Convention of 1835*, p. 75.

83. *Cf. supra*, p. 45.   84. Seawell, *Law Tales*, p. 211.

85. Browning says that free Negroes of ante-bellum North Carolina indulged in inbreeding "to an appalling extent. Marriage bonds reveal the following typical cases: The marriage of Robert Chavis and Greezy Chavis in 1852, Sewall Chavis and Sarah Chavis in 1855, and Daniel Chavis and Emily Chavis in the same year." He then comments, "Naturally this practice tended to produce a low type of mentality, and doubtless it is at least a partial explanation of why some of the children of once wealthy and intelligent free people of color no longer play a vital part in Negro life." Browning, "Free Negro," *loc. cit.*, p. 33.

86. Melbourn, *Life*, p. 19.

sought association with slaves and white persons because of the restrictive legislation which gave these groups the appearance of forbidden
fruit. At any rate, free Negroes were never content with the social
intercourse that was afforded by their own group and were continuously seeking contact with slaves and white persons.

The white citizens of North Carolina, in their erection of the "Free
Negro Code," built a social wall around the free Negroes over which
it was most difficult to climb. They were not so much concerned with
the restriction of the free Negroes as they were with the peace and
contentment of their slaves. The wall was essentially for the purpose of
protecting the slave population from the "evil and insidious influences"
of the free Negro population. In this effort, they performed a distinct
disservice to the social development of the free Negro in North
Carolina.

In regulating the relationships between slaves and free Negroes, the
citizens of North Carolina displayed clearly their attitude toward the
free Negro population. In 1787 the General Assembly passed an act
which provided that if a free Negro married a slave without the written permission of the master, "he shall be liable and held to pay to
the master or mistress of such slave the sum of ten pounds; and on
failing to pay such sum, shall be held to service to the master or
mistress . . . for and during the term of one year."[87] Thus, the responsibility for bringing about such a relationship was placed squarely
upon the shoulders of the free Negro; and the penalty was so considerable as to discourage an infraction of the law.

After the act of 1787 was passed, many free Negroes married
slaves.[88] The first wife of Thomas Blacknall was a slave. The efforts
of free Negro husbands to secure the manumission of their slave wives
disclose the fact that the act did not prevent such unions.[89] The records
do not show that there were flagrant violations of the requirement that
a free Negro must secure the written permission of the master before
marrying the slave. It seems that before the militant period of the
antislavery movement began, white masters were not vigorously opposed to the marriage of their slaves to free Negroes in certain cases.
In some instances, the master would have the opportunity to secure
the labor of the free Negro without assuming the heavy responsibilities
that went with the ownership of slaves. Nor was such a relationship

87. Clark, *State Records*, XXIV, 891.
88. For example, Thomas Newton married Sarah, the property of John Devereaux,
in 1811. County Records of Craven County for 1811.
89. *Cf. supra*, pp. 29 ff.

unattractive to the free Negro man. He could enjoy the bliss of the marital state without having to provide a home and food for his wife, since that was furnished by the master.[90]

After the *Appeal* of David Walker aroused the citizens of North Carolina to the possibility of a great slave-free Negro uprising, the marital relations of slaves and free Negroes were further restricted. In 1830 the General Assembly passed a law which prevented free Negroes from marrying slaves altogether. In part, the law provided,

> That it shall not be lawful for any free Negro or free person of color to intermarry, or cohabit and live together as man and wife, with any slave; and any free negro or person of color, so intermarrying, or cohabiting or living as man and wife with a slave, shall be liable to indictment, and, upon conviction, shall be fined and imprisoned or whipped at the discretion of the court. . . .[91]

Thus, free Negroes were prevented from marrying outside their relatively small group. The silence of the court records on this matter is quite suggestive. It is difficult to believe that all free Negroes observed this law to the letter. One is inclined to believe, moreover, that this law was never rigidly enforced. The question of marriage to a slave would hardly have arisen between a free Negro and a master unless the free Negro and the white person were fairly well acquainted. This acquaintance may have developed into friendship as a result of an employer-employee or a landlord-tenant relationship. Under such circumstances, it would be difficult to convince the master that this particular marriage was not quite all right. If this possibility is multiplied scores of times throughout North Carolina between 1830 and 1860, one can see how the law of 1830 may have proved ineffective.[92]

There were several other areas in which the relationships between slaves and free Negroes were carefully regulated. In 1785, the General Assembly passed a law which provided that if a free Negro was convicted of a felonious crime with a slave, or received stolen goods from a slave, or harbored a runaway slave in his house, he was to pay ten pounds to the town in which he resided.[93] Upon conviction the free

90. *Cf.* Woodson, *Free Negro Heads of Families,* liv, lvi.

91. *Revised Statutes,* I, 590.

92. It will be remembered, moreover, that marriage involving a slave did not need the sanction of the State, since slaves were not capable before the law of entering into a contract. In view of this fact, many slaves and free Negroes may have simply agreed to live together without going through the formalities of a marriage ceremony.

93. It is interesting to observe that the law did not mention free Negro offenders who may have lived in rural areas—where the majority of the free Negroes lived. Perhaps it was only the urban free Negro that made trouble in these matters.

Negro had to make a promise that he would not reside in the town or within ten miles of the town after ten days had elapsed.[94]

In 1787, the law was extended to cover various social relationships between slaves and free Negroes that may or may not have been harmful in a political or economic sense. The law provided,

> That if any free negro or Mulatto shall entertain any slave in his or her house during the Sabbath, or in the night between sun-set and sun rise, he or she shall . . . be subject to a fine of twenty shillings for the first offence, and forty shillings for every subsequent offence. . . .[95]

The social restrictions in this act were far-reaching in their effect. It is difficult to understand why North Carolina saw fit to pass such a law as early as 1787. The free Negro population had given the State no trouble at all, and it was still too small to be formidable in any state-wide insurrectionary movement. The law, it seems, simply suggests the extreme caution with which the citizens of the State dealt with their free Negro population and the distrust with which individual slave owners viewed the slaves which belonged to others.

In 1794 the General Assembly passed another act which further regulated the association of free Negroes and slaves. This time it forbade masters to give permission to slaves or free Negroes to have other Negroes on the plantation "for the purpose of drinking, or dancing, under the penalty of forfeiting twenty dollars, on conviction of such offence."[96] The laws of 1787 and 1794 worked a real hardship on the free Negroes of North Carolina, since they relied rather heavily on the visits to slave cabins for recreation and social contact. This was especially true of the free Negro of the lower economic and social level, who did not feel superior to the slave.

In 1826 the General Assembly passed an act aimed at destroying any economic relationships that may have existed between slaves and free Negroes. The act enumerated a large number of articles which it forbade free Negroes to receive from slaves without written permission from the masters of the slaves. Among the articles were cotton, tobacco, wheat, rice, oats, corn, rye, pork, bacon, beef, leather, raw hides, iron, castings, farming utensils, nails, meal, flour, spirituous liquor or wine, peas, salt, fish, flax, flaxseed, hogs, cattle, sheep, wool, lumber, staves, tar, pitch, turpentine, fodder, shingles, hoops, white oak heading, and potatoes.[97] Any free Negro so offending was to be "prose-

---

94. Clark, *State Records*, XXIV, 728.
95. *Ibid.*, XXIV, 891.   96. *Revised Statutes*, I, 580.
97. *Laws, 1826-1830*, p. 7. In 1845 a free Negro sought to test the constitutionality

cuted in the County or Superior Court and on conviction, shall receive not exceeding thirty-nine lashes on his or her bare back."[98] Obviously, this law was for the purpose of preventing any trading between slaves and free Negroes and thereby to discourage slaves from stealing from their masters.

In 1827 a law was passed which provided that if any free Negro was found guilty of selling, bartering, or delivering to a slave "any fire-arms, powder, shot, or lead, except by the order of the owner or manager of such slave," he may be prosecuted by indictment in the county or superior court, and upon conviction was to receive thirty-nine lashes on his bare back.[99] In 1830 the Legislature passed the following act,

> Be it . . . enacted, That it shall not be lawful for any white person or free negro or mulatto, or person of mixed blood . . . to play at any game of cards, dice, nine pins, or any game of chance or hazard whether for money, liquor or property, or not, with any slave or slaves. . . .[100]

The law further forbade whites and free Negroes to permit slaves to game on the premises of whites or free Negroes.[101] While the law was obviously for the purpose of preventing the demoralization of the slave population by anyone, regardless of race, it meant that even free Negroes who may have had the best of intentions were prevented from indulging in innocent games with their slave friends.[102]

The laws regulating the relationships between slaves and free Negroes were, therefore, of two kinds: those which sought to protect the property of the master and those which sought to prevent a demoralization of the slave population through contact with free persons. One may suggest that the first group of laws was justified in view of the poor economic circumstances under which the bulk of the free Negro population existed. The fields of corn and wheat and the gardens and orchards of fresh vegetables and fruits must have been tempting to

---

of the law. Having been found guilty in the County Court of Granville of buying a peck of corn from a slave, Lewis, the property of Fleming Beasley, Cozens, the free Negro, sought to have the judgment arrested. Judge Nash of the Supreme Court said that the Court could see no reason why the judgment should be arrested, since it was a clear violation of a valid act of the Legislature. State v. Cozens, 28 N. C., 69-70.

98. *Laws, 1826-1830,* p. 8. In 1833 the list of "enumerated articles" was enlarged to include mutton, cloth, woolen yarn, wearing apparel, and gold and silver bullion. *Laws, 1833-1834,* p. 38.   99. *Laws, 1825-1830,* p. 19.

100. *Laws, 1823-1831,* p. 14.   101. *Ibid.,* p. 15.

102. The town of Raleigh had its own ordinance which prohibited free Negroes (and not whites) from gaming with slaves. Free Negroes found guilty of gaming with slaves were to be fined not less than four dollars and not more than twenty-five dollars. *Raleigh Ordinances of 1854,* p. 64.

many a hungry free Negro. In his effort to prevent pilfering by free Negroes, however, the plantation owner seemed to have overlooked a much more dangerous threat to his ripened fields. There were many more whites throughout North Carolina than there were free Negroes who were in need of all the products raised on the plantation.[103] It is quite difficult to believe that their respect for law and order restrained them from bargaining with slaves for these necessaries of life. Upon failing to secure them from the slaves, they may even have been equal to the task of obtaining them directly—under the cover of night.

With regard to the laws which sought to break the lines of communication between the slaves and free Negroes and thereby insure a continued peaceful existence of the peculiar institution, it may be said that the whites of North Carolina had even less justification. It has already been suggested that the activities of the free Negro were never a dangerous threat to the slave system in North Carolina.[104] In view of this observation which seems indisputable, the white citizens displayed little humanity or wisdom in dealing with the social and economic aspects of the free Negro problem. The free Negro's opportunities for social contact were so meager that dancing, drinking, gaming, and the like were important factors in his social life.

If the free Negro could not participate in whatever normal outlets he could find, his opportunities for social contact were appreciably reduced. These activities were as important to the free Negro as the elaborate spring balls were to the white elite or the camp meetings to the rural elements. Without these opportunities, he was likely to be completely frustrated. So often, a group which suffers legal and economic disadvantages may find compensation in recreational and social outlet. The free Negro had fewer and fewer of these opportunities as the period neared its close. He was confined to his own small and not too select group. By thus reducing the orb in which the free Negro could act and removing the valves of reasonable social expression, the whites of ante-bellum North Carolina paved the way for the development of a restless and frustrated element in the population which contributed a disproportionate number of the crimes committed in the latter portion of the period.[105]

In his relationship with whites, the free Negro found that there were numerous restrictions, legal and extralegal. Among the earliest restrictions were those which prevented a free Negro from marrying a white person. These restrictions have already been treated in an

103. Cf. Johnson, Ante-bellum North Carolina, pp. 67-73.
104. Cf. supra, pp. 73 ff.   105. Cf. supra, p. 95.

earlier chapter.[106] It is sufficient here merely to say that despite the legislation that was passed from time to time during the period, intermarrying continued. The large mulatto element in the free Negro population of the state is the best proof of the determination to evade the law.[107]

The most effective restrictions on the relationships between the free Negroes and the whites were in the form of unwritten agreements among the white citizens that their open contact with free Negroes should be as little as possible. Of course, there were numerous exceptions to this tacit rule;[108] but these, like most exceptions, did not do very much to break down the generality. Undoubtedly, the practice of apprenticing free Negroes to white masters had the effect of developing strong friendships between some whites and free Negroes. The manumission of slaves by benevolent masters, moreover, placed in the free Negro population some individuals who could count on the friendship of their former masters. The attitude of the white population in general, however, was that the free Negro population was a degraded and despised element in the society of North Carolina; and, as such, it had no place in the ordinary relationships among human beings.[109]

The economic, legal, and social disadvantages under which the free Negroes of North Carolina existed were reflected in their conduct from day to day and in their feeble efforts to accommodate themselves to their assigned status in society. Because of their economic plight, they suffered from inadequate housing,[110] insufficient diet, and consequently poor health. A glance at the reports on the causes of deaths among free Negroes in 1860 will suggest a number of inadequacies in the social life of the free Negro. Of the seven free Negroes who had died in Cumberland County in the previous year, four were less than one year old and all were less than thirty-five. Some of these deaths were caused by consumption, typhoid fever, and croup.[111] Three of the four free Ne-

---

106. *Cf. supra,* pp. 35 ff.

107. It is not contended that the entire mulatto element is the result of the intermarriage of whites and free Negroes. A part of it, however, is the result of such relationships.

108. For example, Lewis Sheridan, of Bladen County, had numerous business contacts with white persons in and out of the State. *Cf. supra,* pp. 35 ff. John Chavis was intimately acquainted with a large number of white citizens in and near Raleigh.

109. *Cf. infra,* Chapter VI on "An Unwanted People."

110. In describing the housing of free Negro farmers, David Dodge says "they built flimsy log huts, travesties in every respect of the rude dwellings of the earliest white settlers." David Dodge, "Free Negroes of North Carolina," *Atlantic Monthly,* LVII (January, 1886), 24. See also E. Franklin Frazier, *The Negro Family in the United States,* pp. 208-212.

111. Population schedules of the eighth census, Vol. 11.

groes who died in Edgecombe County were under fourteen years of age and were victims of "diareah."[112] These unfortunate conditions will go far in explaining infanticide,[113] desertion,[114] and crime among the free Negro population.[115]

Thousands of free Negroes were not conscious of their peculiarly degraded condition, while others were not extremely disturbed about it. The conduct of free Negroes at the time that Fayetteville was burned was so exemplary that it received special commendation. In an extra edition of the *Observer,* the editor said:

> The slaves and other colored population deserve great credit for their conduct on that eventful day. There was nothing like riot or disorder among them, but they all seemed to work with a zeal and intrepidity which manifested a hearty sympathy in the common cause....[116]

In such conduct one cannot find a manifestation of discontent or disloyalty. Even in their degraded status it seems that the free Negroes felt that they had a stake in the life and development of North Carolina.

Nor did all free Negroes suffer legal, economic, and social privations of a serious nature. There was a considerable number of Thomas Days, John Stanlys, and James Sampsons. Among this element of the free Negro population were individuals who were not only satisfied with their own position but with the general structure of North Carolina society as well. That these, as well as many below their level, met with some degree of success in making their adjustment can be seen in a letter written by a prominent New Bern citizen in 1854:

> The displays made by them [the free Negroes] on Sunday is perfectly astounding. They dress elegantly and have taken the Episcopal Church. The pastor has a tremendous Sunday School of the Negro Elite.... There are a large number of our young men and several of our merchants who have negro wives or "misses" and keep them openly, raising up families of mullatoes. The depravity

---

112. *Ibid.,* Vol. 16.

113. In 1826 Nancy Quin, a free Negro, was before the New Bern Superior Court on a charge of infanticide. The verdict of the jury was not reported in the newspaper. Raleigh *Register,* May 9, 1826.

114. Among the many desertions of free Negro husbands, that of Ephraim Haithcock is perhaps typical. In 1854 his children were bound to Jesse McDaniel because he had deserted his family. Minutes of the Court of Pleas and Quarter Sessions for Alamance County, 1854.

115. *Cf. supra,* pp. 95 ff.

116. *Fayetteville Observer,* June 3, 1831.

of the place is becoming shocking and our preachers may preach forever and they will produce no change.[117]

Even if the above description is not typical of the conduct of free Negroes in other parts of the State, it is interesting that so many were integrating themselves into the social life of the State as to evoke concern from so important a person as Attorney J. W. Bryan. While the same thing was occurring in other parts of the State, the more typical picture would be one which contained free Negroes reacting to their status in various ways. There were free Negroes who struggled against innumerable odds with some degree of success. Their very success evoked sufficient comment to make it possible for the student of the period to learn of their struggles and successes. Then there were those who sought in vain to improve their condition, but the tide of community disfavor was so strong against them that it was impossible for them to attain any notable degree of success. Finally, there were those who resigned themselves to their anomalous and degraded status and in their existence reflected all the limitations to which they were subjected. Their criminality and their general backwardness tell the story more vividly than words can describe of a people whose maladjustment was a state of existence imposed upon them by a society whose general attitude toward them was one of contempt, disdain, and reprehension. The onus for their inability to rise intellectually, socially, and economically must be placed, to a considerable extent at least, upon the shoulders of those who dominated the society in which the free Negroes lived.

117. The John H. Bryan Papers. J. W. Bryan to J. H. Bryan, June 7, 1854.

CHAPTER VI

An Unwanted People

We hear but one opinion expressed, not only by the press of our State, but by every one with whom we converse, in respect to free negroes. All are unanimous in the opinion that the approaching Legislature ought to pass an act to remove them beyond the limits of the State . . . we know the humanity of North Carolinians, and we know that all imaginable leniency will be exercised by the legislature in making arrangements for their speedy removal. Let the North have them. And let their curses rest upon the North, because of their removal from a land flowing with milk and honey to a land where they can scarcely procure the necessaries of life. On the heads of the Northern fanatics rests the responsibility.

> *Goldsboro Patriot*, reprinted in the
> *North Carolina Standard*, Nov. 20, 1850.

America is more our country than it is the whites—we have enriched it with our *blood & tears* . . . and they will drive us from our property and homes, which we have earned with our *blood*.

> David Walker, *Appeal in Four Articles*—
> Article II, "Our Wretchedness in Consequence
> of the Colonizing Plan."

North Carolina "Liberalism"

A CASUAL OBSERVER of ante-bellum North Carolina would doubtless have concluded that the State, as a whole, displayed a rather liberal attitude in its treatment of the free Negro. Though it is clear to the student of the period that a careful observation would have induced a more qualified conclusion, such an observation is quite understandable. One student has suggested that the agrarian philosophy of Jefferson, which dominated the thought of the State between 1789 and 1816, may have affected the point of view of the citizens on many social and political questions.[1] If this is true, there can be little doubt that it found some manifestations—unconscious, perhaps—in the attitude that was developed toward free Negroes in the early period.

In the matter of restrictive legislation concerning free Negroes, North Carolina lagged behind most of the Southern states. It will be remembered that North Carolina was the last State in the South to

1. D. H. Gilpatrick, *Jeffersonian Democracy in North Carolina, 1789-1816, passim.*

disfranchise free Negroes.[2] As early as 1805, Virginia prohibited Negroes from carrying arms without a license,[3] while North Carolina did not pass such a law until 1840.[4] Virginia excluded free Negroes as bearers of arms in the militia in 1757;[5] not until 1812 were they excluded from the North Carolina militia. In 1810, the Georgia Legislature passed a law requiring that all free Negroes in the State should have white guardians.[6] North Carolina never passed such a law. South Carolina's law forbidding free Negroes to enter the State was passed in 1821.[7] Virginia had such a law as early as 1793,[8] while North Carolina's exclusion law was not passed until 1827.[9] Likewise, in other legislation affecting the free Negro, North Carolina lagged behind the other states of the South.[10]

The press of the State was not unaware of the five- to fifty-year lag of North Carolina in the matter of free Negro legislation. It maintained a strict vigilance of the attitude of other states toward the free Negro as reflected in their legislation and told its readers of the changes that were going on from time to time. On occasion, they pointed out how other states, North and South, were taking steps to rid themselves of this portion of the population. Thus, the law of South Carolina which prevented free Negroes from coming into the State was described by the liberal *Raleigh Register* as an "accomplishment."[11] In 1822, when Massachusetts was considering a bill to exclude free Negroes, the deliberations were fully reported in the *Register*.[12]

The manner in which the harsh treatment of free Negroes in other states was reported in North Carolina seems to suggest two things. In the first place, the press was indulging in a bit of praise for the State in showing how much more harshly free Negroes were treated elsewhere. In the second place, however, there was a subtle warning that the people of North Carolina should consider even more seriously the presence of the free Negro and take greater steps to prevent his becoming an active menace. When the *Indiana Farmer* made a vigorous protest against the presence of free Negroes within the State and re-

2. Cf. *supra*, p. 116.
3. Shepherd, *Statutes of Virginia*, III, 274.
4. Cf. *supra*, p. 76.   5. Henning, *Statutes at Large*, V, 17.
6. Hurd, *Law of Freedom and Bondage*, II, 102.
7. *Raleigh Register*, January 26, 1821.
8. Shepherd, *Statutes*, I, 239.   9. Cf. *supra*, p. 43.
10. Compare the time and the severity of the enactments of North Carolina with those of other Southern states in connection with peddling, the use of spirituous liquors, and gaming with slaves. No instance has come to the attention of the writer of North Carolina's ever taking the lead in free Negro legislation.
11. *Raleigh Register*, January 26, 1821.   12. *Raleigh Register*, July 6, 1822.

quested that something be done to prevent their increase, the *Carolina Observer* reprinted the article in full.[13] It was with a note of triumph that the *North Carolina Standard* told how a North Carolina free Negro was happy to return to his native State when he found how his people were treated in Ohio.[14] The Wadesboro *Argus,* the editor of which tried to dissuade the free Negro from going, remarked that there was something rather strange about a "spurious philanthropy that can open its arms to a runaway slave—the property of a neighbor, but cannot treat with common humanity the same class of men when they happen to be legally free!"[15]

It was not long before the *Standard* made clear its position on the free Negro problem. One week after it told of the haste with which the free Negro immigrant to Ohio returned to North Carolina, the *Standard* carried an editorial in which the remark was made that some plan should be devised to prevent the increase of free Negroes and ultimately to remove them entirely from the State. The editor said that, although there were some respectable free Negroes in the State, they would have to leave too, since any such law would of necessity be a general one. To support his point of view, the editor cited the actions of states in the North and in the South that were ridding themselves of this class through restrictive legislation. In conclusion he said,

A friend at our elbow suggests that nothing would please him better than to see every free colored person in this state taken up bodily, and set down in the old-fashioned, *law-and-order* State of Massachusetts. Such an event would create a delectable stir among the descendants of the Puritans. It might serve to cool their affection for fugitive slaves, and incline them to restore the stolen property of the Southern people.[16]

Thus, the articulate element in North Carolina was conscious of the fact that it was lagging behind the other states in the enactment of harsh legislation affecting free Negroes. The State had by no means been idle in the matter, for it had erected a Free Negro Code that touched on almost every aspect of the lives of this despised element. But during the early years of the nineteenth century, the State was far behind its neighbors in the setting up of a Free Negro Code; and in the last thirty years of the period it displayed only a slight and spasmodic inclination to pass additional laws concerning the free Negro

13. *Carolina Observer* (Fayetteville), August 2, 1826.
14. *North Carolina Standard,* October 30, 1850.
15. Reprinted in the *Raleigh Standard,* October 30, 1850.
16. *Raleigh Standard,* November 6, 1850.

even when the hostility toward him was increasing in every part of the South. From the point of view of the North Carolina Legislators, their Free Negro Code was almost complete.

If the editors of the North Carolina newspapers had reason to be disturbed in the lag of their State behind others in the matter of free Negro legislation, they had even more reason for alarm over the way in which existing legislation was enforced. The laxity of law enforcement in North Carolina was widely known, even among free Negroes. The free Negro who talked with Olmsted in South Carolina spoke of the lax enforcement of the laws in North Carolina in comparison with those of South Carolina.[17] Booker T. Washington said that, despite the restrictive legislation in North Carolina, "conditions were more lenient than those of any other Southern state. The result was that many free Negroes crossed into North Carolina and settled, undisturbed, in the northern and southern counties."[18]

Governor Stokes had reference to the lax enforcement of the Free Negro Code in North Carolina when he told the General Assembly in 1831 that there was no need of multiplying the laws affecting the free Negro. He suggested that a more efficient and accountable police, assisted by companies of paid volunteers and detached militia, would accomplish more than additional legislation in controlling the free Negroes.[19] In 1850 the *North Carolina Standard* called for a more rigid enforcement of the Free Negro Code.[20] In 1854 the New Bern *Atlantic* called the attention of the community and the Grand Jury to the flagrant violation of the law by slaves and free Negroes.[21] Apparently, the laws were attended by such lax enforcement that they were of no effect at all, in many instances.

It is difficult to measure the effect which lax enforcement of the law had on the attitude of free Negroes toward law and order. There can be little doubt that since the feeling was abroad that many of the laws went unenforced, free Negroes easily yielded to the temptation to violate them. Only in those areas where an efficient patrol was maintained were free Negroes regularly chastised for their unbecoming conduct. This lax enforcement explains, in part at least, the prevalence of drunkenness and thievishness among the free Negro population.

17. Olmsted, *Seaboard Slave States*, I, 210.

18. Booker T. Washington, "The Free Negro in Slavery Days," *The Outlook*, XCIII (September 18, 1909), 109-110; cf. *supra*, p. 42, and Bassett, *Slavery in the State of North Carolina*, p. 45.

19. *Journal of the House, 1831-1832*, p. 145.

20. The *North Carolina Standard*, November 6, 1850.

21. Newbern *Atlantic*, October 25, 1854.

The demoralization of law and order was far-reaching; for them, as always, a law flagrantly violated was no longer a law.

The lag of North Carolina behind other states in enacting free Negro laws and the lax enforcement of the existing laws was not due altogether to any peculiar liberalism in the social philosophy of the people. It is true that the presence of the Quakers in large numbers and the work of manumission societies may have done a great deal in ameliorating the conditions among free Negroes. The search for a more adequate explanation for these conditions, however, will carry one much deeper into an examination of the economic and social pattern of the State.

It was on large plantations that an impersonal relationship developed between the master and the slave which, in turn, led to suspicion, distrust, and rigorous discipline. In such circumstances, the plantation owners clamored for and secured legislation which established black codes of extreme severity. In areas where a number of plantations had more than, say, fifty slaves, there was likely to develop a morbid fear of conspiracy and insurrections that demanded not only harsh legislation but also a rigid enforcement of the existing laws. The economy of North Carolina, however, was one of small farms. One authority points out that "the prevailing system of slavery in the State was that of close relationship between master and slave, for of the total slaveholders fully sixty-seven per cent worked side by side with their slaves."[22] In such an economy, it was easy for the master to feel that he had his own problems of discipline well in hand. He knew his slaves and was fully apprised, he felt, of their various social relationships. The result was that he was often tolerant of his own slaves; and the only fear that he entertained was that of his neighbors' slaves whom he did not know as intimately as he knew his own. Under these circumstances it is not difficult to conceive of a situation in which many slave owners refused to enforce the law in regard to their own slaves, which resulted in general laxity over a large area.

The general economic development of the State may have had a great deal to do with the enactment and enforcement of free Negro legislation. In the 1820's, when the State was experiencing a severe economic depression, the resulting worry and pessimism made the citizens more sensitive to disturbing factors such as the Vermont Resolution denouncing slavery and David Walker's *Appeal*. Consequently, on such occasions there was some degree of congeniality to more severe treatment of the free Negro. In the later period, however, the economy

22. Johnson, *Ante-bellum North Carolina*, p. 492.

of North Carolina was undergoing a transition. The size of farms was decreasing and the number of farms was increasing.[23] This was followed by a trend toward improved and diversified farming. The effort of the agricultural element to adjust itself to the changing conditions led to some degree of bewilderment and indecision as to the place of the free Negro in the changing economy. After the wave of fear that following the Nat Turner insurrection had subsided there was a noticeable relaxation in the enforcement of the Free Negro Code. Gradually, as the adjustment neared completion, there developed the feeling that the free Negro had no place at all in the social and economic life of North Carolina, and the sooner the State was rid of him the better.

At no time during the period was the patrol system a satisfactory method of enforcing the laws affecting the slaves and free Negroes. Both slaveholders and non-slaveholders were inclined to consider patrol work onerous. Although the patrol laws were strengthened from time to time, there were numerous complaints during the period of the inadequacy of the system and the negligence of the patrollers. In 1802 a citizen complained that the commissioners of Raleigh did not "appoint a sufficient number of patrollers so as to patrole the streets every night."[24] In 1850 a correspondent of the *North Carolina Standard* declared that the county courts did not appoint patrols and those that were appointed were faithless.[25] As late as 1860, a petition to the Legislature criticized the patrol system as "unpaid and inefficient."[26] With such an inadequate system of law enforcement, it is not difficult to understand that the Free Negro Code of North Carolina frequently went unenforced.

The small farmer constituted the largest element in the white population of ante-bellum North Carolina. The larger portion of this class cultivated its own land, with the help of its families and an occasional hired hand during the rush periods. Since these yeomen were engaged in a considerable amount of diversified farming which made them less dependent on the outside world than the large slaveholders,[27] they

23. Taylor, *Slaveholding in North Carolina*, p. 47.
24. *Raleigh Register*, May 4, 1802.
25. *North Carolina Standard*, November 2, 1850.
26. Quoted in Johnson, *Ante-bellum North Carolina*, p. 517.
27. Observe the remark made by Charles Fisher of Rowan County in 1828: "Many of our citizens in the eastern part of the state for several years past have been in the practice of purchasing flour made in the North and feeding their negroes with pork shipped from New York, while every fall droves of Tennessee and Kentucky hogs are sold in the Southern and Middle counties," quoted in Taylor, *Slaveholding in North Carolina*, p. 36. Compare this with the plentiful supply on a Wake County yeoman's farm described in Johnson, *Ante-bellum North Carolina*, p. 66.

were not as hard hit by the competition with the large plantations as were the yeomen of the states of the lower South, where the one-crop system prevailed. This trend toward self-sufficiency on the part of the North Carolina yeoman had the effect of decreasing his interests in the problems which more directly affected the slaveholding and urban population. It stands to reason, therefore, that from lack of interest the free Negro was not a special object of the yeoman's displeasure.

The rural nature of the bulk of the North Carolina population also had the effect of softening the treatment of the free Negro. Public opinion has, for centuries, been an important factor in the formation of policies with regard to various public questions. In ante-bellum North Carolina, however, such a large portion of the population lived in rural areas, where articulation was particularly poor, that it was most difficult to ascertain the attitude of the public toward a specific problem. The newspapers of the period contain little material that reveals the attitude of the great rural population toward the free Negro. There were mass meetings at the county seats to endorse or denounce candidates for public office.[28] Now and then, a North Carolina rustic would express his views in a letter to the editor of his county paper; but nowhere is there any evidence of extensive articulation on the part of the rural element. Regardless of what the attitude of the major portion of the white population was toward the free Negro, it was not freely expressed in the press and on the platform of ante-bellum North Carolina. In the absence of any crystallized opinion from this element, there were large areas in the State—predominantly rural—where enforcement of the laws affecting free Negroes was altogether lacking in uniformity; and often, there was no enforcement at all.

Despite the fact that the State lagged behind other states in the enactment and enforcement of a harsh Free Negro Code, there was a growing feeling against the very presence of the free Negro. The feeling was the product, for the most part, of urban agitation. Though the towns contained only a small percentage of the total free Negro population of the State, they were the only places where the free Negroes were seen in sufficiently large numbers to cause much concern. During the last forty years of the period this concern was manifested in two ways. First, there was the desire of some whites to send free Negroes to Africa, where they would have better opportunities to develop into self-respecting human beings. Secondly, there was the inclination of many to rid the State of this group because of its undesirability. Though these two groups differed in their professed motives, the effect

28. See for examples the newspapers of the State for October, 1828, or October, 1836.

was the same: that of removing the "unwanted people" from North Carolina.

THE COLONIZATION MOVEMENT

The manner in which the colonization movement was received in North Carolina and the character of leadership in its local units are suggestive not only of the attitude of the State toward slavery but are also indicative of the extent to which there was sentiment against the presence of the free Negro. On June 12, 1819, the Reverend William Meade, agent for the American Colonization Society, organized a branch of the Society in Raleigh. It was known as the "Raleigh Auxiliary Society for the Colonization of Free People of Colour of the United States." Governor John Branch was elected president, and Joseph Gales, editor of the *Raleigh Register*, was elected Secretary. Among the managers were some of Raleigh's most influential citizens, John Haywood, Archibald Henderson, T. P. Devereaux, Dr. A. S. H. Burges, and the Reverend William McPheeters.[29] Concerning the organization of the Raleigh branch, the Reverend Mr. Meade said in his report,

> The Supreme Court being in session, many of the judges and lawyers were collected from different parts of the state, who cordially joined the Society, and testified to the general prevalence of good will to it throughout the State. At a meeting for forming the constitution, the highest talents, authorities, and wealth of the state were present and unanimously sanctioned the measure.[30]

In addition to the Raleigh Auxiliary several other branches were set up in the State. In the same year, the Reverend Mr. Meade set up a large organization in Fayetteville, where he had only to go to the homes of the citizens and take down their names.[31] At Chapel Hill he found an organization already flourishing.[32] Within a few years, there were five auxiliaries in North Carolina, and by 1829 there were eleven such organizations.[33] There is small wonder that the Reverend Mr. Meade asserted that North Carolina was a fertile field for the colonization movement.[34]

The auxiliary societies in North Carolina were interested not only in having slaves emancipated and sent to colonies in Africa, but were

---

29. *Raleigh Register*, July 18, 1819.   30. *Raleigh Register*, July 2, 1819.
31. *Ibid*.   32. *Ibid*.

33. See the *Raleigh Register* for May 6, 1825, for an account of the organization of the auxiliary in Edenton.

34. *Raleigh Register*, July 2, 1819. In 1825, the Raleigh branch was still flourishing, with the same principal officers.

also desirous of sending Negroes, already free, to the distant land. In Fayetteville, the agent for the Colonization Society interviewed free Negroes and sought to interest them in going to Liberia. They expressed interest and said they would be desirous of going when the colony was well established. In his report Meade said,

> They proposed to me to let them publish the 2nd annual report I carried with me for the benefit of their brethren who were scattered through their State, and even offered to subscribe to the Society. I answered them that we had better publish a small pamphlet for their use; and if any of their brethren were poor and wanted to go, then they who were better off, might help them.[35]

In close coöperation with the American Colonization Society in its program were the Quakers, who had come to the conclusion that colonization was the best solution to the problem of the free Negro. In the Yearly Meeting of the Society of Friends of North Carolina for 1826, the following significant observation was made:

> It appears from the proceedings of our meeting for sufferings, as presented to this Meeting, that there have been conveyed to free governments since last year, about 300 of the people of colour under the care of this Yearly Meeting. . . . Upwards of 40 have been taken to Liberia; 119 to Hayti; 11 to Philadelphia; and the remainder to Ohio and Indiana.[36]

Quakers supported the proposal to the General Assembly in 1830 to establish a fund for the removal of free Negroes from the State of North Carolina. On December 23, the bill was read the first time and passed by the Senate.[37] When it was read the second time on January 5, 1831, Senator Williams of Franklin moved that the bill be indefinitely postponed. It was agreed to by a vote of 35 to 24.[38] The Quakers did not give up. In the following autumn, they outlined a plan for colonization to the General Assembly and asked the coöperation of that body. In part, they said,

> Your memorialists for many years past have viewed with pleasure the exertions of the Colonization Society and believe it is an institution which merits not only individual patronage, but is well worthy of the countenance and encouragement of the Legislature of this State. The Society has already established a flourishing colony from small beginnings and with very inadequate means,

35. *Raleigh Register*, July 2, 1819.
36. *African Repository*, II (1826), 288-289.
37. *Journal of the Senate, 1830-1831*, p. 83.
38. *Ibid.*, p. 135.

they have . . . mainly depended on individual benevolence for carrying into effect the objects of the Society. . . . Your memorialists very Respectfully submit to your consideration whether the interest of our State would not be essentially promoted by aiding the said Society in their benevolent exertions by annual donations or other pecuniary aid. . . . The Society of Friends have already removed to Liberia and elsewhere about seven hundred persons of colour at an expense of about Thirteen Thousand dollars, that they still have in different parts of the State about five hundred persons of colour who they intend to remove from the State in a short time. . . . Your memorialists believe if a Society comparatively few in number and with limitted means will be able to remove twelve hundred persons beyond the limits of the State it would be entirely practicable for the Citizens of the State through their representatives to effect the entire removal of the free persons of colour from this State in a few years.[39]

Though this appeal from the Yearly Meeting of the Society of Friends impressed some members of the Senate, it was laid on the table December 13, 1831. The Quakers continued to support the colonization movement after 1831, but there was little hope that they would ever secure the coöperation of the General Assembly.

Other religious and benevolent organizations of North Carolina supported the colonization movement. In Fayetteville, several such organizations held anniversary meetings in 1835 and published a pamphlet containing endorsements of the plan to send the free Negroes to Africa. At a meeting on March 20, the Reverend Dr. McPheeters offered the following resolution, which was carried:

Resolved, That the scheme of African colonization, under prudent management, commends itself to the patronage of philanthropists, and the prayers of the whole Christian community. And that, in the opinion of this meeting, the American Colonization Society, in the wise and vigorous prosecution of its legitimate object, is destined to prove a blessing to two continents, by promoting the civil, moral, and religious condition of their inhabitants respectively.[40]

The Presbyterians of the State seemed well-disposed toward colonization. In 1821 the Synod reported that three or four congregations had organized auxiliary societies.[41] As late as 1849, the Synod went on record as "affectionately commending the American Colonization So-

39. Ms. in the Legislative Papers for 1831-32.
40. African Repository, XI (1835), 280.
41. Raleigh Register, October 19, 1821.

ciety to all our churches and Christian denominations; to all philanthropists and patriots and to all citizens of North Carolina."[42]

In the following decade, the attitude toward colonization was not completely favorable. Despite the fact that after the Nat Turner insurrection contributions to the Society decreased noticeably,[43] the agent commented in 1840 that North Carolina was still well disposed to the colonization of the free Negro, and several masters were manumitting their slaves with a view to colonizing them in Africa.[44] By this time, however, the national organization had become involved in politics and as the result of the inefficient leadership and poor administration of the colonization program, the organization became discredited in many parts of the country.[45] Its prestige suffered greatly in these years in North Carolina. In the annual report of 1845 the observation was made that there was no state society in North Carolina and that for several years no agent had visited the State.[46] Before the end of the period it had regained some of its lost prestige in North Carolina, and many of its supporters had resumed their activities.[47]

The Supreme Court of North Carolina seemed to have been well-disposed toward the colonization movement. In two decisions involving the American Colonization Society, the highest tribunal of the State decided in favor of the Society. In 1839, John Rex of Raleigh died and left all his slaves free on condition that they go to Liberia under the care of the American Colonization Society.[48] The proceeds from the sale of slaves not desiring to go and from the sale of his property were to be placed in a fund to settle the former slaves in Africa. A residue, largely the proceeds from the sale of his stock in a tanning establishment, was to be used to endow a hospital for the poor in Raleigh. The commissioners of the city held that the proceeds from the sale of his slaves and his property would fall into the residue and could not be used for the benefit of his slaves. Judge William Gaston, speaking for the Court, held, however, that the whole fund was to be used for the removal and settlement of the slaves and none of it should fall into the residue. It further held that "the devise was good; was for a charitable purpose; and it is not against the policy of this State to permit the emancipation of slaves, provided they be removed and be kept removed out of the State."[49] In 1845 Chief Justice Ruffin reaf-

---

42. *African Repository*, XXV (1849), 27.   43. *Cf. infra*, Table VI.
44. Early Lee Fox, *The American Colonization Society, 1817-1846*, p. 188.
45. *Cf.* Fox, *American Colonization Society, passim.*
46. *African Repository*, XXII (1846), 39.
47. *Cf. infra*, p. 205.   48. *African Repository*, XV (1839), 79.
49. Cameron et al. v. The Commissioners of Raleigh, 36 N. C. 353 (June, 1841).

firmed the earlier opinion of Judge Gaston by holding that a bequest of slaves to the American Colonization Society was a valid bequest under the laws of North Carolina.[50]

The press was especially cordial to the idea of colonizing free Negroes out of North Carolina. The *Raleigh Register* led the press of the State in advocating the scheme. When the agent for the American Colonization Society arrived in Raleigh to organize an auxiliary, its editor declared, "We wish him success, as we believe the object is of great importance to this country."[51] At the first meeting the editor of the *Register,* Joseph Gales, was elected to the post of secretary,[52] an office which he held for more than six years.[53] The columns of the *Register* often contained favorable comments concerning the colonization movement, and, as the program got under way, it displayed even greater enthusiasm for the work of the Society than in earlier years.[54]

The *Carolina Observer* of Fayetteville was also enthusiastic over the plan for colonizing Negroes out of the State. In 1826 it told of the immigration of 119 free Negroes, under the care of the Quakers, to Haiti. There was no doubt concerning the attitude of the paper toward this expedition, for it closed the account with "Prosperity attend them!"[55] In 1853, the *Observer* published a long article instructing free Negroes how to make application for passage on a ship soon to embark for Liberia.[56]

The Raleigh *Star* published several items favorable to the colonization plan. In 1826 it said that it had information from Liberia which showed that "not an individual from North Carolina has suffered materially or in health, in consequence of migrating there. Most of them are building houses and cultivating their lands. . . ."[57] The *North Carolina Standard* was likewise favorably disposed toward the colonization scheme. In 1840 it spoke of the advisability of free Negroes emigrating from North Carolina to Trinidad. It described the island in glowing terms and offered to send pamphlets to interested persons.[58]

The influential leadership of the colonization movement in North Carolina and the support given it in the press had the effect of rallying to the cause a large number of people who manifested their interest by contributing to the fund for the emigration of Negroes from North

50. Cox v. Williams, 39 N. C. 11-12.   51. *Raleigh Register,* June 11, 1819.
52. *Raleigh Register,* June 18, 1819.   53. *Raleigh Register,* July 1, 1825.
54. See, for example, the issues for May 6, May 20, and July 1, 1825.
55. *Carolina Observer,* June 21, 1836.
56. *Carolina Observer,* March 7, 1853.
57. Raleigh *Star,* November 17, 1826.
58. *North Carolina Standard,* December 4, 1840.

Carolina. Among the donors were ministers and congregations of many denominations, the Society of Friends, temperance societies, benevolent associations, auxiliary societies, educational institutions, free Negroes, and other individuals from every walk of life. Table VI, a list of the total contributions by years, suggests that there was a great deal of fluctuation in the amount which North Carolinians contributed from year to year.

TABLE VI. CONTRIBUTIONS OF CITIZENS OF NORTH CAROLINA TO THE AMERICAN COLONIZATION SOCIETY[59]

Year	Amount	Year	Amount
1825	$214.00	1843	$ 29.26
1826	937.74	1844	29.00
1827	541.00	1845	334.14
1828	266.65	1846	.....
1829	468.31	1847	12.78
1830	116.00	1848	10.00
1831	242.00	1849	601.81
1832	93.00	1850	815.97
1833	26.00	1851	1,535.82
1834	5.50	1852	230.20
1835	18.00	1853	53.00
1836	55.55	1854	342.25
1837	388.60	1855	188.58
1838	48.87	1856	945.47
1839	391.55	1857	2,476.20
1840	1,910.44	1858	8,918.64
1841	226.14	1859	15.00
1842	182.06	1860	770.00
		Total	$23,439.53

The contributions of the first seven years represent, for the most part, the work of the members of the auxiliary societies at Raleigh, Elizabeth City, Hillsboro, Fayetteville, and Greensboro. The 1830's were lean for the reason that North Carolinians were in no mood to make contributions to the cause of the free Negro. The fear engendered by the Southampton insurrection divested the citizens of the benevolence which they displayed in the first years of the colonization movement.

The use of an agent to make collections—an innovation in North Carolina in 1840—had a favorable effect on the contributions from North Carolina. Whenever an agent was present in the State, the contributions were larger than in the other years.[60] Even without active

59. This table was compiled from statistics gathered from the first thirty-six volumes of the *African Repository,* covering the years 1825-1860.

60. See Appendix V for a list of the contributors and the amounts given.

auxiliary societies in the decade of the 1850's the contributions were, with the exception of three years, the largest of any decade. This conclusion is reached without considering the large contributions made to the American Colonization Society in 1857 and 1858 in the wills of masters who desired to have their slaves sent to Liberia.[61]

The auxiliary societies, which functioned well during the early years of the colonization movement, contributed more than $600. The churches of North Carolina contributed $777.46 to the Colonization Society. Of this amount, the Presbyterians and Methodists contributed the largest portions. At approximately 180 public meetings held in the interest of the colonization movement, $5,222 were raised. Two groups of individual contributors stand out. Fourteen slave owners of North Carolina left $13,846 to the American Colonization Society to transport their slaves out of the State.[62] Prominent also among the contributors were ministers, whose numerous small contributions amounted to $231.25.

By contributing $23,439 to the American Colonization Society, the citizens of North Carolina made it possible for 390 Negroes to go to Liberia and live for six months at no expense to themselves. While this made it possible for only a small fraction of the Negroes in North Carolina to be removed from the State, the contributions were significant. They indicated that several thousand citizens of the State were interested in the colonization scheme, and under the circumstances of greater wealth and of better management from the national organization, North Carolina would have gone much further in the direction of removing all of its free Negro population.

With the aid of the citizens of North Carolina, therefore, the American Colonization Society undertook to carry many Negroes from that State to its colonies in Africa. Thanks to finances and supplies from other sources, the society was able to send more than three times the number that was financed by the North Carolinians.[63] Between 1825 and 1860, the American Colonization Society sent 1,363 Negroes from North Carolina to Liberia.[64] In forty-two sailings, the Society sent Negroes from North Carolina ranging from one, as in the case of the

61. Appendix V.

62. This figure might have been larger had there not been so much opposition to such a disposition of an estate by relatives of the decedents. For example, in 1849 T. Capehart of Murfreesboro, North Carolina, left $3,000 to send sixty slaves to Liberia, but it was never listed in the contributions because litigation held it up until the end of the period. African Repository, XXV (December, 1849), 381.

63. The Fayetteville Observer, May 7, 1853, said, "The price of passage and six months' support in Liberia is sixty dollars for each one."

64. See the African Repository, XXXIII (1857), 155 and successive issues to 1860.

brig *Montgomery* in 1830, to 143, as in the case of the brig *Nautilus* in 1828.[65] In the number of Negro emigrants, North Carolina was surpassed in 1857 only by Virginia and Maryland, which had sent 3,315 and 1,500 respectively.[66]

The former slaves who went to Liberia from North Carolina came, for the most part, from the eastern part of the State. In 1825 the former slaves of David Patterson of Orange County sailed.[67] When the *Saluda* sailed October 16, 1841, it had four former slaves from Washington, North Carolina.[68] The former slaves of Thomas W. Lassiter of Halifax, North Carolina, sailed on November 5, 1845.[69] At other times, former slaves from Cumberland, Franklin, Pasquotank, Beaufort, and Perquimans counties sailed for Liberia.[70] Some of these slaves enjoyed accomplishments of which a free man would have been proud in ante-bellum North Carolina. Many were described as literate, industrious, and prudent. In one sailing of fifty-eight former slaves, there were fifteen farmers, two seamstresses, two washers, one cook, one shoemaker, and one coachman.[71] The free Negro population of North Carolina would have been substantially augmented if it could have received into its folds these and other former slaves of similar character.

The emigration of free Negroes from North Carolina under the auspices of the American Colonization Society is one of the most interesting aspects of this problem. That the Society was interested in the migration of Negroes, already free, as well as liberated slaves, can be seen in the efforts of the agent to contact prospective free Negro emigrants in Fayetteville in 1819 and in Wilmington in 1838.[72] This question arises: What was the attitude of the free Negro toward colonization? A leading authority on the free Negro in Maryland has suggested that "a great many, probably half, of the Negroes [of Maryland] were untouched by the appeals of the Society."[73] Indifference developed into opposition, and by 1851, when several worthy free Negroes were about to leave for Liberia, not a Negro church in the entire city of Baltimore was available to hold a service in their honor.[74]

65. *African Repository*, XXVII (1851), 149.
66. *African Repository*, XXXIII (1857), 155.
67. *Carolina Observer*, July 14, 1825.
68. *African Repository*, XVII (1841), 329.
69. *African Repository*, XXI (1845), 379.
70. See, for example, Volumes XXVI and XXVII of the *African Repository*.
71. *African Repository*, XXVI (1850), 104.
72. *Cf. supra*, p. 140.
73. Wright, *Free Negro in Maryland*, pp. 291-292.
74. *Ibid.*, p. 292.

It is difficult to ascertain the attitude of the free Negroes of the lower South toward colonization. Louis Mehlinger has wisely suggested that had free Negroes been opposed to colonization they would have been afraid to make known their views, because the movement was often promoted by leading white members of their community.[75] It seems, therefore, that the only way of ascertaining the attitude of the free Negro toward colonization is by observing the extent to which the movement received support from free Negroes. Although the Colonization Society of Mississippi was, as Professor C. S. Sydnor says, organized for the avowed and sole purpose of sending free Negroes to Africa,[76] relatively few migrated. The only considerable contingent of free Negroes to leave Mississippi for Africa were six who sailed on the *Rover* from New Orleans in 1835[77] and fifteen who went in 1860.[78] Professor Sydnor concludes:

> The total number of negroes to go to Liberia from Mississippi was about 571, which was approximately one twentieth of all the emigrants sent from the United States by the American Colonization Society and its auxiliaries. It is probable that at least 500 of these were slaves freed by their owners with the object of colonizing them.[79]

No opposition to the colonization movement was openly expressed by the free Negroes of North Carolina. One can be certain, of course, that there were many free Negroes who viewed settlement in a faraway land of which they knew very little as too great an undertaking in this life. Others, however, came to the same conclusion that Louis Sheridan reached: namely, that life for the free Negro in North Carolina was intolerable and that the prospect of full freedom and prosperity in a new land was well worth the risks involved. From time to time free Negroes left North Carolina of their own volition and sought happiness in the homeland of their ancestors.

When the brig *Nautilus* left Norfolk in 1827, there were 164 free born Negroes of North Carolina aboard, mainly from Wayne, Pasquotank, and Perquimans counties. The *Carolina Observer* remarked, "The good wishes of the people of this state attend them."[80] A decade later the *African Repository* sought to interest a philanthropist in col-

75. Louis R. Mehlinger, "Attitude of Free Negroes toward Colonization," *Journal of Negro History*, I (1916), 279.

76. Charles S. Sydnor, *Slavery in Mississippi*, p. 204. The constitution of the Society is printed on p. 206.
77. *Ibid.*, p. 220.
78. *Ibid.*, p. 231.
79. *Ibid.*, p. 231.
80. *Carolina Observer*, December 27, 1827.

onizing a free Negro family of North Carolina. A part of the appeal read,

> A free coloured man of excellent character, residing in North Carolina, is desirous of emigrating to Liberia. His wife and six children would accompany him; and he has two married daughters, who, with their husbands, wish to go with him. He has but little property, and none of it could be spared to aid in paying his expenses.[81]

This was the same year that Louis Sheridan sold his enormous estate, freed his slaves, and went with them to Liberia.[82]

In the decade of the 1840's several free Negroes went to Liberia for the specific purpose of seeing what it was like. In 1844 Matthias Freeman paid the American Colonization Society $29.00 for passage to Liberia because he was "anxious to see the colony for himself ... if he is pleased with the place and his prospects there, he will return or send over for his family."[83] John B. Johnson of Edenton went out on September 3, 1847, for the same purpose.[84] A careful perusal of the succeeding volumes of the *Repository* fails to yield any additional information concerning these men. There is no record of their return to North Carolina or their impression of Liberia. They were in Liberia at the time Lewis Sheridan was discovering that the officers of the Society stationed in Liberia were "fleecing" the colonists for everything they could.[85] Perhaps they were not pleased with their prospects there. If so, the *African Repository* would not be expected to herald their return as it did their departure. To have returned to North Carolina and advised the free Negroes to remain in the State would have greatly incensed the citizens, who, by that time, were anxious to get the free Negroes out of the State. Regardless of what eventually happened to Freeman and Johnson, we can be certain that their impressions did not receive wide publicity.

In the succeeding years, a large number of free Negroes went to the African colony. In February, 1848, Moore Worrell, a free Negro farmer and carpenter, left North Carolina for the African colony.[86] In July, 1850, Sarah Palin, a free Negro woman of Elizabeth City, sailed from Baltimore with fifty-four other emigrants. On October 2, 1850, the New York Colonization Society shipped thirty-two emigrants

81. *African Repository*, XIII (August, 1837), 258.
82. *Cf. supra*, pp. 144-145.
83. *African Repository*, XIX (1844), 220.
84. *Ibid.*, XXIII (October, 1848), 308.
85. Southall, "Arthur Tappan," *loc. cit.*, p. 171.
86. *African Repository*, XXIV (1848), 94.

from New York to Bassa Cove, Liberia. "Among them was Daniel Williams, his wife and ten children, all of New Bern, North Carolina. He was born a slave, but his wife and, therefore, all his children were born free." He was an engineer and tanner. The eldest son was a mason. All except two small children could read. Five were Methodists.[87]

The information concerning the emigration of free Negroes for the decade ending in 1860 is fairly complete and presents an interesting picture of what was happening to a representative number of the best trained and most active of the free Negroes in North Carolina. Table VII shows that the number of free Negroes who left North Carolina during these years was not very large, but it gives one an opportunity to observe the colonization movement in North Carolina in relation to the movement on the national scene.

TABLE VII. EMIGRANTS TO LIBERIA, 1851-1860[88]

Vessel	Sailing	Number on Board	Number from North Carolina	Free Negroes from North Carolina
Liberia Packet....	July, 1851	52	3	
Morgan Dix......	Nov., 1851	149	13	7
Liberia Packet....	Dec., 1851	?	10	10
Ralph Cross......	May, 1852	126	16	16
Jos. Maxwell......	Nov., 1852	150	105	92
Linda Stuart......	Nov., 1852	171	39	37
Banshee..........	Apr., 1853	161	52	26[a]
Banshee..........	Nov., 1853	277	4	
Sophia Walker....	May, 1854	252	15	14[b]
Lamartine........	Dec., 1854	48	1	
Elvira............	May, 1856	321	41	28[c]
Mary Stewart.....	Dec., 1856	217	13	
Mary Stevens.....	May, 1857	207	125	18
?	May, 1858	108	63	
Mary Stevens.....	Nov., 1860	80	17	17
[a] All from Raleigh.............. [b] All from Elizabeth City........ [c] All from Wilmington..........		?	517	265

The emigration of more than 250 free-born Negroes from North Carolina takes on new significance when one studies the character and accomplishments of the individuals who left. The seven free Negroes who sailed on the *Morgan Dix* in 1851 were an interesting group. Two could read and write; three were farmers, one was a carpenter, one

87. *African Repository*, XXVI (1850), 343.

88. This table was compiled from information printed in the *African Repository* for the years 1851-1860: Vols. XXVII to XXXVI.

was a cook, and one was a washer; two were Methodists and one was a Baptist.[89] Of the sixteen who left on the *Ralph Cross* in 1852, two were literate, and half of them were members of the Methodist Church in Elizabeth City.[90] In the largest contingent of free Negroes to depart at one time—the ninety-two who went out in November, 1852—twenty-four were literate. There were seven carpenters, two plasterers, one wheelwright, one blacksmith, and one bricklayer. Sixteen were Methodists, seven were Presbyterians, and four were Baptists.[91] Later in the month, when the *Linda Stewart* left, North Carolina lost a free Negro preacher, a blacksmith, a carpenter, and a miller. Five of the thirty-seven were literate, and nine were affiliated with various religious sects.[92] Among the twenty-six Raleigh free Negroes who went to Liberia in 1853 there were two blacksmiths, two bricklayers, and one printer.[93]

Thus, those free Negroes who could have done a great deal to strengthen their group were leaving the State toward the end of the period. It is no mere accident that the majority was from the towns. Doubtless it was in those urban centers that the free Negro was least welcome and that he, in turn, saw the boldest manifestations of hostility to him. The urban free Negro, though inconsiderable in number, had made his presence felt in the skilled trades and had provided his family with some decent social experiences. When he began to feel the pressure of law and the community bear down upon him he sought some outlet; he fled his beloved State, somewhat reluctantly, and went to a strange and inhospitable land—not in the West, but in the East.[94] The free Negro population of North Carolina could ill afford to lose any of its more progressive element. In the migration of many of its artisans (and its only printer!), it sustained a loss that was completely irreparable in the last decade of the ante-bellum period. The willingness of these free Negroes, who had a stake in the development of their State, to risk all they had in starting over again is a frank testimonial of the extent to which life was becoming unbearable for the free Negro in ante-bellum North Carolina.

89. *African Repository*, XXVII (1851), 379.
90. *Ibid.*, XXVIII (1852), 183.   91. *Ibid.*, XXIX (1853), 23.
92. *Ibid.*, XXIX (1853), 29.   93. *Ibid.*, XXX (1853), 180.
94. Some free Negroes went into the free states. See, for example, the *Carolina Observer*, January 6, 1836, and the *North Carolina Standard*, October 30, 1850. The writer is unable to make any statement regarding the extent to which free Negroes of North Carolina emigrated from their State to the free states.

THE GROWING HOSTILITY TO FREE NEGROES

During the last decade of the period, the relatively small number of citizens who were capable of some degree of articulation made known their attitude toward the free Negro in no uncertain terms. By this time the North Carolina slaveholders had become disturbed over the efforts of the North to overthrow their political, social, and economic system; and they were doing everything possible to preserve it. Up to 1850, the policy of the State had been to deal with the problem of the free Negro by regulating his activities within the State. This remained the policy to the end of the period. But during each year of the last decade a greater effort was exerted to get the Legislature to enact laws for the removal of free Negroes from the State. Many citizens had become convinced that the only way to deal with free Negroes was to eliminate their presence altogether. The Quaker petitions to secure the aid of the State in the removal of free Negroes in 1829 and 1830 were merely the precursors of a flood of such petitions which began twenty years later. By 1850 North Carolinians were seeking to solve the problem of slavery, in part, by ridding themselves of their free Negro population.

Before the Assembly convened in 1850, there was considerable agitation for the enactment of a law to remove all free Negroes from the State. The *Goldsboro Patriot,* by this time violently anti-free Negro, sought to sum up the situation in November of that year:

> We hear but one opinion expressed, not only by the press of our state, but by everyone with whom we converse, in respect to free negroes. All are unanimous in the opinion that the approaching Legislature ought to pass an act to remove them beyond the limits of the State. We admit that, to the Legislature, the duty may be a painful one. For, none will deny that, in removing this class of people from the scenes of their childhood where they enjoyed health, plenty and happiness, a deep and lasting wound will pierce the heart of all. But necessity, stern necessity, admonishes us of the expediency of such an act. And while we here give it our unqualified approval we cannot but regret that the unaccountable fatuity of the Northern Abolitionists, urges us to this conclusion. The safety of our people and a proper regard for the welfare and future subordination of the slave population demand it at the hands of the Legislature.[95]

During the 1850-51 session of the General Assembly, two petitions were presented which sought relief from the free Negro problem. One was

95. Printed in the *North Carolina Standard,* November 30, 1830.

signed by seventy-seven citizens of Duplin County, where 345 free Negroes were living at that time.[96] These citizens contended that the presence of free Negroes in their vicinity had a tendency to foster a spirit of discontent among their slaves. They asked, therefore, that an appropriation be made to transport the free Negroes to Liberia "and that all of them be compelled to go except those who prefer to be sold and become slaves."[97] The other petition signed by James Graham, of Lincoln County, where there were only thirty-six free Negroes,[98] was couched in more vigorous phrases. In part it read,

> It is desirable that you should adopt a course of policy, and pass a system of laws to induce, if not compell, the free Negroes of North Carolina to emigrate to the Abolition and Free Soil States. It appears to me that *Negrophobia* which is . . . rousing up a large number of people in the non-slaveholding states cannot be cured more effectually than by giving them some strong black medicine out of their own black bottle. . . . Every man who has a southern heart in his bosom must see the propriety and necessity of such legislation.[99]

Mr. Graham then proposed that the General Assembly help finance the removal by passing a law making the owners of land on which free Negroes reside "liable to pay all the taxes, contracts, damages, penalties, fines, and costs, and other legal liabilities which colored persons may contract . . . while living thereon."[100] Both of these petitions were turned over to the Committee on Propositions and Grievances in the Senate, but no action was taken on them.[101]

In 1852 fifty-five citizens of Sampson County, led by Gabriel Parker and Silas Herring, asked the Assembly to enact legislation looking to the removal of free Negroes from the State. Their argument was similar to the other petitioners; but the several alternatives suggested a degree of desperation not expressed in the earlier petitions.

> We . . . hereby desire to call your earnest and direct attention to the evils that exist in our midst, arising from the bad conduct and evil disposition of very many of the free negroes amonst us.[102] We conceive them as a general mass to be a perfect nuisance, to

96. Census Bureau, *Seventh Census (Population)*, p. 307.
97. Ms. in the Legislative Papers for 1850-51.
98. Census Bureau, *Seventh Census (Population)*, p. 307.
99. Ms. in the Legislative Papers for 1850-51.
100. *Ibid.*
101. See the endorsements on the petitions.
102. There were 477 free Negroes in Sampson County in 1850. Census Bureau, *Seventh Census (Population)*, p. 308.

civilized society. They . . . attempt in divers ways to equalize themselves with the white population, notwithstanding the legal restrictions . . . already thrown around them. Which course of procedure, and their communications with the slave population, renders them (the slaves) to be disobedient, and turbulent. . . . For the redress of these grievances and various others . . . we would respectfully solicit your honorable body to adopt some legal measures for their removal from among us, if you can consistently with your obligations to fundamental law, either by passing such caustic laws as to compel them to emigrate, or by raising a fund by taxing them, to be appropriated to their colonization in Africa, or by petition to the general government for a location for them in the far West, or any other place that you in your wisdom may deem prefferable.[103]

When the House Committee on Propositions and Grievances reported on the petition from Sampson County they refused to recommend it for action because they felt that such legislation at that time was unwise and inexpedient.[104]

The year 1858 marks the beginning of the last great effort of North Carolina to solve its free Negro problem by some kind of definite action. By this time the entire South, including North Carolina, was so preoccupied with the sectional struggle that it had no time to regulate free Negroes by ordinances and patrols. In order that the system of slavery would be more impregnable than ever, there were many citizens who felt that a rapid and complete elimination of the free Negro population was absolutely necessary. One of the most vigorous expressions of this point of view was made by the Cleveland County Grand Jury. When it met in July it made the following presentment:

We, the Grand Jury of Cleveland County, North Carolina do present, that free Negroes in general are a nuisance to society; and that it would be expedient to have a law requiring them to leave the State, and for a failure to do so, that they should be exposed to public sale, the proceeds arising therefrom be applied to the Literary Fund of our State. Adopted by unanimous consent.[105]

In September of that year, the *Newbern New Era* urged free Negroes to go to Haiti. It quoted the *New York Advertiser* as saying that two Haitians were in the country for the purpose of looking up free Negroes who would be interested in migrating to Haiti. It said that

103. Ms. in the Legislative Papers for 1852-53.

104. *Ibid.* A resolution, based on this petition, was introduced in the House of Commons, but at the first reading it was laid on the table. Ms. in the Legislative Papers for 1852-1853.

105. *Newbern Weekly Union,* July 7, 1858.

the Emperor of Haiti was willing to make an attractive offer to free Negroes who were desirous of migrating. The *New Era* thought that this offer would be of interest to many free Negroes in the State and advised them to look into it.[106]

When the Assembly met in November, the first bill to be introduced in the House—the third bill to be introduced in the Senate—was one jointly sponsored by Representative Henry Walser of Davidson and Senator Humphrey of Onslow entitled, "A Bill concerning Free Persons of Color." The proposed law provided that it would be unlawful for free Negroes to come to North Carolina under any circumstances. After defining the policy of the State in the treatment of free Negroes who violated this portion of the act, the proposed statute then turned its attention to the existing free Negro problem. It provided,

> That two years shall be allowed . . . to all free persons of color who are now in this State, to remove out of the same; and all those who shall be found here after that time, without the permission of the General Assembly, shall be arrested and sold as provided in this act. . . .
>
> Be it further enacted, that the Governor of the State do issue his proclamation, commanding all free persons of color who are now in the State, to remove from the same before the 1st day of January, 1860. . . .[107]

Colonel Humphrey also introduced a bill entitled, "A Bill to permit free persons of African Descent to select their own masters and become slaves." If the first bill passed, it would be possible under this proposed law for free Negroes who did not choose to migrate to a strange land to give up what freedom they possessed and become slaves. In a lengthy bill of five sections, Senator Humphrey outlined the procedure by which free Negroes over fourteen years of age, then in the State, "or who hereafter may be within its limits," were to renounce their claims to freedom.[108]

The introduction of these and similar bills in the General Assembly evoked a considerable amount of comment from the citizens of North Carolina. From Buncombe County came a hearty endorsement of the Humphrey bills signed by ninety-two citizens of Asheville.[109] They

106. *Newbern New Era*, September 21, 1858.

107. Ms. in the Legislative Papers for 1858-1859. The bill was printed and distributed to the members of the Assembly.

108. *North Carolina Standard*, November 24, 1858.

109. Humphrey's neighbors in Onslow County had already sent in a petition describing the evils of the free Negro population and urging that the Assembly give serious attention to this problem. Ms. in the Legislative Papers for 1858-1859.

were firmly convinced, they said, that something should be done "to alleviate at least if not entirely remove the injuries" occasioned by the free Negro population. "In view of these facts, we have seen with much pleasure the bills recently introduced into our Legislature by Colonel Humphrey of Onslow. . . . We heartily commend them to the support of our Commoner and Senator and urge them to use every constitutional means to secure the objects, which they are designed to effectuate."[110]

Accompanying the petition from the citizens of Asheville was a personal letter from one of the signatories, James A. Patton, to the representative from Buncombe, Dr. J. S. T. Baird. In urging a favorable consideration of the Humphrey bills, Patton vividly described conditions in his vicinity.

> You must be aware that if any section of our country or State *is troubled* with free Negroes, ours is the most vexed in this way. The continuous inroads of free Negroes from the surrounding counties and States, has brought so many upon us that they cannot longer be borne. . . .
>
> The petition was carried around by Mr. Clayton and finds its warmest advocate in him. He informs me that it was not refused *by a single man.* We are earnestly desirous that you do something. If the bills on hand are unconstitutional (I do not see wherein), then do the best you can.[111]

Some individuals were not as heartily in favor of the Humphrey bills as were the Asheville citizens. The editor of the *Oxford Leisure Hour* favored the measures, but placed some qualifications upon his endorsement:

> The resolutions . . . need some amendment—some modification and also a provisional clause. That nine-tenths of the free negroes are a moral curse to any community, is a fact which any observing person will acknowledge, and that something of a positive nature and stringent character is necessary to be done, no one will or can deny, but what that *something* is, ah! there is the rub, and for ourself we cannot devise any plan more satisfactory . . . than the series of resolutions already before the Legislature. We think, though, that some provisions should be made for the removal of the negroes—or that portion of them who prefer to be colonized rather than go into voluntary servitude. To throw the improvident

110. Ms. in the Legislative Papers for 1858-1859.

111. James A. Patton to Dr. J. S. T. Baird, December 1, 1858. Ms. in the Legislative Papers for 1858-1859.

wretches solely upon their own means of removal would be to command an impossibility, or rather would be restricting them virtually to but one course—would be tantamount to forcing them into slavery, whether willing or not. Whether the Humphrey resolutions pass or not, we hope some measures will be adopted to relieve, in some degree the "crying evil."[112]

The Walser-Humphrey bills were before the Assembly from December 1, 1858, to February 1, 1859. They were printed and distributed to members of the Assembly and received wide publicity in the press of the State. On the night of February 1, 1859, they were read for the second time in the House. Upon the motion of Mr. Tilman Farrow of Hyde to postpone the bills indefinitely the House decided in the affirmative by a vote of sixty-two to forty-four.[113] No vote was ever taken on the matter in the Senate.

Thus, North Carolina demurred on the proposition to eliminate its free Negro population. There can be little doubt that the problem raised by the *Leisure Hour,* namely, that of the expense of colonization, was a factor in the hesitation of the members of the Assembly to pass such drastic legislation. It was one thing to say to the free Negroes to get out of the State. It was quite another thing to see that they were actually removed. The costs would have been almost prohibitive in a state that was already experiencing difficulty in meeting its obligations. There can also be little doubt that the humanity of the legislators was a factor. The pupils of John Chavis and the neighbors of Thomas Day, James Sampson, and Thomas Blacknall must have felt keenly the harshness of a law that failed to recognize that here and there among the free Negro population were individuals that were a credit to their community. To have expelled them summarily or to have enslaved them forcibly was further than they were willing to go.

At no other time, before or after 1858, did North Carolina come so close to expelling its free Negro population. In 1860, a group of citizens of Currituck County urged the Assembly to expel the free Negroes or force them into slavery. They said that they were "troubled by no qualms as to the right of the legislature either to expel them from the State, or to reduce them to a condition of slavery. Disfranchised by this State by the convention of 1835, the Supreme Court of the United States . . . by a late decision has decided that they are not citizens under the Constitution. . . ."[114] The men from Currituck said that the first

112. Quoted in the *North Carolina Standard,* December 28, 1858.
113. *Journal of the House, 1858-1859,* p. 453.
114. The petitioners were here referring to the Dred Scott decision.

duty of the citizens of North Carolina was to provide all necessary means to ward off the threatened danger of a half-slave, half-free Negro population. This could be accomplished, they contended, by the removal of the free Negro population.[115] Nothing came of the petition of the 114 citizens of Currituck. The citizens of North Carolina were so concerned over the recent election of Abraham Lincoln to the Presidency and what it meant to them that they were not inclined at that time to enact legislation dealing with such problems. The question of the relation of North Carolina to the Union was the burning issue of the day. For the time being, at least, the problem of Abraham Lincoln loomed larger on the horizon of North Carolina than the problem of the free Negro.

As the free Negro found himself in the midst of an ever-growing hostility, he began to seek avenues of escape, the very nature of which bear witness to the delicacy of his position in North Carolina society toward the end of the period. The prospect of further integration of the free Negro group into the life of the community without losing its identity was slight indeed; and the free Negro began to give that up as a possible solution. Two other avenues of escape were open to him: migration to some area beyond the limits of the State or enslavement within the State. In the last decade of the period, the free Negro sought both of these avenues.

The reaction of the free Negro to the plan sponsored by the American Colonization Society has already been discussed.[116] Among those who did not support the movement were free Negroes who were desirous of going outside the State but not as far as Africa and individuals who because of their poverty or their unwillingness to leave the State at all were ready to accept enslavement. In Raleigh, fourteen prominent free Negroes told the Legislature in 1851 that they were willing to leave the State and settle in the West. The language and point of view expressed in the petition are so interesting that they merit extensive quotation:

> The time has come when a portion of your people deem it necessary and prudent to cast themselves at your feet. This portion is the free Coulourd people in the State of North Carolina—who in judging the future by the past do Humbly unite in praying and in petitioning this Honourable Assembly to memorilize Congress in their behalf—to grant them a portion of the Western Territory as a Colony. Your petitioners feel themselves at a loss for proper

115. Ms. in the Legislative Papers for 1860.
116. Cf. supra, pp. 206 ff.

words and language to express their feelings and apprehensions—
But their motive being pure, they hope to find favor and clemency
in your honourable wisdom.

The free Negro petitioners reminded the Assembly that many of them
were the offspring of slaves and free Negroes who died in the Revolution, "but the blessings of which from political policy are withheld
from them." They said that they were real Americans and knew no
other home and therefore wanted to remain under the care and protection of the United States. They denied that they were the "Eating
cancers and the morbid incubus on the public peace."

> Were your petitioners strangers they would hesitate to express a
> choice in the matter. But being children of the American soil and
> trained to mechanical and farming arts, they would dare that
> choice, and if this should meet with favor in your wisdom they
> pray that your kindness will urge a lugubrious clime and a pro-
> ductive soil—that the milk flowing therefrom may rebound to the
> glory of the giver.
>
> Your petitioners think they feel and see in this their prayer
> much Balm to heal the growing malidy, and a spirit that may give
> peace and happiness to themselves and country.[117]

This dramatic plea on the part of fourteen free Negroes of Wake
County was read in the House on January 23, 1851. No indication of
its having been referred to a committee appears on its endorsement.
It was laid on the table on the same day that it was read.[118]

Another way out of the difficulties which beset the free Negro was
to seek enslavement. As early as 1854 one free Negro indicated his
desire to become a slave. John Stewart had purchased his freedom
from his Raleigh master and had gone to Cincinnati to live some years
before 1854. In the latter year when he was arraigned on a charge of
stealing to which he entered a plea of guilty he remarked, "Since I
came here . . . I have been kicked about and abused by all classes of
white men; can't get work from no one; and to borrow money . . .
that is out of the question." He declared that as soon as he served his
time on the chain gang he would go South and become a slave
again.[119]

117. Ms. in the Legislative Papers for 1851-1852.   118. *Ibid.*

119. *Greensborough Patriot*, December 2, 1854. The very same article appeared in
the *Patriot* five years later! In the later article the *Patriot* printed the following comment which it took from the *Newbern Progress*: "Serves him right. Had no business
with freedom or Ohio either. . . . Slaves are better off in Raleigh than poor free men in
Cincinnati. We hope that all others who may buy their freedom and go there may meet
with the same or a worse fate." *Greensborough Patriot*, November 11, 1859.

Toward the end of the period, a large number of free Negroes sought to escape the hardships which they were experiencing by becoming slaves. Although the Humphrey bill of 1858, which provided for the enslavement of free Negroes, did not pass, free Negroes proceeded to enslave themselves by securing the passage of private bills. At the same session both Houses passed "A Bill for the Relief of Emily Hooper of Liberia." It provided,

> That Emily Hooper a negro, and a citizen of Liberia, be and she is hereby permitted, voluntarily, to return into a state of slavery, as the slave of her former owner, Miss Sally Mallet of Chapel Hill. . . .[120]

The *Western Democrat* of Charlotte remarked that this free Negro woman was the daughter of an official of the Liberian government, and although she "ranked among the 'big fish' of the free Negro Colony, is sick of freedom and prefers living with her mistress in the Old North State than to being fleeced by abolition friends (?) in Liberia."[121] By this time, some North Carolinians were so anxious to extol the virtues and blessings of slavery that they did it even at the expense of the African colony which they had been praising.

The events of November and December of 1860 undoubtedly had a profound effect on the attitude of the free Negro toward life and the future. As a resident of North Carolina, where the slaveholders were talking freely of secession and of the complete subjugation of the free Negro, many of the latter group began to feel that in order to avoid the cruel treatment that they were destined to receive at the hands of the slaveholders, it would be better to become identified with the system than to fight against it. Thus, Theophilus King became the slave of William Frazier of Greene County.[122] Celia Lynch of Martin County was satisfied that her "state of freedom did not conduce as much happiness as she saw in those who were in a condition of servitude." In order, furthermore, that she would have a "legal protector in health, in sickness, and old age," she expressed the desire to become the slave of Dr. J. T. Watson. A bill for her relief was passed February 1, 1861.[123] At the same session, Nelson Patterson became the slave of William Marsh of Davie County, who was already the owner of his wife.[124] On January 19, 1861, Ellen Ransom, "in order to procure for herself a good and lasting hom," became the slave of Leonidas Perry

120. Ms. in the Legislative Papers for 1858-1859.
121. *Western Democrat*, January 11, 1859.
122. Ms. in the Legislative Papers for 1860-61.
123. *Ibid.*   124. *Ibid.*

of Franklin County.[125] On the same day, Janett Wright became the slave of John Clark of Guilford County.[126] On February 9, 1861, Wright Locus became the slave of James Henry Beal of Nash County.[127]

Not only were individual free Negroes seeking enslavement at the end of the period, but several acts are on record of groups of them requesting the status of slaves. On February 20, 1861, a bill was passed permitting Julia Dickinson and Susan Lewis to become the slaves of J. G. Holiday of Northampton County.[128] At the same session, eight free Negroes by the name of Garnes became the slaves of Joseph A. Hartley of Jones County.[129] Without indicating how many children she had, Leah White secured the permission of the General Assembly for her and her children to become slaves and to choose their master in open court.[130]

The General Assembly did not always act favorably on the petitions of free Negroes who desired to be enslaved. On December 6, 1860, a free Negro by the name of Wyatt of South Carolina sought enslavement to C. A. Featherston of Gaston County, but the bill was laid on the table of the House, and action was never taken.[131] In a similar manner, the request of Peggy Ann Morten to be "Divested of all Rights and privileges of a free person of Color" and become a slave of Henderson Adams of Davidson County was denied.[132] Although Kessiah Trueblood submitted a lengthy petition setting forth her dissatisfaction with being a free servant of Dr. H. P. Ritter, and her desire to become his slave, her plea was laid on the table of the House and was not taken up again.[133] One is unable to find in the pleas of the free Negro petitioners any facts on which the legislators could have decided in some cases to permit enslavement and in other cases to deny it. In the absence of any information on which a conclusive presumption can be based, one is inclined to believe that the influence of the prospective master or the sponsor of the bill had a great deal to do with its passage.

The free Negro's presence was, thus, looked upon with growing suspicion in North Carolina. The innumerable manifestations on the part of the citizens of their desire to be rid of the group bear testimony to their conclusions that the free Negro was an anomalous personality which could never be integrated into the social and economic pattern of North Carolina. The free Negro's studied reactions to these man-

125. *Ibid.*   126. *Ibid.*   127. *Ibid.*
128. *Ibid.*   129. *Ibid.*   130. *Ibid.*
131. *Ibid.*   132. *Ibid.*   133. *Ibid.*

ifestations gave evidence of a feeling of frustration and futility. Accepting the decision of the white population concerning their undesirability, many sought to remove themselves from the despised class either by migration or by enslavement. Others, by far the majority, simply waited—with an attitude of resignation—to see if the future would be as unkind in its treatment of them as the present.

CHAPTER VII

Conclusions

A man having no freedom cannot be conceived of except as deprived of life.
Tolstoy, *War and Peace,* second Epilogue.

BETWEEN 1790 and 1860, the free Negro population of North Carolina grew from 5,041 to 30,463, an increase of 604 per cent for the seventy-year period. With the exception of the last decade, it grew faster than the white or the slave populations in the State. In addition to the increase that accrued from natural causes, the free Negro population was augmented from time to time from a number of other sources. The manumission of slaves by benevolent masters and the practice of miscegenation brought to the free Negro group a large number of recruits. The success of runaway slaves in losing themselves in the free Negro group and the immigration of free Negroes from other states served also to swell the number of free Negroes in North Carolina. Finally, free Negroes themselves contributed to the growth of their group through the purchase of friends and relatives and subsequently manumitting them. It was one thing to inherit or acquire freedom and quite another thing to maintain it. The Negro's right to freedom was continuously questioned, and not infrequently he had to go into court and by certificates, affidavits, and the like prove his right to enjoy the privileges of a free man.

Free Negroes were, for the most part, concentrated in the eastern part of the State, where the majority of the white and slave population lived. In the counties bordering on Virginia and South Carolina were to be found a large number of free Negroes whose very presence in these areas bespoke the more liberal treatment of free Negroes in North Carolina than in the neighboring states. Free Negroes in North Carolina were, moreover, a rural people. At no time during the period did more than one tenth live in the population centers, many of which were hardly worthy of the name of towns. Their rural habitations caused them to suffer from the disadvantages that resulted from limited economic opportunities and inadequate social contact. At the same time, however, their living in the rural areas had the effect of making their presence less objectionable, since they were seldom seen in large numbers.

The effort of North Carolina to discipline the free Negro and to prevent his overturning the established order resulted in the reduction of the free Negro's position to one of quasi-freedom. The waves of fear of servile insurrections that swept North Carolina in the 1820's and the irritation growing out of economic depression in the same years had the effect of erecting a Free Negro Code that was fairly complete before the insurrection of Nat Turner at Southampton. That these fears were not well-founded is borne out by the conduct of free Negroes in North Carolina during the ante-bellum period. Only now and then did they assist slaves to escape. Their general violations of the law did not reflect any will on their part to overthrow the slave system. Instead, they merely reflected the social and economic privations under which the majority of them labored throughout the period.

Despite the fact that the free Negro's activities were carefully circumscribed in the code that was established, he enjoyed some of the rights and privileges of a free man. The courts were open to him, although his competency as a witness was often questioned. He could demand jury trial in certain cases, and usually had the benefit of counsel. Down to 1835 he could exercise the privilege of the franchise. After this period, he was without citizenship in any real meaning of the term. In the society of North Carolina, he was merely an anomaly whose legal disabilities were surpassed only by his economic and social disadvantages.

Had it not been for the system of apprenticing free Negro children to white masters for the purpose of training them to make a living, the economic influence of the free Negro would have been even less than it was. The training of free Negro children in a large number of occupations made it possible for many of them to make a living after they had served their apprenticeship. By the end of the period, free Negroes were engaged in almost a hundred occupations, the majority of which required some considerable skill. The opposition of white artisans to free Negro competition doubtless served to limit the number of free Negroes to be found in the skilled trades. The majority of the free Negroes who were gainfully employed in the ante-bellum period, however, were engaged in occupations which required little or no skill. As farmers, farm laborers, and common laborers, they were able to eke out a living if they could find an opportunity to ply their trade.

At no time during the period was the free Negro's right to own real or personal property successfully challenged. In 1860, however, he was forbidden to acquire and control slaves. The serious economic handicaps, many of which were brought on by legislative enactments, made it impossible for many free Negroes to accumulate the necessary capital for the acquisition of property. Their ownership of $1,045,643 worth of real and personal property in 1860—a per capita wealth of only $34—is a testimonial to their economic sufferings, which increased with the years. The ownership of slaves by a small number of free Negroes—benevolent gestures in some instances—serves to emphasize by contrast the poverty of the entire group.

The same circumscriptions that served to hamper the free Negro in the legal and economic spheres were present as he sought a place in the social life of the State. The walls of restriction that almost completely encircled him cut many of the lines of communication between him and the larger community. This condition forced upon him a self-sufficiency which doomed him to continued ignorance with all its concomitant evils. What literacy there was among the free Negroes came largely from the apprenticeship system. There were also religious sects, such as the Quakers, Methodists, and Presbyterians, who were engaged in the task of training free Negroes, but they touched only a very limited number. That some free Negroes were still being educated toward the end of the period is seen in the fact that more than 200 were in school in 1850. The name of John Chavis will always be connected with the education of the free Negro in ante-bellum North Carolina. For thirty years this free Negro preacher and teacher of both races gave to his fellows the rudiments of a literary education as well as the principles of good and constructive living in those difficult times.

Spiritual food was almost as difficult for the free Negroes to acquire as were the material necessaries of life. They had neither the compactness nor the economic strength to support separate churches; and the accommodations for them in the white and slave churches were poor indeed. Here and there, free Negro preachers exhorted small groups of their fellows. But they were virtually silenced by the law of 1831. After that time, they had to integrate themselves into the religious life of their communities as best they could. Although great limitations were placed on their opportunities to affiliate with white and slave churches, there can be no doubt that many of them belonged to such congregations.

In the matter of social relationships, the State expected the free Negro to be as self-sufficient as he was expected to be in education and religion. Social contact with white persons and slaves was generally frowned upon; and laws were passed which were for the purpose of carefully regulating these relationships. During the entire period, free Negroes persisted in maintaining certain social relationships with whites and with slaves. In such violations of the legal restrictions of the State and the mores of their communities, the free Negroes displayed no untoward inclinations to criminality. They were merely struggling to find an outlet for their pent-up emotions and natural sociability.

The lag of North Carolina behind the other states in the enactment of harsh free Negro legislation and the laxity with which existing laws were enforced suggests a type of liberalism that existed in few other states in the South. This liberalism did not stem from any humanitarianism peculiar to the State. Rather, it grew out of several factors present in the social and economic pattern of North Carolina. The economic instability of the slave system, the unsettled state of economic and social life, the presence of a large yeoman class, and the inarticulateness of a predominantly rural population go far in explaining the comparatively "liberal" treatment of free Negroes.

Nevertheless, there was a growing hostility to the very presence of the free Negro in North Carolina. This hostility found expression in various ways. The supporters of the colonization movement felt that the condition of the whites as well as of the Negroes would be improved if the free Negroes were colonized beyond the limits of the State. To others, the important thing was to get rid of the free Negro. They conceived this to be a *sine qua non* to the perpetuation of the economic and social development of the State. In the end, the frustrated free Negro sought colonization, slavery, or anything else that would remove him from the group whose presence was becoming more and more opprobrious to the citizens of ante-bellum North Carolina.

VI. NORTH CAROLINA IN 1860

Appendices

APPENDIX I

FREE NEGRO APPRENTICES IN 1860[1]

AT THE END of the period, almost two thousand children were apprenticed to the citizens of North Carolina. A few were apprenticed to free Negroes; but more than nine tenths were the wards of white citizens. The unpublished schedules of the eighth decennial census seldom give information concerning the occupations for which free Negro children were preparing. It is supposed, however, that the distribution was similar to that in the earlier period.[2] The eastern counties, where the larger portion of the North Carolina population, both white and black, was concentrated, was also the area in which the largest number of free Negro apprentices lived. Below is a list of the number of free Negro apprentices by counties:

County	Number	County	Number	County	Number
Alamance	36	Forsyth	8	Onslow	14
Alexander	3	Franklin	23	Orange	51
Alleghany	8	Gaston	23	Pasquotank	70
Anson	14	Gates	19	Perquimans	28
Ashe	5	Granville	33	Person	16
Beaufort	56	Greene	34	Pitt	26
Bertie	46	Guilford	73	Polk	12
Bladen	29	Halifax	51	Randolph	49
Brunswick	17	Harnett	1	Richmond	13
Buncombe	8	Haywood	3	Robeson	12
Burke	7	Henderson	9	Rockingham	22
Cabarrus	15	Hertford	34	Rowan	10
Caldwell	16	Hyde	3	Rutherford	6
Camden	18	Iredell	9	Sampson	47
Carteret	15	Jackson	..	Stanly	1
Caswell	19	Johnson	15	Stokes	27
Catawba	4	Jones	4	Surry	12
Chatham	14	Lenoir	27	Tyrrell	22
Cherokee	6	Lincoln	27	Union	8
Chowan	1	Macon	14	Wake	92
Cleveland	25	Madison	4	Warren	9
Columbus	9	Martin	50	Washington	17
Craven	16	McDowell	28	Watauga	2
Cumberland	55	Mecklenburg	35	Wayne	65
Currituck	33	Montgomery	10	Wilkes	19
Davidson	30	Moore	22	Wilson	26
Davie	13	Nash	70	Yadkin	2
Duplin	16	New Hanover	7	Yancey	3
Edgecombe	26	Northampton	56		

1. From the unpublished population schedules of the eighth census.
2. Cf. supra, pp. 125 ff.

APPENDIX II

FREE NEGRO PROPERTY OWNERS IN 1860

THE FOLLOWING tables are presented with a view to furnishing a more graphic picture of the free Negro property owner in 1860. While the majority of free Negroes were with little or no property, the first table shows that more than fifty had holdings of real and personal property valued at $2,500 or more. These free Negroes, exceptions to the general rule, were important factors in raising the per capita wealth of free Negroes up to the distressingly small amount of $34.

The second table is for the purpose of indicating the number and distribution of free Negro owners of real and personal property. A larger number of free Negroes owned more personal property than real property. Often, however, free Negroes owned both types of property. The third table indicates the number and distribution of free Negro farmers who owned all or part of the land which they tilled. The fourth table is the aggregate value of the real and personal property owned by free Negroes in each county.

The statistics used in the construction of all of the following tables were gathered from the unpublished schedules of the eighth census in the Archives of the North Carolina Historical Commission and in the Bureau of the Census.

1. FREE NEGROES HAVING PROPERTY VALUED AT MORE THAN $2,500

County	Name	Occupation	Value
Alamance	Ned Corn	Farmer	$ 2,800
	Dixon Corn	Farmer	5,250
Anson	Thos. Jones		6,700
Beaufort	Eliz Picar		2,500
Brunswick	Solomon Webb	Farmer	2,810
Buncombe	Jas. Graham	Farmer	2,800
Caswell	Thos. Day	Cabinetmaker	4,000
Cleveland	E. H. Revel	Farmer	4,826
Craven	Catherine Stanley	Dress Maker	4,000
	Wm. Martin	Farmer	2,500
	Willis Lewis	Farmer	2,750
Edgecombe	Mary A. Jones	Housekeeper	5,500
Franklin	Thos. Blacknall	Farmer	7,300
Gaston	Jno. Mendenhall	Farmer	3,197
Gates	Jno. Knight	Confectioner	5,905
	Nesrim Cuff	Farmer	3,475
Granville	Will Evans	Farmer	3,932
Guilford	Ann Piles	Clerking	5,000
Halifax	David Reynolds	Farmer	4,000
	Jno. Howard		2,500
Hyde	J. A. Collins	Farmer	9,000

1. Free Negroes Having Property Valued at More than $2,500 (Continued)

County	Name	Occupation	Value
Macon.............	Willis Guy.............	Farmer...........	$ 2,695
McDowell..........	Silvester Michael........	Farmer...........	5,000
Mecklenburg........	Jerry Bethel............	Barber...........	3,550
Nash..............	Alison Taboon..........	Farm Laborer.....	5,554
New Hanover.......	James Erwin...........	Musician.........	3,100
	David Lansington, Jr.....	Carpenter........	2,500
	Jas. Sampson...........	Carpenter........	36,000
	E. Hites...............	Carpenter........	4,000
Northampton........	Hester Butch..........	Farm Hand.......	3,450
	Jas. G. Jordan..........	Farmer...........	4,700
Orange............	David Moore...........	Barber...........	4,400
Pasquotank........	Jesse Silvester..........	Farmer...........	2,670
Person.............	Wm. Stewart..........	Farmer...........	3,000
Pitt...............	Ansa Norris............	Carpenter........	3,000
Richmond..........	Jesse Freeman.........	Farmer...........	20,300
Robeson...........	Wiley Locklier.........	Farmer...........	5,200
	Nelson Smith..........	Farmer..........	2,500
	Hardy Bell............	....	14,000
	Geo. Dial.............	Farmer...........	4,900
	Jas. Oxendine..........	Farmer...........	9,825
Rockingham........	Edmond Miller..........	Wheelwright......	8,150
Sampson...........	Jesse Jacobs...........	Farmer...........	3,712
Tyrrell............	Cogge Bryan...........	Farmer...........	2,535
Wake..............	Abram Scott...........	Farmer...........	3,766
	Lydia Mangum.........	Farmer...........	20,816
	Enoch Evans..........	Farmer...........	11,830
	Oscar Alston...........	Farmer...........	17,644
Warren............	M. Green.............	Farmer...........	2,600
	Jno. Burchett..........	Farmer...........	2,500
Washington........	Mary Alee.............	Baker...........	2,750
Wayne.............	Washington Reed........	Farmer...........	3,300
	Chas. Winn............	Blacksmith.......	2,800

2. NUMBER OF FREE NEGRO PROPERTY HOLDERS

County	Realty	Personalty	Total Number of Property Holders
Alamance	17	48	49
Alexander	2	2	2
Alleghany	..	3	3
Anson	6	19	19
Ashe	6	19	19
Beaufort	41	15	47
Bertie	11	29	29
Bladen	21	51	51
Brunswick	19	52	52
Buncombe	7	18	18
Burke	1	12	12
Cabarrus	6	12	12
Caldwell	4	13	13
Camden	1	2	2
Carteret	7	10	10
Caswell	14	46	47
Catawba	1	1	1
Chatham	6	28	28
Cherokee	1	4	4
Chowan	12	41	41
Cleveland	5	5	5
Columbus	25	45	45
Craven	87	168	179
Cumberland	34	112	112
Currituck	5	16	16
Davidson	2	17	17
Davie	..	11	11
Duplin	6	29	29
Edgecombe	16	24	24
Forsyth	7	35	36
Franklin	17	49	50
Gaston	3	8	8
Gates	11	33	33
Granville	40	77	80
Greene	7	15	15
Guilford	19	81	81
Halifax	85	452	463
Harnett	..	4	4
Haywood	..	1	1
Henderson	1	1	2
Hertford	80	197	201
Hyde	1	1	1
Iredell	1	2	2
Jackson	..	1	1
Johnston	13	27	27
Jones	4	7	7
Lenoir	2	23	24
Lincoln	1	7	7
Macon	7	17	17
Madison	..	2	2
Martin	19	1	19
McDowell	1	1	1
Mecklenburg	18	49	49
Montgomery	1	5	5
Moore	3	18	18

2. Number of Free Negro Property Holders *(Continued)*

County	Realty	Personalty	Total Number of Property Holders
Nash	24	105	105
New Hanover	62	96	128
Northampton	26	78	80
Onslow	7	24	24
Orange	6	23	23
Pasquotank	51	259	261
Perquimans	19	64	64
Person	6	10	10
Pitt	8	23	23
Polk	2	11	11
Randolph	14	65	66
Richmond	22	53	53
Robeson	67	163	163
Rockingham	11	8	16
Rowan	3	4	5
Rutherford	1	1	1
Sampson	14	36	39
Stanly	3	5	5
Stokes	2	3	3
Surry	6	18	18
Tyrrell	7	12	13
Union	1	4	4
Wake	54	220	222
Warren	20	57	58
Washington	13	50	51
Watauga	3	8	8
Wayne	22	54	56
Wilkes	10	39	39
Wilson	13	35	36
Yadkin	4	22	22
Yancey	5	11	11

3. Number of Free Negro Farmers Who Owned Real Property

County	Number	County	Number	County	Number
Alamance	10	Forsyth	1	Onslow	6
Alexander	1	Franklin	7	Orange	3
Alleghany	..	Gaston	1	Pasquotank	27
Anson	3	Gates	7	Perquimans	13
Ashe	6	Granville	20	Person	5
Beaufort	21	Greene	1	Pitt	1
Bertie	5	Guilford	7	Polk	2
Bladen	9	Halifax	62	Randolph	7
Brunswick	6	Harnett	..	Richmond	17
Buncombe	3	Haywood	..	Robeson	54
Burke	..	Henderson	1	Rockingham	3
Cabarrus	4	Hertford	14	Rowan	..
Caldwell	4	Hyde	1	Rutherford	1
Camden	1	Iredell	1	Sampson	5
Carteret	2	Jackson	..	Stanly	2
Caswell	8	Johnston	5	Stokes	2
Catawba	..	Jones	1	Surry	2
Chatham	5	Lenoir	..	Tyrrell	2
Cherokee	1	Lincoln	..	Union	1
Chowan	1	Macon	4	Wake	17
Cleveland	3	Madison	..	Warren	11
Columbus	20	Martin	10	Washington	3
Craven	22	McDowell	1	Watauga	2
Cumberland	3	Mecklenburg	1	Wayne	4
Currituck	2	Montgomery	1	Wilkes	9
Davidson	1	Moore	2	Wilson	7
Davie	..	Nash	11	Yadkin	7
Duplin	2	New Hanover	8	Yancey	..
Edgecombe	5	Northampton	14		

4. AGGREGATE VALUE OF PROPERTY OWNED BY FREE NEGROES—1860

County	Realty	Personalty	County	Realty	Personalty
Alamance	$13,500	$7,415	Johnston	$ 4,060	$ 4,853
Alexander	500	390	Jones	1,500	1,875
Alleghany	......	600	Lenoir	625	2,250
Anson	3,798	7,660	Lincoln	100	270
Ashe	2,200	2,495	Macon	4,050	5,100
Beaufort	12,410	6,960	Madison	......	615
Bertie	1,280	3,615	Martin	5,549	1,200
Bladen	6,289	5,112	McDowell	4,000	1,000
Brunswick	6,487	6,239	Mecklenburg	8,875	3,720
Buncombe	3,540	3,184	Montgomery	362	1,285
Burke	200	785	Moore	550	1,975
Cabarrus	1,072	2,050	Nash	8,939	10,889
Caldwell	1,295	1,284	New Hanover	37,720	35,060
Camden	1,000	768	Northampton	12,824	15,359
Carteret	3,150	950	Onslow	1,735	3,475
Caswell	4,208	5,530	Orange	2,800	13,375
Catawba	50	75	Pasquotank	20,440	22,195
Chatham	1,680	2,960	Perquimans	5,000	8,601
Cherokee	350	515	Person	5,180	3,080
Chowan	3,600	2,793	Pitt	2,100	5,560
Cleveland	3,150	4,652	Polk	700	1,446
Columbus	9,135	8,990	Randolph	5,290	8,745
Craven	29,865	21,137	Richmond	10,750	20,930
Cumberland	11,500	7,722	Robeson	37,555	42,159
Currituck	1,270	1,745	Rockingham	2,750	1,900
Davidson	1,200	1,428	Rowan	1,300	970
Davie	......	1,040	Rutherford	225	100
Duplin	3,360	3,777	Sampson	10,014	4,742
Edgecombe	7,100	10,350	Stanly	950	835
Forsyth	1,530	1,665	Stokes	325	550
Franklin	6,535	6,013	Surry	925	1,144
Gaston	2,700	2,300	Tyrrell	725	1,615
Gates	5,125	18,755	Union	300	975
Granville	15,987	13,845	Wake	22,204	45,362
Greene	2,475	2,920	Warren	9,931	13,935
Guilford	5,425	13,445	Washington	5,843	5,077
Halifax	30,948	42,778	Watauga	475	595
Harnett	......	375	Wayne	13,380	9,900
Haywood	......	75	Wilkes	2,710	3,835
Henderson	150	100	Wilson	4,984	3,999
Hertford	15,482	16,624	Yadkin	840	2,912
Hyde	1,000	8,000	Yancey	1,525	1,803
Iredell	330	150			
Jackson	......	125	Grand Total	$480,986	$564,657

APPENDIX III

FREE NEGRO OWNERS OF SLAVES

IT WILL BE interesting to observe the trend in the ownership of slaves by free Negroes during the period. Though the free Negro ownership of slaves was never an important factor in the economic life of North Carolina, the very existence of such a situation presents an engaging picture well worth observing. The fluctuation in the number of slaves owned by free Negroes—as well as the fluctuation in the number of owners—reveals an uncertainty and instability in the ownership of such property that tends to emphasize, further, its lack of consequence as an economic factor. The important humanitarian implications cannot be discerned in the figures, but that they were present is a fact that becomes quite apparent to the student of the subject.

FREE NEGRO OWNERS OF SLAVES—1790[1]

County and Name	Number	County and Name	Number
BEAUFORT		NORTHAMPTON	
John Brayborn	6	Peter Stewart	5
BERTIE		James Roberts	2
Samuel Johnston	11	David James	2
CRAVEN		John Waldin	1
Samuel Simmons	1	Jethro Bass	3
Ann Russel	1	Council Bass	2
John Allen	2	Byrd Cornet	3
CURRITUCK		ONSLOW	
James Thomas	1	Jemboy	6
HALIFAX		Virgil Dry	5
Samuel Hawkins	1	RICHMOND	
Polly Bird	1	Moses Turner	1
NEW HANOVER		ROBESON	
Pages	2	James Lowry	3
Hannah	1	Gilbert Cox	8
Hesse	3	Cannon Cumbo	1
		WARREN	
		William Bradley	1

1. U. S. Census Office, *First Census, 1790.*

FREE NEGRO OWNERS OF SLAVES—1830[2]

County and Name	Number	County and Name	Number
ANSON		Thos. Hollister..........	1
Thomas Jones..........	3	Delia Street............	2
BEAUFORT		Donom Mumford.......	10
Hull Anderson..........	4	Ann Austin.............	1
James Bonner..........	2	Brister Warrick........	8
Edny Brown...........	1	John R. Green..........	6
Betsy Walker..........	3	Matilda Lisbon.........	2
Church Moore..........	2	Jane Garret............	1
John Brown............	2	John S. Stanly..........	18
Clarissa Newton.......	4	John C. Stanly.........	14
Abram Allen..........	1	**CUMBERLAND**	
Eli Moore.............	3	Wining McIver........	1
Easter Rose...........	1	Polly Jackson..........	1
Thos. Walker..........	2	Bella Hadley..........	1
Thos. Bowen..........	2	Lucretia Artis.........	1
BERTIE		William Tutte..........	1
Mary James...........	1	Judy Jordan...........	1
Sally James...........	1	Esther Alvis...........	3
Penelope Hill..........	3	Daniel Munroe.........	1
Jane Ash..............	5	John Wood............	4
Willie Tutle...........	1	Sally Freeman..........	1
BLADEN		Thomas Grimes........	1
Gooden Bowen........	44	Elsey Hammonds.......	5
Eliza Spendlove.........	1	Phillis Dennis.........	4
Molsy Spendlove.......	3	Margaret Revels........	2
Michael Blanks.........	1	Betty Mallet..........	1
Samuel Allen...........	4	Jas. Dunn.............	3
Ann Spendlove.........	1	Geo. W. Ragland......	1
Catherine Smith.......	1	Chas. Mallett..........	36
BRUNSWICK		Chester Lott...........	2
John A. Potter..........	4	**DAVIDSON**	
Jimboy McKenzie.......	2	Tabitha Hotden........	1
CAMDEN		Jesse Cain....	1
Samuel Griffin.........	1	Sarah David...........	1
Thomas Spelmon.......	4	**FRANKLIN**	
Owen Spelmon..........	2	John Armstrong........	1
CASWELL		Sally Taltom..........	1
Thomas Day...........	2	**ORANGE**	
Mary Jones............	1	Fred Hartgrove.........	3
John Wilson...........	4	Lucy Peters............	1
Allen Caswell..........	3	**PASQUOTANK**	
James Worsham........	1	Will Morris............	2
CHATHAM		Aaron Price...........	1
Jerry Anderson.........	1	Alfred Harvey..........	1
CHOWAN		**PERQUIMANS**	
Richard N. Grean.......	4	Dorothy Bagie..........	1
Marey Hornablow......	2	Charlotte Randel.......	1
Jeffrey Iredell..........	1	Mills Winslow.........	7
Lucey How............	3	Jacob Robins...........	1
John Littlejohn.........	1	Judith Overton........	1
Gustavus A. Johnson....	4	Charlotte Nixon........	2
James Bozman.........	1	James Wadkins........	4
CRAVEN		Winney Overton........	1
Jas. G. Stanly..........	10	Nancy Modlin..........	1
Jas. Y. Green...........	4	Penny Overton.........	2

2. Woodson, *Free Negro Owners of Slaves in 1830*. In each case, the figures were checked by the writer.

Free Negro Owners of Slaves—1830 *(Continued)*

County and Name	Number	County and Name	Number
Levina Overton	1	Simon Larington	1
Theny Overton	1	Phillis Bagadeir	1
Nelly Overton	1	Wm. Buffo	1
Jeremiah Williams	3	Leuris Pajay	4
Robert Tucker	2	John Walker	44
Thos. Charles	6	Roger Hazell	5
John Mitchell	3	Jas. Campbell	2
Thos. Blacknel	7	Henry Sampson	5
Benj. Hicks	4	ONSLOW	
Milbry Mitchel	2	Caesar Loomiss	2
Rosetta Evans	2	Benj. Jarman	5
EDGECOMBE		Rose Winslow	3
Elizabeth Scott	3	Luke White	5
Wm. Thompson	5	Sampson Lawrence	7
Henry Morgan	1	PITT	
GATES		Ned Brown	3
Jottro Martin	1	RICHMOND	
Nisom Cuff	1	Pleasant Mask	8
Thos. Hansford	1	ROBESON	
GRANVILLE		James Lowrie	5
Jacob Fain	1	SAMPSON	
Nelson Cousins	1	West Pope	1
HALIFAX		STOKES	
John Jourdan	1	Wm. Shepperd	1
Absalom Richardson	1	Ralph Mason	1
Miles Howard	2	WAKE	
Tabitha Jones	1	Allen Jones	6
Wesley Mills	2	Pope Burwell	1
Lucy Worrel	1	Charles Jones	3
Sally Taylor	1	John Malon	3
Amy Johnson	3	Samuel Green	7
Peggy Taylor	1	John Scott	4
Malissa Cain	1	Marsh Wilson	1
Ann Curtis	3	Nancy Swims	1
Pompey Jones	2	Abigail Evins	4
Olive Hammons	1	Wm. Smith	2
HERTFORD		John Dunn	5
Meede Melton	2	Silvans Smellings	2
Penelope Mandley	1	Prudy Taylor	1
Jaston Renalds	2	Wm. Holmes	3
Lewis Jordan	3	Phil Seawell	5
David Roberts	2	Sally Woodward	1
Jeston Renalds	1	Polly Maxwell	4
David Boon	1	WARREN	
LENOIR		Wm. Cosey	1
Nellie Dutton	1	John Day	1
MARTIN		Stephen Holmes	1
Jno. Critchion	24	Jacob Burt	1
Larry James	1	Isaac Evans	1
Martha James	1	Tabby Evans	1
NASH		Matthew Evans	5
Humphrey Revill	14	Thos. Green	1
NORTHAMPTON		WASHINGTON	
Anthony Wheeler	2	Nancy Boston	1
Ruthy Boone	1	WAYNE	
NEW HANOVER		Joel Burnet	3
Geo. Ware	1	WILKES	
Wanely Mosely	1	Negro Anthony	1
Mary Cruise	3		

County and Name	Number	County and Name	Number
CLEVELAND		CRAVEN	
E. H. Revel..............	2	Catherine Stanly........	7
CASWELL		HERTFORD	
Thomas Day...........	3	Henry Vaughan.........	1
ANSON		FRANKLIN	
Thomas Jones..........	5	Thomas Blacknall.......	3
GRANVILLE		John Hogwood..........	1
Will Evans.............	3		

3. From the unpublished population schedules of the Eighth Census.

APPENDIX IV

FREE NEGROES IN COUNTY POOR HOUSES—1860[1]

NOT ALL OF THE county institutions for the care of the indigent poor had accommodations for free Negroes. It is difficult to believe, moreover, that those which existed were adequate. The unpublished census schedules for 1860 abound with the names of free Negroes who give every evidence of being worthy of such institutional care; but the following list indicates that only a relative few received such care.

County	Number	County	Number
Cabarrus................	1	Onslow................	1
Cumberland.............	1	Orange................	2
Davidson................	1	Pasquotank............	8
Edgecombe..............	1	Randolph.............	1
Guilford................	5	Rockingham...........	3
Halifax.................	1	Rowan................	1
Hyde...................	1	Wake.................	1
Green..................	1	Washington............	2
Northampton...........	7	Wayne................	1

1. From the unpublished population schedules of the Eighth Census.

APPENDIX V

Contributions of North Carolinians to the American Colonization Society[1]

The list of contributors to the colonization movement is, in itself, a story of the successes and failings of the Society in the State of North Carolina. While the motives of the contributors are seldom disclosed, one can reasonably conclude that they were generally in accordance with the motives of the national body. All contributors had at least one belief in common: that North Carolina's troubles would be noticeably diminished if the free Negro were removed from the State. Nothing brings out clearer than the following list the fact that the contributors were a most heterogeneous lot. Often their attitude toward the free Negro was the only thing that they had in common.

Contributions of North Carolinians to the American Colonization Society

Name	Amount	Location
1825		
Rev. Jas. Caldwell	$ 10.00	Chapel Hill
Aux. Soc. Raleigh	100.00	Raleigh
H. D. Gould	5.00	Iredell County
Jas. Williamson	3.00	Roxboro
Aux. Soc.	50.00	Elizabeth City
Aux. Soc.	46.00	Hillsboro
1826		
W. Hooper	5.00	Chapel Hill
Dr. Caldwell	10.00	Chapel Hill
Presby. Church	20.00	Fayetteville
Rev. Douglas' Church	8.00	Milton
Aux. Soc.	150.00	Raleigh
Aux. Soc.	35.00	Hillsboro
John French	149.74	Collections
Aux. Soc.	10.00	Greensboro
Nat Mendenhall	500.00	Guilford County
Mary Mendenhall	50.00	James Town
1827		
Thos. Mendenhall	300.00	Guilford County
Aux. Soc.	100.00	Elizabeth City
Rev. T. Clinton	9.00	Greensboro
Rev. Caldwell	10.00	Chapel Hill
Rev. Hammer	10.00	Fayetteville
Rev. W. Opaisley	20.00	James Town
Jas. Williamson	2.00	Roxboro
Presby. Church	10.00	Wilmington
Donations	80.00	Wilmington

1. From the first thirty-six volumes of the *African Repository*, 1825-1860.

Name	*Amount*	*Location*
1828		
Jas. Nourse	139.65	Collections
Jas. Caldwell	10.00	Chapel Hill
Presby. Church	13.00	Hillsboro
Aux. Soc.	60.00	Pasquotank
Collections	5.00	Cabarrus County
Collections	5.00	Oxford
Aux. Soc.	31.00	Greensboro
Rev. W. Hooper	3.00	Chapel Hill
1829		
Rock River Congreg.	10.00	Mecklenburg Co.
Ann Smith	20.00	Granville County
Rev. Jas. Caldwell	10.00	Chapel Hill
Collection	2.31	Rutherfordton
Collection	5.00	Asheville
J. Williamson	6.00	Roxboro
Collection	15.00	Raleigh
Natle Mendenhall	400.00	–Quakers–
1830		
D. Southall	10.00	Murfreesboro
Rocky Congreg.	10.00	Cabarrus Co.
Anonymous	5.00	
Female Academy	10.00	Salem
St. John's Church	16.00	Fayetteville
Rev. D. A. Penick	15.00	Milton
Rev. C. Bradshaw	2.25	Asheville
Presby. Church	20.00	Raleigh
H. M. Kerr	5.00	Duncan Creek
Mrs. L. Kraush	3.00	Salem
J. Williamson	3.00	Roxboro
Presby. Church	16.75	Fayetteville
1831		
Collection	5.00	Rutherford
Ann Smith	5.00	Williamsboro
Collection	10.00	Fulton
Presby. Church	7.00	Raleigh
Aux. Soc.	3.00	Raleigh
Temp. Soc.	31.00	Asheville
Benevolent Assn.	10.00	Poplar Tent
J. Williams	3.00	Roxboro
Jas. I. Grey	145.00	Halifax Co.
Gideon Harvey	3.00	Halifax Co.
Rev. J. Caldwell	20.00	Chapel Hill
1832		
H. M. Kerr	5.25	Rutherfordton
Jas. Forman	.75	Rutherfordton
J. Williamson	3.00	Roxboro
Presby. Church	20.00	Hillsboro
Jas. T. Grey	43.00	Granville Co.
Collection	4.00	Asheville
Presby. Church	17.00	Newbern

Name	Amount	Location
1833		
Mr. Williams	1.00	
Collection	12.00	Salisbury
Jas. Caldwell	10.00	Chapel Hill
Jas. Williamson	3.00	Roxboro
1834		
J. Janvier	2.50	
Jas. Williamson	3.00	Person Co.
1835		
Aux. Soc.	15.00	Raleigh
Lewis Sheridan	3.00	Bladen
1836		
John Moore	4.00	Rutherford
Rev. Jas. Purvis	3.00	Johnston Co.
Aux. Soc.	24.00	Raleigh
Presby. Church	20.00	Fayetteville
A. lady	.50	Wake Co.
3 ladies	2.05	Wake Co.
1837		
2 colored persons for passage, etc.	120.00	Stokes Co.
Presby. Church	89.80	Raleigh
Presby. Church	55.83	Fayetteville
Method Church	21.41	Fayetteville
Rev. Buxton	10.00	Fayetteville
J. Evans	5.00	Fayetteville
C. P. Mallett	14.00	Fayetteville
Presby. Church	62.56	Wilmington
Method Church	10.00	Asheville
1838		
Aux. Soc.	15.87	
Episcopal Church	22.00	Hillsboro
John Moore	5.00	Rutherford
A. J. Battle	6.00	Rocky Mount
1839		
John Moore	5.00	White Rock
Tour of state	386.55	—Rev. Eli Hunter
1840		
John Rex	520.00	Raleigh
Collection by Rev. McKinney	127.19	Elizabeth City
M. E. Church	12.93	Washington
Capt. Taylor	10.00	Washington
Mr. Fowle	5.00	Washingto.
Chas. Moules	5.00	Washington
B. Rungen	5.00	Washington
A. Friend	5.00	Washington
Collection	104.40	Newbern
Colored People	9.00	Washington
Dr. Freeman	3.00	Washington
Collection	20.09	Plymouth
Collection	3.00	Chowan County

Name	Amount	Location
Collection	51.26	Hertford
Collection	7.25	Halls Creek
Collection	29.10	Pasquotank
Collection	6.87	Gates Co.
Collection	10.19	Gates Co.
Collection	27.25	Gatesville
Collection	58.25	Perquimans
Collection	453.54	—whole state
Miss Collins	15.00	Edenton
Collection	58.00	Halifax Co.
M. E. Church	11.43	Warrenton
Collection	52.76	Raleigh
Collection	36.05	Hillsboro
Collection	37.46	Greensboro
W. W. Price	3.00	Caswell Co.
John Kerr	5.50	Wentworth
Quakers	215.92	Greensboro

1841

Name	Amount	Location
Jas. Purvis	8.00	Wilkesboro
Jno. Moore	5.00	
Collections by Rev. McKinney	112.31	
Colored People	6.83	
Church	36.00	Milton
Collections by Rev. McKinney	50.00	
Well Wishers	8.00	

1842

Name	Amount	Location
Collection	24.50	Raleigh
Jesse Harper	20.00	Randolph
Collection	33.00	Stokes
Collection	10.81	Greensboro
Collection	12.00	Deep River
M. E. Church	3.25	Jamestown
Presby. Church	5.00	Orange Co.
Collection	11.00	Franklin Co.
Collection	8.50	Lewisburg
Collection	8.00	Granville
Collection	46.00	Paris

1843—by Rev. Jas. Higgins

Name	Amount	Location
Collection	26.26	Fayetteville
Baptist Church	3.00	Wilmington

1844

Name	Amount	Location
Matthias Freeman for passage	29.00	Smithfield

1845—by Rev. J. B. Penny

Name	Amount	Location
Collection	68.00	Raleigh
Collection	66.14	Fayetteville
Jas. Bell for passage	200.00	Halifax

1847

Name	Amount	Location
Collection	7.28	Greensborough
Presby. Church	5.00	Pioneer Mills
Thos. Kennedy	.50	Waynesboro

Name	Amount	Location
1848		
Thos. Kennedy	10.00	Waynesboro
1849		
Jesse Rankin	10.00	Lexington
Collection by Rev. H. Brown	106.48	(Scattered)
Church	28.00	Pioneer Mills
Collection	6.56	Lexington
Bethel Church	2.60	Greensboro
Presby. Church	18.52	Hillsboro
Unity Church	28.00	Lincoln Co.
W. G. Bingham	30.00	Clover Garden
Presby. Church	4.00	Sugar Creek
Presby. & Method	25.26	Fayetteville
Colored People	3.48	Wilmington
Collection	51.44	Wilmington
Presby. Church	42.15	Newbern
Churches	21.21	Washington
Collection	29.50	Raleigh
College	8.00	Wake Forest
Presby. Church	13.00	Fairfield
Collection	13.25	Hillsboro
Collection	13.00	Milton
Presby. Church	4.00	Guilford Co.
John Newlin	5.00	Lindsley's Store
Collection	12.00	Hopewell
Presby. Church	5.57	Statesville
Collection	3.80	Black Creek
Collection	43.25	Cabarrus Co.
Collection	42.24	Mecklenburg Co.
Collection	10.00	Rowan Co.
Collection	18.50	Guilford Co.
Euphronia Church	3.00	Moore Co.
1850—by Jesse Rankin		
Collection	35.00	Lexington
Dan McGilvary	5.00	Pittsborough
Collection	9.00	Yanceyville
Wm. Mebane	5.00	Mason Hall
Collection	8.00	Bethesda
Collection	63.75	Rockingham Co.
Collection	5.75	Madison
Collection	20.75	Leaksville
Dr. W. F. Bason	3.00	Salisbury
J. A. Worth	10.00	Gold Hill
Collection	53.50	Randolph Co.
Collection	3.00	Union Factory
Collection	9.50	Asheborough
Collection	8.00	Franklinville
Collection	6.25	Cedar Falls
Collection	5.75	Cabarrus
Collection	16.50	Concord
Collection	4.20	Davidson Co.
Collection	11.00	Rowan Co.

Name	Amount	Location
Collection	16.00	Salisbury
Collection	5.00	Clemmonsville
Martin and Vestal	1.00	Huntsville
Collection	9.00	Salisbury
Dr. Hugh Kelly	10.00	Gold Hill
Collection	15.00	Statesville
Collection	2.00	Bethany Church
Collection	18.25	Tabor Church
Collection	7.00	Lexington
Collection	12.50	Jamestown
Collection	24.00	Greensboro
Collection	11.00	Wilkesboro
Jos. Newton	1.00	New Market
B. L. Beall	10.00	Taylorsville
Rocky River Church	14.00	Pioneer Mills
Collection	1.25	Jamestown
Collection	17.50	Deep River
Collection	7.62	New Garden
Collection	25.00	Salem
Collection	17.50	Bethania
Collection	8.00	Lexington
Collection	8.00	Statesville
Collection	31.50	Taylorsville
Collection	21.00	Salisbury
Collection	10.50	Gold Hill
Collection	30.00	LaGrange
Collection	2.50	Gold Hill
Collection	64.75	Wadesborough
Collection	11.00	Rockingham
Centre Church	24.15	Robeson Co.
Eliza. Eccles	59.50	Fayetteville
Collection	4.00	Murchison
Asheborough	3.00	Asheborough
Collection	24.00	Greensboro
B. Watkins	2.50	Leaksville

1851

Name	Amount	Location
Collection	4.00	Cabarrus Co.
Sharon Church	5.00	Mecklenburg Co.
Collection	67.50	Charlotte
Collection	21.00	Sugar Creek Church
Collection	17.00	Pleasant Hill
Collection	17.00	Steel Creek
C. C. Graham	3.00	Lincoln Co.
Collection	2.50	Davidson Co.
S. C. Miller	5.00	Statesville
Collection	71.10	Salisbury
Davidson College	8.00	Mecklenburg Co.
Bethany Church	5.00	Iredell Co.
Collection	8.50	Huntsville
Collection	14.00	Lexington
Dr. D. C. Mebane	2.00	Greensboro
Collection	5.75	Alamance Co.

Name	Amount	Location
Newlin's Factory	5.50	Orange Co.
Collection	37.95	Hillsboro
Collection	12.00	Bethmont
Collection	44.50	Chapel Hill
Collection	101.70	Raleigh
Collection	30.00	Smithfield
Collection	15.25	Goldsboro
Collection	24.25	Everittsville
Quakers	19.00	Neuse River Meeting
Collection	18.50	Duplin Co.
Collection	9.00	Bladen Co.
Collection	6.75	New Hanover Co.
Collection	99.50	Wilmington
Collection	7.00	Salisbury
Collection	3.00	Third Creek Church
J. D. Hall	2.00	Lincoln Co.
Sugar Creek Church	1.00	Mecklenburg Co.
Dr. S. D. Schofield	3.00	Hillsboro
Collection	17.00	Greensboro
J. R. McIntosh	2.00	Moore Co.
Collection	3.00	Lexington
W. P. Beall	.50	Taylorsville
Collection	60.00	Oxford
Collection	14.90	Henderson
Collection	2.75	Franklin Co.
Collection	39.50	Louisburg
Collection	56.50	Warrenton
P. P. Lawrence	10.00	Tarboro
Collection	13.55	Tarboro
Collection	71.45	Washington
Collection	73.65	Newbern
Collection	4.00	Kinston
J. C. Lamb	1.00	Jamestown
Collection	10.00	Warrenton
Collection	10.00	Yanceyville
R. S. Smith	10.00	Red House
Collection	22.50	Milton
Collection	18.00	Harmony
Collection	8.00	Roxboro
Collection	9.00	Goshen
Jno. C. Taylor	2.00	Oxford
Collection	33.60	Nutbush
Collection	14.85	Grassy Creek
Collection	5.00	Shiloh
Collection	16.00	Spring Cove
Collection	30.00	Greensboro
Collection	3.00	Davidson Co.
S. C. Boyden	1.00	Rowan Co.
E. R. Stimson	1.00	Iredell Co.
Collection	18.10	Randolph Co.
Collection	17.75	Chatham Co.
Collection	12.07	Moore Co.
Collection	78.50	Cumberland Co.

Name	Amount	Location
Collection	8.00	Fayetteville
M. Carnion	5.00	Cabarrus Co.
Collection	12.50	Mecklenburg Co.
Collection	1.00	Salisbury
Collection	2.50	Gold Hill
Collection	8.00	Albemarle
Collection	11.00	Wadesboro
Collection	49.00	Richmond Co.
Collection	57.40	Robeson Co.

1852—by Rev. Jesse Rankin

Collection	4.00	Cumberland Co.
Collection	28.00	Lexington
Samuel Cox	1.50	Randolph
Rev. C. Caldwell	1.00	Guilford
Collection	11.00	Gold Hill
Collection	48.75	Concord
Collection	48.45	Mecklenburg Co.
Collection	6.50	Davidson Co.
Collection	2.00	Greensboro
Collection	26.50	Graham
Collection	12.50	Hausfield's Church
Rev. S. Shell	1.00	Macksville
Collection	13.00	Lexington
Collection	6.00	Charlotte
Samuel Rankin	10.00	Rowan
Collection	6.00	Robeson Co.
Miss Jane Haden	1.00	Davie
Rev. Jesse Rankin	3.00	Rowan

1853

Dr. Dixon	3.00	Wilmington
Jonathan Worth	5.00	Asheboro
Nicholas Williams	10.00	Huntsville
S. C. Miller	5.00	Poplar Grove
Collection	30.00	Wilmington

1854

John Kelly's will	240.00	Orange Co.
Church	14.25	New Bern
J. B. Grasty	2.00	Yanceyville
A. Friend	1.00	Hillsboro
Jno. Newlin	5.00	Lindley's Store
Rev. Neal McKay	20.00	Somerville
Jas. C. Johnson	60.00	Elizabeth City

1855

Andrew Chapel	4.00	New Bern
Henry Turner	20.00	Raleigh
Collection	42.58	Raleigh
Miss M. C. Moore	4.00	Chapel Hill
Collection	12.00	Charlotte
W. J. Bingham	10.00	Oaks
Collection	50.00	Salisbury
Collection	10.00	Guilford Co.

Name	Amount	Location
Collection	1.00	Cabarrus Co.
Rev. T. N. Paxton	3.00	Marion
Rev. Sam Paisley	10.00	Watson's Bridge
W. A. Caldwell	5.00	Greensboro
Jno. Bullock	6.00	Williamsboro

1856

A Friend	1.00	Gregory's
Prof. S. Pool	4.00	Chapel Hill
Jno. Newlin	5.00	Lindley's Store
Rev. T. Atkinson	25.00	Raleigh
Collection	40.00	Salisbury
Andrew Hunt	10.00	Lexington
Mrs. P. Corlew's will	755.00	Halifax
Collection	10.00	Jackson
Collection	29.47	Murfreesboro
L. Jones, Jr.	60.00	Bryant Swamp
Andrew Chapel	5.00	New Bern

1857

Collection	141.50	Edenton
Method. Church	11.20	McBirdes
Collection	18.50	South Mills
G. S. Cherry	5.00	Washington
Collection	13.00	Perquimans Co.
F. D. Thomas, For passage	35.00	New Bern
J. J. McKay's will	2,210.00	Bladen Co.
Collection	32.00	New Bern
Jno. Thompson	10.00	Edenton

1858—by Rev. W. H. Starr

Nathan Winslow	10.00	Perquimans
James L. Bryant estate	534.54	Bertie Co.
W. H. Nelson estate	1,989.10	New Bern
J. J. McKay for his former slaves	6,000.00	Bladen Co.
Jas. L. Bryan	385.00	Bertie Co.

1859

Rev. A. Empie	10.00	Wilmington
Rev. D. A. Penick	5.00	Pioneer Mills

1860

Heirs of Mrs. Janet Hollister	770.00	New Bern

Total	$23,439.53	

Bibliography

PRIMARY SOURCES

1. *Manuscripts*

Alamance County, Minutes of the Court of Pleas and Quarter Sessions, 1849-1860. 2 v. In the Archives of the North Carolina Historical Commission.

Beaufort County, List of Taxables, 1847-1852. 2 v. In the Archives of the North Carolina Historical Commission.

Beaufort County, Minutes of the Court of Pleas and Quarter Sessions, 1824-1829; 1832-1838. 2 v. Beaufort County Courthouse, Washington, N. C.

Bell (Major) Papers, 1853-1864. In the Manuscript Collection of the Duke University Library.

Bertie County, Minutes of the Court of Pleas and Quarter Sessions, 1803-1858. 9 v. In the Archives of the North Carolina Historical Commission.

Bladen County, Miscellaneous Material, October 13, 1773. A list of free Negroes on the king's land. In the Archives of the North Carolina Historical Commission.

Brown (Neill) Papers, 1792-1867. In the Manuscript Collection of the Duke University Library.

Bryan (James W.) Papers, 1704-1860. In the Manuscript Collection of the Library of the University of North Carolina.

Bryan (John H.) Papers, 1798-1860. In the Manuscript Collection of the Duke University Library.

Bryan (John H.) Papers, 1773-1860. Interesting observations on the free Negroes of New Bern. In the Archives of the North Carolina Historical Commission.

Buncombe County, Minutes of the Court of Pleas and Quarter Sessions, 1822-1824. 1 v. In the Archives of the North Carolina Historical Commission.

Burton (Hutchings G.) Papers, 1826. 1 v. In the Archives of the North Carolina Historical Commission.

Caldwell (David F.) Papers, 1830-1860. In the Manuscript Collection of the Library of the University of North Carolina.

Carteret County, Minutes of the Court of Pleas and Quarter Sessions. 14 v. In the Archives of the North Carolina Historical Commission.

Craven County, Minutes of the Court of Pleas and Quarter Sessions, 1807-1868. In the Archives of the North Carolina Historical Commission.

Craven County, Bonds for Emancipated Slaves, 1782-1831. 1 Ms. box. In the Archives of the North Carolina Historical Commission.

Craven County, Apprenticeship Papers, 1800-1860. Includes the apprenticeship bonds for free Negro children. 9 Ms. boxes. In the Archives of the North Carolina Historical Commission.

Cumberland County, Minutes of the Court of Pleas and Quarter Sessions, 1800-1860. 28 v. In the Archives of the North Carolina Historical Commission.

Edgecombe County, Minutes of the Court of Pleas and Quarter Sessions, 1797-1856. 16 v. In the Archives of the North Carolina Historical Commission.

Fisher (Charles and Charles F.) Papers, 1758-1860. In the Manuscript Collection of the Library of the University of North Carolina.

Free Negro Papers, 1801-1850. Register of Free Persons of Color, Rustberg (Campbell County), Virginia. In the Manuscript Collection of the Duke University Library.

Gates County, Minutes of the Court of Pleas and Quarter Sessions, 1786-1820. 9 v. In the Archives of the North Carolina Historical Commission.

Guilford County, Miscellaneous Material, 1774-1854 (scattered dates). 1 Ms. box. In the Archives of the North Carolina Historical Commission.

Halifax County, List of Taxables, 1784-1863. 1 Ms. box. In the Archives of the North Carolina Historical Commission.

Johnson (Austin) Papers, 1836-1861. In the Manuscript Collection of the Duke University Library.

Legislative Papers of North Carolina, 1770-1860. About 450 Ms. boxes. This is an indispensable source for this work, containing petitions, correspondence, and proposed bills concerning the free Negro. In the Archives of the North Carolina Historical Commission.

Mangum (Willie P.) Papers, 1825-1840. (Typescript.) Contains the letters of Chavis to Mangum. In the Archives of the North Carolina Historical Commission.

Mangum (Willie P. and A. W.) Papers, 1804-1832. In the Manuscript Collection of the Library of the University of North Carolina.

Miscellaneous Papers, n.d. Advice on how to emancipate slaves. In the Manuscript Collection of the Duke University Library.

Negro Antislavery Papers, 1812-1860. In the Manuscript Collection of the Duke University Library.

Norfleet Papers, 1784-1865. In the Manuscript Collection of the Library of the University of North Carolina.

Orange County, Minutes of the Court of Pleas and Quarter Sessions, 1800-1857. 14 v. In the Archives of the North Carolina Historical Commission.

Owen (John) Letter Book, 1828-1830. 1 v. In the Archives of the North Carolina Historical Commission.

Pasquotank County, Minutes of the Court of Pleas and Quarter Sessions, 1800-1860. 8 v. In the Archives of the North Carolina Historical Commission.

Perquimans County, Petitions for Emancipation of Slaves, 1713-1814. 1 Ms. box. In the Archives of the North Carolina Historical Commission.

Perquimans County, Miscellaneous Papers, 1709-1831. 1 Ms. box. Emancipation Bonds. In the Archives of the North Carolina Historical Commission.

Pettigrew Family Papers, 1684-1837. In the Manuscript Collection of the Library of the University of North Carolina.

Ravenscroft (John Stark) Papers, 1829. In the Manuscript Collection of the Duke University Library.

Robeson (James A.) Papers, 1854-1864. In the Manuscript Collection of the Duke University Library.

Slavery References, 1787. Connecticut Court Records of an attempt to steal a free Negro from North Carolina. In the Manuscript Collection of the Library of the University of North Carolina.

Stokes (Montfort) Letter Book, 1831-1832. In the Archives of the North Carolina Historical Commission.

Venable (A. W.) Scrap Book, 1849-1850. In the Manuscript Collection of the Duke University Library.

Wake County, Apprenticeship Papers, 1830-1860. 1. Ms. box. In the Archives of the North Carolina Historical Commission.

Williams (John Buxton) Papers, 1804-1870. In the Manuscript Collection of the Duke University Library.

Yancey (Bartlett) Papers, 1817-1828. In the Manuscript Collection of the Library of the University of North Carolina.

York (Brantley) Autobiography, 1876-1888. In the Manuscript Collection of the Duke University Library.

2. *Books and Pamphlets*

Andrews, Evangeline Walker, ed., *Journal of a Lady of Quality*. New Haven, 1921.

Clark, Walter, ed., *The State Records of North Carolina*. 16 v. Winston, 1905. These volumes contain much important material on the free Negro for the early national period.

Coffin, Levi, *Reminiscences*. Cincinnati, 1880. By the "President" of the Underground Railroad, who had some interesting experiences with free Negroes in North Carolina.

DeBow, J. D. B., *Industrial Resources, Statistics, etc. of the United States*. 3 v. New York, 1854.

Edwards, Richard, comp., *Statistical Gazeteer of the State of Virginia and North Carolina*. 2 v. Richmond, 1856.

Forster, William, *Memoirs of William Forster*. London, 1865. The autobiography of a prominent English Quaker, who was interested in the education of free Negroes of North Carolina.

Grimes, John Bryan, *Abstract of North Carolina Wills*. Raleigh, 1910.
———, *North Carolina Wills and Inventories*. Raleigh, 1912.

Helper, Hinton R., *The Impending Crisis of the South: How to Meet It*. New York, 1857.

Hurd, John Codman, *Law of Freedom and Bondage in the United States*. 2 v. Boston, 1858. Valuable for its comparisons of the laws of various states.

Jay, William, *On the Condition of the Free People of Colour in the United States*. New York, 1839. A vigorous denunciation of those who treated the free Negro harshly, written by a foe of the American Colonization Society.

Journal of a Convention Assembled . . . to Adopt Such Measures As Were Deemed Necessary to Procure an Amendment to the Constitution of North Carolina. Raleigh, 1823.

Lane, Lunsford, *Narrative of Lunsford Lane, Published by Himself*. 2nd ed. Boston, 1842. An exciting and perhaps an exaggerated autobiography of a Raleigh free Negro who was run out of the State in 1842.

Lefler, Hugh T., ed., *North Carolina History Told by Contemporaries*. Chapel Hill, 1934.

Melbourn, Julius, *Life and Opinions of Julius Melbourn*. Syracuse, 1847. The autobiography of a well-educated free Negro who finally left North Carolina and settled in England.

Methodist Episcopal Church, *Minutes of Annual Conferences, 1773-1845*. 3 v. New York, 1845.

Methodist Episcopal Church, South, *Minutes of Annual Conferences, 1846-1861*.

Nell, William C., *The Colored Patriots of the American Revolution*. Boston, 1855. Valuable as an example of propaganda. It discusses, for example, the careers of several Negroes who were born *after* the Revolutionary period.

New York Colonization Society, *Sixth Annual Report*. New York, 1838.

Olmsted, Frederick Law, *A Journey in the Seaboard Slave States, with Remarks on Their Economy.* New York, 1856. The author makes several keen observations on the free Negroes of North Carolina.

Paris, John, *A History of the Methodist Protestant Church.* Baltimore, 1849.

Phillips, Ulrich Bonnell, ed., *Plantation and Frontier Documents, 1649-1863.* 2 v. (John R. Commons, ed., *Documentary History of American Industrial Society.*) Cleveland, 1909. Contains authentic accounts of slave conspiracies in North Carolina.

Presbyterian Synod of North Carolina, *Minutes of the Thirty-Eighth Annual Session, 1851.* Raleigh, 1851.

Purefoy, George W., *History of Sandy Creek Baptist Association, 1758-1858.* New York, 1859.

Reichel, Levin T., *The Moravians of North Carolina.* Philadelphia, 1857.

Saunders, William L., ed., *The Colonial Records of North Carolina.* 10 v. Raleigh, 1890. These volumes contain all of the important materials of the colonial period.

Shillitoe, Thomas, *Journal of Thomas Shillitoe.* 2 v. London, 1839.

Travis, Joseph, *Autobiography.* Nashville, 1855. The life of an important Methodist minister, who was familiar with the problems of the free Negro Methodists of North Carolina.

Wagstaff, Henry M., ed., *The Minutes of the North Carolina Manumission Society, 1816-1834.* (James Sprunt Historical Studies, XXII.) Chapel Hill, 1934. Sheds much light on the growth of the free Negro population in North Carolina.

Walker, David, *Walker's Appeal, in Four Articles; Together with a Preamble, to the Coloured Citizens of the World, but in Particular, and Very Expressly, to Those of the United States of America, Written in Boston, State of Massachusetts, September 28, 1829.* Boston, 1830. This is one of the most violent pieces of antislavery literature to appear during the period. It was written by a free Negro who formerly lived in Wilmington, North Carolina.

3. *Newspapers and Periodicals*

African Repository, 1835-1860. The official organ of the American Colonization Society, containing, among many useful items, the annual reports of the Society.

Asheville News, 1854-1859. This paper represented the point of view of the western part of the State. It was Democratic and violently anti-free Negro.

Atlantic (New Bern), 1854.

DeBow's Review, 1850-1860.

Fayetteville Observer, 1819-1860. Sometimes published as the *Carolina Observer.* It was a Whig newspaper that depended largely on the *Raleigh Register* for its news and its point of view.

Greensborough Patriot, 1826-1860. For the first fifteen years this newspaper represented the liberal Quaker point of view. In the eighteen-fifties, however, it became Democratic and violently anti-free Negro.

Newbern Journal, 1855.

Newbernian (New Bern), 1844-1850.

New Era (Wilmington), 1858-1859.

New Era and Commercial Advertiser (New Bern), 1858-1859.

North Carolina Standard (Raleigh), 1834-1860. This newspaper was the leading Democratic paper of the State. It was consistently against the free Negro.

Raleigh Register, 1799-1860. This was the leading Whig paper of the State. It often displayed a sympathetic attitude toward the free Negro.

Star (Raleigh), 1809-1855.

Union (New Bern), 1857-1858.

Western Democrat (Charlotte), 1853-1860. This paper was not averse to raising the issue of the free Negro in the State political campaigns. It was opposed to the free Negro.

4. *Public Documents*

Constitutional Convention of 1835, *Journal of the Convention.* Raleigh, 1835.

Constitutional Convention of 1835, *Proceedings and Debates of the Convention.* Raleigh, 1835. Invaluable in ascertaining the attitude of various sections of the State toward free Negroes as reflected in the remarks of the delegates.

Hening, William Waller, *The Statutes at Large; Being a Collection of All the Laws of Virginia.* Vol. 5. Richmond.

North Carolina, *Laws of the State, 1790-1860.* Sessional. Published by the State.

North Carolina, *Journals of the House and the Senate of the General Assembly, 1800-1860.* Published by the State.

North Carolina, *Reports of Cases Argued and Determined in the Supreme Court of North Carolina, 1798-1860.* Published by the State.

North Carolina, *Revised Code.* Boston, 1855.

North Carolina, *Revised Statutes.* 2 v. Raleigh, 1837.

Proceedings of the Friends of Convention. Raleigh, 1822.

Raleigh, North Carolina, *Ordinances and By-Laws of the Board of Commissioners.* Raleigh, 1854.

Shepherd, Samuel, *The Statutes at Large of Virginia.* Vol. 3. Richmond, 1836.

United States Census Office, *First Census, 1790; Return of the Whole Number of Persons Within the Several Districts of the United States.* Washington, 1802.

United States Census Office, *Second Census, 1800; Return of the Whole Number of Persons Within the Several Districts of the United States.* Washington, 1802.

United States Census Office, *Third Census, 1810; Aggregate Amount of Each Description Within the United States of America.* Washington, 1811.

United States Census Office, *Fourth Census, 1820; Census for 1820.* Washington, 1821.

United States Census Office, *Fifth Census, 1830.* Washington, 1832.

United States Census Office, *Sixth Census, 1840; An Enumeration of the Inhabitants of the United States.* Washington, 1841.

United States Census Office, *Seventh Census, 1850.* Washington, 1853.

United States Census Office, *Eighth Census; The Population of the United States in 1860.* Washington, 1864.

United States Census Office, *Population Schedules of the Eighth Census.* (Unpublished.) These volumes contain information on the occupations and property holdings of free Negroes.

Secondary Works

1. Books and Monographs

Adams, Alice D., *The Neglected Period of Anti-Slavery in America, 1808-1831.* Boston, 1908.

Amis, Moses, *Historical Raleigh from 1792.* Raleigh, 1902.

Aptheker, Herbert, *Negro Slave Revolts in the United States, 1526-1860.* New York, 1939. A vigorous attempt to show that the Negro was not docile. Unfortunately, the author never achieves objectivity.

Arthur, John Preston, *Western North Carolina, 1730-1913.* Raleigh, 1914.

Ashe, Samuel A'Court, *History of North Carolina.* 2 v. Raleigh, 1925.

Bassett, John Spencer, *Anti-Slavery Leaders of North Carolina* (Johns Hopkins Studies, Series XVI, No. 6). Baltimore, 1898.

———, *Slavery in the State of North Carolina* (Johns Hopkins Studies, Series XVII, Nos. 7 and 8). Baltimore, 1899. Contains a sketch on the free Negro; based, however, on interviews and hearsay narratives rather than on documentary evidence.

———, *Slavery and Servitude in the Colony of North Carolina* (Johns Hopkins Studies, Series XIV, Nos. 4 and 5). Baltimore, 1896.

Bernheim, G. D., *History of the German Settlements and of the Lutheran Church in North and South Carolina.* Philadelphia, 1872.

Birney, William, *James G. Birney and His Times.* New York, 1890.

Boyd, William K., *History of North Carolina: The Federal Period, 1783-1860*. Chicago, 1919.

Brawley, Benjamin, *Negro Builders and Heroes*. Chapel Hill, 1937. Contains a sketch of the life of John Chavis.

Carroll, Joseph, *Slave Insurrections in the United States, 1800-1865*. Boston, 1938. A sober account; inaccurate in connection with some problems.

Catterall, Helen T., *Judicial Cases Concerning American Slavery and the Negro*. Vol. 2. Washington, 1929. A reliable treatise for locating the important cases that have bearing upon the subject.

Chamberlain, Hope S., *History of Wake County, North Carolina*. Raleigh, 1922. Too sketchy, but the best history of a very important county.

Cole, Arthur C., *The Whig Party in the South*. Washington, 1913.

Collins, Winfield H., *The Domestic Slave Trade of the Southern States*. New York, 1904. Contains an accurate discussion of the kidnapping of free Negroes.

Coon, Charles Lee, ed., *North Carolina Schools and Academies, 1790-1840*. Raleigh, 1915.

Cummings, John, *Negro Population in the United States, 1790-1915*. Washington, 1918. Contains important statistical information on the development of the free Negro population.

Eaton, Clement, *Freedom of Thought in the Old South*. Durham, 1940. A significant contribution to the literature of the ante-bellum period. Professor Eaton discusses in detail the effects of certain events and publications on the attitude of the white community toward the free Negro.

Fox, Early Lee, *The American Colonization Society, 1817-1940*. Baltimore, 1919. The only satisfactory treatment of the subject.

Frazier, E. Franklin, *The Free Negro Family*. Nashville, 1931. Rather sketchy; based on secondary materials, for the most part.

———, *The Negro Family in the United States*. Chicago, 1939. Contains a section on the place of the free Negro family in the life of the ante-bellum South. This is more accurate and thorough than his *Free Negro Family*.

Fries, Adelaide, *Forsyth County*. Winston, 1898.

Gilpatrick, Delbert H., *Jeffersonian Democracy in North Carolina, 1789-1816*. New York, 1931. An accurate discussion of the extent to which the economic and political life of the State was affected by the agrarian and democratic philosophy of Jefferson.

Greene, Lorenzo, and Woodson, Carter G., *The Negro Wage Earner*. Washington, 1930.

Hamilton, Joseph G. deR., *Benjamin S. Hedrick* (James Sprunt Historical Publications, Vol. X, No. 1). Chapel Hill, 1910. A discussion of a professor at the University of North Carolina who was dismissed because of his opposition to slavery.

———, *Party Politics in North Carolina, 1835-1860* (James Sprunt Historical Publications, Vol. XV, Nos. 1 and 2). Chapel Hill, 1916. This work is an accurate narrative of the political development of the period. Details in the careers of the important men are given.

Harrell, Isaac, *Gates County to 1860*. Durham, 1916. One of the most ably written county histories for the purposes of this work. The free Negro is discussed extensively.

Hawkins, Wm. George, *Lunsford Lane*. Boston, 1863. A biased biography written by an erstwhile abolitionist. Contains some accurate facts, nevertheless.

Jenkins, W. S., *Proslavery Thought in the Old South*. Chapel Hill, 1935.

Johnson, Guion Griffis, *Ante-bellum North Carolina*. Chapel Hill, 1937. The most valuable single volume in the field. Mrs. Johnson's exhaustive work is indispensable to students of the period.

Johnston, James Hugo, *Miscegenation in the Ante-bellum South*. Chicago, 1939.

Klain, Zora, *Quaker Contributions to Education in North Carolina*. Philadelphia, 1924. One of the best discussions of the social program of the Quakers.

Knight, Edgar W., *The Academy Movement in the South*. n. p., n. d.

Lamb, Elizabeth, *Historical Sketch of Hay Street Methodist Church, South, Fayetteville, North Carolina*. Fayetteville, 1934. Contains a good account of the founding of Methodism in Fayetteville by the free Negro, Henry Evans.

Lefler, Hugh T., *Hinton R. Helper*. Charlottesville, 1935. This biography goes far in explaining why Helper, a nonslaveholding white, developed such a bitter hatred of slavery.

Lloyd, Arthur Young, *The Slavery Controversy, 1831-1860*. Chapel Hill, 1939.

Moore, George Henry, *Historical Notes on the Employment of Negroes in the American Revolution*. New York, 1907.

Norton, Clarence Clifford, *The Democratic Party in Ante-bellum North Carolina, 1835-1861*. Chapel Hill, 1930.

Phillips, Ulrich B., *American Negro Slavery*. New York, 1918.

Russell, John Henderson, *The Free Negro in Virginia, 1619-1865*. Baltimore, 1913. The first definitive work in the field. It is a good example of what can be done with the problem of the free Negro when it is handled by the trained historian.

Savage, W. Sherman, *The Controversy over the Distribution of Abolition Literature 1830-1860*. Washington, 1938. An important subject that has been inadequately dealt with.

Seawell, Joseph Lady, *Law Tales for Laymen and Wayside Tales from Carolina*. Raleigh, 1929.

Shaw, George Clayton, *John Chavis*. Binghamton, 1931. Highly sentimental and poorly documented. The author leans heavily on the researches of Knight, Bassett, Weeks, and Charles L. Smith.

Smith, Charles Lee, *History of Education in North Carolina*. Washington, 1888.

Spero, Sterling, and Harris, Abram L., *The Black Worker*. New York, 1931. Contains an introductory chapter on the Negro laborer before the Civil War.

Stockard, Sallie W., *History of Guilford County*. Knoxville, 1902.

Sydnor, Charles S., *Slavery in Mississippi*. New York, 1933. One of the few works that treat adequately the colonization movement in a Southern State.

Taylor, Rosser Howard, *The Free Negro in North Carolina* (James Sprunt Historical Publications, Vol. XVII, No. 1). Chapel Hill, 1920. Sketchy; of little value because of the lack of details and the lack of the use of important sources.

———, *Slaveholding in North Carolina: An Economic View* (James Sprunt Historical Publications, Vol. XVIII, Nos. 1 and 2). Chapel Hill, 1926. An objective discussion of the economic aspects of slavery in North Carolina.

Turner, Edward R., *The Negro in Pennsylvania*. Baltimore, 1910.

Weeks, Stephen B., *Southern Quakers and Slavery*. Baltimore, 1896. An accurate narrative by one of the early Southern historians.

Wesley, Charles H., *Negro Labor in the United States*. New York, 1926. A reliable survey by a sober and competent historian.

Wilkes, Laura E., *Missing Pages in American History; The Services of Negroes in the Early Wars of the United States*. Washington, 1919.

Wilson, Joseph T., *The Black Phalanx; A History of Negro Soldiers of the United States in the Wars of 1775-1812; 1861-1865*. Hartford, 1888. Too sentimentally written to be of great value to the objective student of history.

Woodson, Carter G., *Education of the Negro Prior to 1861*. Washington, 1919.

———, *Free Negro Heads of Families in the United States in 1830*. Washington, 1925. Contains important statistics as well as an authentic introductory chapter.

———, *Free Negro Owners of Slaves in the United States in 1830*. Washington, 1924.

Wright, James M., *The Free Negro in Maryland, 1834-1860*. New York, 1921. A pioneer work in the field. Very good.

2. *Articles*

Bassett, John Spencer, "The States vs. Will," *Trinity College Historical Society Papers*, II (1898), 12-20.

——, "North Carolina Methodism and Slavery," *Trinity College Historical Society Papers*, IV (1900), 1-11.

——, "Suffrage in the State of North Carolina, 1776-1861," American Historical Association, *Annual Report for the Year 1895*, pp. 271-295.

Battle, Kemp Plummer, "George Horton, Slave Poet," *North Carolina University Magazine*, VII (1888), 229-232.

Boyd, William K., "North Carolina on the Eve of Secession," American Historical Association, *Annual Report for the Year 1910*, pp. 165-177.

Browning, James Blackwell, "Free Negro in Ante-bellum North Carolina," *North Carolina Historical Review*, XV (1938), 23-33. Too sketchy to be of any real value.

——, "The North Carolina Black Code," *Journal of Negro History*, XV (1930), 261-273.

Cadbury, Henry J., "Negro Membership in the Society of Friends," *Journal of Negro History*, XXI (1936), 151-213.

Carr, John W., "Manhood Suffrage Movement in North Carolina," *Trinity College Historical Society Papers*, XI (1915), 47-78.

Clark, Walter, "Negro Soldiers," *North Carolina Booklet*, XVIII (1918), 57-62.

Connor, Henry Groves, "The Convention of 1835," *North Carolina Booklet*, VIII (1908), 89-110.

Craven, Avery C., "Poor Whites and Negroes in the Ante-bellum South," *Journal of Negro History*, XV (1930), 14-25.

Dodge, David, "Free Negroes of North Carolina," *Atlantic Monthly*, LVII (1886), 20-30.

Hartgrove, W. B., "The Negro Soldier in the American Revolution," *Journal of Negro History*, I (1916), 110-131.

Holt, Bryce R., "The Supreme Court of North Carolina and Slavery," *Trinity College Historical Society Papers*, XVII (1927), 7-73.

Jackson, Luther P., "Free Negroes of Petersburg, Virginia," *Journal of Negro History*, XII (1927), 365-388.

——, "The Virginia Free Negro Farmer and Property Owner, 1830-1860," *Journal of Negro History*, XXIV (1939), 390-439. Professor Jackson concludes that the free Negro farmer and property owner of Virginia was an "economic reality."

Dunbar-Nelson, Alice, "People of Color of Louisiana," *Journal of Negro History*, I (1916), 361-376, and II (1917), 51-78.

Gruening, Martha, "David Walker," *Dictionary of American Bi-ography,* XIX, 340.

Knight, Edgar W., "Notes on John Chavis," *North Carolina Historical Review,* VII (1930), 326-345. The best account of Chavis that has come to the attention of the writer.

Mehlinger, Louis R., "Attitude of Free Negroes towards Colonization," *Journal of Negro History,* I (1916), 276-301.

Padgett, James, "The Status of Slaves in Colonial North Carolina," *Journal of Negro History,* XIV (1929), 300-327. A valuable summary of the colonial period.

Rogers, W. McDowell, "Free Negro Legislation in Georgia," *Georgia Historical Quarterly,* XVI (1932), 25-37.

Shugg, Roger W., "Negro Voting in the Ante-bellum South," *Journal of Negro History,* XXI (1936), 357-364.

Sherrill, P. M., "The Quakers and the North Carolina Manumission Society," *Trinity College Historical Society Papers,* X (1914), 32-51.

Southall, Eugene Portlette, "Arthur Tappan and the Anti-slavery Movement," *Journal of Negro History,* XV (1930), 162-197. An exposé of the intrigue and corruption in the American Colonization Society.

Taylor, Rosser Howard, "Slave Conspiracies in North Carolina," *North Carolina Historical Review,* V (1928), 20-34. Contends that free Negroes had no part in the slave conspiracies in North Carolina.

Turner, James K., "Slavery in Edgecombe County," *Trinity College Historical Society Papers,* XII (1916), 5-36.

Washington, Booker T., "The Free Negro in Slavery Days," *The Outlook,* XCIII (1909), 107-114.

Weeks, Stephen B., "History of Negro Suffrage," *Political Science Quarterly,* IX (1894), 671-703.

——, "The Slave Insurrection in Virginia in 1831," *Magazine of American History,* XXV (1891), 448-458.

Wilson, C. D., "Negroes Who Owned Slaves," *Popular Science Monthly,* LXXXI (1912), 483-494.

Winston, James E., "Free Negro in New Orleans, 1803-1860," *Louisiana Historical Quarterly,* XXI (1938), 175-185.

Woodson, Carter G., "The Beginnings of the Miscegenation of the Whites and Blacks," *Journal of Negro History,* III (1918), 335-353.

——, "Freedom and Slavery in Appalachian America," *Journal of Negro History,* I (1916), 132-150.

Index

Abel, Willie, 35

Abolitionists, 211. *See also* Anti-slavery movement

Abshur, Lila, 31, 160

Adams, Abraham, 22n

Adams, Henderson, 220

Advertisements, for runaway slaves, 39-40; for kidnapped free Negroes, 54-55; by sheriff of slave suspect, 40; for stolen horse, 96; of slaves for hire, 133-34

Africa, 198-99, 217; free Negroes sent to, 202-10

African Repository, 207-08

Agriculture. *See* Farmers; Farm hands; Farms

Alabama, free Negroes disfranchised, 116

Alcohol. *See* Drinking; Spirituous liquors

Alexandria, Virginia, free Negroes in, 19n

Alleghany County, 158n

Allen, Abram, 76n

American Colonization Society, 140, 217; activities in North Carolina, 199-210; North Carolinians contribute to, 203-05

American Revolution, effect on emancipation, 10-12; slaves and free Negroes in, 102, 218

Amusements. *See* Recreation

Anglicans, promote education among Indians and Negroes, 165. *See also* Episcopalians

Anson County, immigrants in, 8; activities of Baptists in, 180

Anti-slavery movement, 8, 62-63; Quakers and, 23-26; David Walker and, 64-67

Appeal in Four Articles. See Walker's Appeal

Apprentices, free Negro children bound as, 122; laws regarding free Negro, 122-23; occupations learned by, 125-26; free Negro girls become, 126; taught to read and write, 129

Apprentice system, and free Negro, 122-31, 189, 223; as form of education, 129-31, 165, 168; purposes of, 129-30; different for whites and free Negroes, 129

Armwood, Levin, 74

Army. *See* Continental Army

Arson, free Negroes tried for, 85, 98

Artisans, free Negro, 136-44; whites and free Negroes compete, 136-39; migrate to Liberia, 209-10. *See also* Labor; Occupations

Asbury, Bishop Francis, 178

Asheborough Bulletin, 56

Ashe County, 14n

Asheville, citizens petition legislature, 137; free Negroes in, 214; citizens desire removal of free Negroes, 214-15

Asheville News, 119-20; 137

Badger, George E., 86, 173

Baird, J. S. T., 215

Baldwin, Billy, 73

Baltimore, free Negroes in, 7; free Negroes migrate to Liberia, 206, 208

Baptists, free Negro, 176-77; migrate to Liberia, 210. *See also* Ralph Freeman

"Barber Jack." *See* John C. Stanly

Barbers, importance of free Negro, 140n

Barringer, D. M., 32, 68, 173

Bassa Cove, Liberia, 140, 209

Bassett, John Spencer, 8, 12, 112

Bastardy, a basis for apprenticeship, 122-23; and race mixing, 37-39, 122

Bateman, D. N., 45n

Battle, James, 118

Battle, William H., quoted or cited, 51-52 and n, 77n, 85

Beal, James Henry, 220

Beaufort County, 16n, 17n, 53, 67n, 96, 128, 149, 153; slaves in, 8; certificates of freedom in, 49; slave conspiracy in, 61; citizens protest use of free Negro mechanics, 138; free Negroes migrate to Liberia, 206

Bell, Christian, 73n

Bell, Hardy, 157

Bertie County, 67n, 99, 161; slave conspiracy in, 61; apprenticeship indenture, 124

Biggs, Asa, 120
Bill of Rights, 77 and n
Black, Martin, 127
Blacknall, John, 36
Blacknall, Thomas, 150, 176, 183-84, 216; slaves owned by, 160
"Black Prophet," 70. *See also* Nat Turner insurrection
Blacksmiths, 92; free Negro, 142
Bladen County, 144, 161; immigrants in, 8; free Negroes in, 14n
Blango, Hosea, 126
Blount, Nathan G., 162
Bolton, Herbert E., 3n
Boon, William, alias William Hussey, 97
Boothe, Edmond, 75
Borden, Benjamin, 127
Borough representation, abolished, 110, 114
Boston, 29n, 64
Bowen, Gooden, slaves owned by, 161
Bowser, Eaton, 142
Boyd, William K., 108
Boylan, William, 46n
Bragg, Thomas, 120
Branch, John, 106n, 109, 113 and n, 199
Branding, as punishment of free Negroes, 87-88
Bray's Associates, 166
Brooklyn Advertiser, 168
Brown, Hugh, 174n
Brown, Patsy, 125n
Browning, James B., 140n; on marriages within free Negro families, 183n
Brunswick County, 44 and n, 84; immigrants in, 8
Brunswick County, Virginia, 56
Bryan, James W., 86, 161, 191; favors disfranchisement of free Negro, 110-11
Bryan, John H., 86, 161; comments on free Negro voting, 108
Bryan, Thomas O., 48
Bryan, William T., 151
Buchanan, Thomas, 140, 144
Buncombe County, 14n; citizens desire removal of free Negroes, 214-15
Burges, A. S. H., 199
Burglary, free Negroes convicted for, 97
Burke County, 14n, 119
Burton, Hutchings G., 43; warns legislature about free Negroes, 62-63

Cabarrus County, 68, 148; property of free Negroes in, 158
Calloway, Reuben, 148n

Calvinism, 177
Camden County, 67n, 75, 113n
Campbellton, 99
Canada, free Negroes move to, 154
Cannon, Clarissa, 130
Capehart, T., 205n
Carolina Observer, 115, 194, 207; supports colonization movement, 203
Carroll, Henry, 98
Carroll, Joseph, 72n
Carter, Mary, 22
Carteret County, 67n, 110
Caswell County, 40, 160n; citizens complain of conduct of free Negroes, 101
Catawba County, 158n; property of free Negroes in, 159
Catawbas, 5
Chapel Hill, 33, 55, 219; colonization society in, 199
Chaplain, Jasper, 129
Charleston, South Carolina, 5; free Negroes in, 7, 19; Denmark Vesey insurrection in, 62
Charlotte, 162, 219
Chatham County, 17, 25
Chavers, Sylvester, 87, 100
Chavers, William, 86
Chavis, Daniel, 183n
Chavis, Emily, 183n
Chavis, Gilbert, 100
Chavis, Greezy, 183n
Chavis, John, 189n, 216, 224; opposed to general emancipation, 73; active in politics, 106-07; education of, 170 and n; Presbyterian missionary, 170, 177; school of, 171-74; letters of, 172n; borrows money, 173; is given tract of land, 173; honored by North Carolina, 173-74; author, 177
Chavis, Robert, 183n
Chavis, Sarah, 183n
Chavis, Sewall, 183n
"Chavis Letter on the Doctrine of the Atonement of Christ," 177
Cherokees, 5
Cheves, Morris, 73
Children, free Negroes seek to emancipate, 29-31; legal status of Negro, 49; stealing of free Negro, 54-56; laws to apprentice free Negro, 122-30
Chowan Baptist Association, 177
Chowan County, 31, 67n; free Negro voters in, 111

Churches, for free Negroes, 176-77; 224

Cincinnati, free Negro goes to, 218

"Citizen of Richmond," 37

Civil Rights, restraint of free Negroes, 81-85; incompetency of free Negroes as witnesses against whites, 82; free Negro voting, 105-06, 111, 113, 118-19

Clark, James, 136 and n

Clark, John, 220

Clergy. See Preachers

Cleveland County, 213

Coffin, Baron, 167 and n

Collet, John, 10

Collins, J. A., 150

Colonization movement, societies, 199-210; assistance of Quakers, 200, 204; free Negroes and, 140, 207-08. See also American Colonization Society

Columbus County, 113n

Common schools, free Negroes not to be taxed to support, 104; free Negroes cannot attend, 168

Concord, 139n

Connecticut, 55, 119n; disfranchises free Negro, 116

Connor, Henry Groves, 111n

Constitutional Convention, movement for, 109; convenes in Raleigh, 109; abolishes borough representation, 110; debates disfranchisement of free Negro, 110-12; votes to disfranchise free Negro, 112; votes to equalize representation, 114

Constitution of 1776, 12-13, 105

Continental Army, Negroes serve in, 102

Continental Congress, 59

Cook, Caroline, 32n

Cooke, Thomas, 152

Corbin, Mrs. Jean, 20

Cotten, John, 36

Counsel for free Negroes, in county courts, 85; in superior courts, 85; in Supreme Court, 86

County Court, manumission of free Negroes in, 21-22; clerk forbidden to issue marriage license to mixed couples, 37; records contain information on Negroes' freedom, 48-49

Court of pleas and quarter sessions. See County court

Courts and the free Negro. See County court; Superior court; Supreme Court

Craven County, 30, 44, 48, 67n, 68, 104, 111, 128, 140, 144, 152; slaves in, 8; free Negroes in, 16 and n, 17n, 44n; man

convicted for stealing free Negroes, 55; apprentice records, 125-26; apprentices, 130; citizens protest use of free Negro mechanics, 138; property of free Negroes in, 158; free Negroes in school in, 169

Crawford, William H., 106

Creditors, treatment of free Negroes by, 162

Crichlow, John, slaves owned by, 161

Crimes of free Negroes, 95-101, 188, 190. See also Punishments

Crudup, Josiah, 106, 182n

Cully, Augustine, 86

Culpepper, J., 181

Cumberland County, 67n, 77, 144; immigrants in, 8; free Negroes in, 17 and n; disturbances among free Negroes in, 100-01; free Negroes migrate to Liberia, 206

Currituck County, 67n, 75, 128-29; citizens seek to expel free Negroes, 216-17

Curry, Benjamin, 151

Cutter, John, 149

Daniel, Joseph J., quoted or cited, 84, 113, 152-53, 156; opposes disfranchisement of free Negro, 110

Davidson County, 25, 180, 214, 220

David Walker's Appeal. See Walker's Appeal

Davie County, 56, 158n; free Negro enslaves self, 219

Davis, Lawrence, 94

Day, Aquilla, 45 and n

Day, Thomas, 73, 144, 176, 183, 190, 216; free Negro cabinetmaker, 45, 142; sends petition to legislature, 45; slaves owned by, 160

Dean, Samuel, 128

Death penalty, 91; for burglary, 97; for rape, 98-99; for murder, 99

Deaths of free Negroes, causes of, 189-90

Debt, imprisonment of free Negroes for, 89-90; sale of free Negroes for, 162

Declaration of Independence, 66

"Declaration of Rights," 81, 84, 89

Democratic party, in elections, 116-20

Dempsey, Whitmell, 50

Denmark Vesey insurrection, 62

Dennis, Joseph, 140

Desertion, 190 and n

Devereaux, John, 184n

Devereux, T. P., 92, 199

Dewey, John, 163

Dewey, Oliver J., 108

Dicken, Benjamin, 154

Dickens, William, 96

Dickinson, Julia, 220

Dismal Swamp. *See* Great Dismal Swamp

Divorce, difficulty of securing, 37-38; proceedings bring out race mixing, 37-39

Dockery, Alfred, 119-20

Dodge, David, 189n

Dogs, proposals to dispossess free Negroes of, 78 and n

Dove, John, 128

Dred Scott Decision, 216n

Drinking, free Negroes accused of excessive, 79; legislation to curb free Negroes', 80

Dunstan, Hillard, 142

Duplin County, slave conspiracy in, 71; justices of peace request award for free Negro, 74n; citizens protest presence of free Negroes, 212

Dutch, in North Carolina, 5-6, 8

Eborn, A., 149

Edenton, 40, 110n; law regulating slaves and free Negroes in, 59-60; Negroes tried for conspiracy, 61-62

Edenton Whig, 102

Edgecombe County, 16n, 67n, 154, 190; slaves in, 8; free Negroes taxed, 10

Editors, comment on disfranchisement of free Negro, 116-20; Joseph Gales, 199. *See also* Newspapers

Education, of apprentices, 129-31, 165, 168; of free Negroes, 164-74, 169n

Edwards, Weldon, 110

"Elder Ralph." *See* Ralph Freeman

Elections, influence of free Negroes in, 106, 116-20

Elizabeth City, free Negroes to give bonds, 70n; colonization society in, 204; free Negroes migrate to Liberia, 208

Emancipation, presumed after thirty years of freedom, 52 and n. *See also* Manumission

Emigration, of free Negroes, 200-10. *See also* Colonization movement

England, 157

English, in North Carolina, 5-6

Enslavement of free Negroes, 218-20

Episcopalians, free Negro preacher among, 182; free Negroes of New Bern become, 190

Evans, Henry, 142; organizes Methodist Church, 178-79

Everitt, Thomas, 40

"Extent of Atonement," 177. *See* John Chavis

Factories, free Negro labor in, 143

Farmers, 125; free Negro, 135, 148-50; houses of free Negro, 189n; begin diversified farming, 197; migrate to Liberia, 209-10

Farm hands, free Negro, 147-49

Farms, size of, 196-97

Farrow, Tilman, 216

Fayetteville, 44, 98, 110, 110; free Negroes in, 14, 16n; citizens request manumission of slave, 30n; man sells free Negro as slave, 56; law regulating slaves and free Negroes in, 59-60; magistrate disturbed by *Walker's Appeal,* 66; rumors of insurrection near, 71; lawyers, 86; free Negro Methodists in, 178-79; fire, 190; colonization movement in, 200, 204

Fayetteville Argus, 119

Fayetteville Observer, 56, 136; commends conduct of free Negroes, 190

Featherston, C. A., 220

Felonies, 90-91

Fighting, among free Negroes, 95, 100-01

Fines, as punishment of free Negroes, 88; free Negroes to be sold for, 89

Firearms, possession by slaves, 76; possession by free Negroes regulated, 76-78

Fisher, Charles, 26, 115-17, 197n

Florida, free Negroes disfranchised, 116

Forster, William, 167

Forsyth County, 25

Fort, John, 174n

Foy, Enoch, 45n

Franchise. *See* Elections; Voting

Franklin County, 67n, 81, 100, 127-28, 150, 160; free Negroes migrate to Liberia, 206; free Negro enslaves self, 219-20

Frazier, William, 219

Fredericksburg, Virginia, free Negroes in, 7

Freedom, Supreme Court upholds Negro's, 49; of Negro questioned, 51-54; color as a factor in presumption of, 52-53

Freeman, Archy, 73

Freeman, Jesse, 157

Freeman, Matthias, visits Liberia, 208

Freeman, Rachel, 98

Freeman, Ralph, free Negro Baptist preacher, 180-81
Freeman, Richard, 50
Freeman, Ruffin D., 56
Freeman, William, 56
Free Negro Code, 68, 70, 72n, 73-74, 95, 138, 184, 193-95, 197-98, 223
Free Negro in Maryland, 3
Free Negro in Virginia, 3
Free pass, runaway slave with, 40
French, in North Carolina, 5-6
French and McNeil, lawyers, 85
Friends, Society of, 211; emancipates slaves, 11, 23-26; opposed to slavery, 23; organizes manumission societies, 25-26; and the colonization movement, 200, 204; educates Negroes, 166-168, 224; Negro membership in, 175
Fundamental Constitutions of Carolina, 7

Gales, Joseph, 199, 203
Gambling, of slaves and free Negroes forbidden, 187 and n
Garrison, William Lloyd, 26
Gary, R. B., 45n
Gaskill, Bennett, 128
Gaston, Richard, 160
Gaston, William, 109; quoted or cited, 23, 25, 49, 89-91, 127, 151, 202-03; opposes disfranchisement of free Negro, 111-12, 114-15
Gaston County, 220
Gates County, 44n, 67n, 75; literacy of free Negroes in, 169; free Negro Baptists in, 176
Geography, of North Carolina, 4-5
George, Robert, 97n
Georgetown, South Carolina, 97n
Georgia, 79, 193; leaders disturbed over *Walker's Appeal,* 66-67; free Negroes disfranchised in, 116; slavery in, 147
Germans, in North Carolina, 5-6, 8
Giles, John, 116; opposes disfranchisement of free Negro, 111-12, 111n
Globe, 166
Goldsboro Patriot, 211
Good, John, 140
Goode, Trueman, 99-100
Gordon, Polly, 129
Gragson, John, 95 and n
Graham, James, 212
Granville County, 44n, 67n, 84, 91, 102, 128, 160n, 170, 187n; petition from, 10; free Negroes in, 17 and n; free Ne-

gro farm hands in, 149n; property of free Negroes in, 149n
Great Dismal Swamp, rules for free Negroes working in, 74-75; free Negroes in, 132-33
Green, Amelia, 30
Green, John Y., 142
Green, Mary, 153-54
Green, Robert, 31, 182
Green, William, 81 and n
Greene County, 16n, 67n; free Negro enslaves self, 219
Greensboro, free Negroes in, 16n; colonization society in, 204
Greensborough Patriot, 26, 120, 218n
Griffin, Ned, 102
Griffin, Rigdon, 130
Grimson, Benny, 96
Guilford County, 17, 25, 39, 44n, 72, 151; citizens concerned about insolvent free Negroes, 88-89; free Negro enslaves self, 220

Hackey, F., 149
Hails, Ellen, 123
Hails, Emanuel, 48, 123
Haithcock, Ephraim, 190n
Haiti, 91; North Carolina free Negroes migrate to, 200; free Negroes urged to go to, 213-14
Halifax, 81, 110 and n; free Negroes in, 14, 16-17, 19n; free Negroes migrate to Liberia, 206
Halifax, Virginia, 45
Halifax County, 67n, 113, 150; concentration of free Negroes in, 14-17 and n, 16n; slave conspiracy in, 61; free Negro voters in, 106, 111; free Negro farm hands in, 149n; property of free Negroes in, 148
Hall, John, quoted, 24
Hall, Lemuel, 29
Hambleton, John, 152n, 153
Hambleton, Rebecca, 152n
Hammonds, Cordy, 95
Hammonds, W. B., 182n
Hanover Presbytery, 170
Hansell, William, 97
Harnett County, 158n
Harris, Henry, 85, 98
Harris, Jack, 97
Harris, John, 77n
Harrison, William H., 117-18
Hartley, Joseph A., 220

Hatch, Alfred, 28
Hayes, James, 99
Haywood, George W., 98
Haywood, James, 108
Haywood, John, 199
Haywood, Manley, 98
Haywood, William, 99, 107, 117 and n
Haywood County, 43, 158n; free Negroes in, 44n
Health, of free Negroes, 189
Henderson, Archibald, 172, 199
Henderson, John, 172
Henderson County, 158n
Hendrick, Thomas, 129n
Herring, Silas, 212
Hertford County, 67n, 100-01; free Negroes in, 17n; free Negro voters in, 106, 111; free Negro farm hands in, 149n
Hill, Joseph A., 45n
Hillsboro, 110n; colonization society in, 204
Hillsborough Academy, 71
Holiday, J. G., 220
Holloway, John, 45
Holmes, Ezra F., 151
Holmes, Owen, 115
Holmes, William, 95
Hooper, Emily, 219
Hostler, James, 32-33
Housing, 189
Humphrey, Lotte W., 214-16, 219
Hunt, Louis, 100
Hunt, Nathaniel, 40
Hunter, Isaac, 29, 142; secures manumission in New York, 145; asks permission to remain in Raleigh, 46 and n
Hyde County, 67n, 150, 158n, 216
Hyman, Edward, 153

Immigration, from Virginia, 8; of free Negroes, 42-45; legislation against free Negro, 42-43; vote on law regulating free Negro, 43-44; persistence of free Negro, 45-48
Imprisonment, for debt, 89-90; as punishment of free Negroes, 90-91
Incendiary publications, legislation against, 68, 90. See also Walker's Appeal
Indentures, apprenticeship, 124-25 and n, 128, 165 and n; of apprentices rescinded, 128-29. See also Apprentices; Apprentice system
Indiana, North Carolina free Negroes move to, 200

Indiana Farmer, 193-94
Indians, 5, 52
Infanticide, 190 and n
Insurrections, reaction to Nat Turner, 71-72; effect on attitude toward free Negroes, 72-73
Intermarriage, law against, 10, 35; persistence of, 36-37. See also Race mixing
Internal improvements, employment of free Negroes in, 137
Iredell County, 115
Irish, in North Carolina, 5-6

Jackson, Andrew, 106
Jackson County, 158n
Jacobs, Asa, 84
Jails, free Negroes escape from, 97-98. See also Imprisonment
Jefferson, Thomas, 65, 192
Jeffrey, Osborn, free Negroes serving with, 102
Jerry, emancipation of, 32
Johnson, John B., 208
Johnson, Micajah, 56
Johnston, James Hugo, 35
Johnston, Polydore, 34
Johnston, Samuel, slaves owned by, 161
Johnston County, 67n, 98
Jones, Allen, 92
Jones, Dr. Calvin, 87
Jones, Charles, 9
Jones, Dave, 99
Jones, John, 39
Jones, Mary Ann, 154
Jones, William, 128
Jones County, 67n; slave conspiracy in, 61; free Negroes enslave themselves, 220
Jowers, Atlas, 94n
Jury, free Negroes have trial by, 84-85
Justices of peace, 80n; of Duplin request award for free Negro, 74n; issue licenses to free Negroes, 69

Kease, Diana, 128
Kease, Southey, 49n, 126, 151, 153n
Keese, Elizabeth, 127
Kentucky, free Negroes disfranchised in, 116
Kiff, Jones, 99
King, Benjamin, 171 and n
King, Joel, 165n
King, Samuel, 115

King, Theophilus, 219
Kitchen, William, 102
Knight, E. W., 170 and n, 171n

Labor, apprentice, 121-30; unskilled free
Negro, 121-22, 132-36, 133n; hiring
out of slave, 133-34; competition of free
Negro and slave, 133-34; wages of un-
skilled, 136; skilled free Negro, 136-47;
wages of skilled, 143-44; farm, 147-49.
See also Occupations
Lane, Lunsford, 29 and n, 92n, 145-47;
secures manumission in New York, 46;
sentiment in Raleigh against, 46; mes-
senger to the governor, 146n
Lassiter, Thomas W., 206
Latham, John W., 153
Laughton, Price, 127
Lawlessness. See Crimes; Fighting; Mob
violence
Lawyers. See Counsel for free Negroes
Lee, Mary A., 143
Legislative Papers, 23-24
Leigh, Joshua, 53
Lenoir County, 67n; citizens want to regu-
late free Negro peddlers, 131
Lewis, Susan, 220
Lexington, Virginia, 170
Liberia, 138, 140, 144-45; North Carolina
free Negroes migrate to, 200-10; price
of passage to, 205n; North Carolinians
desire to deport free Negroes to, 212;
free Negroes enslave themselves, 219-20
Lightfoot, William, 99
Lincoln, Abraham, election of, 217
Lincoln County, 14n; citizen requests de-
portation of free Negroes, 212
Linda Stewart, The, 210
Linegar, Isaac, 175
Liquor. See Drinking; Spirituous liquors
Lisbon, Robert, 30-31 and n
Locke, John, 7
Locofocos, 120
Locus, Wright, 220
Locust, Valentine, 54
Lomax, Roland, 100
London, 157
Lords Proprietors, 7; receive complaint
concerning free Negroes, 9
Louisiana, free Negroes in, 19; Walker's
Appeal in, 67; legislature concerned
about the Nat Turner insurrection, 71-
72; disfranchises free Negroes, 116
Lovelace, Archibald, 32n

Lutheranism, 6
Lynch, Celia, 219
Lynch law. See Mob violence

McDaniel, Jesse, 190n
Macdowell, John, 175
McDowell County, 119, 158n
McKay, William, 162
Mackie, Bill, 128
McKinley, Mary, 28
McNeil and French, lawyers, 85
McPheeters, William, 199, 201
McRae, Duncan, 86
Macon, Nathaniel, 109; favors disfranchise-
ment of free Negro, 111
Madison County, 158n
Magee, Joseph, 180
Maiming, as punishment of free Negroes,
87
Mainer, Salisbury, 97
Mallet, Sally, 219
Malone, John, 30 and n
Mangum, Lydia, 157
Mangum, Preston, 172
Mangum, Willie P., 106, 170, 172-73,
172n
Manly, Charles, 172
Manly, Joe, 87, 100
Manly, Matthias E., quoted, 93, 153-55
Manumission, 222; laws regulating, 10,
20-34; of slaves by free Negroes, 12,
29-32; by will, 20; by legislative enact-
ment, 20, 29-34
Manumission societies, 25-26, 196
Marriage, laws regulating, 10, 185, 188-
89; of free Negroes and whites, 10, 35-
37; extra-marital relations, 36-39; of
slaves not legal, 155; within the family,
183n; of free Negroes and slaves, 184
Marsh, William, 219
Martin County, 16n, 40, 67n, 158n, 161;
slave conspiracy in, 61; swamp hands
in, 133; property of free Negroes in,
159; free Negro enslaves self, 219
Maryland, 82n; free Negroes in, 6-7, 14,
17n; urban free Negroes in, 19; law
permitting slaves to testify against free
Negroes, 83; disfranchises free Negroes,
116; free Negroes migrate to Liberia,
206
Mason, Thomas, 178
Massachusetts, 79, 193-94
Masters, William B., 152
Matthews, Frederick, 90-91, 95 and n

Mayho, William, 49

Meade, William, 199

Meares, William B., 179

Mechanics, number of free Negro, 135; competition between white and free Negro, 137-39 and n; citizens protest use of free Negro, 138-39; proposals to regulate free Negro, 139; citizens use free Negro, 140; term discussed, 140n

Mecklenburg County, property of free Negroes in, 159

Mehlinger, Louis, 207

Melbourn, Julius, 157, 183

Memphis, Tennessee, 5

Mendenhall, George C., 146n

Merchants, free Negro, 144-45, 157

Meritorious services, 20; a basis for manumission, 22-23

Methodists, educate slaves and free Negroes, 166, 224; free Negro, 177-79; organized by Henry Evans, 178; contribute to colonization, 205; migrate to Liberia, 209-10

Militia, free Negroes serve in, 101; function of free Negroes in, 101-02; exclusion of free Negroes from, 103

Mills, Joe, 99

Milton, free Negro cabinetmaker in, 45, 142; citizens sent petitions to General Assembly, 45

Ministers. See Preachers

Misdemeanors. See Crimes

Mississippi, disfranchises free Negroes, 116; colonization movement in, 207

Mob violence, in eviction of free Negroes from land, 93; against Lunsford Lane, 47; against free Negroes, 84, 92-93

Montgomery, The, 206

Montgomery County, 44n, 180

Moore, Churchill, 152n

Moore, Ezekiel, 76

Moore, John, 126

Moore, Lovey, 126

Moore County, 17, 127, 180

Moravianism, 6

Moravians, begin to emancipate slaves, 11

Morehead, James T., 85

Morehead, John M., 85, 109, 117-18

Morgan District, 14n

Morgan Dix, The, 209

Morphis, Sam, 33

Morten, Peggy Ann, 220

Mouseau, Sarah, 125n

Mulattoes, 189-90; slave, 35-36; free Negro, 35-39; run away from masters, 39-40; have easy chance to establish freedom, 53

Murder, punishment for, 91; of free Negroes, 162; free Negroes charged with, 99-101

Murfreesboro, 205n

Nash, Frederick, quoted, 51, 77-78

Nash County, 21, 67n, 117, 152; free Negro enslaves self, 220

Nat Turner insurrection, 70-72, 197, 202, 204, 223

Natural rights, to freedom, 25; applied to free Negro, 94

Nautilus, The, 206-07

Neale, Benjamin, 152

Negroes in North Carolina, status of first, 7n. See also Slaves

New Bern, 5, 16, 31, 110n; free Negroes in, 14, 16n, 190-91; ordinance forcing free Negroes to work out taxes, 94; free Negroes voting in, 107; citizens object to free Negroes voting, 107-08; free Negro peddlers from, 131; free Negro barbers in, 140; free Negro dressmaker in, 143; free Negroes migrate to Liberia, 209

New Bern Atlantic, 168-69, 195

Newbern New Era, urges free Negroes to go to Haiti, 213-14

Newbern Progress, 218n

Newbern Spectator, disapproves of disfranchisement of free Negroes, 117

New England, 62

New Hanover County, 51, 115, 153, 157, 161, 179; slaves in, 8; property of free Negroes in, 158-59

New Jersey, disfranchises free Negroes, 116

Newlin, James, 33

New Orleans, free Negroes in, 19; free Negroes migrate to Africa, 207

Newsom, Elijah, 77-78

Newspapers, on disfranchisement of free Negroes, 115-16; and party politics, 117-20; express opinion on free Negroes, 193-95, 211; support colonization movement, 203

Newton, Thomas, 30, 148, 184n

New York, 31-32, 45-46; Anti-slavery Convention, 92; free Negro convict escapes to, 97

New York Advertiser, 213

New York Colonization Society, 208-09

Norfleet, J. B., 133

Norfolk, Virginia, free Negroes in, 7, 19n

Northampton County, 44n, 67n; slaves in, 8; free Negroes taxed in, 10; concentration of free Negroes in, 14; citizens desire to take dogs from free Negroes, 78n; free Negroes fighting in, 100; free Negro farm hands in, 149n; free Negroes enslave themselves, 220

North Carolina Historical Commission, 174

North Carolina Manumission Society, 25, 53-54, 167

North Carolina Standard, 117, 136, 194-95, 197; attacks manumission society, 26; attacks free Negro population, 101; supports colonization movement, 203

North Carolina Yearly Meeting, 25, 175, 200. *See also* Society of Friends

Norwood, John W., 85, 162

Notes on Virginia, 65

Observer. See Fayetteville Observer

Occupations, of free Negro apprentices, 125; unskilled, 132-36; tabulated, 134-35; skilled, 136-47; maritime, 141 and n; in the building trades, 141-42; of free Negro women, 143; agricultural, 147-50

Ohio, treatment of free Negroes in, 194; North Carolina free Negroes move to, 200

Olmsted, Frederick Law, 132, 136, 195

Onslow County, 67n, 214 and n

Orange County, 44n, 160n; free Negroes in, 16; manumission society in, 25; sheriff holds runaway slave, 40; free Negroes migrate to Liberia, 206

Orange Presbytery, 173, 177

Osborn, Charles, 25

Outlaw, David, 162

Outlaw, George, 124-25

Owen, John, 66-67, 144

Owens, Fred, 128-29

Oxendine, Charles, 86

Oxford Leisure Hour, 215-16

Palin, Sarah, migrates to Liberia, 208

Parker, Gabriel, 212

Parks, Lewis, 56

Parks, William, 56

Pasquotank County, 67n, 75, 78, 97, 131; free Negroes in, 16-17; free Negro voters in, 111; apprentice records, 126;

free Negro farm hands in, 149n; property of free Negroes in, 159; free Negroes migrate to Liberia, 206-07

Patrick, Henry, 98

Patridge, Thomas, 123

Patrols, governor recommends stronger, 43; established, 59; need for better, 72; unsatisfactory, 197, 213

Patterson, David, 206

Patterson, Nelson, 219

Patton, James A., 215

Paul, Henry R., 128

Paul, Martha, 36

Pearson, R. M., 39 and n, 52n, 84, 94 and n, 154

Peartree, John, 128

Peddlers, regulated, 131-32; discrimination in law between white and free Negro, 132

Pee Dee Baptist Association, 180

Penalties. *See* Punishments

Penitentiary, need of, 41, 90-91

Pennsylvania, disfranchises free Negro, 116

Pennsylvania Colonization Society, 144

Perquimans County, 67n, 78, 111, 175; free Negro farm hands in, 149; free Negroes migrate to Liberia, 206-07

Perry, Leonidas, 219

Person County, 96

Petersburg, Virginia, free Negroes in, 7, 19n

Pettiford, John, 142

Pettigrew, Charles, 61

Pettigrew, Ebenezer, 61

Pettigrew, William, 61

Philadelphia, North Carolina free Negroes move to, 200

Physical combat. *See* Fighting

Pickard, Robert, 130

Pitt County, 14n, 41, 67n

Pittman, Henry, 99n

Plantations, impersonal relations on, 196

Plymouth, 143; free Negroes in, 16n

Politics. *See* Elections; Voting

Pollock, London, 97

Population of North Carolina, by nationalities in 1790, 6; concentration of free Negro, 14; growth of free Negro, 14-19

Powell, Elijah, 152-53

Powers, Levin, 127

Preachers, proposal to silence free Negro, 70n; arrested for anti-slavery utterances, 72; neglect slaves and free Negroes, 174; free Negro, 176-82, 224; activities curbed by law, 180; migrate to Liberia, 210

Presbyterians, educate slaves and free Negroes, 166, 224; free Negro, 176; approve colonization, 201-02; contribute to colonization, 204

Princeton University, 170

Prison. See Imprisonment

Pritchard, H., 162n

Property, owned by free Negroes, 150-62; 223-24; free Negro driven from, 151-52; rights of free Negroes questioned, 153-57; left to free Negroes in wills, 153-55; in slaves, 155-57, 159-61, 224; value of, 157-59, 224

Prostitution, in Raleigh, 39n

Protestant Episcopal Church. See Episcopalians

Prue, Alfred, 127-28

Public schools. See Common schools

Punishments, forms of, death penalty, 86, 91, 97; whipping, 86-87; maiming, 87; branding, 87-88, 100; fines, 88-90; imprisonment, 90-91, 100; stocks, 91; of whites and free Negroes different, 91

Quakerism, 6; influence of, 196

Quakers. See Society of Friends

Quin, Nancy, 190n

Race mixing, 35, 114; Supreme Court on, 38-39; laws against, 10, 35; seen in relations of white women and Negro men, 37-39; a social problem in North Carolina, 37

Race relations, laws regulating, 10, 35-36, 188-89; incompetency of free Negro as witness in case involving whites, 82; insolvence of free Negro, 94 and n; debates on free Negro in Constitutional Convention, 110, 112; public opinion on, 193-95, 211

Raleigh, 42, 107, 157, 187n, 202, 218; free Negroes in, 14, 16n; citizens request manumission of slaves, 30; citizens protest manumission of slaves, 34; citizens petition legislature in behalf of Isaac Hunter, 46; Commissioners require free Negroes to register, 62; laws enforced against free Negroes, 73; Commissioners require free Negroes to obtain permits, 75-76; ordinance concerning drinking, 80; citizens condemn mob violence, 92-93; free Negroes commit murder near, 100; wages of unskilled laborers in, 136; names park for John Chavis, 174; citizens organize colonization society, 199; supports colonization movement, 203-04; free Negroes desire to leave State, 217-18

Raleigh Register, 37, 54, 117, 168, 193, 199; approves of free Negro immigration law, 44; incensed over stealing of free Negro, 55; reports slave conspiracy, 71; condemns beating of free Negro, 92; disapproves of disfranchisement of free Negroes, 115-16; comments on school of John Chavis, 172

Raleigh Star, 203

Ralph Cross, The, 210

Randolph County, 17, 25, 44 and n, 180; men sell free Negro, 56

Ransom, Ellen, 219

Rape, 91, 98-99; slave accused of, 37

Rayner, Kenneth, 118

Recreation, of free Negroes, visiting slaves restricted, 186; dancing and drinking prohibited, 186; gambling with slaves prohibited, 187

Reddick, R. H., 149

Reid, Margaret, 159

Reid, William, 176

Reminiscences of the Bench and Fayetteville Bar, 106

Rencher, Abraham, 173

Representation, inequality of, 108; as an issue in the Constitutional Convention, 114; vote compared with vote to disfranchise free Negro, 114

Respess, Isaiah, 41

Revels, John, 140

Rex, John, 202

Reynolds, David, 150

Richmond, Virginia, 5; free Negroes in, 7, 19n

Richmond County, 44n, 47, 157

Riddick, N. J., 75

Ritter, H. P., 220

Robeson County, 44n, 86, 100, 157; free Negroes in, 17 and n; citizens request that no free Negroes have firearms, 78; citizens request regulation of sale of liquor to free Negroes, 79; property of free Negroes in, 158-59; free Negroes in school in, 169

Rogers, Benjamin, 173

Rover, The, 207

Rowan County, 111, 115, 143; citizens oppose election of Van Buren, 116-17; citizens protest use of free Negro mechanics, 138-39

Ruffin, Thomas, 33; quoted or cited, 22-23, 24-25, 38, 49-50, 128, 202-03

Rural areas, free Negroes in, 16, 185n, 198, 222; inarticulate, 198. See Farmers

Rural life, persistence of, 5, 18-19

Russell, John H., 3

Russell, William, 108'

Rutherford County, 14n, 158n

Salisbury, 110n, 140; free Negroes in, 16n

Saluda, The, 206

Sampson, James D., 142, 157-58, 190, 216

Sampson County, 67n, 212n; slave conspiracy in, 71, 73; free Negro farm hands in, 149n; property of free Negroes in, 159; citizens desire to deport free Negroes, 212-13

Sandy Creek Association, 180

Saunders, Romulus M., 118

Savannah, Georgia, 66

Schools, enrollment of free Negroes in, 169. See also John Chavis; Education

Scotch-Irish, in North Carolina, 5-6, 8

Seawell, Henry, 63, 115

Sectionalism, in North Carolina politics, 108-09; reflected in vote to disfranchise free Negroes, 113-14

Seditious publications, law against circulation of, 68. See also Walker's Appeal

Sex relations. See Marriage; Race mixing

Sharrock, Mary, 125n

Sharrock, Samuel, 124

Shepard, Charles, 108

Shepard, William, 55

Shepherd, Jesse G., 86

Sheridan, Louis, 144-45, 158, 189n, 207-08

Sheriffs, hold runaway slaves, 40; receive letter from governor on incendiary publication, 67

Sherrill, P. M., 25

Shillitoe, Thomas, 167-68

Shober, Emanuel, opposes disfranchisement of free Negro, 111 and n

Shooting, by free Negro, 95

Shugg, Roger W., 106

Skeeter, Jacob, 133

Slave conspiracies, in the eighteenth century, 59; law guarding against, 60-61;

in northeastern North Carolina, 61; in Chowan River section, 73

Slaveholding, 7-9; 196-98; rank of North Carolina in, 9; free Negro, 155-56, 159-61

Slavery in North Carolina, importance of, 9; not profitable, 9n; effect on status of free Negroes, 58-59; free Negroes return to, 218-20

Slaves, position of, 7; numbers, 8, 14; drained from North Carolina, 8; encouraged to run away, 10-11, 41; purchase their freedom, 28-29; free Negroes tried for stealing, 41; free Negro group increased by runaway, 41; law against teaching of, 88n, 168; incompetent to make contracts, 155; right of free Negroes to own, 156-57; owned by free Negroes, 159-61; religious life of, 174, 176; relations of free Negroes with, 184-88; tolerance of, 196; influence of free Negroes on, 213; proposal that free Negroes become, 214; free Negroes become, 218-20

Small, Benjamin, 97

Social movements, antislavery, 8, 23-26, 62-63; emancipation of slaves, 19-34; temperance, 79; colonization, 199-211

Societies, manumission, 25-26, 196; colonization, 199-211

Society for the Propagation of the Gospel, 166, 175

Society of Friends. See Friends, Society of

Southampton County, Virginia, 71

South Carolina, 41, 79, 193, 195, 222; free Negroes in, 6-7, 14, 19; concentration of free Negroes on border of, 39n; strengthens its Free Negro Code, 42; Walker's Appeal in, 67; governor concerned about Nat Turner insurrection, 72; free Negroes disfranchised in, 116; slavery in, 147; free Negro seeks to enslave self, 220

Spaight, Richard D., 12, 68, 109

Spellman, Aaron, 123

Spencer, Thomas, 36

Spirituous liquors, petitions and legislation on free Negro use of, 79-80; 81n

Spivey, William, 96n

Stabbing, of free Negroes, 96, 99-100, 162

Standard. See North Carolina Standard

Stanly, Alfred, 108

Stanly, Catherine, 143

Stanly, Edward, 108

Stanly, John C., 115, 160n, 190; emancipates slaves, 23, 31-32; permits slave to carry gun, 76; takes free Negro apprentices, 126, 128; conducts barber shop, 140; large holdings of, 149-50, 158; slaves owned by, 160; difficulties of, 161-62

Stedman, William, 45n

Stewart, John, 218

Stockard, John, 45n

Stocks, as punishment of free Negroes, 91

Stokes, Montfort, 71-72, 91-92, 97-98, 195

Stokes County, 44n, 111

Strange, Robert, 86

Stringer, Dorothy, 103-04

Stringer, Hezekiah, 123

Stringer, May, 51

Suffolk, Virginia, 75

Suffrage, of free Negroes under Constitution of 1776, 12-13, 105; free Negroes deprived of, 113

Sunday, law concerning Raleigh free Negroes on, 75-76; free Negroes of New Bern on, 190-91

Superior Court, powers over manumission, 20, 27; free Negroes tried before, 85-86; counsel for free Negroes before, 85-86, 98

Supreme Court, upholds manumission of slaves, 22, 28n; attitude toward free Negroes, 49-53, 93-95; counsel for free Negroes before, 86; rules against Quakers holding slaves, 24; decides against manumission by will, 28; interprets free Negro immigration law, 47; defines Negro, 50; upholds law regulating use of firearms by free Negroes, 77-78; upholds law on insolvent free Negroes, 89-90; upholds apprentice law, 127-29; protects property rights of free Negroes, 151-52, 156

Surry County, 44n, 54

Suydem, James, 129n

Swain, David L., 33, 109

Sydnor, C. S., 207

Symons, Thomas, 9

Taburn, Washington, 91-92

Tappan, Arthur, 144

Tappan, Lewis, 145

Tarboro, 154; free Negroes in, 16n

Taxes, 14n; free Negroes exempted from paying, 103-04; paid by free Negroes,

103-05; planters pay poll, on free Negroes on plantation, 104; capitation tax on free Negroes proposed, 104-05

Taylor, John Louis, quoted, 24, 52-53

Taylor, Mice, 162

Taylor, Rosser Howard, 73

Temperance movement, 79

Tenants, free Negro, 149

Tennessee, 41, disfranchises free Negroes, 116

Testimony, limitations on free Negro giving, 82-84; of free Negroes in New York, 118-19

Tetterton, Asa, 126

Thefts, 96-97

Tinker, Stephen, 55-56

Titterton, Polly, 49

Towns, in North Carolina, lack of, 14; free Negroes in, 14, 16, 18-19; compared with those of other states, 19

Tradesmen. See Peddlers

Trinidad, 203

Trueblood, Kessiah, 220

Turner, Nat. See Nat Turner insurrection

Tuscaroras, 5

Tyrrell County, 67n; swamp hands in, 133

Vagrancy, Raleigh ordinance forbidding, 75-76

Valentine, Abednego, 92

Valentine, Nancy, 55

Van Buren, Martin, 106; in North Carolina politics, 117 and n

Vance, Zebulon B., 32

Vendors. See Peddlers

Vermont, 42, 196; resolution against slavery, 62-63

Virginia, 41, 49, 193, 222; free Negroes in, 6-7, 14, 19; concentration of free Negroes on border of, 39n; North Carolina free Negroes from, 42-45; free Negroes sold in North Carolina as slaves, 56; *Walker's Appeal* in, 67; law permitting slaves to testify against free Negroes, 83; disfranchises free Negroes, 116; slavery in, 147; free Negroes migrate to Liberia, 206

Voting, free Negroes prevented from, 10, 105, 113, 115n, 116, 193, 223; qualifications for free Negro, 105; of free Negroes, 105-06, 111; debate to prohibit free Negro, 110-12; of free Negroes after disfranchisement, 118-19

Wadesboro Argus, 194

Wages, of unskilled labor, 136; of skilled labor, 143-44

Wake County, 14, 16, 34, 37, 54, 63, 97, 115, 157, 173; free Negroes in, 14, 17 and n; grand jury, 30; free Negro children stolen, 55; free Negro escapes from jail in, 97; property of free Negroes in, 159; free Negroes in school, 169; free Negroes desire to leave State, 217-18

Walker, David, 64, 164

Walker, John, slaves owned by, 161

Walker's Appeal in Four Articles, discussed, 64-66, 185, 196; disturbs Southern leaders, 66-70

Wallard, Dan, 124

Walser, Henry, offers bill to remove free Negroes, 214-15

Warren County, 44n, 67n, 110

Warrenton, 97; free Negroes in, 16n

Washington, Booker T., 195

Washington, General George, 102

Washington, George, slave, 28

Washington, North Carolina, law regulating slaves and free Negroes in, 59-60; free Negroes migrate to Liberia, 206

Washington Academy, 170

Washington and Lee University, 170

Washington County, 67n, 143

Watkins, Patsy, 49n

Watson, Isaac, 87, 97

Watson, J. T., 219

Watson, John, 128

Watters, William P., 50

Wayne County, 17n, 44, 55, 67n, 96, 174; free Negroes migrate to Liberia, 207

Weapons, free Negroes must have license to carry, 75-78, 76n; use of, 95-101

West Indies, 60-61

Western Carolinian, 118

Western Democrat, 219

Whig party, 117-20

Whipping, as punishment of free Negroes, 86-87

White, Leah, 220

White, Mona, 124

White, Sidney, 128

White population, in 1790, 5-6

Whitehead, William B., 75

Whitfield, A. H., 98

Wiggins, Anthony, 99

Wiggins, Dorset, 41

Wiggins, Solomon, 124

Wilkes County, 14n, 44n, 118

Williams, Betsy, 99

Williams, Daniel, migrates with family to Liberia, 209

Williams, John, 82

Williams, Thomas, 200

Wills, emancipation by, 20; free Negroes receive property in, 153-55

Wilmington, 5, 32, 64, 73-74, 110n, 140-41, 153-54; Safety Committee, 10-11; free Negroes in, 14, 16, 17; citizens request manumission of slave, 33; law regulating slaves and free Negroes in, 59-60; police discover *Walker's Appeal,* 66; free Negroes to give bond, 70n; mob violence in, 93; property of free Negroes in, 158

Wilmington Aurora, praises beating of free Negro, 93

Wilmington Journal, 132

Wilmington Recorder, 141

Wilson, Jesse, 111

Windsor, 61

Witherspoon, John, 170n

Witnesses, incompetency of free Negroes as, 82

Women, employment of free Negro, 143

Woods, Benjamin, 148

Woodson, Carter G., 166, 168n

Woolard, Sarah, 128

Worrell, I. W., 133

Worrell, Moore, migrates to Liberia, 208

Wortham, George, 170

Wortham, James, 173

Wright, C. G., 86

Wright, James, 122-23

Wright, James M., 3

Wright, Janett, 220

Wright, Joshua, 153

Wright, William B., 85-86

Yates, Thomas Hall, 33

Yeomanry, 6, 139, 149-50, 197-98

AMERICAN HISTORY TITLES IN THE NORTON LIBRARY

Samuel Flagg Bemis *The Latin American Policy of the United States* N412

Ray Allen Billington, Ed. *The Reinterpretation of Early American History* N446

Fawn Brodie *Thaddeus Stevens* N331

Robert E. Brown *Charles Beard and the Constitution* N296

Roger H. Brown *The Republic in Peril: 1812* N578

Edmund Cody Burnett *The Continental Congress* N278

Richard L. Bushman *From Puritan to Yankee: Character and the Social Order in Connecticut, 1690-1765* N532

George W. Cable *The Negro Question: A Selection of Writings on Civil Rights in the South* N420

Mark Lincoln Chadwin *The Warhawks: American Interventionists Before Pearl Harbor* N546

Dudley T. Cornish *The Sable Arm: Negro Troops in the Union Army, 1861-1865* N334

John Paton Davies, Jr. *Foreign and Other Affairs* N330

Dwight Lowell Dumond *Antislavery* N370

Herbert Feis *Contest Over Japan* N466

Herbert Feis *The Diplomacy of the Dollar* N333

Herbert Feis *The Spanish Story* N339

Herbert Feis *Three International Episodes: Seen from E. A.* N351

Robert H. Ferrell *American Diplomacy in the Great Depression: Hoover-Stimson Foreign Policy, 1929-1933* N511

Robert H. Ferrell *Peace in Their Time: The Origins of the Kellogg-Briand Pact* N491

John Hope Franklin *The Free Negro in North Carolina, 1790-1860* N579

Dewey W. Grantham *The Democratic South* N299

Fletcher Green *Constitutional Development in the South Atlantic States, 1776-1860* N348

Michael Garibaldi Hall *Edward Randolph and the American Colonies, 1676-1703* N480

Holman Hamilton *Prologue to Conflict: The Crisis and Compromise of 1850* N345

Pendleton Herring *The Politics of Democracy* N306

Preston J. Hubbard *Origins of the TVA: The Muscle Shoals Controversy, 1920-1932* N467

Rufus Jones *The Quakers in the American Colonies* N356

George F. Kennan *Realities of American Foreign Policy* N320

Gabriel Kolko *Railroads and Regulation, 1877-1916* N531

Howard Roberts Lamar *The Far Southwest, 1846-1912: A Territorial History* N522

William L. Langer *Our Vichy Gamble* N379

Douglas Edward Leach *Flintlock and Tomahawk: New England in King Philip's War* N340

William S. McFeely *Yankee Stepfather: General O. O. Howard and the Freedmen* N537

James Madison *Notes of Debates in the Federal Convention of 1787 Reported by James Madison* N485

C. Peter Magrath *Yazoo: The Case of Fletcher v. Peck* N418

Alpheus T. Mason *The Supreme Court from Taft to Warren* N257

Burl Noggle *Teapot Dome* N297

Douglass C. North *The Economic Growth of the United States, 1790-1860* N346

Norman Pollack *The Populist Response to Industrial America* N295

Robert E. Quirk *An Affair of Honor: Woodrow Wilson and the Occupation of Veracruz* N390

Robert E. Quirk *The Mexican Revolution, 1914-1915* N507

Robert V. Remini *Martin Van Buren and the Making of the Democratic Party* N527

Charles R. Ritcheson *Aftermath of Revolution: British Policy Toward the United States, 1783-1795* N553

Eric Robson *The American Revolution, In Its Political and Military Aspects: 1763-1783* N382

James W. Silver *Confederate Morale and Church Propaganda* N422

John W. Spanier *The Truman-MacArthur Controversy and the Korean War* N279

Ida M. Tarbell *History of the Standard Oil Company* (David Chalmers, Ed.) N496

Frederick B. Tolles *Meeting House and Counting House* N211

Arthur B. Tourtellot *Lexington and Concord* N194

Frederick Jackson Turner *The United States 1830-1850* N308

Harris Gaylord Warren *Herbert Hoover and the Great Depression* N394

Arthur P. Whitaker *The United States and the Independence of Latin America* N271

Bryce Wood *The Making of the Good Neighbor Policy* N401

C. Vann Woodward *The Battle for Leyte Gulf* N312

Benjamin Fletcher Wright *Consensus and Continuity, 1776-1787* N402

Howard Zinn *LaGuardia in Congress* N488

A MILLIONAIRE AND A
PROJECT CHICK 2

SHONTAIYE MOORE

Cole Hart
SIGNATURE NOVELS

A Millionaire And A Project Chick 2

Copyright © 2021 by Shontaiye Moore

All rights reserved.

Published in the United States of America.

Mailing List

To stay up to date on new releases, plus get information on contests, sneak peeks, and more,

Go To The Website Below...

www.colehartsignature.com

INTRODUCTION
NEAL

"Boobie, grab ya shit! It's a hit! Girls, get down!" I screamed.

I cocked my gun and spun back around to open fire through the closed window. I was too slow. The gunman's first shot was through the back window where my kids were seated.

All I could hear were their screams and frantic cries for help as the entire glass shattered down on them. The next thing that I knew, Boobie's connect, Lawrence, was ripping the car apart with the Draco he was holding.

"Daddy!" I heard my girls continue to shout from the backseat.

Mid-cry, a second round of bullets met the side of the car, this time, tearing through the interior and shattering the passenger side glass. The impact was so forceful, the car vibrated. My life flashed before my eyes, but I quickly shook that shit off.

Out of instinct, I ducked and crouched as low as I could into the seat, only bringing up my arm briefly to bust my gun.

"Shit!" Boobie grumbled as he dropped down and frantically scrambled to retrieve the gun that he kept under the seat, while I let off a few more punk ass shots.

With lowered brows and beads of sweat peppering my forehead, I squeezed down on the trigger a few more times. I was not only angry at myself for being caught slipping, I was also pissed for lacking on my daughters' safety, which now had them in a dire situation. We were severely outgunned, and the little Nine I had was no match compared to the Draco that nigga was holding. I'd only caught a quick glimpse of it, but the sight of that big motherfucker was enough to have me cowering in the seat and whispering a quick prayer to God for mercy.

I'd been shot at before, but a nigga never had me shook like this. It was easy to scream that tough shit, but all that went out the window when a nigga had you boxed in with an automatic weapon strong enough to flip a car. I didn't know what Lawrence's issue was. I just knew that he'd come on some shit. Even though he was masked, his identity was easy to determine. His build, movement, and distinct dreads gave it all away.

Still stiff, crouched down in the seat, and covered in glass, I did my best to peek behind me and check to make sure my kids were okay. I heard their screams and cries, but there wasn't shit I could do. I couldn't defend them, and even though I would give my life to keep them safe, that wasn't good enough at the moment. What I did know for sure was that I was gon' still bust my gun in an effort to protect them. Win, lose, or draw, I was letting off.

After crouching down a few more seconds, I brought my pistol back up through the shattered window and let off another volley of shots just as Boobie was letting his shit go. He'd finally grabbed his tool from under the seat and was able to return fire. In the meantime, I was back to praying to God. This time, though, I wasn't praying for mercy; I was praying for a miracle instead. If Lawrence shot across the front of the car, it was definitely about to be a wrap for us. I held my breath while silently peering over at Boobie. A few seconds passed, and it seemed like my prayers may have worked. The shots stopped.

Although Lawrence was still clutching his gun, he had done the unexpected. He had stopped shooting and had started backing up. Why? I wasn't sure. I didn't hear the police or any sirens. Maybe he'd caught one of those slugs we'd sent his way. I doubted it though. He didn't seem to be in any sort of pain, nor was he grabbing at his body to indicate that he'd been hit. Whatever the case was, I was just thankful that he'd lowered his weapon. To capitalize on his sudden intermission, I motioned to bring my gun back up so I could fire, but Boobie reached over and stopped me. He brought his hand over my gun and pushed it back down.

"Hold up," he mouthed.

I had no doubt that he was thinking the same thing that I was. *What the fuck is this nigga doing?* What was he waiting on?

A few seconds later, Lawrence lowered his weapon completely to his side, ran back to his car, and peeled out of the parking lot.

"The fuck was that?" I shouted out to no one in particular, after I'd exhaled a massive sigh of relief.

I spun to my side to face Boobie, and the look on his face was hard to place. It was a mixture of terror and confusion. My thoughts instantly rushed back to Sage and Violet. A ripple of panic washed over me.

I pushed open the bullet-riddled door, hopped out, and raced to check on them. When I snatched open their door, I couldn't help but fear the worse. I expected to see the two of them limp and covered in blood. Instead, they were balled up together near the door, wearing terrified looks and clutching one another for dear life. Seeing them like that was enough to bring tears to my eyes.

"Sage! Violet! Y'all okay?" I yelled frantically, before reaching in and pulling them across the seat and out of the car. The whole time, my heart felt like it was in the pit of my stomach.

I spun them around and inspected their tiny bodies for any wounds. They had some cuts, but they were okay. I blew out another sigh of relief before pulling them up into my arms.

"I'm scared, Daddy!" Violet sobbed into my shoulder, before throwing her arm around my neck tightly.

"I want Mommy," Sage also cried.

"It's gon' be okay." I did my best to console them, but I knew it was going to take more than some hugs and kisses to make that shit better. I knew that what had just happened was going to leave them with some emotional wounds. I had fucked up, but at least they were safe.

"Boobie, you good?" I asked. He had gotten out the car and was now limping over to where I was standing, holding my daughters.

"Yeah, I'm good. They okay?" he asked, looking and sounding damn near amazed. I knew what he was thinking. *It was a fuckin' miracle.*

"Yeah. They're good. Just scared. We gotta get the fuck outta here though. Twelve 'bout to be crawlin' all through this motherfucker."

I knew someone had definitely called them. I was starting to hear the sirens in the distance. I looked over at the bullet-riddled Benz. We'd be lucky if we could even get the bitch to start. The shit was wild.

Still clutching my daughters, I pressed kisses into the sides of their faces while they continued to whimper. It was no secret that they were still shaken up. Hearing them and seeing them had me ready to dig deep in my bag. They both were bleeding and Violet had a stream of bright-red blood trailing from the top of her head and down the side of her face.

"My girls a little scratched up, but I ain't trying to go to no fuckin' hospital," I admitted.

There was no way I was trying to explain to a doctor what had happened. The way Sage ran her little ass lips, she'd have the whole story ran down to the entire hospital in five minutes tops.

Boobie went to reply but instead, grew silent. A few nosy ass people that were in the drive-thru had gotten out of their vehicles. There were also now a few concerned McDonald's employees pushing through the doors and making their way over to us. I counted about three people holding up cell phones in their hands. They were either recording or calling for help.

"Shit," I mumbled, my eyes doing another quick scan of the parking lot.

There were too many witnesses. There was no point in leaving the scene. Even if we wanted to, they'd pull the cameras. Since the nigga Lawrence had on a mask and was probably pushing some stolen shit, he was good. Besides, even if someone had recognized him, I highly doubted that they would have the balls to step inside of a courtroom once he got wind of it. Boobie's Benz, on the other hand, was definitely registered and could be traced back to him with ease.

"Are you all okay?" a few of the onlookers called out to us.

"You know the drill, nigga. Keep the girls quiet and play dumb," Boobie said, giving me the look.

"Fuck," I muttered.

We were about to make the news.

❧ 1 ❧

ALIZE

I trailed my fingers up and down Lance's broad, chocolate chest while I gazed quietly at the egg-shell-colored wall.

"Watchu thinkin' 'bout?" he asked, tearing me away from my thoughts.

He used the arm he had wrapped around me to pull me closer into his body before pressing his soft lips into my forehead. My face melted into a buttery smile.

"Just my girls."

Yeah, I was smiling from his kiss, but I was also smiling from the thought of my babies. I couldn't wait to show them our new place. Couldn't wait to see their faces light up with joy. With Lance's help, I had saved quite a bit of money and had more than enough to decorate my girls' room in a lavish princess theme. After everything they'd been through, they definitely deserved it.

I'd only been in my new place a few days and was still getting it together the best I could with the little I had. I had my bedroom set, but I was still waiting on the living room furniture, as well as the girls' bedroom set. Despite what I lacked, the place was still coming along so beautifully, and I couldn't have been prouder. A lot of people took small things like stability for granted. I knew I definitely had, but never again. Being homeless would have you appreciating damn near everything.

"I should have known," Lance replied. "You ready to show them the new place?"

"Yeah. They're gonna love it. I just hope the judge gives them back to me tomorrow."

I exhaled a wishful sigh. I had court in the morning, and I was nervous as hell. The lawyer Lance had retained for me was expensive and esteemed. After speaking with him a couple of times, he seemed confident that I would get the girls back in my custody at the very first hearing. However, I was still worried because I hadn't even been to court for the criminal charges against me. I was hoping for the best but deep down, I had prepared myself for the worst. The last thing I wanted to do was walk into that courtroom with my heart set on leaving with my babies, only to have it shattered when I didn't. Even if things did go wrong, I knew when it was all said and done, I would have them back with me, especially because there was nothing that I wasn't willing to do to make that happen.

"Shit gon' go yo' way. If not now, eventually. George gon' handle it," Lance assured me before planting another moist kiss on my forehead. "Trust me," he added.

Trust me. My body shivered from the words. And it wasn't a bad shiver. It was a good one. One that I could wallow in forever. It wasn't *something* about that man, it was *everything* about that man. Lance provided me with a sense of comfort, love, security, and protection. It was like I could relax even in my troubles. When he said he had me, I knew damn well he meant that shit, because he never just said it; he also showed it. And for those reasons, I would gladly submit to him and give him my entire heart. I'd never met a man more loving, wholesome, and deserving.

"I trust you," I finally replied before reaching up and pushing a few strands of hair from my face.

"Good. Because I trust you too and as long as we got that, then we good."

Before I could respond, I was interrupted by the blaring ring of my cell phone. I rose off Lance's chest, climbed my naked body from the bed, and grabbed my phone off the dresser where it was placed. I looked down and saw Judy's number running horizontal across my screen. I frowned curiously. It was a weekday, and I knew that she didn't get home until well after midnight from her shift at the hospital. The girls were usually in daycare until Neal picked them up and took them home. I swiped my finger across the phone and answered.

"Hey, Judy, wassup," I greeted her warmly, despite my apprehension.

"Alize." Judy paused, and I knew that something was wrong. My heart immediately skipped a beat while dread cloaked me.

"What is it, Judy? What's the matter?" I asked. My tone was now urgent.

"There's been an accident," she choked out. "Neal and the girls. You need to get down here."

ॐ

Judy wouldn't tell me anything over the phone. All she kept repeating was that there'd been an accident and that I needed to get to the hospital. Me being me, I wanted to know who, what, when, where, why, and how; however, she wouldn't divulge anything of value. All she'd told me was that the girls were okay but something serious had happened. The term 'okay' just didn't sit well with my spirit. I'd never been so scared in my life.

The old folks used to always say, *God would only give his toughest battles to his toughest soldiers.* I wanted him to take me up out his lineup, because I was tired of being strong. A bitch had been beaten, dragged, *and* stomped on. I didn't have too much more fight up in me. I lived and breathed for my children and if anything happened to them, I didn't know what more I really had to live for.

After hanging up with Judy, I literally raced around my apartment to get dressed and find my keys. Anxiety overwhelmed me with each step I took. It was hard to stay positive when my brain automatically assumed the worst. I needed to know what was going on. I knew it was bad since whatever it was, Judy insisted on telling me face-to-face.

Being the man that he was, Lance refused to let me drive to the hospital alone. He wouldn't take no for an answer. When I began throwing on my clothes and shoving my feet into my sneakers, so did he. I couldn't lie, my thoughts were racing, and I was close to having a panic attack. I was dropping things, stumbling, and running into shit before I could even get out my front door. Lance immediately became my voice of reason.

"Babe, you're too upset to drive. Try to calm down and breathe. I'll get you to the hospital." He was standing at the doorway while I was trying to get out.

"I'm okay. I can drive myself. I just gotta get to my girls and see what's going on."

"And you will. But you ain't going alone. I'm driving. The last thing I need is for you to be wrapped around a fuckin' pole because you not thinking clearly. Give me the keys," he demanded sternly before reaching down and taking them out my hand.

Despite my reluctance, I didn't bother to protest. My man had spoken. I raced out of the building with him right behind me.

After doing nearly eighty miles per hour on the freeway, Lance pulled up to the parking lot of the hospital in ten minutes. After parking illegally, I raced into the emergency room with him right behind me.

"Where are my kids?" I demanded to know after rushing through the doors of the emergency room and spotting Judy and her sister Brenda, also Boobie's mom.

Judy had been sitting quietly in a corner chair of the waiting room when I walked in while her sister sat beside her looking just as worried. Judy stood up as I approached her. The two of them glanced at Lance questionably, but I ignored the looks. I didn't have time for the pleasantries, nor did I owe either one of them an explanation of who he was.

"What happened?" I asked her, before she'd even had the opportunity to answer the first question.

My eyes were wide and filled with worry while I impatiently waited for a response.

"Alize." She sighed before continuing. "Neal and the girls were riding with Boobie when someone shot the car up."

My eyes widened and I grabbed my chest. *What the fuck?* I wasn't expecting that. "The girls are okay," Judy said. "They both have some cuts and scratches, but they're okay."

I exhaled in relief. "What about Neal and Boobie? Are they okay?"

"They're both fine. No one was shot. Thank God."

"Definitely God. You should have seen the amount of bullets," Brenda added.

I could tell that the two of them were just as rattled by the news as I was. They looked worn. Their eyes were red-rimmed, and their faces were puffy from crying. Despite my sympathy for the two of them, my mind shifted right back to my kids.

"I need to go back there and see my babies." I glanced at Lance and then spun around to walk off.

"Alize, wait. You can't go back there," Judy quickly called out.

I ignored her. I wasn't asking her no way. I proceeded to the front desk of the emergency room on my own. Lance was right behind me.

"My name is Alize McKoy and my girls were brought in here."

"Was it by ambulance?" the receptionist asked. She was an elderly woman that was looking *and* moving slow. I knew that she was probably just following procedure, but her snail-like pace and the silly-ass question that she'd just asked, irritated me. I didn't fucking know if they were brought in by ambulance or not. I didn't know shit. I knew damn well that she'd just seen me walk through the doors right in front of her face.

"Ms., I don't know," I replied irritably. "I wasn't with them. I just got a phone call from their grandmother that they were involved in an accident, and I raced down here."

Lance reached over and rubbed my back in an effort to calm me. I appreciated the gesture but the only thing that was going to calm me, was seeing my girls.

"What are their names?" she asked.

Just as I began rambling their names off to the receptionist, I spotted a disgruntled looking Neal exiting the automatic double doors that led from the emergency care area.

"Neal!" I rushed over to him, forgetting all about Lance being behind me. "Where are the girls?"

Neal's eyes fell on me briefly. Instead of responding, he whipped his head sharply in Lance's direction and glared at him. His face hardened into a scowl, while his chest seemed to swell with animosity.

"The fuck this nigga doing here, Alize?" Neal spat.

"What?" I asked in disbelief. "I don't got time for that dumb shit, Neal. Where the fuck are my kids?"

Neal tore his gaze away from Lance and looked back to me.

"Back there with the doctors getting stitched and wrapped the fuck up because this nigga's bitch ass brother," he accused angrily.

"What?" I stared at him blankly, as I was lost.

"Ask yo' new nigga," he added bitterly. "It was his people that shot Boobie's car up," Neal said quietly, but loud enough for Lance to hear. "But yo' bitch ass knew that already ... right?" he added, pausing for a confirmation.

"Lance, what the fuck is he talkin' about?"

I turned around and peered at Lance, who was standing there looking just as dumbfounded as me. I knew he had a brother because of Lindsey. However, Lance rarely spoke of him.

"I don't know what he's talking about," Lance replied. I glanced back at him and he was calm, although, I could detect traces of anger creeping up into his eyes. I briefly studied his face. He was either a damn good liar or he truly had no clue what Neal was talking about.

"You can play dumb in here, but that won't work in the streets. Not for you *or* your brother."

"What is he talking about, Lance?" I asked again, as if that was going to change his previous answer of not knowing.

Lance was still standing quietly. His jaw had tightened, and anger leaped in his eyes. Instead of replying to me, he chose to address Neal.

"I don't know you, and clearly, you don't know me. If you did, you'd know there ain't a drop of hoe in me. I don't take kindly to threats. You better ask yo' boss."

Neal met Lance's icy gaze.

"You keep talkin' that boss shit. Fuck all that. At the end of the day, I'm a ma'fuckin' man, and I don't take kindly to attempts on my fuckin' life. So, fuck you," Neal argued, pointing towards Lance and stepping a few feet closer toward him. "My daughters were in that car. He violated. Yo' folk made it clear he wanted action, so fuck talkin'. And you already got one pass for that slick shit you talked downtown that night, but ain't no more passes being given." Neal turned his attention to me. "Get this nigga the fuck outta here," he demanded, before walking off to join his mom and aunt in the waiting area.

"Lance, please tell me what's going on."

He had to have known something. I didn't know the details of his business, but obviously his brother played some part. Held some kind of important role.

Lance glanced around nervously while I stared him down and waited for a response. He looked reluctant to speak, and for good reason. We were in the middle of the damn emergency room waiting area, where if we didn't keep our voices down enough, almost anyone could hear our conversation.

"I honestly don't know. But I'm definitely gonna find out." He was clearly angry, but I could also tell that his thoughts were swirling.

I shook my head and exhaled a frustrated breath. I was still lost, but from what I'd gathered from the short exchange was that Neal suspected that Lance or his brother had something to do with Boobie's car being shot up. Nothing else made any sense to me. Neal never spoke about his business and neither did Lance. I wasn't privy to the extent of their relationship. All I knew was Lance supplied Boobie and Boobie supplied Neal.

Still desperate to see my kids, I went back up to the check-in desk and waited while the receptionist pulled up their room numbers. After a brief scan through her computer, she was able to give me some information.

"They're in pediatrics, but no one is allowed back there at this moment. If you can have a seat, I'll have someone out shortly to speak with you."

"What do you mean no one is allowed back there? I'm *their* *mother*," I grumbled.

"Ma'am, I have to go by what's in these notes. I understand you're upset, but I have to do my job. I need you to take a seat and I'll get someone out here as quickly as I can to explain everything."

"Okay," I mumbled in defeat.

I had no choice but to comply. I was becoming drained. Not just physically but also mentally.

To minimize drama, Lance agreed to wait outside while I sat with Neal and his family. I tried to get as comfortable as possible in the cold, hard waiting room chairs, but it was difficult. I was angry, fidgety, and worried. To make matters worse, each time I looked up, Neal was staring me down like he had a chip on his motherfuckin' shoulder. I rolled my eyes each and every time I felt his beady, little black eyes peeping in my direction. I would deal with him later since I knew he wasn't going to say too much with his mom and aunt present. I respected my elders, but he knew that I would still turn the fuck up with them right there. I didn't care about them being there or the fact that we were in a public place. We were no longer together, so I wasn't about to pretend for anyone. Especially not when it came to my kids.

A few minutes later, a white lady in a cheap-looking suit walked up with an older, white male that appeared to be the doctor. He was stiff looking and wearing a white lab coat. Despite the lady being front and center, the man began speaking.

"Hi, I'm Doctor Gelof, the chief pediatric physician, and this is Elizabeth Cortese."

"With Child Protective Services," she threw in.

My heart instantly sank at the mere mention of Child Protective Services. *What the fuck were they doing there? Who called them?* My brows immediately dipped from concern and confusion.

"Are you mom?" Doctor Gelof asked me. He extended his hand out, so I reached out and shook it. Since he didn't offer that same courtesy to anyone else, I assumed that he'd already met them.

"I am," I quickly responded. I then turned in the direction of the CPS worker. "Why are you here?" I asked. My intuition told me something was up. "You're not my caseworker, so why are you here?" I asked. I studied her while I anxiously waited for a response.

"It's protocol." She forced a tight smile. "And you're right; I *wasn't* your caseworker, but I am now."

"How are my kids?" I asked, turning my attention back to the doctor.

I knew the conversation with Snow White was about to go left. I could feel it in my gut. I didn't want to hear shit else the thin-lipped bitch in her wrinkly ass suit had to say.

"Your daughters are just fine. They both had minor lacerations on their face and head from the glass. The youngest one has a small gash above her eye that we stitched up. Otherwise, they're okay."

My jaws tightened while I shot Neal and Judy a look of disapproval. Clearly, they were to blame. The girls shouldn't have been out that late anyway with his sorry ass. I turned my gaze back to the doctor, urging him to continue.

"They aren't in any pain and they, of course, are expected to make a full recovery with minimal scars. They are, however, shaken up. Which is expected considering what occurred."

He stopped speaking and looked at Elizabeth, giving her the floor.

"So, I'm here because it was noted that the girls have an active case. They are currently in the care of the father."

"No. They're in the care of their grandmother." I frowned.

"Well, in our system it has them as being in the care and custody of the father. They all reside with the grandmother."

"Right. He just lives at my address while they're in his custody," Judy said weakly.

Anger coursed through my body. That wasn't the fucking agreement when Sage and Violet were taken out of my care. It also wasn't the agreement when I'd spoken to her old ass on the phone from the city jail after being arrested. Judy was supposed to be their temporary guardian. Not Neal's rusty, dusty, irresponsible ass.

"So, that's the problem. The girls are in the custody of the father, who was shot at tonight. According to the officers I spoke with tonight, the father is under investigation."

"Under investigation for what?" I quizzed. I shot Neal another hard look, but he just sat there silently, looking tight.

"I, unfortunately, can't divulge that information. But the investigation itself does create an element of concern."

"What does that mean?" I asked. I wanted her to get to the point.

"Basically, your girls can't leave with him. Their safety is our primary concern."

"Okay. So, they should still be able to leave with their grandma," I said impatiently.

"Not in this situation. Mainly because their father lives in the home with her. According to the officers, anywhere he is, there are major safety concerns."

My eyes darted around the room. My gaze was met with solemn expressions. I now knew why Judy sounded the way she did on the phone. They already knew that CPS was on some bullshit before I arrived. That's exactly why she didn't want to hardly tell me shit over the phone.

"What does that mean for them?" I asked, my voice wavering. I didn't have anyone else that I trusted enough to hand my girls over to. The more the bitch talked, the worse shit was starting to sound.

"Well, normally we ask if there is another family member that could step in, but it seems as though there isn't."

"What about my sister?" Judy asked. I was about to protest since I didn't know Brenda that well, but I didn't have any better options.

Elizabeth glanced at Judy and then turned her gaze to Brenda.

"I understand that you're the aunt, but you're also mother to the other passenger targeted in the shooting, so you, unfortunately, wouldn't be an option."

Elizabeth turned her attention back to me, wearing a sympathetic look.

"At this point, the girls will be placed into state custody. I see that you have a hearing in the morning, that may very well land them back with you; however, the judge will ultimately have the final say."

Hearing her say that my girls were going into state custody was enough to render me speechless. I felt like I was being suffocated. It was like someone had their hands wrapped around my throat, squeezing it. For a brief moment, it seemed like hardly any of my senses were working. I couldn't breathe, see, or hear.

My world had paused, and I not only felt drained, but I also felt empty.

My girls were slipping further and further away from me, and I wasn't sure how to process the emotions that came with that. I was so frustrated I could've screamed. I had been trying so hard, but it seemed like every step I took forward, something or someone would pull me two steps back. There were times when I felt like I wanted to give up. Times where I wanted to die. But as a mother, I would never. I would never stop fighting to get my girls back.

"Can I just see them before I go?" My lip quivered uncontrollably while I fought back a mountain of tears. My heart ached, but I was tired of crying.

"You can. But only for a few minutes," Elizabeth said.

I bit down on my bottom lip to keep from responding the way I really wanted to.

"Thank you," I forced out.

I wanted to smack her pale, white ass. *Only for a few minutes.* She couldn't have been a mother. There was no way. If she was, she'd understand. My babies had just been in a shoot-out, and I was only allowed to see them for a few minutes. I wanted to kiss them, hug them, and console them. That would certainly require more than a few measly fucking minutes. It was what it was though. And it was certainly better than nothing.

After waiting a few more minutes, I was finally escorted to the pediatric section of the emergency room by Elizabeth and a uniformed police officer. It was that moment that I truly felt like less of a woman. A complete bum and failure as a mother. I was being escorted to see my own damn children. The whole experience was tough, but I kept telling myself that I was tougher. I made a vow that I wouldn't let it break my spirits, but I couldn't lie, it was difficult. Even more so when I entered the room, and my babies were sitting on the bed looking like no one loved them.

Violet had a thick bandage going around her head covering

the nasty gash she sustained during the shoot-out. Despite being stitched and covered, I could still see specks of blood peeking through. Sage wore a few bandages on her face from the cuts she incurred but otherwise, she looked normal.

They were happy to see me, but, of course, the tears would pour, and the cries would fill the room when they were informed that they weren't leaving with me, their father, nor their grandmother. They had a million questions that I couldn't truly answer. Questions like when they were coming home, and why they had to go with the white lady. Kisses, hugs, and promises weren't enough. The 'I love you's' weren't enough. They wanted their mother. They wanted their life back ... and so did I.

After an emotional and teary goodbye, I walked out of that hospital in a daze. When I got to the car, I explained to Lance what had happened. Like he always did, he reassured me that everything would be alright. He seemed to think that money could fix everything. I was beginning to question that. I no longer knew if having money at my disposal was enough.

"George will handle it, babe. I don't care how much it costs. You're gonna get your kids back. I promise."

I prayed that he was right, because I truly didn't know how much more I could take. While Lance began the drive back home, I sank into the plush passenger seat of the Jaguar with a defeated sigh. Glancing up at the dashboard, I checked the time. I had gotten Judy's call around eleven and it was now nearly one in the morning. I knew I wouldn't get much sleep worrying about my court hearing scheduled for later that morning. I knew that my mind was going to be bogged down with what else that could go wrong. Something told me that this was only the beginning of my troubles.

❧ 2 ❧

LAWRENCE

I could admit that I was a raw ass nigga. A killer that had been crafted by the gritty streets of Atlanta. I had not only witnessed death on numerous occasions, I'd also personally delivered it. For sure, I was a demon, but I wasn't heartless enough to kill no little ass fucking kids. Because of all the shit I'd been through, I didn't really believe in God. Not until a few hours ago, anyway. It wasn't just good luck that kept breath in those niggas' bodies. Nah, God had definitely shown up in that parking lot earlier and spared that nigga Boobie and whoever the bitch ass nigga he had with him.

Any nigga that knew me, knew that I was TTG—Trained To Go. Always had been, always would be. Anybody that had ever crossed me knew that when I got on a nigga's ass, it was a wrap. One sweep across the rear of that Benz and I blew out the back windows. Another sweep across the side and I was just about to send those niggas to chill with their ancestors. Lucky for them, it was the sound of those screams that kept me off their ass. They weren't just any screams. It was the screams of innocent children. Fortunately for them, even a ruthless nigga like me had boundaries.

I hadn't been tailing the goofy ass nigga Boobie long before he got all nervous and blocked his own self in at McDonald's. I expected a little chase or something. Nope. The scary ass nigga made it too easy for me when he pulled in and hopped right in the drive-thru out of all places. That particular location had a concrete barrier with a little bullshit garden running alongside to prevent a motherfucker from hopping out of the line once they were in it. To put it simply, it was a dummy move. To be a so-called hood nigga, it was clear that he couldn't think quick on his feet. Being as though *I could*, I took the opportunity and hopped out on his ass. When I ran up, I had every intention of killing Boobie for the slick shit he spat over the phone. I also planned to kill anybody he had with him. Niggas anyway. I didn't fuck with hoes and babies. Usually. There were definitely some exceptions to the hoes. If you were a scandalous hoe, then you could definitely catch a bullet. No matter the circumstances, though, I wasn't fucking with no babies. Never had. Never would.

Of course, it would be my luck to hear some screaming while I had the perfect chance to smoke a nigga or two. Despite having the perfect opportunity, I couldn't proceed. I knew that if I continued to let the Draco rip up that little Benz, then there was no guarantee I would be able to spare the little ones. So, I lowered my gun. Trust me, I didn't want to. My trigger finger was itching something fierce. Even with them pussies bussin' back, I backed off, jumped in the unregistered whip I was pushing, and peeled off. I'd get they ass another day.

Back at home and staring out the window of my luxury condo, I was now restless and annoyed. My bitch, Casey, wasn't answering the phone, I had no fuckin' drugs and even if I did have some drugs, I didn't have anyone to sell them to since Lance's soft ass had made good on his threat and snatched away his people. Corey, Tye, Boobie—none of them niggas were trying to fuck with me. I knew it was strictly because Lance had told them not to, and that was cool. If they wanted to be pussies, then that was on them. My problem with Boobie was he had to come out his mouth reckless. I was cool with all three of them niggas saying they were taking their business elsewhere. That wasn't the issue. It was the fact that Boobie felt that he could reprimand a nigga about ethics and how I handled business. The audacity of his little low-class ass coming out his face to me like he was a gangsta. I didn't take kindly to disrespect. I didn't give out passes when it came to that. Ever. Plus, I knew that his bitch ass would have never come out his mouth crazy to Lance. That alone was enough for me to want to put a bullet in his ass.

There were no morals in the dope game anyway. Yeah, I'd ignored them niggas' phone calls when they found out the drugs that I'd sold them were bad. But what the fuck could I do? I wasn't Walmart, so I wasn't issuing no fuckin' refunds. I also wasn't exchanging shit since I didn't have no different product to give them no way. Losses were expected when it came to hustling. I knew firsthand since I'd taken one just like everyone else. I was actually still hoping that I ran into the nigga that had sold me the bullshit. The bad part was, I didn't know shit about the dude. All I had was his first name. Carlos.

I'd met Carlos at a large, high-end club called Drip that I frequented. Although I'd never seen him regularly before in the past, I'd noticed him there the past few times. He was a flashy Spanish cat that usually occupied a VIP section with a few other slick-haired dudes that looked like him. I'd never really paid him much mind until he'd sent a message through the bartender that he wanted to speak with me. I wasn't into being beckoned and shit, but I still made my way to his section to see what he wanted with me. After sizing the nigga up and conversing with him for a little bit, I determined that he wasn't no petty little dealer. He made it very clear that I shouldn't even think such a thing. After that was established, he got right down to business. Said he'd seen me around and had done a little research. I knew he hadn't heard too much since Lance and I didn't really fuck with too many. He knew enough though. Enough that eliminated all doubt I initially had about him.

Any motherfucker could say they knew me and Lance from

back in the day. They'd say we were petty dealers. Poor little niggas, known for throwing hands and bussin' our guns. Niggas that eventually saved some money and made it out the hood. Started a business and got out the way. That's what most people knew. The average folks, anyway. However, any nigga that could speak on our real business had my attention.

Carlos knew that we had most of the city on smash. He knew that we supplied a few niggas that in turn distributed our drugs through the streets of Atlanta. It was no secret that there was a drought. With Lance's connect at a standstill, the streets were suffering. Carlos was supposed to alleviate that suffering. He claimed to have the capability to supply the two of us on a larger scale. I, of course, would inform him that I was a one-man show. Lance believed in loyalty. Me, not so much.

I knew there was no way that Lance would go behind Luis' back and cop from anyone else. I, on the other hand, operated a little differently. I decided to take my chances. And boy, what a bad fuckin' idea that was.

Shaking thoughts of my recent misfortune, I continued gazing out my window while sipping my drink. I shook my glass around out of habit, before bringing it to my lips and taking a smooth sip of the bitter liquid. I was now trying to figure out what was next.

I wasn't worried about Boobie clapping back since I wasn't easily accessible. While they were in the trenches, a nigga like me was behind fences. No one knew where I lived and even if they did, they'd have to be bold to try something where I laid my head. I resided amongst the rich folk of Atlanta. I mean, literally. On some hi-rise, gated community, Bentleys, butlers, and French poodles type shit. I was one of only a couple black motherfuckers in the building. It was actually Lance's idea to get the spot. He always preached discretion, security, and invisibility. I'd never cared for his reasoning until moments when they mattered, like now.

I would gladly admit that Lance was smart, but he was also

one of the most annoying motherfuckers I knew. I mean, literally. Always walking around preaching shit that nobody wanted to hear. I understood that he'd changed. That was cool. But I couldn't stand when a nigga tried to push that shit off on the next man. I enjoyed a fast-paced lifestyle. Appreciated the fruits of my labor. I just wanted to have fun and enjoy life. Not hoard millions and walk around in some Fruit of the Loom drawers and old ass Dickie pants like his ass. He was cheap, while I wanted to indulge. So I could forget about all the pain that I, too, had endured as a little nigga on the street. He wasn't the only nigga with demons. I had them too. We just dealt with them differently. He wanted to *be* better, while I wanted to *feel* better. I'd *done* a lot of things that haunted me. *Went through* a lot of things that haunted me. One in particular, and the most significant, was Lance's fault.

My brother prided himself on being fair and talking things out. That was cool when we were dealing with fair people. However, most street dudes didn't fall in that category. For that reason, it oftentimes took something drastic to happen in order for him to act. By then, the damage was usually done. Sometimes the damage was so great that it was irreparable.

Lance swore that he was smarter than everybody, and he wasn't. He swore that I didn't know shit and that I was a hot head that never thought things through. I disagreed. I thought things through my way and when his back was turned, I'd also do them my way. We'd come to blows a few times about my methods. And even though he'd assisted me in making a lot of money, there were times when I felt like he was stopping my growth. Stopping me from acquiring the authority that I could obtain if he'd get the fuck out my way.

I'd contemplated smoking his ass on several occasions. But since we shared the same big-mouth mammy, that unfortunately wasn't an option. So, I continued to play the way he wanted to play. I didn't mind talking shit out either. It really depended on who it was and what it was about. I just didn't have time to play with niggas. Especially niggas like Boobie. He had a big, strong, solid team. Disrespect from him meant eventual disrespect from his team. I couldn't ever let that come close to happening. My way was simple. A nigga either got on board or he got his shit pushed back. Expeditiously. I was confident that I'd made that very clear earlier.

Weed, liquor, pills, and cocaine kept me numb to all the shit that I'd endured. Growing up, Lance and I had fought many battles for our mama. Checked niggas on situations that she was clearly in the wrong for. For example, she'd steal a nigga's pack, he'd smack her around, and then she'd go grab us, as if she'd been unjustly violated. There were plenty of times I wanted to turn my back on her raggedy ass, but Lance would always tell me that we would never do that. I never understood why he went so hard for a bitch that wasn't doing the same for us. I didn't give a fuck about that mother title. She never seemed to give a fuck about it. Every day she'd choose the streets over us. Sold the food stamps. Wouldn't work. Wouldn't pay the rent. You name it and she did it. We fed ourselves. Clothed ourselves. Hustled from damn near sundown to sunup to make sure our subsidized rent was paid, and we had some food in the fridge. Took care of Lindsey like we took care of ourselves. Little niggas holding shit down. I was tired of doing what Lance felt was the right thing. Doing the right thing had cost me in more ways than one. It had stripped me of my dignity and had made me the demon that I now was. I was brutal and unfair to niggas that violated. I did niggas how they would do me. How they had *done* me.

A violation could be a number of things. For Boobie, it was the verbal disrespect. I'd never been shown any mercy growing up. For that reason, I was merciless.

Feeling myself slip into a darkness that I wanted no parts of, I shook thoughts of my past traumas out of my mind. My thoughts shifted back to something more positive. Someone who had managed to bring temporary light into my dark world. Casey.

I dug my phone out of my pocket and tried to call her back. Like it had done the last half-dozen times I'd called, it went straight to voicemail. I blew out a frustrated breath before tossing back the remaining liquor in my glass. I'd been calling and texting her all day and she hadn't replied once. The fact that her voicemail was full, angered me further. I couldn't even curse her ass out the way I wanted to. I really just wanted to hear her voice. It was like my medicine. Soothing me and bringing me peace. Every street nigga needed a little peace.

Casey had been acting funny ever since I beat the fuck out of her little bitch-ass boyfriend, Blaze. I wasn't sure what she'd expected me to do after the nigga ran up in her spot with his homeboys being disrespectful. He'd shown off, so I'd shown out. Like I said before, I didn't play the disrespectful shit. He got out of line, and I'd tried to break that nigga's face with my Glock. Casey's ass had been acting stank since then. I knew she was in a relationship with the nigga, but she always behaved like she had everything under control. That day, I learned that she didn't. It was all a front. She really had a nigga all up in an entanglement. I just hated how she tried to flip that shit on me like I'd over-reacted.

You can't behave like that in real life. What if you'd killed him? You gotta learn to control your temper. That was all the bullshit she'd spat after the shit went down. I wasn't trying to hear none of that shit. I was who I was, and Blaze was who he was. He wasn't no gangster, so I didn't know why he'd tried to step like he was. It was a learning experience for his ass. Definitely worth the little bullshit charges the cops drew up on a nigga. I wasn't worried about that, though, since I had the best lawyer in the city.

Despite being cased up and about to go to war with some clowns, my mind was clouded with thoughts of a female. Trying to figure out what was up with her. The main issue that I was still trying to address was the fact that she was defending a nigga that she claimed she no longer wanted to be with. A nigga that she was supposedly leaving soon. I was trying to figure out why she hadn't changed the locks on the condo that she claimed belonged to her. Or why he seemed to think that they were still a couple when she was carrying my unborn child. Apparently, she hadn't told him about that yet. Couldn't have. Lately, nothing was adding up with Casey. I'd seen her a few times since I'd beat on Blaze, so this was unlike her. I'd been off house arrest two full days, and she was missing in action.

I pulled my phone back out and pressed the icon to open my Instagram app. I keyed her name in the search bar, but nothing came up. I clenched my teeth and nodded at the realization that I'd been blocked. *You got that*, I thought.

I couldn't lie, the fact that I was blocked was a blow to my ego. I didn't understand why she would block a nigga when I'd just kicked it with her a few days back. She was fine, and now all of a sudden, this. There I was, running around thinking I was that nigga, and I was letting a slick bitch finesse me. Casey had said 'I love you' so much that I'd lost count. I believed that shit. However, over the last couple days, I'd finally realized that she'd lied. The bitch was playing me. Lance had said it so many times, but I refused to believe it. Casey cared about money and who could do the most for her. She probably never had any intention of leaving dude like she said she would. I hated that my brother was right.

Still on Instagram, I typed in Blaze's name. Unlike Casey, he popped right up. Ignoring the fan pages made in his honor, I clicked on his profile. As soon as I began scrolling up and down his page, I felt my blood begin to run hot. Recent pictures of him and Casey made up the first couple rows. I read the captions. One said, 'all mine.' Another said, 'she chose a real one.' I knew for a fact that the pictures were recent since she'd just gotten her hair cut in layers and dyed honey blonde. It was the same style that she was rocking in the photos. I stared down at her image. In one, her curvy caramel figure sported a black and white Balmain bathing suit. In another, she wore a burgundy-colored, wrap-around dress that clung to her body like silk.

I angrily closed out of the app and shoved my phone back into my pocket. Her little scandalous ass was definitely about to be an exception to my "no hoe" rule. I didn't play about disrespect, but I also didn't play about broads fuckin' with my feelings. I could respect a wolf dressed as a wolf, but I couldn't stand a wolf dressed as a sheep. I was definitely going to make it a priority to figure out exactly which one she was.

❦ 3 ❦

CASEY

My eyes widened to the size of quarters, while my heart hammered in my chest at the sight of the dark figure in front of me. I sprang up in the pitch-dark of my bedroom. My eyes quickly adjusted to the darkness, eventually registering the image in front of me.

"What the fuck is wrong with you?" I asked angrily.

I held my hand against my upper body and let out a sigh of relief. It was just Blaze. His creepy ass was standing at the foot of my bed with a phone in his hand. My phone. The light from the screen beamed into his focused face, while he stared down and swiped like his life depended on it. Whatever he was viewing, had all of his attention.

"You find what you were looking for, weirdo?" I asked him groggily, before swinging my feet over the side and climbing out of the bed.

I glanced at the alarm clock beside me and read the bright red numbers. It was well after two in the morning. Unbelievable. I was about sick of him. I couldn't even sleep peacefully, without him creeping into my condo like a damn cat burglar. Yeah, his name was listed somewhere after my own on the lease. However, that was irrelevant since the place was mine and not his. Hearing me address him, Blaze turned his gaze away from the screen and focused on me.

"It's not about what I'm looking for. It's what you leave behind."

I stared at him blankly for a few seconds and headed towards the door so I could walk out. Blaze tossed my phone on the bed, walked to the light switch, and pushed it up. Bright light seeped into my eyes, causing me to squint. I kept walking and didn't even bother responding to the silly shit that he'd just said.

I proceeded to the bathroom so I could empty my bladder. Apparently, the avocado-size baby that I was carrying liked to sit on it non-stop. Just as I was squatting down to relieve myself, there he was. Just as annoying as he wanted to be. I didn't even have my panties to my ankles, or my ass fully situated on the toilet seat before Blaze was barging in the bathroom behind me.

"Can I piss in peace?" I frowned when he didn't respond. "Get the fuck out," I demanded while my frown deepened.

My patience was waning. I was already irritated from being awakened from my sleep. To be questioned on top of that was enough to make me very disrespectful.

"Why is that bitch-ass nigga still calling you?" he asked, not caring that he was invading my privacy.

I sighed. I knew the bitch-ass nigga he was referring to was none other than Lawrence.

"Blaze, I don't have any control over what he does."

"Why haven't you blocked him like I asked?"

"I did block him," I said evenly, shifting my eyes to avoid his gaze.

I fell silent. I had blocked Lawrence on social media, but I hadn't actually blocked his number from my phone because frankly, I didn't want to. The only reason I'd blocked him on my social media accounts was because Blaze had access to all of them. If Lawrence reached out to me there, which he would if he wasn't blocked, Blaze would surely see it, since his corny ass checked my messages and read through my comments religiously. Since he and I were "supposedly" taking time apart and weren't around each other that much, I figured I could get away with not blocking him on my phone. I instead just set my phone to do-not-disturb whenever Blaze was close by.

I should had known better though. Instead of giving one another space as agreed, Blaze wanted to keep doing that poppin' up shit, which annoyed me. Like a typical rich, high-profile man, he wanted to do what he wanted to do and fuck whoever when he got good and ready, while I sat in the house pretending to be the only one or crying my eyes out because I knew I wasn't the only one. He had the wrong bitch for that. I was a firm believer in, you seek, and you shall find. That first unannounced visit to my home got him beat the fuck up and chased around by Lawrence, while this second pop-up had him sitting there with his lip dropped, looking stupid.

"Then why are his calls still coming through?" Blaze continued to probe. "Why do you even still entertain this nigga? Are you still fuckin' him, Casey?"

I rolled my eyes and stared straight ahead before I began to piss loudly into the toilet. I no longer even cared that he was still standing there. Blaze was a rich clown that I tolerated solely for the money. Don't get me wrong, he was fine. Standing six-foot-five, with a toned, sun-kissed body, he was only a few notches short of perfection. He rocked a tapered cut with spinning waves and wore a dark beard that neatly framed his handsome face. He looked good, smelled good, and he was quickly becoming a fashion icon because of the expensive, designer threads that adorned his body, courtesy of his stylist. He was a damn good baller and had a serious future ahead of him. Despite all those wonderful qualities, the bad ones stuck out to me. He couldn't fuck, he couldn't fight, *and* he lacked substance.

I was pretty and all, but I was also a hood bitch, straight out the slums of Baltimore, so the last couple things mattered more than all the other shit. Shit that should have been most impor-tant, but it wasn't. A female like me needed to be stimulated to be fulfilled. Blaze was hardly fulfilling. It was disappointing since I'd dedicated most of my teenage years and all of my adult life to snag a man like Blaze.

Needless to say, I grew up fast and quickly learned that with my looks, I didn't have to rely so much on education. It wasn't like I was gonna get much of one anyway up out of Baltimore City. Their school district was and still is the pits. Instead of focusing on the shitty education accessible to me, I focused on perfecting my charm to relax in the beds of hustlers and eventually high-caliber ballers. It wasn't hard to get what I wanted since the majority of them were superficial. They simply wanted what other men desired but couldn't have.

Average height, slender but still curvy, I was what most would consider effortlessly beautiful. With my thick, coiled tresses cascading down my back, infectious smile, and angelic features, I was definitely noticeable. I wasn't the typical pretty face on the arm of a hustler. I didn't look like everyone else. I didn't want to. While they wore perms, weaves, and blow-outs, I let my dense, untamed curls blow freely in the wind like the Disney star, Zendaya. I was also charismatic, observant, and street smart. I was self-taught and well versed in the game of seduction. I understood the power of sex appeal and desire.

As a teen, I used who I needed with grace and charm, before discarding them the first chance they slipped up. I would become 'the one that got away,' instead of 'the bitch that used me.' As soon as I turned eighteen, I moved to the black millionaire mecca: Atlanta. I focused on maintaining a low profile and wholesome reputation, all while keeping my eye on the prize. It wouldn't take me long to accomplish what I'd arrived for. I secured the bag early when I ran into Blaze at a draft party. Fresh out of college and a soon-to-be rising star, I was able to sink my fangs into him without him even noticing. Fast forward to the present, and I now had everything I wanted. The car. The crib. The lifestyle. The money. I just didn't have the man that my soul craved.

I met Lawrence about a year later at another high-end party. He was thick, chocolate, and fine as fuck with his wild dreads standing wild on his head. He pursued me right off the bat, and even though I was interested, I was initially hesitant. He was persistent though. He wouldn't take no for an answer. He kept himself visible by constantly commenting under my pictures and continuously hopping in my DM. I ultimately caved in and the two of us met up. One thing led to another, and his thick, fine ass was right at the tippy top of my wish list.

Lawrence was handsome, strong, masculine, and most of all, respected. He was the perfect man for a ghetto broad like me. Unfortunately, he was a drug dealer, and any smart chick that had got it out the mud like I had, knew that there was no future with a drug dealer. Especially not one that actually enjoyed dealing. It would have been different if he expressed a desire to quit, but he never did. And I didn't even bother encouraging him to change his life since he'd made it clear that he was born and bred for a life of crime. I wasn't that simple chick that thought she could change a nigga. I simply accepted people for who they were.

As hardened as he was, Lawrence still expressed his feelings to me all the time. He said he loved me, and to be honest, I believed him. I'd actually grown to love him too. I think. He not only satisfied me sexually, but he also satisfied me mentally. He understood me and gave me something my soul needed. But I wasn't ready to give up security over no love. I had too much at stake. Back home in Baltimore, I had an ailing mother and a teenage brother that I provided for and had been providing for a few years now. I wasn't out there dealing with niggas for nothing. Since becoming serious with Blaze, I'd been able to move them to the county and my brother was able to attend a private school that had him on track to actually attend college. Something rare for a young man where we were from. They depended on me, and I couldn't let them down. There was no way.

I had to figure something out though. And soon. Blaze was

hounding me, and I was damn near four months pregnant and doing my best to hide that shit. It wasn't Blaze's baby. It was Lawrence's. My plans were to get rid of it and keep doing me; however, Lawrence's nosy ass noticed everything. Especially since up until recently I spent a lot of time with him because Blaze traveled a lot.

My eating habits. My sleeping habits. All that had changed. And Lawrence had taken notice. He'd asked me a few times was I pregnant. As much as we were fucking with no protection, he knew it was certainly a possibility. Of course, I would deny it whenever the question was asked. One day I was sitting on the toilet relieving myself, when he barged in and shoved a pregnancy stick right up under me. It was tasteless as hell, but Lawrence was the kind of guy that did what he wanted. If he wanted answers, he got them. The two pink lines that appeared shortly after the piss dried up, confirmed everything.

I begged him to be silent about the pregnancy, all the while promising to tell Blaze on my own time. He reluctantly agreed. Lawrence knew that I had a situation, but he also thought that I was eventually going to leave Blaze for him. Just like a nigga that wanted to have his cake and eat it too, I'd convinced him that I would. Now that Blaze had found out about Lawrence, things were getting messier by the day.

Blaze was threatening to cut me off and was being trivial by making ridiculous requests *and* doing silly shit like popping up unannounced and practically controlling my social media accounts. He was also insisting that we spend more time together. I knew that was only to be spiteful and petty. He was posting me all over his social media account with bullshit captions, just to make it clear to Lawrence that he and I were still very much a couple, and he was still dicking me down. Blaze just wanted to desperately prove that he was the bigger, better man. Unwilling to throw away my meal ticket, I allowed him.

Blaze standing in my face demanding answers to questions that he already knew was the least of my worries. I had to figure out how I was going to explain things to Lawrence when I finally faced him. I'd been ignoring him because of the way I had to play my cards, but I knew that he would eventually surface now that he was off house arrest and able to move around freely.

I knew Lawrence's background of trauma, and I hated that I was hurting him. He'd been hurt enough. Experienced hurt that some of the closest people in his life didn't even know about. Even if I did really love him like I thought I did, our lives weren't like the movies. We couldn't just ride off into the sunset because we loved one another. I wasn't about to have a drug dealer's baby. I had people I loved depending on me, and he simply wasn't stable. And he wasn't just a drug dealer; he was also a hot head that stayed immersed in drama. Embroiled in street beefs. As much as I loved him, I knew there was no future there. Despite that, my heart and body craved him something fierce.

Finally done relieving myself, I looked over to Blaze, who was still standing there waiting for a reply.

"No, I'm not still fucking him, Blaze," I finally answered, softening up my tone and expression. It was a manipulation tactic that I often used. I mustered up my sincerest looking expression and eyed him. "That was a mistake. A one-time thing, and now he and I are over. You have nothing to worry about. Now could you get out so I can wipe my ass and wash my hands?"

Blaze paused for a moment, staring into my eyes like that was going to reveal if I was lying or not.

"Yeah. But you better be telling the truth. Because if I find out anything different, it's really over this time," he threatened before walking out.

I sighed. I'd definitely dug my own hole. It was crazy how a chick like me could get caught up the way that I had. But that's what good dick and/or love did. It made a person dumb. I had to figure out how I was going to terminate the rapidly growing baby in my belly without anyone else finding out. There was no way that I was getting an abortion in Atlanta, and the way Blaze watched my every move, it was difficult to fly out and have it done somewhere else or even back home in Baltimore.

It also didn't help that since Blaze was now posting me like crazy on his social media accounts, motherfuckers were starting to recognize my face. He had over three million followers and my own following was growing rapidly by the day. It would be just my luck that somebody took a picture of me going into an abortion clinic. I'd not only have to deal with Blaze finding out that I was pregnant and getting rid of it. I'd also have to deal with Lawrence finding out that I had gotten rid of his baby just to keep it a secret from Blaze. My head hurt just thinking of the love triangle that I'd fallen in. I had to figure something out soon. Before it was too late.

✺ 4 ✺

ALIZE

I t was only a little after nine in the morning, and I hadn't even walked up the steps to the courthouse, yet my day had already started off fucked up. Before the alarm clock could sound off for us to get out of bed, Lance got a call that Luxe had been shot up. His business, out of all places.

Since I had to meet with the lawyer before court, I didn't have time to race over there with him, meet the police, and survey the damage. Of course, Lance would fill me in. To put it mildly, the place had been riddled with bullets and nearly every rental vehicle on the showroom floor had been destroyed. Hundreds of thousands in damages. If not more. A Rolls Royce, Bugatti, Porsche, and countless other luxury vehicles intentionally destroyed by bullets. The building was severely damaged. Glass was everywhere, and to make matters worse, the front of his building had been spray painted with the bone-chilling words: *It's war.* Considering the fact that there had been a shootout just a few hours earlier, it was only natural for the police to assume that the two incidents were related. *How* and *why* were now the big questions for them. Lance had no doubt that it was an act of retaliation, because of the spray-painted message. Which, by the way, was just plain stupid. That basically told twelve that either something took place before, or something would take place after, since war itself was something usually ongoing once it was declared. Just pure senselessness.

My nerves were getting the best of me, and my stomach swarmed with butterflies as I walked into the courthouse. My gut had been unsettled all morning, which I took as a sign that things weren't going to go as hoped. Much to my dismay, my gut had been correct.

"Unfortunately, at this time, the two children in question, Sage and Violet Henson, will remain in the custody of the state. I will consider releasing them into the mother's custody once she's able to verify a safe environment. That includes the home and outside of the home. Also taking into consideration the new information given, I need to see that she has adequate daycare set up, as well as a stable job."

I was now standing at the defense's table facing the judge with my lawyer beside me.

"But I have a job!" I shouted out to the judge in response to his last statement.

"Counselor, control your client!" the judge barked back, shooting daggers in my direction while adjusting his robe to remind me that he was the one in charge.

"This shit isn't fair. I've done everything they asked," I mumbled a little more quietly, but the judge still heard it because his scowl hardened some.

George quickly lifted his finger up to shush me.

"I'll go over everything with you to ensure that you understand everything they're requiring. You aren't to speak until spoken to directly."

I exhaled heatedly through clenched teeth. It was the audacity for me. A bunch of white, oily head motherfuckers telling me how to care for my children *and* telling me when the fuck I could and couldn't talk. None of it sat well with me. Noticing my discontent, the judge glared at me and decided to address me directly.

"Ms. McKoy, let's get something straight. Your anger is clearly misplaced. Let me give you a few words of parenting advice. I strongly suggest that you evaluate the individuals you have around your innocent children. That includes relatives. My job is to uphold the law and I do that very well. I do that by asking questions to ensure I have all the facts. With that being said, your children's father is under investigation and was the target of murder because of his alleged criminal activities. Today, *your* place of employment was riddled with bullets, which leads authorities to believe that it was related. Now, with your place of employment being closed while this matter is being investigated, you lack employment. You also lack direct care because the children wouldn't be allowed with their father, nor would they be allowed at the grandmother's home because it's also the home that he resides in and is also likely to be targeted in the future. You're lucky that I'm not assuming that someone also wants *you* dead as well because of him. And that would be an easy assumption since it was your workplace that was shot up this morning. And to be clear, if bullets happen to fly near you, or somewhere you're affiliated with in the near future, you can kiss your kids goodbye. Now, at this time, there is no record of a daycare on file. You need to arrange care. Whether it's a childcare center or a reliable family member that's not directly related or affiliated with their father. To be frank, your life lacks stability, which creates instability for your children. Now, your primary job is a mother. A job that you seem to be lacking at. Once you fulfill your job as a mother, I will then consider allowing you access to your children. If you take your job seriously, then you'll have your kids back sooner, rather than later. But please don't forget that *your* actions are what caused them to be taken in the first place. They're *your* responsibility. You're in charge of keeping them safe, cared for, and supervised. Until you can show us that you are capable of doing that, then we will do it for you."

I glared at him with hate flowing through me. He'd definitely just read me for filth. He had me furious. But at the same time, I was also hurt. Hurt because everything that he'd said was basically true.

"Is that understood?" he asked me, his thunderous voice sounding through the courtroom.

For a second, I almost wanted to sink down and dissolve into the floor. That's how embarrassed I was. However, at the end of the day, I was just a mother that wanted her kids back. So, I swallowed my pride and answered. Despite the fact that I felt like I was dying inside.

"Yes, Your Honor."

"Good. I'll see you back in four weeks. If all the criteria have been met, then your girls will be able to go home with you."

I wanted to pass the fuck out. Four weeks! My children had to live in someone's foster care for four fucking weeks. I mumbled an insincere thank you, waited for my paperwork with my new court date, and then scurried out with my lawyer. Although I'd managed to maintain my composure and suppress my anger in front of that judge, I knew that was going to fly out the window as soon as I walked out the door of that building. I was ready to turn up.

❄❄❄

I wasn't thinking straight when I left that courthouse. I only remembered storming out of there while George trailed behind me swinging his briefcase and trying to explain what had just happened. I couldn't even register everything he was saying. All I knew was that I wasn't going home with my kids and that I had to go back to court in a month. All I could think about was the fact that Neal was the reason why I'd been set back. My whole life was continuing to crumble because of him! I wanted my babies. My chest ached from sadness while the rest of my body swirled with rage.

Adrenaline was rushing through me the entire time my heels clicked out of the courthouse and through the parking lot.

George was still trying to talk, but I paid him no mind. I, instead, popped my trunk and kicked off the pumps I was in. Tossing them inside, I dug out my gym shoes and jammed my bare feet into them. He was still rambling as I jumped in the Jaguar and roared out of the parking lot so I could head straight to Judy's house. I would get with him later.

Despite a twenty-minute drive, the grief and anger hadn't subsided by the time I got to my destination. I was so disappointed. Although the girls didn't know anything about the court process, it still hurt to know that every day that passed was another day without their mother. I could only imagine how they felt. It just wasn't natural for a child to be away from their mom.

The whole time I drove, I wept. When I finally got to Judy's block, I raced down the street and aggressively pulled up directly in front of her cute little, well-kept home. Since I didn't see Neal's car parked outside, I didn't bother to turn off the car. Still wearing my court clothing, a white blouse and stretchy pencil skirt, I stormed to her front door. I knew she was there. It was too early for her to be at work, and her car was parked in the driveway. I pounded on the front door a few times and then waited impatiently for her to answer. About ten seconds later, I was ready to bring my fist back to the door, but she snatched it open.

"Alize, why are you banging on my door like that?" she questioned with an unusual frown.

My eyes automatically scanned her body from head-to-toe. Even though it was the dead of summer, she was still dressed in a thick house coat and wore a black bonnet on top of her hair. She was a plump, brown-skinned woman with kind eyes and tiny mole-like specks sprinkled on her cheeks.

"Sorry. Do you know where Neal is?"

I cut right to the chase, skipping the pleasantries. I didn't even bother to hide the frustration on my face.

"Why? Is everything okay?" she asked, her brows lowering in concern.

"You know everything is not okay," I snapped impatiently.

Her expression quickly transformed from concern to dissatisfaction. I wasn't trying to be disrespectful but at the point I was at, I no longer cared how I came off. The judge had been correct earlier. My anger was definitely misplaced, but I couldn't help it. In reality, I couldn't blame Judy for anything because the fact of the matter was, she'd only stepped in to help. Although it was the right thing to do, she wasn't obligated. Neal and I were to blame. Despite those facts, I was human, and I was still angry with her. That anger stemmed from the fact that when she'd picked up the kids the day that I'd gotten arrested, she told me that she would assume temporary custody of them. I wanted them somewhere safe and with someone that loved them. Yet, she allowed them to be released in Neal's custody, knowing damn well he wasn't responsible. She wasn't green and she understood that we were dealing with the court system. It just didn't make any sense to me.

"I had court this morning and the judge didn't give me back the kids."

Judy stared at me. Her expression transformed again. This time to compassion.

"Alize."

I quickly cut her off. "I know. There isn't much you can say, and I'm sorry how I came off to you because none of this is your fault. I'm just frustrated. I know you were only trying to help by getting the girls, and I understand that you have a life too and have to work, so they have to be with their dad sometimes. I didn't come here for all of that. I just want to know where Neal is. My job got shot up today and the way things are looking, it was retaliation from Boobie's car getting shot up. I'm from the hood too, Judy, so I understand the streets. But *my job*, out of all places? Just like you, I don't get involved with who Neal has issues with. He don't like so-and-so, cool. He don't like my new man, that's cool too. But to try and retaliate on a man's business that he knows I'm employed through, is foul. Now, usually I would let men handle men's issues, but they brought that shit up in court. It cost me my girls. Now they're saying I need to have stable employment lined up *and* childcare. It's a setback. How long ... I don't know. They're giving me two weeks to find a new job and line up daycare. They're also telling me that the kids can't be around Neal, *or* anyone closely related to him. Including *you.*"

I stared at her just to see the impact that last statement had made on her. Like I expected, she looked hurt. After a moment of silence, she cleared her throat and began speaking.

"Now you know I try to stay out of Neal's business. The less we know, the better. I also try to stay out what y'all got going on between y'all, by keeping my opinion to myself. But you and I both know that a lot of this shit could have been avoided."

Judy hesitated, and I could see that my words prior to her speaking were weighing on her heart. I knew she wanted to say more about everything, but she really wasn't the meddling type.

"When he's not here, he's usually at the girl Melissa's house. *Usually.* You didn't hear that from me."

"Thank you, Judy," I grumbled, before spinning around and heading back to my car.

With each day that passed, I was beginning to have less and less respect for Neal. The nigga was still fuckin' the home-wrecking hoe, Melissa, but worried about who and what I was doing. Luckily, I was never serious about going back to him. If I had been, I would have been in for a rude awakening since he never stopped dealing with her.

"Alize," she called out to me before I could hop in.

"Huh?"

"Neal filled me in on a few things, and my advice to you ... is there is no happy ending in a situation like that. Choose your girls."

My eyes lingered on her for a moment, and then I hopped in

my car without bothering to respond. I would always choose my kids; I just didn't see why I couldn't have the happy ending too.

After shaking off Judy's words, I cranked up the Jaguar and peeled off. I was on my way to Oakland City so I could have a quick little chat with my baby's daddy.

Shortly thereafter, I spun up into the parking lot of Melissa's apartment complex. I parked smack dab in front of her building. My eyes darted angrily around the parking lot. Just like I expected, Neal's Charger was proudly parked a few spots down. Just the sight of it and knowing he was laid up in there kee-kee'ing and cackling made my anger intensify. I wished I'd brought a brick so I could launch that bitch right through his front window.

I hopped out, slammed the door of Lance's Jaguar, and sped to the front door, my chest rising and falling as unfiltered rage began to build back up and course through me. Adrenaline over-whelmed my body and my thoughts raced from all the feelings that I'd been doing my best to suppress. I was frustrated, angry, and fed up with so many things. The fact that I was trying to do right but kept getting kicked to the fuckin' ground had me ready to spaz out and lose it all. What was life worth without my girls? I just wanted my kids! The babies I'd nursed, burped, and pushed out my pussy. I also wanted to be happy without inter-ruption. Free to live and love. That's the least I deserved. What I had, wasn't even close. I didn't understand how some bum bitches had it so easy, while so many solid ones with good inten-tions struggled.

Yeah, I'd fucked up. I could admit that I'd brought most of that shit on myself. But I was trying! I loved my girls, and I was trying so hard. I'd gotten a job, saved money, found a good man, and even got up in a fly ass apartment, only for egos and greed to fuck my shit up! Knowing that my babies were sleeping in a house with some fucking strangers had my heart ready to bust out my chest. I couldn't deal. I hated everyone! I hated Judy for doing what she felt was best for her hoe-ass son and not her grandkids. I hated Boobie because he was a bitch, and I hated Neal because he was also a bitch! A bitch who didn't think. His actions affected Sage and Violet like mine did. Then the nigga had the nerve to be laid up with dick-eating Melissa when his kids were in a foster home! I was fed up! I wanted action!

Now standing directly in front of Melissa's apartment on the first floor, I took my fist and started pounding on the door like I was the police. I was to the point where I wanted all the smoke. I prayed she snatched open the door and wanted to rumble. Since I didn't have my fuckin' babies, I had all the time in the world to box it out with her and any hoe that was ready to step with her.

"Yo, what the fuck is wrong with you?" Neal asked as he snatched the door open clad in a Milano short set with matching slides.

I expected to see Melissa first since I assumed that he would try to hide in the back somewhere, like the hoe-ass nigga he was. Neal's dark eyes locked angrily with mine as he waited for a reply, but I didn't bother to answer. I cocked back and started throwing hands.

Right! Left! Right! Left! I used all the strength in me to try and take his nappy-ass head off his shoulders. His eyes widened in bewilderment as he pushed me back off him. I staggered a few feet, but it wasn't enough to stop me. I kept throwing punches while a few nosy neighbors snickered as they peeked from their doors. A few that had been standing around outside made their way closer to get a front-row seat of the ghetto, domestic scuffle. I definitely was giving them something to watch too.

After taking an embarrassing blow that split his lip, Neal snatched me up and bear hugged me, pinning my arms into my sides tightly. That was cool. I still had my teeth. I sunk them motherfuckers down into his shoulder like Jaws and tried to tear a chunk out his ass. I bit him so hard I damn near ripped a hole out the Milano shirt he was wearing.

"Ahhhh! You retarded ass bitch!" Neal shouted as he abruptly released me.

He whipped his head to the side and examined his shoulder with large eyes.

"Have you lost yo' fuckin' mi—"

He didn't get to finish his statement, because I was back on his ass! This time, though, he no longer cared about the neighbors watching, so he did what a hoe would do. He pushed me back and then rushed towards me so fast, he damn near slid out his slides. Grabbing me by a fistful of hair, he yanked me down to the pavement. Since I was still wearing my court clothes, my bare knees burned as they scraped against the pavement. Despite the pain, I wasn't fazed. If anyone knew Alize McKoy, then they knew I was a real bitch. A real bitch that never stopped fighting.

With fury, I scrambled right up, and just as I'd jumped back up on the soles of my Nikes, Neal stopped me by hopping on top of me and pinning me back down to the ground. I immediately tried to throw some more punches, but he placed his knees over my arms so I couldn't move. This time, though, he kept his upper body away from my reach by using one hand to hold my head down.

"Yo, would you calm the fuck down before I gotta hurt yo' ass out here!" he yelled into my face. "The fuck is wrong with you?"

My chest heaved so hard I couldn't even reply. Adrenaline was roaring through me. That didn't stop the tears though. I had so much rage in me. So much hurt! I wanted to let it out. I wanted to hurt somebody like I was hurting. I wanted to tear some shit up!

As Neal stared down at me with a scowl painting his face, I couldn't believe that he was the same man that I once loved. The same man that I'd given my entire heart to and allowed to fertilize my womb. I now couldn't stand the sight of him. I hated him because he'd put me through so much when he'd already known what I came from. Neal continued to pin me down while I screamed and cried, all while wriggling around to get free.

"Alize, you need to calm down before somebody calls twelve. You trying to get both of us locked the fuck up?" he growled into my face.

"I don't care!" I sobbed. "What fuckin' good are we anyway? Why would you let them shoot up my job, Neal?" I choked out. "My fuckin' job! When you know that every little piece of my life is under scrutiny." A river of tears ran from my eyes while my chest continued to heave heavily.

"Keep your voice down!" he demanded. His eyes cut around to see who was listening. "Y'all better mind ya fuckin' business before I come over there!" he spat threateningly to the nosy folks lingering nearby. They quickly and quietly walked off.

"I don't know who you been talking to, but I don't know shit about that."

The look on his face told me that he was being dishonest.

"You're lying. They knew everything when I went to court this morning. Instead of giving Sage and Violet back, they put them in a fucking foster home! A foster home, Neal!" I sobbed uncontrollably. "They said I can't provide them a safe environment. Because of you!" I screamed out like I was a possessed bitch, startling him.

"They were gonna give them back to me," I whimpered. "What were you thinking?" I sobbed weakly. My energy was waning, so my cries were softer, however, no less painful.

Neal's face softened, and that told me for a fact that he knew. He always did that. His face always showed remorse when he knew he was wrong.

"I didn't have shit to do with it, Alize. And even if I did, that nigga's brother tried to kill ya fuckin' kids and you still wanna fuck him?" he said in disbelief. "At some point, you have to pick a side, Alize," he said before pausing. "You gotta choose."

He paused again. He was still holding me, but he had

adjusted his body some so that the full weight of his body wasn't on me.

"You gotta stop this," he pleaded.

I didn't bother to reply since I didn't want to hear shit he had to say if he wasn't going to tell the truth. Plus, I knew that he was trying to use the fact that I was vulnerable against me. I let my head fall to the side while I stared off and allowed the tears to continue running.

"You gotta end this bullshit you on. You running 'round with the opps. End that shit so we can get our girls back ... together." He paused for a moment and then continued when I failed to respond. "Okay?" Neal asked, staring down at me.

"Get off of me." I sniffled softly.

Neal hesitated a moment, but he eventually climbed from off top of me slowly. Breathing heavy, he kept talking.

"I'm serious, Alize. Shit might get crazy, and you need to be out the way. Everything will work out with the girls. I can help you with whatever you need. The lawyer. The rent on your new place. I just need you to promise to stay away from that nigga."

Neal watched me with pleading eyes as I got off the ground and remained silent. There he was, over a hoe's house and telling me that I needed to stay away from someone. It was laughable.

"I'm serious, Alize," he repeated for the second damn time. "I know you want the girls back, so that means you need to be out the mix of things and somewhere safe."

I glared at him. "I guess you're supposed to ensure that?" I scoffed. "I'll take my fuckin' chances. Don't worry about me *or* the girls. You made it perfectly clear that you don't give a fuck about them *or* their well-being. You should focus on your own safety. Not mine, because trust me, I'm good."

"Lance gon' make sure of that, huh?" He eyed me evilly.

"He makes sure of everything," I shot back, before heading back to the car.

Neal didn't even bother to reply. He simply turned around and headed back into Melissa's place. She hadn't even brought her ass outside to see what was going on with *her* nigga. Just the simple fact that I'd brought the drama to her doorstep should have warranted her appearance. She was so weak, it was pitiful. I was completely done with Neal. I was done asking for any type of help when it pertained to his children. I would no longer beg him to be reasonable. His karma would be the bitch he ended up with, or ... *how* he ended up.

❦ 5 ❦

LANCE

Last night had been a shit show, and the start of today was no different. I had been blowing Lawrence's phone up all morning, and his bitch ass still refused to pick up. I knew he saw my calls and texts. He was definitely avoiding me, but he'd soon have no choice but to face me. Even if I had to scour the streets looking for him, I would. Luckily, there weren't too many places that he could be.

After leaving the hospital in the wee hours of the morning, I took Alize home but later slipped out when she fell asleep. I had a million questions that only one person could answer, and that person was Lawrence. I knew Neal was telling the truth when he revealed that Lawrence had shot Boobie's car up. It sounded like some shit he'd do. I just needed to know why. I also needed to know how the fuck he planned to rectify the situation, if there was even a way to do so. Had it been my life that someone had taken a direct shot at, there was no rectifying. To make matters worse, kids had been thrown up in the mix. Shit was about to get really ugly, and I needed to know what the fuck my brother planned to do about it.

Lawrence had placed me in a tough situation. My back was literally against the wall, and I wasn't sure what I was going to do yet. That alone placed me in a tough spot because I'd been targeted. I knew that Luxe being shot up was retaliation. It was the law of the streets. Simple mathematics. A nigga sent shots; they send shots back. This time, I didn't want any parts. This was one of the times where I preferred to sit down and talk shit out. I didn't even care if Lawrence was right or wrong in whatever the issue was he had with Boobie and his team. I just wanted to hurry up and resolve it because of Alize. Her kids had been in the car when it got hit and as a result, had been injured. All at the hands of my brother. I'd be wrong to tell them to let it go. Why would they? The problem was, this time, I really needed them to.

I needed them to end the beef immediately. I needed them to say that they wouldn't harm my brother. But if I said that, it was also like saying fuck Alize's girls. Fuck the fact that he'd damn near killed them. They didn't deserve that shit. That was an entirely different conversation that I hadn't even had with Alize. I had promised her that I'd look into what was going on, but I hadn't even gotten the facts yet. I hadn't talked to Boobie yet either. But I was definitely going to. Boobie was reasonable and I knew that he, too, was a businessman. He knew like I knew that no one could make any money if we were fighting. That was like a person walking to their favorite grocery store, but they were shooting inside. There was no way that people would keep coming there to shop if their life was in danger. The workers would also stop showing up if their lives were in danger. The business would suffer and eventually shut down.

I had no doubt that Lawrence could hold his own. He was a street nigga that had soldiers on call. However, Boobie had a big team. A team of young niggas that were ready and willing to go to war. Not just because of the attempt on Boobie's life, but also because of the gall and blatant disrespect to the streets as a whole. Not only had Lawrence made the streets hot by selling them a boatload of bullshit, he'd also killed a bunch of their customers and caused them to lose money each day that they sat without drugs. It was like throwing gasoline on an already raging fire. In the streets, you couldn't just do shit and constantly get away with it. They'd already made it clear that they wanted smoke. Every part of my heart wanted to say fuck him, fall back, and hunker down with my girl and her kids until shit blew over. However, I'd also be wrong to cower in a corner while war was waged against my flesh and blood.

Things were bad, and I wasn't sure if I had the ability to fix it. I had so much going on that my head was not only spinning, it was also pounding against my skull. I'd just gotten the call from Alize saying that her court hearing was disastrous. Her girls were still in the custody of the state, and they brought up the fact that Luxe had been shot up. Since that was her workplace, they wouldn't consider it as stable employment. It was like neither of us could win.

Childcare wasn't an issue since I could help her with that; however, she'd made it clear that she no longer wanted help with the job part. I was slowly starting to realize that having an abundance of money wasn't always enough to eliminate every little problem in a person's life. I could literally go deposit fifty grand in Alize's account to prove to the courts that she had the means to take care of her kids, but they would still want to know where the money came from. Who it came from. What it was for.

They wanted Alize to show them proof *and* a solid plan that she could not only take care of her children now, but also in the future. It didn't seem fair because I knew Alize's character. However, it was fair considering everything her girls had been through. They'd been evicted, left unattended, and last but not least, involved in a drive-by shooting that left them injured and likely traumatized.

I was going to do everything in my power to make sure nothing else affected them. I had no doubt that shit was definitely about to go down. I just prayed that Alize didn't push me away.

I shook thoughts of my brother. I had a brand-new tragic incident that I had to deal with. Tye had been murdered.

With my eyes fixed on the road, I raced down the expressway, my Michelin tires gripping the asphalt. I'd just gotten the troubling phone call from a nigga named Eazy, informing me that Tye had been shot coming out of his side-chick's house. All she heard was gunshots and the car peeling off.

I couldn't help but think Lawrence was behind that shit too. First Boobie and now Tye. Two out of the three niggas we dealt with. That shit wasn't just fuckin' ironic. The only thing that made sense to me was Lawrence. Maybe he was angry that I'd orchestrated the ending of their business relationships. Of course, that was no reason for him to go around killing niggas. But then again, I forgot that I was the voice of reason between the two of us. I was the one that thought logically and fairly. Lawrence was the opposite.

My jaw tightened while I continued the drive to the address Eazy had given me. I needed to get up with Lawrence's ass. And soon! Because if he was responsible for Tye's death, in addition to the attack on Boobie, he was waging a war that he would not win. All it took was for those two teams to band together and it would be nothing to take him out. My biggest concern was one couldn't have war without casualties.

Lawrence wasn't thinking about the innocent people that would die as a result of the conflict he'd created. He had no regard for who would be a target in order to take him down. What he failed to realize was that the streets saw us as a unit. It was Lance *and* Lawrence. If they aimed for Lawrence, then they were definitely going to aim for me as well. Even if I wanted no parts, I had been deemed a player. I had to round up my circle.

❧❧

It was barely noon, but the day had been long. Tye was dead and things were growing tense. When I pulled up, he was literally being zipped up and carried away in a thick, black body bag. His family along with a gang of niggas were present. The latter not even attempting to hide the fact that they considered my brother a suspect. Of course, word had gotten around quickly that Lawrence had rode down on Boobie and his cousin Neal. They even knew about the kids being in the car and my business being shot up. All the shit was on the news and the reporters had made sure to tell everyone that police believed it to be an ongoing feud over drugs. I also couldn't help but suspect that the teams were chatting amongst one another. Although Tye, Boobie, and Corey didn't deal with each other directly and operated from different parts of Atlanta, they were all familiar enough with one another to conversate. I didn't clarify or confirm anything, nor did I protest the accusations too hard about Lawrence's involvement. Their loved one had just been slain, and I didn't want to say anything to trigger anyone. Shit was fresh and people were hurt. I wasn't a punk, but I wasn't stupid either. I offered my condolences and assistance before getting the fuck out of there. When I left, I couldn't help but feel like I would definitely need to watch my back moving forward. From *all* angles.

The streets were buzzing. I not only had Boobie calling me, I also had Corey calling me. To kill two birds with one stone, I made plans to meet the two of them at once in a mutual location. I knew for them that trust was definitely an issue.

Now back at Alize's place, I once again felt like public enemy number one. After the hospital and court, her mind was now bogged down with slew of unanswered questions. She wanted to know what role my brother had played in the shoot-out. I honestly didn't know the answers, and that didn't sit well with an agitated Alize.

"That's ya brother. Now all of a sudden you can't get ahold of him?" she questioned, pacing back and forth in her bare living room, while I sat on the floor, back against the wall.

"No. I can't. We haven't been on the best of terms lately."

become. He was damn near forcing me to choose my girl and say fuck him all together. I was trying to keep from doing that. I was trying to choose them both. But I wasn't about to sit up and lie, Alize was getting chose no matter what. Brother or not.

Lawrence was not only ungrateful, but he was also moving dangerously. I didn't have no big ass squad on call. I was a mafuckin' millionaire that passed off big drugs. I wasn't in the trenches no more. I wasn't no little nigga, and I didn't want any parts of the so-called war that had started. I just wanted to take care of my family and be with Alize, so we could work on starting our own family. I also knew that the sooner Alize's custody issues were over, the sooner I could get her out of Atlanta and tucked away somewhere. That way, if shit did eventually get hectic on the streets, it wouldn't affect her or her kids ever again.

"Alize, please," I asked again.

She looked at me but then looked away. I walked up on her slowly and looped my arms around her waist, pulling her into my chest. I felt her head relax into my chest, and then I heard her exhale in defeat. She loved her girls, but I knew that she loved me too. She pulled her head away to face me. With dry tears threatening to stain her face, she finally answered.

"I'll give you a day or two. But please fix this so they aren't taking you. Because as long as they are, I can't be around you. I love you, but I can't risk it. I want my babies back, Lance, and I won't let nothing get in the way of that," she admitted softly.

"I'll take care of it," I assured her.

"And why is that, Lance?"

She stopped pacing and stared at me. I sighed. No matter how much I cared for her, I couldn't fill her in on street shit. In response to her question, I gave her a simple shrug.

"We just weren't seeing eye-to-eye on some important issues."

"Important issues like what?" she asked before going back to pacing.

"When is the furniture supposed to be delivered?" I asked, trying to change the subject. "If I knew they were gonna take this long, you could have been staying at my place."

Alize stopped pacing again and glared at me.

"Fuck the furniture, Lance. And fuck staying at your place. You think I care about being comfortable when my kids are in a foster home? I'm here because I expected to be bringing my kids back. Do you know how fucking disappointed I am? How disappointed they probably are? Sleeping in a strange house and a strange bed?" She bit down on her bottom lip when it began quivering. "You better pick a better time to ask dumb ass questions, because now ain't it!" she snapped.

I was instantly remorseful. It wasn't the time. She had real questions and deserved real answers.

"Yo, I'm sorry. You right." I rose up off the floor and walked over where she was standing with her arms now folded across her body. I reached out to hug her, but she snatched away.

"I don't want a motherfuckin' hug, Lance."

I backed up and sighed. My fear was coming true. All the stress and tension were having an impact on our relationship.

"Babe, look. I'm sorry. I love you and I don't want you to push me away."

I took a step toward her, but she was still guarded. Her arms were still folded tightly against her chest and her face was balled up angrily.

"What choice are you giving me?" she said, her expression

softening. Her eyes fluttered a few times, demonstrating that she was on the brink of tears.

"What's that supposed to mean?"

"It means what it sounds like. I have to do what's best for my girls. If that means walking away from you, then that's what I have to do."

I frowned. That wasn't what I wanted to hear. The thought of losing Alize made me sick.

"Why is walking away from me a solution to your problems?"

"Because the judge told me that if some shit goes down again, anywhere near me, then I won't get my kids back. I can't risk that."

I paused. She had run down the whole day to me, so I knew that the judge and her caseworker had already been informed about the shooting at Luxe.

"Neal and Boobie consider you the opps. They expect you to ride with your brother if he truly is the one behind all this. And even though you won't tell me that, I believe that he was. I've known those two for years, and they're not gon' lie about some shit like that."

"But I would?" I questioned, my eyes narrowing.

I had some choice words for her after her comment. To be honest, I didn't even know why I was getting upset. Maybe because she was basically telling me that she took her bitch-ass baby daddy's word over mine. I wasn't no sucka nigga, though, so I wasn't about to say no sucka shit.

"I'm not saying that. What I am saying is that instead of lying, you won't say anything. And to me, that isn't much better."

Alize took a deep breath, and finally lowered her arms to her sides. Her expression relaxed and eventually softened. However, when she began to speak, her voice shook, as it was heavy with emotion.

"Babe, I know that's your brother. I know you're a protector and protecting him is what comes natural in a situation like this. But I'm also a protector ... and I have to do what's best for my

kids. I love you, and walking away from you would be hell. But I could still live life and go on with my girls. If girls ... then I wouldn't want to go on. Because what would life be without them?"

Visibly emotional, her eyes began to well up and to slip out the corners of her eyes. I knew that the she'd just spoken were from her soul, and that only her more. To hear a woman stand in my face, and she loved her kids more than any man, spoke volu the type of woman that I wanted to raise my own was also the type of woman that I wasn't trying to

"Alize, what exactly are you saying?" I asked. was going to ask for space, but I wasn't going for

"I'm saying that we have to spend some everything blows over. Until all of this is resolv

I swallowed the hard lump that had formed was right, but I couldn't stop the wave of s running through me. I didn't want to lose little time to try and resolve things.

"That's not what I want."

"That's not what I want either, but w have?"

"You can give me a little time to handl my brother and let me talk to Boobie. I from escalating."

I hoped anyway. I hadn't told her about Lawrence's possible involvemen things worse. The less she knew the b

"Please," I begged.

She let out a sigh while giving me a nigga wasn't used to no. I loved heart, and she gave me peace. She passionate mother, she was lovin importantly, she gave her all. I w the more he fucked up, the m

❧ 6 ❧

ALIZE

After that bitch basically threw me on the streets with my kids, most people would call me a damn fool to fuck with my aunt Melva. I couldn't even lie, I was desperate as hell to even be talking to her, let alone, asking her sorry ass for help. Help wasn't even a word that I wanted to use to describe what I needed. I actually refused to even let the word come from my mouth. I asked her something more like, "*You tryin' to make some money?*"

Fuck what people said. The fact was that I needed childcare and I needed it quick. I didn't mind taking my kids to a daycare. The problem was that I had two that needed daycare immediately and I couldn't find an adequate center to take them both. I wasn't worried about the cost because I had a couple dollars saved and, of course, I had Lance. I was solely focused on the quality. And quality was definitely not something that I could afford to slip up on, especially after the judge's words to me earlier that day.

Although the girls had been going to a daycare in Oakland City when they were with Judy and Neal, I couldn't take my chances taking them back there, because it was tied to the two of them. Fuck that. I wasn't taking any chances. Most of the popular daycare centers had zero openings and the little in-home shits, I didn't trust.

I was aware that Aunt Melva wasn't shit, but one thing she was about, was her money. It was clear that she had never fucked with me. However, despite her feelings, she'd never laid a finger on me, and she always made sure that I was clean, clothed, and fed. She wasn't a good person, but I knew she would be a good babysitter for my Sage and Violet. And to be honest, she was really the only sufficient option that I had.

All I needed was for my girls to be watched, fed, and cared for, and I needed her to show up and attest to that in court. Commit to the courts that she would be a responsible caregiver for the two of them. Hell, she was already in the court systems before, since she had been my legal guardian. In my opinion, that made it better. Because according to them, she was already qualified.

Before approaching Aunt Melva with the job, I ran it by Lance to see what he thought. It was sad that I was running it by my nigga and not their daddy, but that was a whole notha story for a whole notha day. After explaining my relationship with Aunt Melva, he agreed that it was a good move. He, however, was adamant about monitoring her closely with video surveillance. If she agreed to it, then it was a go. If she didn't, he said that I should keep it moving. Other than that, he thought her providing care to the girls was a good idea.

Lance didn't hesitate to try and cut me a check. However, I wasn't with all that check shit. I wanted to get the ball rolling, and I didn't have time to wait for a check to clear. When I expressed that, he didn't even bat an eye as he handed me one of his bank cards. I was instructed to take out enough to pay her what I owed her and enough to have security installed in and around her home. In addition, when the time came, I was also going to pay her a ridiculous amount weekly to make sure that babysitting for me was well worth it. I wanted the benefits to outweigh everything. Overweigh her apparent dislike for me and whatever ill feelings she had toward my mother.

"So, when are we starting?" she asked with greed lighting up her tired eyes.

"Well, I have to get the security and everything set up first. That should take place over the next week. I have to tie up a few other things, so it'll be three or four weeks. The agreement and money are all for sure though," I reassured her.

I wasn't about to go into detail about my situation. I had learned that the less folks know of your business, the better.

"Okay, so when are you giving me the thousand from that trip to Vegas?" she asked me.

My jaw immediately tightened. I couldn't help but become slightly irritated. Her mouth and her lackadaisical attitude annoyed the hell out of me. As usual, she didn't seem to have a damn care in the world. Even after treating people the way she did. I studied her. She was laying in her favorite spot on the couch with an old, flower-patterned throw covering her body, while I was sitting on the adjacent love seat.

"I'll give it to you as soon as they start coming. I want to make sure you're still on board because honestly, I feel like the amount you claim I owe you is excessive. Especially because at the time you charged me that, I was down bad and barely had anything. I'm only giving it to you now because my situation has changed and also because I need something in exchange," I admitted. "You'll get it when they start coming."

I wasn't trying to be rude, but I was at the point where I was going to speak my mind and keep it real. She wasn't getting shit if she wasn't trying to do what I needed her to do. And I didn't want to take the chance of paying her early with the possibility of her backing out later down the line.

After my response, Aunt Melva lowered her eyes briefly. "Yeah, well whether you feel it was excessive or not, that was what you agreed to. But that's fine. I can wait," she said smugly, before turning back to the television.

I hated people that acted like her. People that had a rebuttal for everything. It didn't matter if they were dead ass wrong. Let them tell it, they were right. On some random shit, I wanted to ask her what the hell she did that allowed her to lay on her ass all day? I never understood it. She always had so much to say about my mom and everybody in the neighborhood but couldn't tell anyone what she did that afforded her the luxury to lay on her wide, flat ass all day. And yes, it was wide and flat like a damn pancake.

I'd never known Aunt Melva to work. She was the bonnet-wearing, biscuit-making homemaker, minus the man. She cooked, cleaned, watched her stories, and every now and then, watched other people's kids. She had her occasional struggles where she complained about a past-due bill, but I could never recall an eviction notice. I could never recall a time she went without food, water, or utilities. Now that I was an adult and actually thinking about it, I was very curious. If I were on good terms with Melvina, I would have called and asked her. Of course, that wouldn't happen since I still planned to put my hands on her whenever I saw her. Thoughts of my trifling cousin brought me to the fact that it was time to get going.

"Cool," I finally replied to Aunt Melva's slick comment.

Since she wasn't paying me no mind anyway, I stood to my feet and got ready to leave. She was focused on watching television, with her dry, tightly coiled hair standing up on top of her head. I was convinced she never combed it. She just wet that shit in the shower, pushed it to the front of her head, and wrapped a scarf around it. Hence the reason her ass had no man. My guess was that even the niggas her age didn't want a mean, old hussy that didn't comb her damn hair.

"I'll drop back by to let you know when they'll be setting up security, and keep you posted on when the girls will actually start. I'll make sure you get everything then."

"Mmm hmmm," she mumbled.

I rolled my eyes and headed out. I didn't bother to say bye. I never knew what her problem was with me and frankly, I no longer gave a shit. All I knew was that if she wanted to make some money, then she'd make sure she took good care of my kids while I worked. I'd never known her to mistreat anyone else other than me, and that was verbal. Besides, I wasn't Niecy, and I was going to make sure that I reminded her of that fact. Aunt or no aunt, I would beat her ass black and blue about mine. Point-blank, period.

Closing the front door behind me, I stepped on the porch and paused, quietly peering at the new-model Audi that was parked in front of the house. My eyes shifted from the car itself and fell on the familiar figure sitting inside. My blood began to run hot. The Devil was busy as hell that day. This was the second time today that my emotions would take over, forcing me to step out of character. I felt like a dog that was having a bone wagged in my face.

For a minute, I almost thought my eyes were deceiving me. Thought that maybe my mind was playing tricks on me. I blinked twice and realized they weren't.

Sure enough, it was my dear cousin, Melvina. Oblivious to my presence, she opened her car door and began stepping out. However, she stopped. She had one leg out the door and the other inside of the car. My eyes focused on her. She looked a little disheveled. Like she'd recently woken up. Almost a little distraught. She was preoccupied and completely unaware of the fact that there was a threat present. She had no idea that I was about two-point-five seconds from her ass.

For a split second, I thought about letting bygones be bygones. But then I quickly remembered that the days of letting fuck shit slide, were over. I also had a special hatred for people who tried to kick a person when they were down. Melvina had done more than kick me. That bitch had mortal combat, karate-kicked my ass.

I began making my way down the steps, hoping that Melvina would look up and notice me; however, she still had her head down and buried in her phone. Probably arguing with some nigga. I figured the least I could do was alert her of my presence and let her know that I wanted smoke. That was the fair thing to do. Give her a few seconds to defend herself.

"Bitch, you might as well put that phone and purse down," I said calmly, but loud enough to get her attention.

I tossed my keys behind me on the porch and began approaching her car. It was going down whether she wanted it to or not. I wasn't worried about Aunt Melva tripping. I knew that once we got to rumbling that she wasn't going to do shit but break it up. Now that the tables had turned, Aunt Melva wasn't going to take no sides. That was just the way she was. Even growing up, when Melvina and I would have our little childish showdowns, she'd pull us apart, but that was about it. Our beef didn't have shit to do with her. She wasn't about to let shit get in the way of her money no way.

"Alize, ain't nobody got time for that shit today."

Melvina sniffled before waving me off and sitting her phone down on the passenger seat. She could suit herself, because I was on a roll that day and I wasn't trying to hear it. Just like she had time to lock me out that Vegas hotel room and cancel my flight, I had time to lock my fingers into a fist and cancel that ass. Her actions had caused my life to spiral into the pits of Hell, and I had made a vow that she would see me because of it.

"You don't get to decide who has time for what," I said calmly before walking around the front of her car and punching her right in her shit while she was still seated.

I'd given her a heads up, along with the opportunity to get her dumb ass up. She knew me, just like I knew her. I didn't do no bluffing. When I told a bitch to drop her shit, she'd better drop it. The fight was still going down whether a hoe chose to listen or not.

"Bitch!" Melvina screamed after being socked directly in her mouth.

I guess the impact of my fist had shook some sense into her.

I didn't respond, nor did I give her a chance to say anything else, because I quickly slid my fingers deep into them long ass bundles and snatched her ass up out of that Audi.

Judging by the lack of fight she was putting up, along with her blood-shot, deeply hooded eyes, I could tell that she was either high off something or had simply had a rough day. I didn't know if it was weed, pills, or what, and frankly I didn't care. She could have been stressed and crying her eyes out and it wouldn't have made a bit of difference to me. When a motherfucker went around doing dirt, they should always be prepared to step.

I was surprised since I knew for a fact that Melvina could hold it down. It just wasn't in her that day. She was making it too easy for me. Still gripping her by her hair, I brought my arm back and drove my fist all up in that trifling face, over and over, while she thrashed around wildly. I felt the skin on one of my knuckles tear as it scraped against one of her teeth. I didn't care. Her face was my canvas, and my fists were the paint brush.

I knew that I was going to have to eventually control the violent streak that I was on. I had to get that shit under control, because catching assault charges on top of the child neglect charges I already had, definitely wouldn't be a good look. But just like earlier, when I hopped on Neal, rage consumed me. Along with all the emotions that I'd been struggling with since the day that I'd lost my girls. The feelings of betrayal, hopelessness, and despair. It was too much for my body to hold inside when I got around the people that had played a role in hurting me. It just felt too good to release all those emotions. I knew it wasn't all Melvina's fault, but I still felt like she held some blame. She didn't have to do me like she'd done me. She was my family. But then again, sharing a little blood didn't mean shit to some people.

While I focused on beating Melvina to a pulp, I felt myself transform. My jaws were now hard, my face was tight, and my eyes had narrowed into snake-like slits. Melvina's face had also transformed. It was twisted up in pain.

"Bitch, you thought I was gon' let that shit from Vegas slide!" I screamed as I tore her ass up. I was literally dragging her by her hair away from her car and into her mama's yard. I took a few weak little hits to the side of the face as she finally began trying to fight back. It was hardly enough to slow me down. The way I was dogging her, you'd think she was just some random chick off the street.

"Fuck you, bitch! Get the fuck off of me!" I almost wanted to laugh out loud. There she was getting drug and she still was gon' pop her shit.

Melvina let out a blood-curdling scream while I continued delivering hard blows to her like I was on a gym bag. I was trying to temporarily strip that hoe of the only thing she seemed to care about: her looks.

"Make me get off you, hoe!" I hollered into her face, before tightening my grip on her hair and shaking her by the head on some dumb shit. Yeah, I was that type of petty chick. I'd beat yo' ass and then pin you down just to scream in your face and spit on you.

"Alize! What the hell!" I heard Aunt Melva yell out.

I didn't bother to look back. I heard the door slam, and I knew she was headed over. I could hear the patter of her feet as she approached us.

"Break that shit up!" she hollered.

I had stopped hitting Melvina, but I still held her tightly by her hair. Hearing my aunt's voice actually made me squeeze her hair up more into my fingers. I was mad because I wasn't done. I wasn't tired yet and I wasn't satisfied.

"Alize! Turn her loose!" Aunt Melva yelled out again, this time a little more forcefully.

When she finally got close enough, she grabbed my arm to pull me away. She then reached for my hand to begin trying to break the mangled grip I had on her daughter. She wasn't strong enough, but I did her a favor and let her go. Melvina was lucky. I wanted to bring my leg back and kick her in the face, but I didn't want to disrespect Aunt Melva to that extent.

I spun around and walked back to the porch to grab my keys. My chest rose and fell as my body sucked in oxygen. I began heading back to my car. It was parked a few doors down up the street. Of course, Melvina hadn't noticed it because I was no longer pushing my Hyundai. If she had, she probably would have kept it moving.

"What the hell wrong wit' y'all?" Aunt Melva continued to argue as I walked off.

I glanced back and saw Melvina getting up from the ground slowly. Aunt Melva was already heading back into the house. She hadn't even bothered to help Melvina up.

I didn't bother replying to my aunt's comment. I hopped in my car and drove off. Besides, there wasn't anything wrong with me. I was just sick and tired of people playing with me, and I had shown them that. I had shown them that I wasn't weak anymore. I had proved what I had been trying to prove my whole life. But I was done with that. I no longer had shit to prove to anyone. I was evolving. I knew that God tested a person the most when it was their time to evolve. I also knew that in order to evolve, one had to eliminate. I wanted a peaceful life, and whatever had to go, was going.

❧ 7 ❧

MELVINA

I'd literally just had the worst day of my life, and running into Alize's bum ass didn't do shit but make things ten times worse. So much for getting back in her good graces. Clearly, she wasn't having that.

Despite being mad as hell, I knew that ass whooping wasn't nothing but karma. I'd expected it to make its way through at some point, but I'd never expected for that bitch to roll down on me in such a short period. That hoe had literally descended upon me and struck like lightning. I had no energy, a pounding headache, and now I had a busted lip and black eye to add to my already fucked up day. I'd only stopped by my mama's house to drop her off a few dollars that she kept worrying me about. I shouldn't have gone. I had no business being anywhere but in my bed. When I pulled up to her crib, I wasn't in my right frame of mind. I was upset, and rightfully so.

Just a few horrible hours ago, I'd woken up groggy from a Percocet and alcohol-induced slumber, only to find myself getting fucked from behind. Every time I thought about it, I felt as if I were reliving it.

My ass was tooted up in the air, while my face was buried deep into the thick, expensive comforter covering the hotel bed. Once I brought my face up and my eyes cut across the room, I damn near lost it.

I wouldn't have been so alarmed, but the nigga Murda Maine that I'd been fuckin' with for the past month or so, wasn't the one deep inside of me going ham against my walls. Of course, he was the one that I had come to see. That wasn't anything new. Ever since my trip to Vegas with Alize, I'd been seeing him regularly. This time, however, he'd come to Atlanta. I was in his hotel room, but it wasn't his penis that was sliding in and out of my body. The percs had my head spinning, so I was blinking and looking around all crazy. Maine's high-yellow ass was seated on the couch engrossed in some video game with his cousin Billy, as if he didn't have a care in the world.

Meanwhile, the nigga behind me was fucking me like he was my man. Like his dick belonged inside of me. I mean, the nigga was sweating and grunting like no one else was in the room. He even had his palm pressed down against my spine to arch my back. I couldn't make this shit up.

Had I been some little, young, around-the-way broad, I probably would have just gone with the flow; however, Maine knew that a chick like me wasn't into that. I dealt with individual niggas and got high dollar for my pussy. I didn't care about a nigga being able to say, *I fucked her.* But I never wanted anyone to be able to say, *we fucked her,* or *we ran a train on her.* Yeah, I was a sack chaser, but I wasn't no broke smut bucket that got passed around.

My mind was racing and trying to figure out what the fuck type games they were on. My heart was thumping in my chest when I looked back and realized I was getting dug out by Maine's brother, Ruger! I didn't know whether to scream, cry, or pass the hell out. I guess he'd been going at it for a while, because by the time I blinked a few times and realized what was really happening—that I was being unknowingly smutted out—Ruger's moist body was growing stiff after ejaculating inside of me.

Still naked, I snatched myself off his limp and thankfully wrapped pole and then immediately started going off. I cocked back and slapped the fuck out of Ruger before hopping off the bed and running towards Maine.

I'd only wacked his ass a few times, but that, of course, didn't last long, because he quickly slid both hands around my throat and proceeded to choke me until I slid to the floor and was ready to go limp. Luckily, Billy would intervene and pull him off me. Despite being breathless and dizzy, I began screaming and cursing him out.

"Are you niggas fuckin' crazy? I didn't agree to no shit like this!"

"Bitch, you thought a nigga ain't peep how much money you been finessing a nigga out. All that bread I been giving you and all that bread you been taking behind my back. Yo' hoe ass ain't even have the decency to bring another bitch or two for my patnas. I can't stand a bitch that take, take, take and think all she gotta give in return is some weak ass pussy. I figured yo' little thirsty ass could take one for the team," he spat.

There I was, thinking I was finessing his ass by overcharging him and running his pockets while he slept. The whole time, the nigga was plotting on his get back. The sad part was shit like that happened all the time. A rich nigga would send for a chick like me with plans to smut her out amongst his team. I prided myself on peeping those types of plots, but somehow, I'd been fooled. I'd been so focused on being greedy that I never fathomed becoming a victim.

"Get ya shit and get the fuck out!" he screamed.

I guess I wasn't moving fast enough because before I knew it, Maine was hurling my shit toward me and pushing me out the door. Barefoot and half-naked, I stood at the door of the hotel room, crying and getting dressed. I had never been so fuckin' humiliated in my life.

Now back at home, all I could do was reflect and figure out how I planned to make Maine's ass pay. And I meant literally. It was simple. Maine wasn't rich, but he was close. He was booking shows left and right all over the country, so the paper was definitely piling up. I was certain that he wouldn't want a rape case derailing his career.

I grabbed a few painkillers out the bathroom's medicine cabinet, cupped my hand in the sink, and threw them back. I didn't bother to shower. I was on my way to the closest emergency room to get a rape kit done. I didn't plan to file charges. Not if I didn't have to. I knew that more than likely, I wouldn't need to. The kit was really the only thing I needed. Murda Maine had fucked with the wrong bitch.

8

LINDSEY

"I do everything that y'all ask of me! I just graduated at the top of my class! The whole entire time, helping you build your business. I'm not out here running the streets and I don't cause Mommy any trouble. Now you're telling me that I have to sit in the house and wither away because of some bull-shit you and Lawrence got going on!"

I argued at Lance as I stood in the center of the living room, directly in front of the television that he had called himself watching to ignore me. If I didn't get some answers soon, I was about to smack that motherfucker into the floor.

"First of all, watch your fuckin' mouth!" my mother cut in, before springing up to her bare feet from her spot beside him on the couch. "Keep it up and you'll be eating that motherfucking floor!" she said with a huff before slowly easing back down to her seat with her narrowed eyes fixed on me.

I sucked my teeth and tightened my lips into a ball in response. I wasn't really worried about her hitting me. She was usually all bark and no bite anyway. And at that point, I no longer even cared whether she did or she didn't. I'd rather be beat anyway than sit in that boring ass house all summer long. I was eighteen years old. I wanted to live. Not die of boredom in a dry ass town like Marietta, surrounded by nothing but a bunch of wrinkly, old ass white people. It was typical of Lance to move us to a dirt fucking road, while he sailed through Atlanta.

"I'm sorry, Mommy, but somebody has to tell me something!" I whined like the big, spoiled ass teenager I was.

I was used to getting my way. I did everything that I was supposed to do, just so me not getting my way rarely occurred.

"Nobody needs to tell you anything else. You were already told enough," Lance said calmly. He stopped looking around me and finally met my gaze.

After studying his face, I realized that he wasn't budging. He looked too serious and he was far too calm. I stomped to the loveseat across from the couch they were on and plopped down. I knew I was being a brat, but I truly didn't give a damn. The shit he was saying wasn't fair! Despite pouting and not wanting Lance to say shit else to me, he began moving his lips.

"Since you want somebody to tell you something, here goes. For the second time, Luxe was shot up because Lawrence got involved in some shit. You can't go anywhere. That's it and that's all."

Lance turned back towards the television and went back to the bullshit show he had been watching before I stood in front of it.

"Whatever, I'm done talking to you," I countered.

I wasn't giving up just yet. I mustered up the saddest face I could and turned to my mom.

"Mommy, I've been talking about the Baller Bash for months. It's the biggest party every year in Atlanta. I've waited for years to go. Please just let me go. I wouldn't be alone. Natalie and Kristina would be there too. I have a brand-new wig. No one's gonna even know who I am," I begged.

My mother went to reply, but Lance started talking again.

"The answer is *no*! No! No! No! What the fuck can't you understand about that?" he snapped loudly, his face crinkling to a frown.

I jumped to my feet and took off upstairs, slamming my door after I got in my room. I heard my mother stomp behind me to the steps and scream out, "Slam another motherfucking door!"

I threw up my middle finger in response and fell back on my California King-sized bed. Yeah, I had a bomb ass life. I had money, drove in fancy cars, and I rocked nothing but designer. Designer clothes, shoes, and shades. I wore thousand-dollar wigs and barely cleaned my room because I had a maid come in twice a week. Despite all the perks, it was bullshit like this that made me want to be a regular little, poor bitch. Lance's black, crispy ass controlled everything. And yeah, I was black too, but he was blacker, so whatever. My brother's word was law in my family, and it annoyed me. Don't get me wrong, I loved him because he was usually good to me. Usually. He had high standards for me, and I always met them. I helped him with his business, and I was directly responsible for his social media presence. I never just took. I found ways to contribute. I felt used. I'd helped him all those years, did well in school, and all I wanted was what I was promised. The ability to enjoy life a little. Go out and do what young females did. Travel and live a little. Like I said, the luxuries were good, but at times, the restrictions and loss of control didn't seem worth it.

I knew my brothers were killers and kingpins. It had never been spoken in the house, but I knew. Lawrence's black, scary, Side Show Bob looking ass, definitely looked like a killer for sure, and Lance had way too much money to be anything other than a drug dealer. And he was too respected in the streets to not have killed a few folks. According to my mama, people would try Lawrence before they tried Lance, so, I knew he was the truth for sure. I didn't hang out in the hood, so I could only go off what she said and what I saw when I did have the rare pleasure of seeing either of them interact with someone they knew from way back. Also, the way folks fell under Luxe's comments showing admiration and respect for my brother informed me that he was definitely respected. It didn't take a rocket scientist to figure out how they operated.

Yeah, yeah, yeah, Lance had a business and all that, but he didn't acquire it by saving up at a regular job. He didn't have a degree, nor did he have a high school diploma. And Lawrence didn't have shit but money, so he had to be slinging drugs. I was far from stupid. If they wanted me to be, then they shouldn't have put me in an expensive ass private school and given me the best education money could buy.

After laying in my bed and pouting for a few, I decided to get up and take a shower. Lance would be leaving soon to head home to Alize, and my mom would be going to bed at her usual nine o'clock. I didn't care what they said, I wasn't missing the Baller Bash. Once I finished that shower, I was going to lay down for a while and pretend to go to sleep. As soon as my mama drifted off, I was gone. Wasn't nobody about to stop me from living my best life.

❄ 9 ❄

NEAL

Tucked in the corner of Boobie's office, I sat slouched down in his tattered, leather office chair not giving one fuck about what his ass was talking about. He had called a little bullshit, emergency meeting about the shooting that took place earlier, which to me was absolutely pointless. It was what it was. The biggest issue he had was the fact that he didn't know it was going down until after the fact.

"I run shit!" he argued in the center of the room, doing a full turn so he could stare everyone down. "Nobody should be calling no plays like that except me!"

He slapped his hand against his chest all dramatically, causing me to chuckle loudly at the theatrics.

He spun around and glared at me. "Nigga, you got something to say?" he asked sharply.

"Yeah, I actually do." I matched his gaze. "Is it okay to speak? I mean, since you run shit and all."

Boobie's eyes narrowed but he urged me to continue.

"Say what you gotta say."

"Okay. Well, what I'm trying to figure out is, why you worried about us retaliating on a nigga that don't give a single fuck about any of us? He's made that clear on multiple occasions.

He went behind his brother's back and sold us some bullshit. Said fuck us after the fact. Then the nigga gets mad over who knows and shoots your car up with a fuckin' Draco."

I paused and peered at him for emphasis. I needed his simple ass to help me make it make sense.

"And you mad because niggas sent shots back?" I asked in disbelief. "The nigga almost killed my kids. *My kids*, Boobie. And you mad because we sent shots back to let niggas know that we not playing? Dude think you soft," I told him. "And if he thinks you soft then he also thinks your whole fuckin' team is soft."

My eyes cut around the room to address the dozen or so men that were standing inside.

"Y'all soft?" I asked.

Together, they all mumbled some form of no.

"I don't see what the problem is." I shrugged.

"The problem is you don't run shit. You take orders from me," Boobie angrily reminded me, his eyes flickering with fury.

I matched his icy gaze while my face hardened. I was tired of motherfuckers saying that. Until Lance called me a worker that day in front of Alize, Boobie had never been hollering that shit.

"Aren't you the same nigga that told me I was second in command?" I eyed him for confirmation, since he knew he said that shit religiously. "You got these niggas running back and forth to me all day, but now when I make a decision, it's a problem."

"Yeah, it is!" Boobie nodded. "Especially when it's *that* type of decision. One that nobody asked yo' ass to make."

Clearly frustrated, Boobie eyed everyone in the room.

"All y'all niggas, get out. I'm gon' holla at my folks real quick, one on one."

Everyone quickly exited the room. Once it was just me and him, he closed the door.

"You got a problem or something?" he asked sharply.

I ain't gon' lie, I definitely had a problem. I also had an attitude, and I was uninterested in what he had to say. My posture and demeanor spoke volumes. My eyes were slits, my face was tight, and I was now seated upright with my fingers locked together holding up my chin.

"Nope," I replied evenly.

That was a lie. I was pissed that Boobie wanted us to go out like some hoes. The nigga Lawrence was able to fire on us and bully us, but we couldn't do shit about it because Boobie didn't want to piss off big bro Lance. The shit was weak! The nigga had taken my bitch and now was controlling the nigga that controlled me. I had a big fucking problem with that.

"I think you do have a problem. And since you have a problem, you're doing your best to create problems for everyone else. So, since that's the case, I need you to fall back and lay low, nigga," Boobie said to me. "You have every right to feel the way you do. You're right. Lawrence definitely violated, but to keep this shit from getting crazy, I want to speak to Lance before we make any rash decisions."

"*Lay low?*" I asked Boobie. I wasn't really paying attention to none of the other shit he was saying.

"Yeah. Lay low. You fuckin' shit up for me. Niggas can't make any money if they have to focus on going at it."

"Niggas can't make no money anyway because we don't have shit!" I reminded him.

"Even if we did, Neal, how the fuck can niggas make money if they shooting day and night and trying to watch their backs?"

Who's fuckin' fault is that, Boobie!" I yelled, jumping up from my seat. "That nigga shot at us! He tried to kill us, nigga! You letting shit like that slide now?"

My face was torn all the way up and all kinds of twisted. I wanted an answer.

"No, I'm not. But I call the shots! You don't!" he said, a little too forcefully for my liking. "You don't get to decide when we ride out on niggas. You understand that?" he argued while wagging his finger in my face like I was some punk ass kid. "That shit you pulled is gonna have every nigga around us with a fuckin' death wish."

"A death wish from who? We got hella niggas that's ready to step, if that's what them niggas Lawrence or Lance want! Watchu scared of that nigga or something?" I accused.

"I ain't scared of shit. But I also ain't no fuckin' dummy! Them niggas got long paper compared to us. They can sit somewhere on a fuckin' hill, make a couple of phone calls, and get us touched! When you going to war with niggas like that, you gotta be strategic or you wind up murked. Our issue is with Lawrence! Not Lance! If you paid attention, then you would know that they're two totally different niggas. Lawrence is a crazy hot head. Yeah, he'll bust his gun, but Lance is a different type of cannon. A lot more strategic. That shit that went down last night, didn't have shit to do with him. He probably didn't even know about it. If I don't have to go at it with Lance, then I won't! You aiming at the wrong target."

"Fuck that pussy, Lance! My gun bust like his do and his body bleed like mine!"

Boobie stared at me, his eyes wide in disbelief. "You slow or something? Lance ain't the fuckin' problem. Lawrence is. But he will be a problem if you aim for him again. Let's keep it real. It seems like you more worried about Lance because he's shoving dick down Alize's throat!"

That comment did it for me. It not only got under my skin; it instantly painted an image in my brain that made my skin crawl. I sprang to my feet, ran up, and shoved Boobie so hard, he soared back into the wall. I jumped back, expecting him to be ready to throw hands. However, he snatched his gun off his waist, cocked it back, and pointed it directly in my face.

"Family or no family, don't ever put yo' motherfuckin' hands on me again."

My jaw tightened and my breaths picked up speed as I stared down the barrel of his gun.

"Get out." He motioned towards the door with a wave of his

gun. "Now, go home and lay low like I asked you to in the beginning."

I didn't bother responding. I tore my gaze away from him and headed towards the door. I couldn't believe my own cousin pulled a gun out on me. We'd had disagreements that escalated to scuffles back in the day. But this was different. This was a different side of Boobie that I'd never seen before. He could say that he was just trying to protect his little empire, but I didn't see it that way. He wasn't trying to do what was best for the team. He was trying to do what was best for himself. If that was the game that he wanted to play, then so be it.

10

MELVINA

It took roughly three hours for the nurses to collect all the information and evidence for the rape kit exam that I'd walked into the hospital and requested earlier that day. After providing them with my medical history, I had gone through the grueling and invasive process of being poked, swabbed, and photographed from head to toe. They'd taken pictures of the light bruising left behind from Ruger smacking my ass, and they took close up photos of my pussy that confirmed the tearing and bruising from having been penetrated against my will.

Yeah, I'd fucked Maine earlier that day as well. Right after I'd popped that perc. That, of course, I was sure would show up in the blood work that they ran on me. I didn't admit to taking any type of drugs willingly because I knew that if I decided to go to the police, then they would use the information given to the nurses as well. I couldn't slip up and be inconsistent. I told them I only suspected of being drugged because I woke up in a mentally altered state. I even blamed my busted lip and black eye on the sexual assault, even though it had come from Alize. For me, it was go big, or go home. And at the end of the day, it was my word against theirs. In the world we lived in, it was guilty until proven innocent, especially when being accused of some shit like rape.

I'd specifically asked for no police. I didn't have any intentions of having them charge Ruger. I just wanted leverage. I just wanted Maine to know that I wasn't playing and had done shit by the book. Just in case he wasn't on board to see things my way. It was about more than just money. It was bigger than that. It was the fact that I was violated and humiliated. Yeah, I wasn't the most wholesome chick in the world, but at the end of the day, Ruger penetrating me should have been a choice that I was allowed to make. I was the only person that could say who was and wasn't allowed into my body. Earlier, I had been stripped of that right. Completely demoralized. I wanted retribution. I wanted to teach him a lesson.

Now that I was home, I was able to relax. I had just scrubbed away all traces of Maine *and* Ruger from my body and was now slathering my body down with lotion while listening to some soft music. Tonight was the Baller Bash, but I wasn't going. Alexis had been calling and texting me all day about it. I'd just recently called her back, informing her that I'd be sitting this one out. Sporting a black and purple eye, I was not only beat physically, I was also beat spiritually.

The whole ordeal with Maine had me feeling some type of way. I wasn't sure what to call it. It was a mixture of anger and resentment. I had been wronged and it wasn't really shit that I could do about it. Nothing significant anyway, that would bring me satisfaction. It was a terrible feeling. Probably the same feeling that Alize had when I did her the way I did her.

I couldn't blame Alize for whooping my ass. I'd absolutely deserved it. It was some fuck shit. But I'd only done it to teach her a lesson. I'd initially claimed that I did it to make her stronger and force her to see things for what they were, but that was bogus. I'd done it out of spite, and I'd done it because I wanted to show her that I had the power. That was the same exact shit that Maine had just done to me. Karma was definitely a bitch.

For the next few minutes, I finished moisturizing my body. When I was done, I grabbed my phone and crawled into bed. I went through my text messages and pulled up the thread for Maine.

It was time to address the situation for what it was. Back in the hospital, I was able to snap a picture of the rape kit box. I'd done that so he knew I was for real. I attached the picture of the kit, along with a picture of my discharge papers, and then pushed send. I then began typing the actual message of what I wanted to say to him. I tapped away until I finally had a message concocted. I looked it over to make sure it was exactly what I wanted to say.

Me: While I was drugged up, your brother violated me while you and your cousin watched. Trust that shit will not go unpunished. This is just the beginning of holding you and your team accountable for your actions. To watch and not act is to condone. Because you did not intervene, you played a role, and for that reason, you are just as guilty as your brother. Despite the nature of the situation, I would like to do this amicably. Have your lawyer contact me so we can sit down and discuss whether I should go to the police or whether we can agree to settle in other ways. If you don't contact me in twenty-four hours, I'll be going to the police and then I'll go to social media and let everyone know that your brother is a rapist and that you and your cousin aided and encouraged it.

I had done my best to make it sound professional. I was satisfied with it. I pushed send and then I tossed my phone down on the nightstand. I got up and turned off my light and then climbed back into bed. It was still early, but after everything that I'd been through, I was taking it down. Before I could position myself comfortably in my bed and drift to sleep, my phone began ringing. I sat up and stared at it for a moment before grabbing it and examining the number. It was private. I took a deep breath and went to swipe it, but I hesitated. I knew it wasn't Maine's lawyer calling back that quickly. I just knew that whoever it was, was contacting me about the message that I had just sent. Going against my better judgement, I answered it and brought the phone to my ear.

"Hello?" I asked nervously.

"Bitch, you want to play? I'll come right the fuck to where you stay at!" Ruger's voice spilled through the receiver, surprising me.

I gripped the phone tightly as his words sank in.

"Ain't nobody force you to do shit," he growled into the phone.

"Don't ever call my fuckin' phone again. Tell Maine to have his lawyer call me or I swear that you, your cousin, and Maine's faces will be on every fucking blog in the country," I countered angrily. "And you also let him know that he can sit down with me and cut me a check, or he can allow his broke, bum ass brother to fumble his bag."

"Bitch, I swear to God, you can fuck around if you want to, but you'll regret it. You not getting shit!"

"Suit yourself," I said calmly before ending the call.

I was no longer tired. I was now wide awake, and I wasn't fucking around. There was a reason that Ruger and Billy were flunkies. Not only were they *not* talented, but they also didn't understand the entertainment industry. If they truly did, then they would have known that one single accusation could catapult him into destruction. I was about to give all three of them a glimpse of what that path looked like.

I opened up my phone and tapped the icon to open Instagram. I began swiping and clicking away, and in less than three minutes, I had a brand-new dummy Instagram account created. I went to the search bar, pulled up The Shade Room, and dove right into their DM. They loved tea and even more, they loved having it early.

I typed up a quick message and pushed send. I knew that

they hired people just to monitor and oversee tips and news-worthy stories. I knew it wouldn't be long before they got back to me. Trust when I say that this wasn't my first rodeo. I'd anonymously exposed a few high-profile men. I'd exposed one celebrity who'd paid me to fuck him multiple times. Luckily, I'd used protection, because one day while he was in the shower, I snooped through his shit and found several pill bottles containing HIV meds that had been prescribed to him. That situation called for more than money. That called for awareness. And that's what I did when I made the whole world aware of the fact that his ass had AIDS but was still slinging dick around to any bad bitch that he could afford. There were others, but that, of course, was the most significant.

A few seconds later, a message appeared from The Shade Room.

Shade Room: We need receipts.

That was simple. I always kept proof, or receipts as everyone liked to call them now. I went to my photos and quickly edited the two pictures I planned to send. I cropped them, blacked out identifying information, attached them, and pushed send. Less than ten minutes later, Maine had made it to The Shade Room. I smiled in satisfaction as I read the short caption.

Up-and-coming Cali rapper Murda Maine could soon be up-and-coming prisoner in a Georgia prison cell. Sources say a young lady is accusing a member of Maine's team of sexual assault. She was apparently drugged before blacking out and waking up to the unidentified man on top of her and penetrating her while two others, including Maine, were in the same room. She's saying that all three played a role in her being drugged and knew that she was being raped because they sat in the room while it happened. The young lady went to the hospital and had a rape kit performed that could soon be handed over to authorities. This story is still developing so at this time, we do not know if charges have already been filed, but we expect them to be. The young lady submitted receipts and she is adamant about getting justice. We'll update everyone as we find out more.

When I was finished reading, I turned my phone off and put it back on the nightstand so I could go to sleep. I knew that what I'd done would either go two ways. Maine and his people were either going to cave in, talk to the lawyer, and cut me a check, or I was going to need to start watching my back ... and my front.

LANCE

"Wasn't nobody expecting to have to deal with no beef shit," Corey solemnly admitted from where he stood across from me.

Corey, Boobie, and I had all met up in Marietta to discuss all the shit that had recently transpired. I'd arranged the spot and I made sure to get there early so I could watch them safely to see if they had niggas trailing them. We were now all standing inside of a small, guarded warehouse where I usually kept all my vehicles for Luxe. It was where I stored those that weren't in the showroom, and it was also where I had new cars delivered so they could sit safely until they were moved.

"I know," I replied to Corey. "And neither was I. I didn't know he was going to be on that type of time."

"I knew you didn't have shit to do with," Boobie admitted.

"So, if that's the case, then why was Luxe hit?" I eyed him. I wasn't angry. I was more curious than anything.

"I didn't have shit to do with that, and on some real shit, I also didn't have any knowledge that it was going to take place. I do accept responsibility for it because it was my people. Neal called that play and because of that, he's not with us right now."

"*Not right now* or not anymore."

Boobie paused. I could tell he hadn't thought that far in advance.

"You know ... When Lawrence made that move behind my back, I addressed him and then benched him. *Permanently.* I take the actions of the people who represent me very seriously."

"My situation is a little different though, Lance. You fucking his kids' mother," he said with zero hesitation.

"Boobie, that's even worse. He acted out of emotions. You want a man like that representing you? A man that acts off impulse and does something drastic enough to ruin your business and possibly get a whole lot of motherfuckers killed? All because somebody fucking his ex?"

"He's family, Lance. And I don't mean no disrespect when I say this, but you know how much you done let Lawrence get away with. He done did a lot of shit to folks. A lot of shit that niggas wanted to get at him about but didn't because of you. So, just give me this one and know that I'm handling it," Boobie replied.

"Okay, but please do. And do it quickly. Because that move Neal made, set Alize back in court today. She can't afford nothing else to happen. I called y'all here to talk as men because I respect the both of you. I don't respect too many motherfuckers." I turned to Boobie. "As far as Luxe. I'll eat the business loss. It's just money. And it doesn't compare to the fact that my brother made an attempt on your life."

"And what about Tye?" Corey asked. "Ya people tried to smoke Boobie, and then Tye got smoked. Am I the next nigga he gon' try to get at?" he asked, although it was more of a statement than a question. I eyed Corey. He never really said too much. He was a short, chubby guy, with a round bald head.

"I honestly don't know what Lawrence is up to. And I want to be clear that none of us knows who killed Tye. I haven't even gotten the chance to ask him anything about that. Lawrence hasn't been answering my calls and even if he did, he wouldn't admit to that because he knows that I wouldn't be with no shit like that. So, he's definitely not admitting to it. Especially not without witnesses. The situation with Boobie is different. Boobie saw him with his own eyes. I can't charge Lawrence for Tye though. We can never be too sure when it comes to that street shit."

"So, what's next?" Boobie asked, now leaning up against a new-model Nissan truck. Likely a rental. "I'm meeting up with a new connect tonight since you out the game. I'm just trying to go back to getting money. I ain't trying to go back and forth with Lawrence's crazy ass. We just need you to talk to him. Cuz I ain't gon' sit here and bullshit with you, Lance. If he run up on us again, me and my patnas gon' have to defend ourselves.

"I wouldn't expect anything else." I exhaled. "But give me a day or two to find him and talk to him. For now, just don't have your people running down on him on some trigger-happy shit. At the end of the day, he's still a nigga that I'll tear through the city about."

"I gotchu." Boobie gave a reluctant nod and we all parted ways.

Back on the road and headed to Alize's, I called my mom to see if she'd heard from Lawrence.

"Have you got up with Lawrence yet?" I asked after the call connected and we greeted one another.

"No. He's still not answering. I just hope he's okay." I could tell that she was worried by her tone. "I'll keep trying him though," she assured me before yawning loudly into the phone. I looked at the dashboard and realized it was getting close to her bedtime. She was clearly tired.

"Alright, Mom. Thanks. Let me know as soon as you get him. And don't make it obvious that I'm looking for him. Just fish to get his location and then call me immediately."

"Lance, how many motherfuckin' times is you gon' keep saying the same shit?" she snapped. "I know what the fuck to say and do. And I'm tired too. I'm sick of Lawrence's ass. Can't even go the fuck to bed, shit."

I couldn't help but smile. Even when things were tense and serious, my mom's crazy ass would always say some slick shit to put a smile on a nigga's face.

"I'll call him a few more times and then I'm going to bed. If I can't get ahold of him tonight, then I'll call him in the morning. I'm not staying up all night worrying myself to death about Lawrence's ass. Some people you just can't help. Child or no child. Brother or no brother. But I'll keep you posted," she told me before hanging up.

I didn't dispute the fact that my mama was worried. But at the end of the day, she was right. Lawrence had his moments where he came and went mentally. He had demons that he just wouldn't let go. He tried to battle them with drugs and alcohol, but it wasn't doing shit but making it worse. Making *him* worse. Normal days, he was his normal self. Happy and lively. Other days, he was moody, agitated, and violent. Lately, the *other* days were starting to outnumber the normal.

Most recently, Casey was the only thing that seemed to keep him happy. Unfortunately, that situation was going downhill. I'd expected that. While she may have cared for Lawrence, she was a sack chaser that didn't know true love. She just knew how to finesse and manipulate on a level that he wasn't accustomed to. So much that it felt like love to him. Casey wasn't leaving no baller for his ass. Lawrence had money, but Blaze's type of money provided security and a lifestyle that came with no risk. I probably knew just as much about her as he did. When she first started bringing her ass around, I'd hired an investigator to do a little background check on her ass. Go figure, right. I should've had one done on Alexis' ass.

But back to Casey. She had a sick mother and a brother in a private school that cost over $25K a year. She had her own place, and she was paying the rent on a fancy little spot in Baltimore for her family. To be frank, she needed Blaze. With Lawrence's brain working the way it did, he couldn't take her for face value. He just couldn't see it. Not right away anyway. With Lawrence shifting to a dark place so quickly, I had a strong feeling that he was beginning to see her for what she really was. So much for happy. I blamed myself for Lawrence's demons.

Back when we were younger and going at it with the older niggas in the hood over me killing Black, Lawrence and I got caught lacking. Black had a cousin that went by the name of Drew. Drew wasn't hardly a menace like his cousin, but he, of course, was still a threat. While Lawrence and I were dropping Black's crew in daily shoot-outs, Drew sat back quiet.

He claimed that he would not involve himself because of the type of man that Black was. Anybody that knew me and knew Black, knew that I only smoked his ass because he left me no choice.

Lawrence didn't buy the whole Drew not getting involved spiel. He had pushed for Drew's death early on. I protested it and as usual, I ultimately had the final say. A week or two later, Lawrence was abducted while coming back from visiting the treatment center our mama was staying at to kick her drug habit. Lawrence was beaten, tortured, bound, and sodomized. Drew and the three other niggas that snatched him up, brought him back a few days later and discarded him next to a dumpster with a trash bag tied around his head.

It was a hellish few days trying to function while assuming my little brother was dead. When he surfaced, I was thankful that he survived. One of our crackhead neighbors found him and drug him into their home. Instead of calling the ambulance, she had someone call me. She didn't want what happened to him and his condition plastered all over the news. That day, a huge part of Lawrence died. He became harder and his soul became darker. He blamed me. He made that clear. It didn't matter that I'd quickly smoked the niggas that did it. Didn't matter that I swiftly delivered justice. I'd beat each of them unconscious, only to wake they asses up from the agonizing pain of being set on fire. I burnt them niggas to death and then dumped their charred bodies in their hood. Shit died down after that, and I'd never been tried again.

I had no doubt that Lawrence was fucked up mentally from that day. I wanted so much to help him, but I didn't know how. There was only so much I could do, and I was to the point that I was tired of even trying. I'd essentially shut him out of the drug world and now he was shutting me out. If that's what he wanted to do, that was fine, but I wasn't going to let his actions keep affecting me and mine.

⚜

Alize moaned loudly as I worked in and out of her slippery canal. With the tip of my tongue, I trailed a path north and south along her back. Her pussy gripped my manhood so tightly, it took everything in me to contain myself and keep from erupting inside of her. While I clenched my teeth together to avoid calling out, she did the opposite.

"Shittttt!" she screamed out, like she didn't have neighbors.

She threw her ass back against my pelvis as if she were challenging me. Being the nigga that I was, I loved a challenge. I slipped my hand downward and cupped her swinging breast. I squeezed her nipple and thrust deep into her pussy, causing her to scream out.

"Lance!"

"Lance what?" I asked her in a raspy whisper loud enough for her to hear, but she didn't reply. "You gon' come for daddy?" I asked her, but still no reply.

"Come for daddy," I begged through pants.

I was dead ass serious. I wanted her to come for a nigga. The way that box was built, I couldn't stay up in it too long. She felt so good that I couldn't control myself any longer. I pulled myself out of her, just as I reached my peak.

A blissful current passed through my lower body, causing my

dick to pulsate and finally erupt all over her bedding. To save face, I pushed her body down into the bed but snatched her backside up into my face.

Holding thick legs up with my arms, I buried my face in her box and went to work, licking, sucking, and slurping all the creamy nectar that covered it. I knew it was nasty, but I was a nasty nigga that aimed to please. If tonguing her wet, sticky pussy down made Alize melt in my mouth, then that's what I would do. Besides, I had cum quick as fuck and I had to give her a reason to not even notice.

"Ahhhhhhhhhh! Shit, Lance! Sssssssss," she hissed. "Mmmmmmm, I'm gonna come."

She moaned and whined while her legs trembled in my arms. I flattened my tongue against her and licked back and forth from her clit, all the way to her ass, occasionally stopping to suck her clit into my mouth. A few seconds later, she began shuddering and finally released a sweet, thick stream of cream on top of my tongue. I moaned in satisfaction and swallowed every drop.

"Fuck!" she yelled out before growing still. A few seconds went by and she started laughing. That was the goofy shit she did after skeeting all up in a nigga's mouth. I smacked her ass and then lowered her body back down to the bed, lying beside her.

"You came already?" she asked with a smirk.

"Mmm hhm," I replied, avoiding her gaze.

She paused a few seconds and then began to giggle. "Yeah, I know. Yo' ass was gone with the wind," she joked. "You get it? Gone with the wind." She slapped my bare thigh playfully while she grinned like the cornball she was.

"Get the fuck outta here." I couldn't help but laugh. I loved seeing her smile. Lord knows we both needed it.

"I don't know why you be trying to play that shit off. I can always tell when you come. Ya shit always feels like it's throbbing or something."

She sat up, leaned over me, and pressed her lips into mine.

With all the problems the both of us had between us, we were at a temporary peace when we were alone together and away from all the griefs of life. Seeing me smile, she gave me another kiss. She slipped her tongue in my mouth and I happily received it. I felt my dick stiffen up.

"You must want another round," I said, briefly pulling my mouth away from hers.

"You know it."

I pushed her back down on the bed, but before I could slide back between her legs and push myself back into her, my phone began to ring.

I grumbled since I didn't want to answer. However, the two of us had so much going on that neither of us could afford to not answer our phones. I hopped off the bed and quickly snatched it up, answering it on the fourth ring. It was my mom.

"Lance! Lindsey's gone!"

"What do you mean she's gone?" I asked, eyes widening.

"She done fuckin' snuck out. You need to get over here. Go find her or something!" she argued.

"Okay. Okay, Ma. Just give me a minute and I'll be over there. And calm down!"

"Just bring ya ass," she said before ending the call.

✥ 12 ✥

ALEXIS

I didn't give a damn that I had to step up into Drip by myself. There was no way that I was missing the ATL Baller Bash that took place yearly at the club. It wasn't nothing but a big ass party, but all the rich niggas were guaranteed to be in attendance. I knew my girl Melvina wasn't feeling well, but I hated that she couldn't go with me. That bitch knew everybody, and she would have definitely made the night a lot more lit and a lot less awkward had she been present.

Instead of being at a nigga's table, my ass was at the bar nursing a Long Island Iced Tea. Since I had no one to watch my back, I planned to drink light the entire night. Wasn't no creepy ass nigga about to catch me slipping. Although the drink I was sipping was free to me, I made sure anything I put my lips to was made fresh and in front of me. Not to brag or anything, but I'd literally been turning down drink after drink since the moment I waltzed my fine ass up in the building. It wasn't anything new since I was accustomed to attention. I just didn't want to get too drunk since I was by myself. Mentally, I was prepared to shoo off men all night. As gorgeous as I was, men were bound to flock to me all night. My body was tight and glowing from the shimmery lotion that I'd applied before I left. I was dressed in a pink, two-piece ensemble that complemented my light creamy skin, paired with a pair of clear pumps that showed off my perfectly pedicured toes. With my long, silky weave pressed and flowing down my back, I resembled a video vixen. I didn't mind sitting quiet and looking pretty. I just needed a rich nigga to star in my video.

It was a shame that the nigga I wanted, no longer wanted me. I sniffled lightly and then remembered why. Despite all the arguments and fights, Lance ended up calling it quits over the little cocaine incident. I could still remember him throwing me out his damn place like I was trash. In my world, cocaine use wasn't a big thing. A lot of bitches sniffed coke in Atlanta. I'd actually been snorting it since I was sixteen or seventeen years old.

The daughter of a white mama and black daddy, I'd been around drugs since I was a little girl. My mother used them in secret, while my daddy sold them. Eventually he'd get busted and my mama would start using them openly. She eventually settled down and married a rich white man who also used coke and partied hard just like her. I was basically the modern version of my mother, minus the man. I'd thought I had that with Lance, but unfortunately, he came from a different kind of world than I did. It wasn't what I expected since a lot of the dealers, rappers, and entertainers used drugs heavily. Shit, I knew for a fact that his brother Lawrence did.

Unlike Lance's, my life consisted of partying and hanging out. I was a lot livelier, while Lance was sort of dark and gloomy. Melvina and I clicked for those reasons. We'd met at a party one night after high school and had been friends since. Melvina had never expressed a desire to settle down. She was cool with having multiple guys and getting paid by each one of them. I, on the other hand, wanted to be a kept bitch.

Shaking myself out of my thoughts, my eyes went back to scanning the club. I hadn't fully given up on Lance but in the meantime, I was still going to actively look for a replacement. I wasn't downgrading though. Lance had millions, so the next nigga needed to have millions. That wasn't too hard in a city like Atlanta, where money flowed.

I bobbed my head to the lyrics of a Lil' Baby song and took small sips of my drink, until a familiar face rolled up on me smiling. A wide smile instantly spread across my own face.

"Lindsey, what the hell are you doing here?" I asked as she leaned over and hugged me while I was still seated.

The powerful smell of alcohol immediately smacked me in the face.

"I'm wit' my girls!" she said a little too loudly with a heavy slur.

My eyes widened from the stench of her breath. I shot a quick smile at the two nerdy-looking, young bitches that were with her. All three of them were trying way too hard to be cute. They had on short skirts and tube tops like they were in a *Grease* movie. They were a hot damn mess. I could tell that Lindsey was the leader of the three. Her skirt and top hugged her body, complementing her lean, chocolate frame. The other two broads definitely didn't have the body to pull the fit off like she did.

"Girl, how much have you had to drink?" I asked, returning my gaze back to her.

Her eyes were glossed over and low, while a thin film of perspiration coated her forehead. She was definitely hot from the liquor she'd consumed.

"Not much. But don't you worry about what I'm drinking," she shot back drunkenly. "I want to know why you're even drinking at all if you're supposed to be pregnant?"

I frowned and moved my head back some and away from hers. She was loud and she was spitting a little. I had also grown instantly annoyed that she felt comfortable enough to question someone my age. But then again, I'd made her feel that she could since I was always blowing up her phone trying to get up with her brother.

"Girl, get yourself together, and this is a virgin Long Island," I lied.

Despite the fact that I wasn't really pregnant, I didn't want her running shit back to Lance. I was going to run with that fake pregnancy shit for as long as I could.

"Good. Because I don't want my niece or nephew coming out with no jumbo head from fetal alcohol syndrome."

I rolled my eyes. Lindsey was one of those people that I could only take in doses. She was annoying and too smart for her own damn good. As drunk as her little ass was, she could remember a white-ass word like fetal alcohol syndrome. A black ass chick with a private school education was something I wasn't used to.

"Lindsey, where's your phone? I want to call your brother to pick you up. He'd kill me if I left you out here like this with those dumb bitches you came with." I flashed the two of them a smile. "No offense."

Not that I cared if they were offended or not. They were both just as tipsy as Lindsey, so they probably weren't paying me much mind.

"Well, he'd kill me if you managed to get through to his phone."

She laughed in my face, showing two rows of pearly whites, perfected by some Georgia orthodontist.

The comment itself pissed me off, but her laughing in my face pissed me off even more. It actually made me want to smack her head off, but I didn't want a death wish. As much as they bickered, I knew that Lance loved his little sister to bits.

"Cool. I don't have to use your phone."

I dug in my purse, pulled out my phone, and jammed it in her face. With her homegirls next to her, I snapped a picture of the three of them. Lindsey was still giggling and looking drunk. Still thinking shit was sweet. I was about to give her a quick dose of reality, all while serving myself.

"I'll just send him this."

I turned my phone towards her and showed her the picture. Her drunken smile slowly dissipated. She reached for my phone, but I pulled it away and out of her reach.

"I'm sure he'll bring his ass as soon as he gets it."

I was the one grinning this time.

✖ 13 ✖

ALIZE

By the time I'd realized that Lance had left his phone behind, I was sure he was too far gone for me to try and run out and catch him. I'd only realized that he forgot it because it started ringing not long after he raced out the door. My intentions were to just let it ring until it stopped; however, whoever it was that was trying to get in touch with him, wouldn't let up. It was becoming annoying, so I went to check and see who it was and then turn off the ringer. I groaned, but eventually got out of bed and climbed to my feet to go retrieve it. I figured it was probably just his mom calling to make sure that he had already left and was on his way.

Once I reached the dresser where he left it sitting, I picked it up and saw Alexis' name pop up. Not a single one of the calls were from Peanut. They were all from Alexis. She'd called five times. I frowned at the fact that he even still had her number saved in his contacts.

I'd honestly never gotten around to speaking with him about his and Alexis' past relationship. I'd never asked him about the alleged pregnancy either. He wasn't a person that really dwelled in the past. He didn't seem to have left that relationship with any wounds or anything. When we were together, he was happy, and it was just me and him. That's what we focused on. Standing there and staring at the phone, I now realized that he and I were going to need to finally have that conversation.

Initially, I respected his privacy and didn't want to get all up in his business. But now that we were actually serious and practically living together, I deserved to know what was up with the two of them. I sat the phone back down and headed toward the bathroom so I could clean the residue and stench of sex off my body. Unfortunately, I barely made it completely out of the room before Lance's phone started to ring again. I turned around and grabbed it. It was Alexis again. I swiped the screen to answer.

"Lance!" Alexis said loudly into the phone.

"No, it isn't Lance. It's Alize. He's not here, but why are you calling my man's phone?" I asked sharply.

Shawty had never been my cup of tea, so I preferred to be blunt versus polite when dealing with her. I could also admit that I was territorial, and I wasn't exactly thrilled that a bitch like her had history with my man. To put it simply, I was about to end all the calling and texting shenanigans. Lance and I were a couple. An item. Boyfriend and girlfriend. I didn't care if she was pregnant or not, she didn't need to be blowing his phone up like that. Neither daytime nor nighttime.

"*Man?*" She scoffed. "Well, Alize, I'm pregnant by your so-called man, so I can call him whenever the fuck I want," Alexis clapped back.

I was just about to let loose on her ass, but she cut me off.

"Just let him know his sister is out here acting a damn fool at The Baller Bash."

"The what?" I asked.

"I forgot you ain't got no damn life." She blew into the phone and then snickered. "The Baller Bash that they have every year at Drip. Just tell him that he needs to come get her. And soon. She's pissy drunk and acting a damn fool. And the little home-girls that she came with left her. So, he needs to come on, 'cause I ain't babysitting her ass all night."

"Why didn't you call Peanut?" I asked out of curiosity since I knew that Peanut probably didn't drive and would have just sent Lance anyway. I figured Alexis hadn't called her because when she called Lance, she had no idea where Lindsey was. Peanut also hadn't called Lance's phone back to update him since he left.

"Who?" Alexis quickly countered.

"*Peanut*," I repeated.

"Who the hell is Peanut, Alize?"

"Girl. Never mind." I rolled my eyes and hung up the phone on her before she could utter another word. I could now see why he gave that dumb bitch the boot. How the hell was she pregnant by a man and didn't even know his mama's name? All I could do was shake my head at the foolishness.

I went to the bathroom, grabbed a rag, and took a quick bird bath so I could run out. I wasn't sure when or if Lance was coming back. Since I was up and had Lance's phone, I figured I would just do everyone a favor and go grab Lindsey myself. I wasn't taking her way back to Marietta, but at least her family would know where she was and that she was safe.

As I grabbed my keys and got prepared to leave, my own phone began ringing in my purse. I quickly dug it out and checked the number. That was odd. It was Ms. Dot, an elderly lady that lived across the street from Aunt Melva. She was like the block grandma. One of those old people that one just naturally showed respect.

As a teen living with Aunt Melva, I'd taken a liking to her. She was sweet and kind, and always passed out those little church candies to all the respectful kids, like me. When I moved out and occasionally popped back in to see Aunt Melva, I would usually also go see her. Lately, I'd had so much going on that I hadn't gotten around to seeing her. It had been some months. She always had my number though. I was just unsure of why she would be calling me randomly at that time of night.

"Hey, Ms. Dot," I greeted her warmly before she could get her words out.

"Uhh, hey there. Is this Alize?" she asked.

Her sweet, aging voice was normally calm, but tonight her tone sounded extremely different. It had a sense of urgency to it.

"It is Alize. How are you, Ms. Dot. Is everything okay?"

"I'm okay, sweetie. I'm sorry to trouble you, but I didn't know how to get ahold of Melvina."

"What did you need with Melvina?" I asked.

"Well, uh, Melva's house is on fire," she finally spit out. "We done called for help, but we need one of you to hurry up and get on over here. It ain't looking too good."

"I'm on my way!"

Forgetting all about Lindsey, I flew out the door and raced over to Aunt Melva's.

⚜

Because traffic was thick, it took me nearly thirty minutes to get to Aunt Melva's Oakland City home. The entire time I drove, I feared the worst. She hadn't been the best aunt, but at the end of the day, she had basically raised me. I still didn't want to see anything happen to her. I prayed that she was okay. As selfish as the thoughts were, I also couldn't help but think about my girls. I wasn't sure where I was going to put them now. It was always something. I was strong, though, and I was determined not to fold.

When I finally pulled up to Aunt Melva's street, I couldn't even get through. The streets had been blocked off with fire trucks, police officers, and a single ambulance van. I parked the Jag up the street and then ran down to the house. When I got close enough to see the damage to the house, I nearly froze in my tracks. While the firefighters had already extinguished the fire, water ran down into the street while smoke still poured from all over the house. The top, the front, the sides. Smoke coming from everywhere. It was surreal. The entire front of the house was burnt black to a crisp. The front was so much more charred than the rest of the house, that I was convinced that the fire had started there. The front porch had literally crumbled to the ground from the flames and water. For a moment, I became lost in the sight. I could only just stand there and gawk at the remains of the house where I had basically grown up. It was like I was in a daze. I finally snapped out of it when I heard my name being called. It was Ms. Dot.

"Alize!"

I followed her voice and saw her standing nearby with a couple police officers. Dressed in a faded housecoat, she waved for me to come over. Although the house and its perimeter had been taped off with yellow 'do not cross' tape, she stood inside of the barriers talking to first responders. I dipped my body under the tape to get inside, and then made my way to join her. As I was walking up, she ushered me with her hand to come closer.

"I think she can answer these questions better than me. This is her niece. I called her. Alize, I'm gonna let you talk to these nice men, honey. I gotta get back inside," Ms. Dot said before scurrying off. I nodded a thank you before turning my attention to the officers.

"Where's my aunt?" I asked them instead of introducing myself.

"She's in the ambulance, being transported to the burn center at Grady Memorial."

The officers both looked at me solemnly before one continued.

"Your aunt suffered some extensive second and third-degree burns. I have to advise you as a professional that the burns are life threatening, although I do feel personally, that she was pulled out in time. We think she'll make it. Grady Memorial has an excellent trauma and burn center, so I'm confident that she will be well cared for."

I swallowed hard and nodded my understanding. I was about to turn and walk off so I could head over to the hospital, but the officers stopped me.

"Ma'am. We have a few more questions to ask but wanted to do so privately. Step over here." Although the tape was up, folks still stood right up on it and close by. He motioned for me to follow the two of them, and we walked off a few feet where we had a little more privacy.

"Did your aunt have any enemies? Or maybe someone that she was seeing that she may have angered? Anyone that would possibly want to hurt her?" he asked.

"Huh? What? No, not to my knowledge. She didn't really date, and she stayed to herself."

They looked at one another and one of them proceeded to jot down a few notes on a tiny, yellow notepad.

"Why are you asking me these questions?" I asked with a puzzled look.

"Because we're treating this incident as a possible arson. So far, everything is pointing to that. We believe the fire was deliberately set."

It suddenly became hard to breath. Like I'd been hit in the stomach with a soccer ball. Just when I took two steps forward, I was being pulled two steps back. Aunt Melva was hurt bad, I had no fuckin' childcare, and my childhood home had been intentionally set on fire. Fucking arson! I wasn't ready to hear no shit like that.

So much for giving Lance time. It sounded like the niggas that Lance had the talk with earlier, didn't seem to hear him. They either weren't listening, or they didn't care. What I didn't understand was why the fuck would they target Aunt Melva's house? That didn't sound like anything Boobie would do, and I didn't think that Neal would cosign no shit like that. It was crazy how dudes would target any and everyone just to prove a statement. I was beginning to think that Lance's brother, Lawrence, was actually the person that was trying to prove that statement.

I'd already told Lance that I couldn't risk anything affecting my chances of getting my girls back. I wasn't big on repeating myself. He and I were over. I was also going to cut off all communication with Neal and his family. I didn't give a damn about who could help me anymore. I didn't care about anyone's money. I was going to do everything I needed to do on my own. It was going to just be me, Sage, and Violet. And as much as that shit was going to hurt in the beginning, it would be worth it in the end.

❦ 14 ❦

NEAL

"Mmmm, just like that," I moaned as Melissa slurped my dick up into her mouth.

I watched her intently while she bobbed on it a few times with the skill of a porn star. Jumping off the dick, she lowered her head down to my balls and used her long, slick tongue to pull them into her mouth.

"Got damn!" I hissed.

I gripped the back of her neck so hard that I nearly choked her. Her top was so good that I wanted to rip her mafuckin' head off and carry that bitch with me everywhere I went. She could literally top me off and make me come in two minutes. She was that good.

"Nasty bitch," I moaned in satisfaction.

I gripped her hair and lifted her face up to see what a mess she'd made. I eased my dick out her mouth, grabbed it with my other hand, and began tapping it up against her lips. I could never understand how a bitch could look so disgusting and good at the same time. Her eyes were wide, her nose was running, and she had thick slobber all on the side of her face and running down her chin. It was a beautiful sight.

Pushing my wood back in her mouth, I let Melissa go back to

work. Shawty was a filthy hoe, but I low-key loved it. That bitch would literally do anything to please a nigga. Dick, balls, toes. She'd lick my ass if I'd let her. I wasn't for the homo shit though. I was straight just off the top. A minute hadn't even passed, and I was ready to explode. My toes were curling, and I was about ready throw my head back in bliss, but a tiny fist started knocking on the door of the bedroom and then the door flew open. My shit instantly deflated.

"Aunt Melissa," a pint-sized voice called out.

Melissa had already snatched a blanket and threw it over her head, covering up my lower body as well.

"Beetle, get the hell out and go sit down!" she yelled out from under the covers.

"But Tay-Tay went in the kitchen and got a snack and now her sick—"

"Close my door and go sit yo' ass down!"

The child whined in return but quickly exited and swung the door shut.

"Why you yelling at them kids like that?" I chuckled while she still leaned over me, hidden under her blanket. I wasn't laughing because I thought she was funny. I was more so laughing because her ass was ghetto, and that shit didn't make no sense at times.

Melissa pulled the blanket off her head and smoothed down her hair.

"Because they don't be wanting shit. Just want to tell something all the time," she argued with a frown. "Especially Beetle's lil' ass. I can't stand that tattle-telling shit. I told my sister 'bout that."

As she rose, I studied her features. A frown definitely didn't look good on her. She wasn't ugly, but she was average at very best. She damn sure didn't look better than Alize. Melissa was just the typical, brown-skinned, thick-body, dusty project chick. Her mouth game and curvy body kept her from actually looking the dusty part. A nigga like me would gladly keep her hair and nails done in exchange to constant access to that throat.

"Well, you the adult and you need to keep your door locked," I reminded her.

Her simple ass kept a house full of kids and didn't think to lock her bedroom door before she decided to suck some dick. She had three of her own tearing through the apartment, and it was common to see another one or two belonging to a friend or relative, running through the place as well.

"Yeah, that's true. But they know damn well they need to knock on my bedroom door. But I'm gonna go wash my face and check on they asses real quick. See what they want. I'll finish you up when I get back."

She slid into her attached bathroom and after a couple minutes of hearing the stream of water splashing against the sink, she emerged. While she walked out, I ran to the bathroom and cleaned myself off as well, so I could run out and hit a lick.

Even though Boobie had told me to lay low, I hadn't. I'd actually never stopped selling that lethal heroin and fentanyl mix that Lawrence had given us. Unlike my cousin, I didn't have another source of income. I had to hustle every day, as I couldn't afford to sit around idle. Sure, Boobie had reimbursed me for the majority of the unsold work. But since he never asked for the work back, I put it in the tuck.

Besides, not every dope fiend was dying from it. A lot of them were, but not every single one. The crazy part was, the most dangerous mix of heroin was the kind of drug the dope fiends flocked for. They wanted some shit that was powerful enough to almost take them out. While it was good for them, as long as they actually came back to, it was bad for the drug dealers who were dealing with loss of clientele from the deaths and dealing with scorching hot streets because of the police investigations. To find out that I was under investigation had me low-key paranoid. I wanted to know who had my name in their mouth.

To my knowledge, none of my youngins had gotten hemmed up by police. If they did, the biggest risk I faced was them telling where they got their drugs from. If Boobie ever got wind of what was going on, he would flip his lid. But that was a chance I had to take, because my hustle didn't stop for no one. My goal was to get rid of what I had left by tomorrow, and then hopefully Boobie would have the distribution plans with the new connect. Even though we went at it earlier, he was still supposed to get up with me and let me know what had happened. At the end of the day, he was right. I had to get a grip on my feelings and stop tripping over Alize and her new nigga.

Meanwhile, we all had to watch our backs in case the nigga Lawrence decided to step again. He'd come for us once already, and I wouldn't put it past him to try again. Especially after Tye was mysteriously killed. None of it sat well with me, and I personally believed Lawrence was behind it all. Probably just wanted niggas gone because he'd been cut out. Just as I finished wringing out the rag I'd grabbed from under the sink, Melissa began screaming for me at the top of her lungs.

"Neal! Help me!"

I knew something was wrong. It was the way she called for me. The urgency in her tone. It was more than just panic that I heard in her voice. It was sheer terror.

I tossed the rag down and ran from her room and into the living room. My eyes lowered to Melissa. She was down her knees, hovered over her little girl, Tay-Tay. She couldn't have been no more than three or four.

"Tay-Tay, baby, wake up! Come on, baby! Get up!" Melissa screamed.

She was borderline hysterical, shaking the little girl's limp body. Her normal brown skin was a grayish hue, while foam began to build up in the corners of her mouth. The rest of the kids were standing back, watching everything unfold.

"Yo! One of y'all call 911!" I screamed to them.

It was roughly four of them. Their ages varied from four to

ten, but I knew damn well one of them knew how to dial 911. Two out of the four raced to find a phone.

"Tell them you need an ambulance and that she's having a seizure! Hurry!" I yelled to establish urgency.

My phone was deep in my pocket, but there was no way in hell that I was digging it out to make the call. I knew exactly what was going on, while Melissa didn't have a clue. While she screamed over her daughter, I wanted to tell her. Tay-Tay was definitely having a seizure, but it wasn't just any old regular seizure. It was a seizure from an overdose. She'd definitely ingested drugs.

As soon as I ran into the living room and saw Melissa over her daughter, I immediately spotted faint traces of white powdery residue around her mouth. Tay-Tay had gotten into the heroin that I had stashed in the kitchen. Of course, Melissa didn't know that I had put it high up in the cabinet, right next to the powdered sugar that I used to cut the drugs down even more than they already were. When Beetle had barged into Melissa's room a few minutes back, she'd said that Tay-Tay had gotten a snack and wasn't feeling well after the fact. They probably had been climbing up on the counters, eventually stumbling upon it. Either way, I now had a huge fucking problem. It was either take flight or stay and help her right until the paramedics arrived so her daughter wouldn't die. *Shit.* I couldn't leave the little girl. I had kids of my own.

I dropped to my knees, beside Melissa. "Is she breathing?" I asked before snatching Tay-Tay up towards me and shaking her as hard as I could without her hurting her. "Melissa, go make sure dem kids called 911. If they haven't, you do it and tell them to get here quick!" I demanded.

Melissa was crying and staring at me all wide eyed. We didn't have time for that shit. I needed her to get the fuck right or her daughter was going to die.

"Go!" I screamed.

Melissa jumped from the thunderous demand, but right after, hopped to her feet and ran out of the room.

"Come on, lil' mama," I said, as I shook her some more.

I paused for a moment and then felt under her nose to see if she was breathing. She was, but it was labored. I gently placed her back down on the floor.

"Did you call them?" I yelled. I was about to start panicking just like she was. Shawty needed help soon.

"They're on the phone!" she screamed out, rushing back out into the living room with her phone in her hand.

"They want to know if she's breathing," Melissa said.

"Yeah, but barely."

Melissa listened to the dispatcher and nodded. "She says we need to start CPR."

"I don't know no fuckin' CPR," I spat. Her dumb ass must've forgot that I was a hood nigga.

Melissa began to cry at the realization that none of us were worth a fucking damn.

"She says that we need to keep her awake and try to keep her breathing until the paramedics get here."

I looked down at Tay-Tay, and she was out of it. Her skin was turning grayer and her lips were losing their color.

"Fuck!" I yelled, before jumping back to my feet.

I raced to the bedroom, grabbed the bookbag that I usually brought with me, and then raced into the kitchen. I scrambled through the cabinets and snatched the big stashed bag of heroin. Stuffing it into the bookbag, I raced through the living room and headed for the door.

"Lance! Please don't leave. Stay with me until the paramedics come!" she begged tearfully.

"I can't. I gotta go."

I gripped the door handle but hesitated. I had to tell her. I didn't know if the paramedics would realize right away that they were actually responding to an overdose. Yeah, they were trained to look for the signs, but not in a fucking three or four-year-old. I had to tell her.

"Melissa, as soon as the paramedics get here, tell them that she needs Narcan."

"What?" she cried.

"Listen!" I screamed. "Pay-a-fuckin-tention! Tell them that she needs Narcan. *Narcan*," I repeated for emphasis. "Don't forget it. They'll give her that and she should be okay. You understand?" I asked her.

"Yeah." She nodded her head vigorously to indicate her understanding. With tears in her eyes, she recited it. "She needs Narcan."

"I gotta go."

I took off out the door, hopped in my car, and got the fuck out of there. My days of fucking Melissa were over. I would have much larger problems as soon as the truth surfaced. I just prayed that Melissa's daughter survived.

❦ 15 ❦

CASEY

I didn't know why I'd let Blaze talk me into going to the Baller Bash with him. I wasn't in the mood. Most of the chicks that rolled up in there were looking for a baller, and I already had one. Besides, I couldn't drink until I made a final decision on whether or not I was going to keep or terminate the pregnancy. Even if I decided to get rid of it, I just couldn't bring myself to be gulping down liquor while carrying a fetus.

I hadn't even been in Drip a full twenty minutes before a familiar face began walking quickly toward me. He looked angry, and he also looked high off cocaine and highly intoxicated. The stench of liquor seeped through his pores while his eyes were wide as saucers. Judging by his state, I knew that the night was about to go left. The energy he brought was dark and surreal. I literally had the urge to empty my bladder onto the floor when Lawrence finally stopped in front of me and Blaze.

"So, this why you not answering the phone?" He eyed me angrily. His voice was laced with disdain while he seemed to tremble from what appeared to be borderline rage.

"Lawrence, please, this is not the time." My eyes cut across the club to see who could hear us. There I was in the middle of a damn love triangle and standing next to Blaze the basketball star.

"Not the time, huh? So, when is the time, Casey? Because you've been saying that this isn't the right time for a long time now. Right? I've decided that now is actually the perfect time. I've been off house arrest for fucking days, and you haven't returned a single call nor a single text. You blocked me on social media but let this pussy ass nigga post you and him running around doing y'all. After all that shit you promised me!"

"Yo, she chose. Why don't you just go on so we can enjoy our night," Blaze said in an attempt to calm a visibly enraged Lawrence. I was about to tell him to walk off and let me speak to him alone, but before I could do that, Lawrence glared at him.

"I suggest you shut yo' bitch ass up or get beat in the middle of this club. I see you tried to be tough tonight and come without an entourage or security. I swear you keep talking, and you'll regret that."

Lawrence looked back to me. "Let's lay it all out there, Casey. Tell him what you told me."

I swallowed hard. Blaze looked at me angrily, but he also looked confused. I knew he was tired of the situation with Lawrence, but I could also tell that he wanted to know what Lawrence was talking about.

Despite what Lawrence was saying, that wasn't a conversation that I was ready for. Hell no. I felt myself getting nauseous. I had to get the fuck out of there. Without saying a word, I grabbed my clutch and tried to storm off, but a strong hand snatched me back by my arm.

I spun around and was face-to-face with Lawrence.

"Don't you fucking walk away from me while I'm talking to you!" he snapped, drawing attention to the two of us. We were now standing near the middle of the floor, and it looked like some shit was about to go down.

"Get the fuck off me!" I demanded. I loved Lawrence, but there were times that the demons inside of him made me fear him. That was the biggest downside of dating hood niggas. The violent streaks.

While Lawrence and I still faced off, Blaze rushed over toward us.

"Take your motherfucking hands off of her," he demanded.

"Or what?" Lawrence asked. To spite Blaze, he held my arm, although after a few seconds, his fingers loosened, and he let me go.

"What you gonna do?" Lawrence taunted, still staring Blaze down with a menacing smirk. "You gonna fight me? Or you gon' get pistol whipped again? Or maybe I'll just murk yo' bitch ass this time for fucking with me. Or maybe I'll murk this curly head bitch." His gaze tore away from Blaze and fell on me. "Murk yo' ass for lying and playing games. Tell him what the fuck is really up!" Lawrence demanded. "Why don't you fucking tell him that you've been talking about leaving his lame ass from the moment you tasted this dick! Tell him how you laid up with his ass night after night but pregnant by me! Tell him, Casey! Tell him that you got my baby in your fucking stomach!" he argued.

I was so embarrassed I wanted to fucking disappear.

"Lawrence, please don't do this. This isn't the time." My voice was wavering and ready to crack because the whole situation was hurting him.

Blaze glared at me so hard it felt like he was about to burn a hole through my damn face. He shook his head in disgust, looked at me, and then looked at Lawrence. He muttered something indecipherable, and then he walked off, leaving me there staring teary-eyed in the face of my lover. I noticed people watching, staring, pointing, and laughing.

"Is this what you fucking wanted? To fucking humiliate me and ruin my life?" I accused tearfully. That's how it felt. The way Blaze looked at me and walked off on me, I knew that there was no coming back from that. I began to cry softly, but Lawrence was unmoved.

"So, being pregnant by me and admitting it to the nigga that you claim you don't wanna be with is ruining your life?" he growled.

Anger danced in his eyes, but his face still bore the look of sadness and pain.

"All the shit that I told you I went through. Opened up to yo' hoe ass, and you still did a nigga dirty. I offered you the same shit that nigga gave you. But you were too busy counting pockets, and you chose him because of it. Bitch, you better get the fuck out my face. I swear to God I want to break your fucking neck so bad. Stomp that baby right out you."

His words sent chills down my spine. It was all I needed to get the fuck out of there. I wasn't sure what to expect from him. I didn't know if he was going to stop me and apologize or possibly run behind me, but he did none of those things. He, instead, continued to stand there and look at me with hate.

"Lawrence," I called out to him with tears in my eyes. I hated that it had come to this.

"Don't you mean Blaze? You might as well go run behind that nigga since that's what you planned to do anyway. Get the fuck out my face before I hurt you," he growled, as his wild, dark eyes cut through me.

I didn't bother to reply. I turned and walked off, picking up my pace so I could catch Blaze before he left.

❧ 16 ❧

LAWRENCE

I was in a terrible mood. I was high as a kite and seeing Casey's lying ass walk through the club without a care in the world infuriated me. Of course, she looked just as beautiful as the day that I'd met her. Despite her beauty, her face repulsed me. Carrying my baby but prancing around on the arm of another man was the utmost disrespect in my book. It was more than just jealousy for me. It was also anger. It was the fact that she had played the shit out of me. To block and ignore me and then have the audacity to waltz up in a public place, during a popular, annual event was the most disrespectful shit I'd ever seen in my life. It was like she didn't have a care in the world. That bitch either had big balls or she let the nigga Blaze use her as a pawn for his own ego. What he failed to realize, was that I wasn't the nigga to try to play games with, or stunt on. But that was the shit that niggas did to try and prove that they were the bigger man. Hoe shit that just might get him and her smoked in the end. I was seriously contemplating it.

Back in VIP, I threw back the remainder of the bottle that I'd ordered, while my eyes roamed through the thick crowd. Since I frequented the club regularly, I was able to get my same table in my normal section. It was tucked in a corner, not far from the entrance, and it provided me the ability to see basically everything that was going on in the club. The club was huge, and although it was usually packed, the Baller Bash made it damn near impossible to move around. In attendance were mostly athletes, entertainers, and a whole lot of Instagram models. While I should have been in a good mood and enjoying myself, all I could think about was how motherfuckers kept trying to play me lately.

I picked my bottle back up and brought it to my lips, becoming instantly annoyed when I remembered it was empty. I looked around for one of the waiters that served VIP and finally spotted the closest one. She was at a small table occupied by a couple chicks that I couldn't really make out. I didn't feel like waiting, so I got up from my table and headed over to where they were so I could catch her before she went to put their drinks in.

"Ay yo, waiter!" I called out. The waiter spun around, looking aggravated.

"Watchu need?" she asked with a stank ass attitude.

My lip curled up. I didn't mind a ghetto broad, but I couldn't stand a ghetto-acting broad.

"Fix yo' attitude when you addressing a nigga!" I barked.

The cocaine and liquor combination had me slightly aggressive. While she stood there sucking her teeth, I decided to order a bottle so I wouldn't have to see her little funky ass again.

"I need another bottle of Belvedere."

My eyes roamed behind her when I heard a loud and highly intoxicated female voice coming from the table that she had just left. I was type fucked up, so my eyes couldn't quite make out their faces. Seeing me observing them, she decided to give her two cents.

"Little young girl can't hold her liquor. I don't know who been serving her. Give me a few minutes and I'll be back with your bottle."

She walked off and I was just about to head back to my table, but I stopped when the two females from the table got up and began heading towards me.

"I gotta pee! I don't need you to use the fucking bathroom!" she snapped drunkenly as she stumbled in my direction. As she got closer, I realized it was Lindsey. Right behind her was Alexis. A bad ass, big butt, light-skinned bitch my brother was fucking on.

"Girl, I'm going with you." Alexis locked her arm under Lindsey's to make sure she was balanced and continued walking. I figured it was a good time to intervene.

"What the fuck yo' little ass doing in here?" I made sure my voice boomed loud enough for her to hear me.

"Thank God!" Alexis said dramatically. "She's too damn much. Her sorry ass homegirls dipped on her and I been in here babysitting ever since. She's all yours."

"Ma know you out here?" I asked, eyeing her in disgust. Lindsey always did the most.

"I'm grown," she countered. I took that as a no.

"Whose table y'all at?" I asked out of curiosity. The VIP section was a pretty penny during an event like the Baller Bash.

"Mine," Lindsey replied. I should have known. Lance spoiled the hell out of her. She had more money than most drug dealers.

"Where her homegirls go?" I turned to Alexis.

My eyes traveled up and down her frame shamelessly. Her body was banging, and her titties were practically popping out the little dress she had on.

"I made them bitches get up because they were running their mouths!" Lindsey answered loudly, her knees seeming to nod underneath her.

"More like they probably bailed on her because of how she's acting. They were all turnt up when I first ran into them. Her ass just seems to be the one that can't handle her liquor." She turned to Lindsey. "Girl, you can't be carrying yourself like that. You need to get it together. I'm about to roll."

"No you not!" I grumbled as she attempted to unlock her arm from Lindsey's.

"You better call that nigga Lance. I ain't her daddy. She not coming with me."

I didn't want to babysit her ass either. I loved my baby sis, but her little spoiled ass got on my last nerve. Plus, I liked to move dolo. With my lifestyle, anything was bound to pop off. I didn't have time to be carrying around dead weight. Family or not.

"She yo' family," she reminded me.

"I don't care nothing 'bout that. I'm not watching her ass. What I can do is help you get her in the car so you can take her home, and I'll pay you for your troubles."

That was about all she was going to get out of me. Alexis rolled her eyes and sucked her teeth before replying.

"I guess that's what I get for trying to help."

Just as we began attempting to make our way out the VIP section and toward the exit, I saw a face that I hadn't expected to ever see again. Carlos. He was dressed to perfection in Tom Ford with diamonds glistening from his neck and wrist. He had his crew with him, of course, but he also had someone that I'd never expected to see alongside of him. Boobie.

Carlos paused. I could have asked him some questions. Questions like, why he would sell me a shit load of garbage. I could have also asked him why he was with someone who I'd previously sold that garbage to. Carlos had definitely snaked me, and it seemed like Boobie was in cahoots since he was trailing behind him, looking like he was going to have the exact conversation that I'd had not long ago. I decided to address Boobie instead, just to stall so I could back up a few feet to my table and grab the gun that I kept stashed. Like I said before, I frequented Drip regularly. So regularly that I had enough pull to not only get in armed, but to actually stash my shit at the same table I always patronized.

"Aye, Boobie, I see you met the plug."

Boobie looked at me blankly, as if he had no idea what I was talking about, while Carlos and his crew stood there silently. Carlos smirked, so I continued talking.

"The one that delivered the same bullshit that got the streets hot."

The expression on Boobie's face instantly changed. As I spoke, Lindsey and Alexis stood closely behind me, aware of the tension but oblivious to the events that were about to unfold. I tilted my head to the side to address them as I began backing up. I hated to put either of them in harm's way, but there was no way that I was letting that nigga Carlos or Boobie slide up out of Drip untouched. I was about to tear some shit up.

"What's going on?" Alexis asked.

"When I say go, run towards the exit and get Lindsey out of here," I said sternly.

I brought my head back around and yelled, "Go!" before dashing over to my table, flipping it over, and ripping down the AK-47 taped underneath it.

❦ 17 ❦

LANCE

My mind had been preoccupied when I raced out of Alize's and headed to my mama's house after she called me. However, as I was driving down the highway and traveling the short drive from Buckhead to Marietta, something clicked in my head. Lindsey had been going off about the Baller Bash earlier that day, and I was willing to be that's where her black ass was. When I went to call my mom, I realized that I had left my phone back at Alize's. I was too far to try to go back and get it. I, instead, rerouted and headed back to downtown Atlanta.

When I finally pulled up to Drip, I was confused. So much that I sat stuck for a moment in disbelief. The parking lot was a war zone. People were running, screaming, ducking, and dodging for cover. *What the fuck is going on?* It was so much happening at once, that my brain couldn't keep up. Then ... I heard the shots. I shook my head in disbelief. I did my best to keep from being overbearing and overprotective, but this was the reason why I didn't want Lindsey running all over Atlanta, all up in the mix.

My eyes darted around the parking lot to see where the shots were coming from. There were a lot of them. From multiple guns. I followed the sounds and eventually spotted the orange sparks as bullets ripped from multiple barrels. My eyes narrowed when they landed on a familiar face. It was Boobie. He was fleeing Drip's exit while firing his gun wildly. Things were getting more complex by the minute. *What the fuck?* was my thought when I saw four Spanish dudes running out behind him and shooting in the same direction. Yep, shit was getting more complicated. It was like a puzzle where pieces were slowly being placed so the picture could make sense. Every nigga that had just ran out the door, I'd seen before. Of course, I knew Boobie, but I'd also seen each one of the Spanish cats before as well. On numerous occasions.

One in particular caught my eye. He was the leader of the quartet. His name was Carlos ... and he was Luis' nephew. Luis, my former plug. I wasn't sure what the fuck was going on, but I was going to get to the bottom of it—after I got my sister the fuck outta there safely.

I bent down, reached under my seat, and retrieved my gun. After cocking it, I hopped out my truck and headed to the entrance. I wasn't trying to kill anybody, but I would if that's what it took to get to my sister. I took a few more steps, but the image in front of me stopped me dead in my tracks. It was just the person I'd been looking for. I now knew who everybody was running from.

When my brother emerged from the bullet-riddled doors of Drip, his face was twisted into a menacing scowl, and he was squeezing down on the trigger of an AK-47. How he even got a gun that size in the building was beyond me. All I knew was that he was on some shit, and there wasn't a single gun out there able to compete against the spray of bullets his was kicking out. While Lawrence created a path, my eyes landed on two screaming females behind him. Alexis and Lindsey!

Lindsey could barely stand on her own and was being held up and damn near drug out by Alexis. My stomach dropped to my feet. Lawrence had put them in so much danger it was fucking pitiful. I was convinced that he wanted to die, *and* he wanted everyone around him to die too! Just when I thought things couldn't get any fucking worse! The whole scene itself was overload. I didn't know whether to start shooting or simply focus on covering my baby sister. I had to make a quick choice, and since I didn't have time to ponder, I sprang into action.

"Go back inside!" I screamed at the top of my lungs to Lindsey and Alexis while I ran full speed into the parking lot through the mess of people with my index finger mashed against the trigger of my Glock. My focus was on whoever was shooting too close to my motherfucking sister. I didn't have beef with any of them, but I refused to allow anyone to harm her. I would lay down old ladies and babies to keep her safe. Lindsey was definitely out of line for bringing her ass out after being told not to, but it wasn't the time to go into her knowing right from wrong.

Hearing and seeing bullets flying at them from a new direction caused Boobie, Carlos, and his patnas to spin around and aim in my direction. I saw Boobie mouth the word *shit*, before he lowered his gun and took off in the opposite direction. He knew he couldn't keep firing at Lawrence because the bullets were flying too close to my sister. He'd seen my sister a few times when he stopped by Luxe, so he knew exactly who she was. Now that I was on the scene, he knew that I would lay him down if he posed a risk to her. I respected Boobie. I didn't want to war with him, and I knew damn well that he didn't want to war with me.

"Go back inside!" I screamed again. This time they heard me, *and* they saw me.

"Lance!" Alexis screamed in terror as soon as her eyes landed on me. She screamed again when a bullet whizzed past her head and penetrated a nearby parked car.

"Fuck!" I growled. My eyes scanned the group of men to see who fired that shot. I brought my arm up and fired in his direction. The bullet plowed through the back of his head and sent him crumpling to the pavement in a heap.

Realizing they were outgunned, they all began running towards a big, black, darkly tinted SUV. However, they kept shooting, so I kept firing on them while I ran through the thick crowd of people and scrambled to get to my sister.

Lawrence was still squeezing down on his AK, while Lindsey and Alexis stayed glued right behind him. The sight infuriated me more. All his stupid, suicidal ass was focused on, was killing niggas and wasn't even the least bit concerned with protecting Lindsey. He wasn't even paying her any mind. He didn't tell her to stop, nor did he attempt to reinforce what I was telling them. He knew, just like I knew, that the best thing they could have done, was hide against something until the bullets stopped flying. To let them keep walking right in the line of fire, was like suicide. I was tempted to put a bullet in the middle of his forehead my fucking self, but I honestly felt that Lawrence had to be in some type of deep, dark trance. Judging by the look on his face, his mind was focused on one thing and one thing only. That was the only thing that made sense.

After pushing past a few more people and managing to avoid being shot, I got to Lindsey and a frantic Alexis. Lindsey was pissy drunk and didn't have a fucking clue what was going on. I wanted to beat her ass out there. The little skirt she wore was hiked up her ass, she reeked of alcohol, and she couldn't even stand up straight. I was going to have to carry her.

"Give her to me!" I said to Alexis.

Even though I was grateful, the shit came out forcefully. It was actually the first time I was happy to see her hoe ass.

"It's too loud. Get me out of here," Lindsey slurred, as I wrapped my arms tightly around her torso so I could lift her up and drag her. She really had no idea of the type of danger she was in. The shit was beyond sad.

"Lance—" Alexis was just about to say something, but the spray of bullets flying inches from us stopped her.

"Go!" I ushered her toward the side a nearby car while I dragged Lindsey with us.

"Get down!"

I pulled Lindsey around the car and tossed her down so I could cover them.

"Stay down until I tell you to get up!" I growled.

"Okay," Alexis cried. A few seconds passed, and Alexis let off an agonizing scream that came from the top of her lungs. I looked down at her to see what was wrong, and then my eyes fell on Lindsey. She was up against the car and slumped over on Alexis. Her eyes were now closed, and blood leaked from a wound in her temple. She had been shot in the head.

I dropped my gun and fell to my knees before quickly examining her. I tapped the sides of her face and tried to lift open her eyes.

"Lindsey!" I cried out. My voice was cracking and I was about to lose it. "Lindsey, wake up!" I looked at her chest and noticed she was still breathing, although only faintly.

"She needs an ambulance," I muttered. "Somebody call a fuckin' ambulance!" I screamed out. "Fuck."

I knew I had to move quick. Otherwise, she wasn't going to make it.

❧ 18 ❦

CARLOS

"You disobeyed me," my uncle Luis yelled angrily in his thick Spanish accent.

I pulled the phone away from my face because his voice boomed so loud through the receiver that it made my ear tingle.

"I did not. I did what you asked me," I countered while doing my best to keep my volume low and my tone respectful. Disrespecting a man like him wouldn't be a smart move.

"*Did you?*" he spat.

"With all due respect, I did. You asked me to come to Atlanta to take care of Tye, and you asked me to make sure that Lance's brother wouldn't be an issue as I stepped in to take over."

I fell silent after that statement. I'd done exactly what he'd asked. He hadn't given me any instructions on *how* to do it, so I'd done things my way. My way just happened to be by supplying Lawrence with a shipment of bad drugs. It made the streets hot and it caused everyone to lose money. Because of the caliber of loss endured, no one was going to want to work with him. Lawrence was out of the question. I would be able to walk in and supply Lance's people as well as gain their connections. Mission accomplished. Unfortunately, my uncle wasn't happy with my method.

"So, you think starting a war was a bright idea?" he argued.

My jaw hardened. I didn't like his tone. I never did. It was condescending. Deep in my heart, I knew my uncle only put me in position because I was blood. And to be honest, it wasn't much of a position. Up until recently, Lance supplied Atlanta. He had done so for years, and apparently, he'd done it well, since my uncle constantly praised his performance and never had a bad word to say about him. That, of course, all changed about a month ago when he found out that Lance had a high-level informant amongst his crew. As soon as that was revealed, Uncle Luis halted shipments to Lance. It only got worse when he realized that Lance pretty much allowed his brother Lawrence to run things. In my uncle's opinion, Lance seemed to no longer have a desire to be the largest heroin supplier in Atlanta. If he did, then he would have been monitoring his people a lot more closely, instead of allowing his brother to do so. According to Uncle Luis, if Lance had been more actively involved, he would have known that Tye had been talking to the feds. It was a critical mistake that Lance nor his brother would ever have the opportunity to make again.

"That wasn't my intention," I finally replied evenly. "I only sold the cut drugs to Lawrence because my sources told me that he was actively looking to find a new supplier for his team. I derailed that plan by dividing him from his team. I assumed that Lawrence would move along, and I could move forward with our plan to step in and supply who was left. It didn't go as planned. Lawrence made it clear that he wasn't happy with everyone severing ties with him. He shot at Boobie while he had his people in the car. Once we clipped Tye, everyone assumed that was also the work of Lawrence. When he saw me with Boobie, he must've connected the dots and realized that I'd sabotaged him."

When I was finished speaking, Uncle Luis exhaled a deep breath into the phone.

"You lost a man. One of *my* men. That won't happen again. I'll send for them in the morning." He paused. "The girl? Did she make it?"

"I don't know," I admitted, although it was something that I should have been working diligently to find out. All I knew was that one of the women Lawrence was with, had been hit. And it was one of my men who delivered the shot.

"You should hope she does, because if she doesn't, then you probably won't make it either. Not without a strong team. I suggest you round one up," he said with finality. "The question for you is, how do you end a war that started because you took something that a man loved?"

"By taking something that a man loves even more and using it as leverage," I replied simply.

"And what do you do when you accomplish that?"

"I kill the man."

Uncle Luis let out a hearty chuckle. "Carlos ... You seem to have it all figured out. But you must remember that this is chess, not checkers. Do you want Atlanta that bad?" he asked, his tone switching back to serious.

"I do."

"Well, you'll have to prove it. In my opinion, it's not worth it because you won't win. Not without my help anyway. And that, you won't be receiving. It's time for you to be a man and take accountability for your mistakes. This one ... you will fight alone. Prove me wrong, nephew. If you can, then I'll provide you the tools you need to run Atlanta. Just like we planned."

"You'll see," I told him before hanging up.

I tossed my phone down on the cushion beside me, before staring out the glass doors that led to the Olympic-size pool in the large rented mansion that I occupied with my men. I knew that my uncle doubted me. And the reason he doubted me was simply because of the blood that ran through my veins. Although

I was his baby sister's son, I was also the son of his former sworn enemy. One of two Spanish drug lords fighting over territory. While my uncle conquered the streets, my father, Miguel, would spitefully focus on conquering the young and beautiful sister of his rival. And that, he did. Despite claiming that they loved one another, the affair and forbidden child they eventually had together wouldn't help them unite. My father wound up dead and my mother wound up the single mother of a son that her brother accepted and cared for, but secretly resented. My uncle Luis would always say that I was messy like my father. Incapable of making rational choices to run things. I had plans to prove him wrong.

FINALE COMING IN SEPTEMBER

Made in the USA
Columbia, SC
01 September 2021

44704969R00083

STARTING & RUNNING

a Coffee Shop

LINDA FORMICHELLI and MELISSA VILLANUEVA

ALPHA

Publisher: Mike Sanders
Development Editor: Christy Wagner
Art Director: William Thomas
Cover Designer: Jessica Lee
Book Designer/Compositor: Ayanna Lacey
Proofreader: Lisa Starnes
Indexer: Celia McCoy

First American Edition, 2019
Published in the United States by DK Publishing
6081 E. 82nd Street, Indianapolis, Indiana 46250

Copyright © 2019 by Linda Formichelli
19 20 21   10 9 8 7 6 5 4 3 2 1
001-313885-SEP2019

Published in the United States by Dorling Kindersley Limited.

ISBN: 9781465483799
Library of Congress Catalog Card Number: 2019936933

Note: This publication contains the opinions and ideas of its author(s). It is intended to
provide helpful and informative material on the subject matter covered. It is sold with
the understanding that the author(s) and publisher are not engaged in rendering
professional services in the book. If the reader requires personal assistance or advice, a
competent professional should be consulted. The author(s) and publisher specifically
disclaim any responsibility for any liability, loss, or risk, personal or otherwise, which is
incurred as a consequence, directly or indirectly, of the use and application of any of the
contents of this book.

Trademarks: All terms mentioned in this book that are known to be or are suspected of
being trademarks or service marks have been appropriately capitalized. Alpha Books,
DK, and Penguin Random House LLC cannot attest to the accuracy of this information.
Use of a term in this book should not be regarded as affecting the validity of any
trademark or service mark.

DK books are available at special discounts when purchased in bulk for sales
promotions, premiums, fund-raising, or educational use. For details, contact: DK
Publishing Special Markets, 1450 Broadway, Suite 801, New York, NY 10018 or
SpecialSales@dk.com.

Printed and bound in USA.

Reprinted from *Idiot's Guides: Starting and Running a Coffee Bar.*